D1767554

The Projection of Britain

For
my family & friends

THE PROJECTION OF BRITAIN

British overseas publicity and propaganda 1919–1939

PHILIP M. TAYLOR
Lecturer in International History
at the University of Leeds

CAMBRIDGE UNIVERSITY PRESS

Cambridge
London   New York   New Rochelle
Melbourne   Sydney

Published by the Press Syndicate of the University of Cambridge
The Pitt Building, Trumpington Street, Cambridge CB2 1RP
32 East 57th Street, New York, NY 10022, USA
296 Beaconsfield Parade, Middle Park, Melbourne 3206, Australia

© Cambridge University Press 1981

First published 1981

Printed in Great Britain by
REDWOOD BURN LIMITED
Trowbridge & Esher

British Library cataloguing in publication data
Taylor, Philip M.
The projection of Britain
1. Propaganda, British – History
I. Title
327.41   DA566.2   80–42274
ISBN 0 521 23843 9

Contents

Preface	page vii
Acknowledgements	xiii
Abbreviations	xv
Introduction	1

Part One
Publicity and diplomacy, 1919–1939

1	The Foreign Office and the press	11
2	The Foreign Office and propaganda abroad	44

Part Two
The projection of Britain, 1919–1939

3	Commercial propaganda and the concept of national projection	83
4	Cultural propaganda and the British Council	125

Part Three
Psychological rearmament, 1935–1939

5	The BBC foreign-language broadcasts	181
6	The Vansittart Committee for the Co-ordination of British Publicity Abroad	216
7	Propaganda for war	260

Contents

Conclusion 293

Notes 301
Select bibliography 339
Index 353

Preface

This book is a pioneering study of a little-known aspect of British foreign policy between the wars. Essentially, it is an examination of the peacetime origins and early development of what are today loosely termed Britain's Overseas Information Services. Accordingly, the book traces the work of the Foreign Office News Department and its important press office, the commercial propaganda conducted by such organisations as the Empire Marketing Board, the Travel Association and the Industrial Publicity Unit, the foundation and rapid expansion of the British Council, and the origins of the BBC's World and External services. It is not, however, designed to provide a definitive history of Britain's world-wide propaganda activities during the twenty years of peace that followed the First World War. Nor does this book aspire to be comprehensive in its treatment of the issues it does examine. Rather, it is intended to be a preliminary investigation into those official and semi-official organisations which were established to 'project' Britain abroad, the reasons for their creation, and the peculiar features which characterised such work.

Despite considerable scholarly interest in this subject during the inter-war period itself, historians, at least in the United Kingdom, have only recently begun to appreciate the importance of studying propaganda and its impact upon public opinion as part of our understanding of the twentieth century. There is still a long way to go before the subject earns the credibility its significance deserves. Few textbooks or general historical surveys dealing with the period devote more than a brief mention to the British government's activities in this direction, and even then it is usually in the context of the First and Second World Wars. Recent research into the subject has not unnaturally tended to concentrate upon the more blatant examples of state propaganda, either in the hands of the totalitarian regimes or its use in time of war. Though inevitable – and desirable –

Preface

this concentration has tended to reinforce the general, if inaccurate, impression that Britain did not conduct such an unpleasant activity in peacetime and that it was simply one of the necessary evils of war. Apart from introductory sections in books such as Marjorie Ogilvy-Webb's *The Government Explains* (1965), Sir Robert Marrett's *Through the Back Door: An Inside View of Britain's Overseas Information Services* (1968), Sir Fife Clark's *The Central Office of Information* (1970), and J. B. Black's *Organising the Propaganda Instrument: The British Experience* (1975), little work has yet been done on Britain's inter-war propaganda, and still less with the benefit of documentary material now available at the Public Record Office at Kew. This book is intended to help fill this gap.

Because it attempts to break fresh ground, the book enjoys a large degree of freedom in its approach and analysis, for this is not a subject on which there are widely held views and interpretations to either modify or refute. This must not be taken to imply that the book deals with a somewhat esoteric subject that was confined to the lower echelons of officialdom, even if it did tend to operate 'on the edge of diplomacy' on a day-to-day basis. Indeed, as will be seen, the question of overseas propaganda occupied a proportion of the time of every Foreign Secretary during the period under review, although admittedly some, most notably Arthur Henderson (1929–31) and Anthony Eden (1936–8), gave the subject more sympathetic consideration than did others. This may have been due as much to force of circumstance as it was to the result of personal interest, because, generally speaking, propaganda was not an activity with which British officials felt comfortable.

On the other hand, much of the text is unavoidably devoted to an account of the organisations involved, although every attempt has been made to avoid the appearance of a straightforward administrative history. It has also been considered necessary to rely heavily upon quotations by the principal characters involved, to see the story through their eyes, because Foreign Office officials are not usually credited with an appreciation of many of the issues examined here. Moreover, strict limitations have been imposed upon the scope of the work, not least because of the twenty-year period which it attempts to cover. The book deals only with official and semi-official publicity and propaganda conducted abroad. It has not been possible to examine other than in passing certain related sub-

Preface

jects such as domestic and imperial propaganda, and the important question of censorship. That the Foreign Office had to give due consideration, in propaganda as in other matters, to all parts of the world from Europe to the Far East is not always explicitly apparent from the text. And whereas every attempt has been made to place the propaganda conducted by the Foreign Office or under its auspices within the broader context of that conducted not only by other government departments but also by other countries, much research nonetheless remains to be done in this field.

The approach is historical, although any study of propaganda admittedly requires some appreciation of sociological methodology as well as an understanding of psychology and political science. But my chief purpose has been to tell a story which has not been fully told before, and I hope, to paraphrase J. R. R. Tolkien, that this tale will grow in the telling until it becomes a history of British peacetime propaganda overseas between the wars and includes glimpses of history that preceded it.

I have found it virtually impossible to give a consecutive account of Britain's involvement in such work during the inter-war period, because of the many and diverse origins from which it developed. Reference to those origins where they pre-date the end of the First World War is made in the opening pages of each chapter, but a chronological spinal cord has been abandoned in favour of a thematic treatment. This approach can often involve a simplification, and sometimes even a falsification, of the subject, because, however convenient it might be for the historian to isolate the different themes, those officials who had to deal with such matters (particularly at the higher levels) were unable to do so but rather had to consider developments in relation to each other. Every attempt has therefore been made to relate the various themes examined here not only to each other but also to much wider issues.

The book is divided into three sections. British overseas propaganda was organised not by reference to individual media – press, radio, film – but to its variable forms: political, commercial and cultural propaganda. At the hub of all Britain's official activities abroad between 1919 and 1939 lay the News Department of the Foreign Office. Part One describes the work of this department, which can be loosely described as political propaganda, and also introduces the leading Foreign Office exponents of increased British

Preface

involvement in such work. Part Two is divided into two chapters which deal with commercial and cultural propaganda respectively, but it might also be said to examine the theory and practice of what came to be known as 'the projection of England'. Like Part One, this section examines its themes within a broad but distinct chronological framework. The mistake of many contemporaries was to assume that commercial and cultural propaganda were two entirely separate types of activity when, in fact, they were mutually complementary. Although commercial and cultural propaganda have been examined in separate chapters, this vital point must be borne in mind, as indeed must the fact that the underlying aim of both forms of activity was ultimately political.

This became much more apparent during the years from 1935 to 1939. Part Three of the book, which deals with the period of the peacetime machinery's most rapid expansion, is divided into three chapters, each of which deals with a specific development within the broader context of the growing political significance of commercial and cultural propaganda. In effect, this third section examines the transition of the 'projection of Britain' into that process which became known as psychological rearmament as the prospect of fighting another war became a distinct possibility. The final chapter, which deals mainly with the preparations for the conduct of propaganda in the event of another war, is slightly anomalous in that it does not deal with Britain's peacetime propaganda activities but has been included because it throws some new light on the preparations, which anyway had serious implications for those organisations already in existence.

It is notoriously difficult to assess the impact of propaganda, particularly when it is directed to foreign audiences. Although some attempt has been made to draw conclusions at the end of each chapter and at the end of the book, the commentaries are designed more to provoke further discussion and research than to provide the reader with any categorical solutions to complex problems.

Finally, a word about the title of the book. Just as Sir Stephen Tallents, who made famous the phrase 'the projection of England' after publishing a pamphlet with that title in 1932, made no apologies to the Scots, the Welsh or the Irish, because, he wrote, 'they may be counted on to take their full share in the study and practice of the new art' for which he pleaded, so also do I make no apologies for

Preface

adapting his phrase for my purposes, because, without Tallents and people like him who were prepared to convert unfashionable theory into unpopular practice, this book would never have been made possible.

Acknowledgements

I am chiefly indebted to Professor David Dilks for first inspiring me as an undergraduate with an enthusiasm for twentieth-century history and for his constant help and guidance during my time as a research student under his supervision. I am also deeply indebted to Nicholas Pronay for his unfailing support and encouragement and for sharing with me his considerable knowledge of propaganda in all its aspects.

Professor W. N. Medlicott, Professor D. C. Watt, Professor M. R. D. Foot, Professor Keith Robbins and Professor A. P. Adamthwaite kindly clarified certain issues which had, before their advice, remained something of a mystery to me. Dr Paul Swann and Dr Richard Taylor were equally prepared to discuss their knowledge of film propaganda, and I have learned much from several enjoyable conversations with them. I am also grateful to Timothy Hollins, Trevor Ryan, Diana Eastment, Caroline Anstey and Judy Adams for sharing with me some of the many treasures they have unearthed in various archives during their time as research students. Professor Norman Hillmer was equally prepared to clarify the imperial context of my research. Katherine Riley always proved willing to pursue various leads, often with great success, and was thus an ideal research assistant.

Mr Iverach McDonald, Mr Irvine Watson, Mr and Mrs Edgar Anstey and the late Mr Kenneth Johnstone kindly granted me interviews and answered my questions with a great deal of patience and with generous hospitality.

The research for this book could not have been completed without the support of the British Academy and of the Gilbert Murray Trust.

Nor could it have been undertaken without the assistance of the following: the staff at the Public Record Office at Chancery Lane, Portugal Street and at Kew in London; the staff of the Brotherton

Acknowledgements

Library at the University of Leeds; and the staff of the London headquarters of the British Council at Spring Gardens, who permitted me to search the council's archives prior to their transfer to the Public Record Office in 1977. Mr John Webster, the council's archivist, deserves particular mention. I am also grateful to J. M. Kavanagh and her staff at the BBC Written Archives Centre in Caversham for making my visit there such a pleasant experience. Mr Gordon Phillips, the archivist of *The Times*, proved invaluable to my search in New Printing House Square. Mary C. LaFogg and Judith Schiff, of the Manuscripts and Archives Branch of Yale University Library, were most helpful in obtaining photocopies of the numerous documents held in the Arthur Willert collection there. Miss V. A. Leeper deserves special mention for sending from Australia copies of her brother's family letters relating to the 1930s. Lady Leeper was also most helpful in relating information concerning the career of her late husband, Sir Reginald Leeper, one of the central figures of this book.

I wish to thank the Controller of H.M. Stationery Office for permission to quote from Crown copyright records; Yale University Library for permission to quote from the Arthur Willert collection; the BBC for permission to quote material held in the Written Archives Centre at Caversham; and Miss V. A. Leeper for permission to quote from her family papers. Apologies are due to any whom I have failed to consult.

My colleagues in the School of History at the University of Leeds were outstanding in their support and tolerance, particularly Roy Bridge, Graham Ross, Keith Wilson, Ellis Tinios and Ed Spiers.

There are also those who, over the past five years, have provided me with memorable moments which have helped to sustain my morale and enthusiasm. They are: David and Frances Murdoch; Dr Frank Lissauer and his wife, Vera; Rodney Dalton; Harry Callahan; Jack Regan and George Carter; John Carpenter; John Ford; Martin Scorsese; Richard Blaine; Bill Shankly; Bob Paisley; Liverpool Football Club.

I am eternally grateful to my parents and to my brother and his wife for their outstanding faith and encouragement.

Finally, this book could not have been written without the light and strength of Susan Heward.

Needless to say, all errors of fact and judgement are mine, and mine alone.

Abbreviations

ABC	Arabic Broadcasting Committee
APA	All Peoples Association
BBC	British Broadcasting Corporation
BC	British Council papers
BFI	British Film Institute
BIF	British Industries Fair
BLI	British Library of Information
BT	Board of Trade
CAB	Cabinet Office papers
CBPA	Committee for the Co-ordination of British Publicity Abroad
CID	Committee of Imperial Defence
DOT	Department of Overseas Trade
EH	Electra House
EMB	Empire Marketing Board
FBI	Federation of British Industries
FO	Foreign Office
GPO	General Post Office
Hansard	*Parliamentary Debates (Commons)*
HMG	His Majesty's Government
INF	Information papers
OEPEC	Overseas Emergency Publicity Expenditure Committee
PID	Political Intelligence Department
PREM	Prime Minister's Office papers
PWE	Political Warfare Executive
RAF	Royal Air Force
SIS	Secret Intelligence Service
SOE	Special Operations Executive
T	Treasury papers

Introduction

'God would not have made them sheep had he not wanted them to be sheared.'
(A line spoken by the actor Eli Wallach in John Sturges's 1961 film *The Magnificent Seven*)

It is a truism, but nonetheless one worth stating, that the conduct of propaganda presupposes the existence of an audience. That audience must not only be capable of receiving information or opinions, but it must also possess the potential ability to respond in a manner desired by the propagandist; otherwise there would be no point in making an appeal of whatever type to it in the first place. During the course of the twentieth century, the capacity and potential ability of the audience have increased dramatically through the spread of literacy and education, the development of mass communications through the advance of technology, and growing political consciousness and participation in the mechanics of power on the part of an ever increasing number of people. Although public opinion remains a somewhat erratic and indefinable concept, it has become something which those who enjoy positions of power and status ignore at their peril. Accordingly, attempts to inform, cultivate, control and manipulate public opinion have resulted in the scientific development of the new arts of publicity, public relations, advertising and propaganda conducted through organisations designed specifically to influence the audience to respond in a manner desired by those in power or by those who wish to secure power.

How do we distinguish between propaganda and other attempts to influence public opinion? The word 'propaganda' itself implies calculated intent on the part of one person or group of people to persuade others to think or behave in a certain way. It is this element of calculated intent which is crucial to our understanding of propaganda and to our ability to detect propaganda when we are confronted by it. A major problem derives from the debasement of the word

Introduction

since the First World War. Before then, propaganda meant simply the means which an adherent of a political or religious doctrine employed to convince the unconverted.[1] Between 1914 and 1918, however, the wholesale employment of propaganda by all the belligerents served to transform its meaning into something more sinister. It came to be associated with base motives to such a degree that everything to do with it tended to be regarded as suspect. From a strictly conceptual viewpoint, this need not necessarily be the case, because the propagandist can be actuated by creditable and even altruistic motives, while the thought or action which he wishes to incite may be designed to promote the general well-being of his audience. If the propagandist is genuinely committed to a cause or point of view, he invariably assumes that his cause or point of view is the correct one. His audience, of course, might not agree, but, in a free society in times of peace, the individual retains the right to accept or reject opinions without serious consequences to his liberty of thought and action. War, not unnaturally, creates a different set of criteria.

Education may be said to be designed to promote the general well-being of an individual through the imparting of knowledge and the cultivation of mental skills that will enable him to form sound judgements for himself.[2] J. A. C. Brown has argued that 'education' teaches people how to think, whereas 'propaganda' teaches them what to think.[3] This simple distinction, as Richard Taylor has suggested, might also be usefully adopted to distinguish between 'information' or 'publicity' on the one hand and 'propaganda' on the other.[4] Because publicity imparts information which might not otherwise have been available, it provides its audience with opportunities to formulate opinions and to act accordingly. It therefore exploits the skills developed through education. By the same token, propaganda may be said to exploit publicity because it tells its audience how to use those opportunities. However, although propaganda is usually held to be something apart from education or information, the distinction in practice is not always quite so clear. Information might be released to inform or to educate an audience, but if, for various reasons, some information is held back from the recipient in order to strengthen the case of those responsible for its release, then the intent is deliberate calculation and may therefore be said to be propagandist. It is thus inadequate to state that propa-

Introduction

ganda is the dissemination of opinions whereas publicity is the dissemination of information, because careful selection and deliberate omission of information in the process of publicity make it propagandist.

What then distinguishes the two processes from each other? It is just as inadequate to accept the view that 'everything is propaganda' as it is to state that propaganda appeals to man's emotions while publicity appeals to man's reason, because, as Bertrand Russell has pointed out, 'the line between emotion and reason is not so sharp as some people think'.[5] Hitler simplified this complex issue by claiming that he was appealing to man's baser instincts, to his emotions and passions, rather than to his reason. This was why he attempted to discover the lowest common denominator of his audience, and why he had little time for appealing to intellectuals, who were suspected of being capable of rising above such instincts through their command of reason. To Hitler, the masses were merely sheep whose purpose was simply to provide his Nazi movement with the woollen cloak of legitimacy. By way of contrast, it was precisely those people whom Hitler chose to ignore that constituted the primary targets of British overseas propaganda between the wars. British propaganda was directed not towards a mass audience, at least not directly, but towards the educated classes of foreign societies. It was designed to influence people in government, the media, education and commerce – individuals, in other words, who were in a position to influence much larger numbers of their own people.

This approach had the advantage of disguise, because it employed indirect methods of reaching a large audience. An educated person capable of forming his own judgements on the basis of information available to him would, however, be less susceptible to the opinions of others than would an individual who had not developed such skills from education. Great caution was therefore required on the part of British propagandists in their techniques of persuasion. It was essential for them to avoid the appearance of conducting propaganda. This could be achieved by disseminating information rather than opinions, although the information disclosed would have to be carefully selected in such a way as to guide the recipient to the desired conclusions. In the words of Sir John Reith, director-general of the BBC for most of the inter-war period, 'news is the shocktroops of propaganda'. The source of official propaganda could also be dis-

Introduction

guised by utilising intermediary channels of communication which had no ostensible connection with that source. Hence the emphasis which British propagandists placed upon the cultivation of personal contacts and their preference for conducting their work through semi-official and private channels. It was equally important for the information or news to be accurate. Lies can be detected and misinformation can be refuted, in which case propaganda becomes self-defeating once the credibility of the source, or the channel of communication, becomes suspect. It was for these reasons that British propagandists learned from an early stage that it was more effective to tell the truth, nothing but the truth and, as near as possible, the whole truth. They also learned that it was essential to let their primary targets believe they were making up their own minds. If the recipient managed to draw the desired conclusions from the basis of information supplied to him, he must be encouraged to believe that it was because reason had dictated his thoughts rather than because he had been told to think or behave in a manner desired by the propagandist. Provided he remained convinced of this, and did not detect that his thought processes had been manipulated or tampered with in some way, then not only would others respect his judgement more but he would continue to remain a valuable instrument of propaganda. It was by these means that much of Britain's overseas propaganda between the wars masqueraded under the disguise of publicity.

Propaganda, then, must be defined by reference to its aims. In order to distinguish it from publicity, it is necessary to determine the reasons why certain information is being released or withheld. Hence the importance of studying the means for controlling information alongside the means employed for its distribution, for censorship and propaganda are Siamese twins, inseparable and inextricable. Publicity may therefore be defined as the supply or release of information of a factual nature which is designed to provide the public in general with an opportunity for each individual member to formulate opinions for himself and to act according to his own conscience. It is a service, designed to keep the public informed of events which may benefit an individual or section of the audience to which it is directed, but without compulsion. Propaganda can be defined as an attempt to influence the attitudes of a specific audience, through the use of facts, fiction, argument or sug-

Introduction

gestion – often supported by the suppression of inconsistent material – with the calculated purpose of instilling in the recipient certain beliefs, values or convictions which will serve the interests of the author, usually by producing a desired line of action. Whether or not it is successful in producing the desired line of action is, however, largely irrelevant to the question of definition. Value judgements such as that propaganda is 'good' or 'bad' are therefore meaningless unless the question of intent is judged by similar criteria.

Clear-cut definitions are one thing, but their application in practice is quite another. During the inter-war years, propaganda was interpreted in a variety of different ways. In 1931, for example, one Foreign Office official suggested that the major reason why greater official sympathy and support for increased British involvement in propaganda abroad had not been forthcoming was that

> The real trouble centres round the use of the word propaganda. This word was in particularly bad odour for some time after the war. In the News Department we constantly avoided using it and there have been occasions when we have written to our press officers and other correspondents abroad asking them to use the word 'publicity' or any other euphemism rather than 'propaganda'. A sufficient time has elapsed, however, for the most objectionable associations with the word to have faded out, and it is now frankly adopted by some commercial and other organisations in place of the word 'publicity' or 'advertisement'.[6]

Yet no sooner had the word appeared to have escaped its dubious wartime connotations than it began to regain notoriety with the aggressive activities of foreign governments, particularly of the dictatorships. 'Propaganda' therefore became something other people did, while in Britain a wide variety of euphemisms were created, the most popular being 'publicity', with 'national projection' and 'national self-advertisement' also frequently occurring. Indeed, one German writer, commenting in 1936 upon the different values attached to the word in Britain and Germany, suggested that 'publicity' was merely a more palatable English word for describing what the Germans unashamedly termed 'propaganda'.[7] While this assertion was not without foundation (the British deliberately label their propaganda organisations 'News Department', 'Foreign Publicity Department', 'National Publicity Bureau' and – even in war – 'Ministry of Information'), there were nevertheless fundamental dif-

Introduction

ferences between the German and British interpretations of the word in practice.

In a leading article defending the establishment in 1934 of the British Council to conduct cultural propaganda, *The Times* proclaimed:

> Those who dislike publicity may dismiss the idea on the plea that it is nothing but veiled propaganda, but none need fight shy of the word 'propaganda' so long as the work associated with it is openly performed and the principles spread are honestly held and are not insinuated into the minds of readers or listeners, but are provided as a contribution to thought and experience for those who wish to learn them.[8]

The British Council or the Foreign Office could undoubtedly find much comfort in these words, but certainly not enough for them to begin using the word 'propaganda' to describe their work in public. 'Cultural diplomacy' was the phrase most officials preferred to use in describing the work of the British Council, whereas when the purely propaganda side of the News Department's work was separated from its press activities in the summer of 1939, it was rechristened the 'Foreign Publicity Department'. Official propaganda known to be such is treated with much greater scepticism than is propaganda which has been disguised in some way. Even when a new organisation was created in April 1939 to conduct industrial propaganda in the foreign press, it was termed the 'Industrial Publicity Unit' despite the fact that its existence was kept secret. It is important to recognise, therefore, that although publicity and propaganda are two different types of activity, British officials tended to regard the words as interchangeable or even as one and the same. However, much of British activity in this direction was a wolf in sheep's clothing; when sheared of its protective euphemisms, propaganda is clearly exposed.

Even so, there was much to distinguish Britain's overseas peacetime propaganda from that conducted by other countries. As mentioned above, news constituted its basic ingredient, while interpretation was generally left to the recipient, although the manner in which the news was presented was usually such that it guided him towards certain conclusions. There was a strong counter-propagandist element in this dissemination of accurate news, because, by correcting misstatements in the foreign press and substituting for them a more accurate and reliable piece of infor-

Introduction

mation, the credibility of the inaccurate source would thereby be severely questioned. Moreover, Britain's overseas propaganda, regardless of its political, commercial or cultural variations, tended to be pro-British rather than anti-foreign in character. While engaging in self-glorification, great care was taken to refrain from criticising the activities of other countries or the nature of their governing regimes. It was defensive rather than aggressive. Unlike many of its continental counterparts, British propaganda attempted to provide an opportunity for foreigners to learn more about Britain and the British way of life without forcing them to 'think British' if they had no desire to do so. It was this aspect which gave British propaganda the appearance of being publicity. As one Member of Parliament stated in 1939, 'The function of propaganda is to state a case, whether it is true or false. It is, therefore, suspect. Publicity states the truth.'[9] Though a gross oversimplification of the issue, this statement does reflect the reluctance of people in British public life during the 1930s to tar their own work with the same brush as that applied to the activities of others. Rex Leeper, head of the News Department from 1935 to 1939 and the leading Foreign Office exponent of increased official propaganda abroad, was more specific in his definition: 'Publicity, as opposed to political propaganda, is the attempt to make known abroad the main features of our political, economic and cultural activities, to give an accurate picture of this country and to refrain from criticising the activities of other countries.'[10] Yet, given that both activities must ultimately be defined by reference to their aims, both publicity and propaganda, however fine the distinction between them in the British context, involve a deliberate attempt to influence opinion on certain issues. As another MP stated after a lengthy Commons debate on the subject in February 1939, 'We have heard much tonight about the Projection of Britain and the British people. Well, but what is that but propaganda? We may dislike the word because it has collected unpleasant associations. But the thing itself may be necessary and right. Let us not be ashamed or afraid of it.'[11]

PART ONE
Publicity and diplomacy, 1919–1939

'...news is the shocktroops of propaganda...'
(Sir John Reith, *Into the Wind* (London, 1949) p. 354)

1
The Foreign Office and the press

Prior to the outbreak of war in 1914, the Foreign Office possessed no formal apparatus for the regular supply of official information to the press. There did not exist any Whitehall equivalent to the Maison de la Presse at the Quai d'Orsay or the Press Bureau at the Wilhelmstrasse. Unlike many of their continental counterparts, British diplomats generally preferred to conduct their business beneath an umbrella of secrecy, while the Foreign Office may be said to have abstained assiduously from creating any machinery that would serve to encourage a greater level of public participation in what was considered to be the private and exclusive realm of international politics.[1] Publicity and diplomacy were, in other words, considered to be incompatible. It was believed that the conduct of British foreign policy required a high degree of freedom from public scrutiny, whether at home, where – should popular interest manifest itself – it was felt that the majority of people were incapable of appreciating the subtle intricacies of complicated diplomatic manoeuvres, or abroad, where premature disclosures concerning policy aims might produce results prejudicial to British interests and prestige.

Such attitudes, broadly speaking, were firmly entrenched within the foreign-policy-making élite of the nineteenth century. However, they began to come under attack with the gradual trend towards universal suffrage, improving standards of education and literacy (which served to both subsidise and reflect the new developments in journalism towards the close of the century) and the advance of communications technology. The implications of these developments for both publicity and diplomacy were to prove dramatic. But with broadcasting and the cinema still in their infancy, the press remained the chief medium through which public opinion at large could be most readily influenced. And because the press more often tended to lead rather than follow public opinion in matters relating

Publicity and diplomacy, 1919–1939

to foreign affairs, the role of newspapers as instruments of official publicity gradually began to assume added significance. While there did not exist any system of formal contact, a type of symbiotic relationship developed between small groups of officials and journalists, each utilising the other's sources of information in pursuit of their respective duties.[2] Information was a vital commodity to both professions. Control over it meant the power to influence opinion, and opinion was becoming an increasingly important consideration in the formulation of official policy with the broadening base of political power.

Nevertheless, parallel to what may be interpreted as this growing awareness of the value of publicity in diplomacy, there developed an equal, if not greater, appreciation of the dangers. To the majority of British officials, attempts to influence mass opinion were considered unethical, unnecessary and tantamount to opening Pandora's box. Indeed, it was partly to help keep the lid sealed that, in the wake of the Fashoda crisis, a standing sub-committee of the Committee of Imperial Defence (CID) was appointed to examine the question of censorship in time of war.[3]

It was the First World War which provided the chief catalyst in the relationship between Whitehall and the press. The war required the mobilisation of elements in society which had hitherto remained uninvolved in the exigencies of national survival. The ability to influence opinion in allied, neutral and enemy countries became a military asset. The need, on the one hand, to harness and, on the other, to exploit the propaganda potential of the press manifested itself in August 1914 with the creation of the Press Bureau and of the Foreign Office News Department. Thus, from the very outset of the conflict, censorship and propaganda became the twin pillars upon which the British government waged its war of words against the Central Powers. By 1918, an elaborate machinery had been constructed for the purpose, centering upon Lord Beaverbrook's Ministry of Information and Lord Northcliffe's enemy propaganda department at Crewe House. By the end of the war, such was believed to have been the success of the propaganda experiment, and of the role played by the press within that experiment, that a reappraisal of government–press relations became unavoidable on the return of peace.

The Foreign Office and the press

Into the den of lions

The Ministry of Information did not survive the war. It had never during its short life been a popular organisation. Many members of the British governing élite had found its work distasteful and 'un-English', while others – such as Austen Chamberlain – had feared the consequences of Lloyd George's policy of large-scale recruitment of its staff from Fleet Street.[4] Men such as Beaverbrook and Northcliffe for their part had initially advocated the continuation of their work on behalf of the government once the war had been won but had in the end decided to resign their posts in order to resume what they considered to be their normal newspaper duties in view of the coming general election and the Paris Peace Conference. As a result, various schemes for the re-education of Germany advanced in Crewe House at the end of the conflict came to nothing, and the entire wartime propaganda machinery was set in the process of liquidation under the direction of John Buchan (later Lord Tweedsmuir), who had himself been in charge of propaganda in 1917 before being superseded by Beaverbrook. It was Buchan's task now to decide which of the various wartime propaganda activities should be wound up and which might be considered desirable to maintain in peacetime.

As a result of Buchan's investigations during the final months of 1918, the majority of the wartime activities were discontinued, quite simply because, in most cases, their rationale had seemingly disappeared. It was, however, decided to transfer responsibility for those activities which Buchan considered desirable to maintain, or for those about which he was uncertain, into the hands of the Foreign Office.

It might reasonably be assumed that this move would almost certainly have resulted in a return to the pre-war system whereby the Foreign Office divested itself of any formal responsibility for the conduct of official publicity. This was not to prove the case. In 1919 it was decided to reconstitute the former News Department and to amalgamate it with another wartime creation, the Political Intelligence Department (PID), under the overall direction of Sir (later Lord) William Tyrrell. Tyrrell's qualifications for this post predated the war; while serving as Sir Edward Grey's private secretary, he had been responsible for meeting press enquries, which often called upon him to defend the sanctity of his superiors. The new joint News and Political Intelligence Department was designed to monitor and record the fluctuating moods of foreign opinion and, if it was considered necessary or appropriate, to attempt to influence that opinion through the use of propaganda. The post-war decisions relating to the latter aspect of the department's work will be discussed in greater detail in the following chapter. In so far as press publicity was concerned, Tyrrell was charged with the task of keeping the parliamentary under secretary of state for foreign affairs 'fully cognisant of all that was passing and would arrange for interviews between him and important journalists when this was found necessary'.[5] In effect, this meant simply a rationalisation of those pre-war contacts which had taken place unofficially. The system of informal contact between individual journalists and officials, as indeed between individual politicians and editors or proprietors, did, of course, continue (and was to achieve a high degree of notoriety during Lloyd George's remaining tenure as Prime Minister).[6] The main difference now was that formal contact had been institutionalised in the form of the News Department. Correspondents wishing to see someone of significance within the Foreign Office would first have to meet with Tyrrell, who would either arrange an interview or deliver any news and comment himself. Otherwise, the parliamentary under secretary would deal with specific matters. A much more obvious difference in Foreign Office–press relations was that now representatives from the British and foreign press corps in London were actually encouraged to call at the News Department's press office to receive daily communiqués containing routine news and information relating to foreign affairs. These decisions marked a little-noticed departure from established peacetime tradition.

The reasons for this diplomatic innovation were partly linked to the post-war decisions relating to the future role of propaganda in the context of British foreign policy. Various officials, particularly those with some wartime experience of propaganda, had, since the return of peace, been contemplating the need for some machinery to secure adequate publicity for the British point of view. The world had changed radically since the outbreak of war in 1914. The unprecedented degree of active public participation, both at home and in the trenches, in the survival of the state – or, alternatively, in its de-

The Foreign Office and the press

struction – led to a general assumption that the war had served to increase the level of popular interest in foreign affairs. One official, for example, who considered that 'the chief means by which the different peoples can arrive at a mutual understanding of each is the press', argued that 'the masses will now demand to know much more than previously of what is going on, and what is being done in the diplomatic field, and it would not only be futile, but dangerous, to attempt to keep knowledge from them'.[7] The contemporary backlash against secret diplomacy, combined with the lessons of the revolutions in Russia, Germany and elsewhere, all seemed to lend support to the argument of groups such as the Union of Democratic Control that public opinion could no longer be ignored in the determination of foreign policy. As another Foreign Office official warned,

> Whatever we may know about the legal or formal constitution of a foreign country, we seldom, if ever, know who 'runs' the country, or who 'runs' it in reference to any particular matter. We therefore do not know who is to be approached in order to deal at once and effectively with any particular difficulty or misunderstanding. In some cases and in some matters the ultimate power is split up in the hands of a very large number of persons and, therefore, the only means of influencing them is through the press or other instrument of publicity.[8]

Seemingly reinforced by President Wilson's call for 'open covenants, openly arrived at' and for the creation of a League of Nations as an expression of 'the organised opinion of mankind', such arguments could not be lightly dismissed.

However, in view of the need for financial retrenchment during the post-war years of economic dislocation, there emerged a powerful body of official opinion, led by the Treasury, which proved more reluctant to accept the claim that publicity had become an integral part of modern diplomacy. As will be illustrated in the following chapters, this body of opinion was sufficiently powerful to limit the extent of the News Department's propaganda activities abroad throughout the 1920s. Its first victim was the Political Intelligence Department, which was closed down in 1920. The News Department survived, in much reduced form, but it too found its work subjected to repeated limitations, so much so that, in late 1920, the Foreign Office was forced, under Treasury pressure, to revert to an improved version of the pre-war system for dealing with the British press whereby responsibility for dealing with visitors from Fleet Street was placed in the hands of the private secretary to the Secretary of State.[9]

During Lord Curzon's tenure as Foreign Secretary, this task was undertaken, somewhat reluctantly at first, by Robert Vansittart, who recalled that during the numerous international conferences which took place after the war, 'the press grinned and enjoyed itself. I, the first embryo of a press department, had to satisfy it and enjoyed myself less. To be daily classed as an official, and therefore cagey, is not conducive to conceit.'[10] Vansittart even admitted that he generally tried to avoid meeting journalists and, in doing so, dissatisfied Curzon, the more so because Lloyd George 'was so well served' by Lord Riddell, owner of the *News of the World*, chairman of the Newspaper Proprietors' Association, and self-appointed public relations officer to the Prime Minister. Vansittart wrote:

Beside this Fleet Street leviathan I was small fry, but Curzon expected me to influence newspaper-men to an extent impossible in the twentieth century... He swung between thinking they knew too much and too little of his domain... Every morning trouble arose on the telephone. 'Why did you put that in?' He did not understand that modern journalists had sources of information other than the Foreign Office.[11]

Indeed, Vansittart's work was made all the more difficult by the fact that one of those alternative sources of information was the Prime Minister's office at 10 Downing Street. Tension between the Foreign Office and what was considered by many of its members to be an unconstitutional rival in the form of Lloyd George's 'garden suburb' often mounted to such a level that Whitehall appeared to be speaking with two entirely different voices on important foreign policy issues.

Relations between Whitehall as a whole and Fleet Street could hardly be said to have been much better. The distinguished journalist Kennedy Jones commented upon what he described as a 'semi-contemptuous attitude' which characterised government–press relations after the war,[12] an impression confirmed by Lord Hardinge, the permanent under secretary at the Foreign Office.[13] Jones wrote cynically of officials who, in his opinion, had been appointed for their ability 'to gauge correctly the exact suppression of truth in each statement, for these statements, though in the main true, are rarely the whole truth and nothing but the truth, and their nature

The Foreign Office and the press

varies according to the friendliness or the hostility of the medium through which they are to reach the public'.[14] Suspicion was, however, mutual, particularly in view of the dispute which existed after the war between the Northcliffe press and the Lloyd George government.[15] Matters came to a head when, on 13 July 1921, *The Times* published a leading article in which the Prime Minister and his Foreign Secretary were bitterly attacked, personally and politically, for their attitude over the forthcoming Washington Conference.[16] Such attacks, as Lord Riddell had already noted, were providing foreign governments with a ready-made supply of anti-British propaganda while 'the British case was not being represented'.[17] Lloyd George was fully aware of the dangers to Britain's image abroad of poor governmental relations with Fleet Street, and with Printing House Square in particular. But as he said in the House of Commons after the July episode,

> In spite of its record in recent years, *The Times* is still supposed in many circles abroad to represent both educated and official opinion in this country... It is therefore essential that the British Government as a whole should mark strongly its disapproval of such an attack upon the Secretary of State for Foreign Affairs at this moment.[18]

The incident had, in fact, provoked an outcry. The Foreign Office's response had been to send instructions to its overseas representatives not to extend their assistance to *Times* correspondents,[19] while, in London, a temporary news embargo was placed upon the Northcliffe press.[20] By November 1921, the official embargo had been lifted, but, as Curzon's assistant private secretary, Allen Leeper, recorded, 'The position here is that the Northcliffe press representatives are received if they call. The *Times* know this but are not at present calling here.'[21] It was quite clear that the Foreign Office's new press system was not working. Some alternative had to be found if the Foreign Office was to reap the benefits of the British press serving as a positive influence in foreign publicity.

It was towards solving this problem that William Tyrrell turned his attention in December 1921. Tyrrell wrote: 'I am not sure that we sufficiently realise the great change which has taken place in our relations with the press since the outbreak of war.'[22] Commenting upon the apparent increase of public interest in foreign affairs, which had produced a corresponding increase in newspaper interest, he argued that there had been a simultaneous decline in the independence of the press due to the influence of four proprietors – Northcliffe, Rothermere, Beaverbrook and Dalziel – upon the editorial policies of the majority of British newspapers. Tyrrell continued:

> If their outlook happens to coincide with the national view, so much the better for the nation, but if these mighty men settle on a personal policy, so much the worse for the nation. In the latter case they will only accept information from here which suits their book, and are quite willing to reject or distort what runs counter to their policy as distinguished from ours.[23]

There was, moreover, the additional problem of Lloyd George's 'garden suburb'. Tyrrell complained that the Foreign Office 'no longer held the monopoly for the distribution of foreign policy'. Sir William Sutherland, one of the Prime Minister's closest advisers at the 'rival establishment', was accused of granting or withholding information supplied to him by the Foreign Office 'as a reward or the reverse for the support of the press in matters of internal policy'.[24] Similarly, Philip Kerr (later Lord Lothian), until recently Lloyd George's private secretary, was accused of publishing confidential material in his leading articles for the *Daily Chronicle*, owned by Lloyd George since 1918.[25]

In an attempt to prevent the government speaking with two, often diametrically opposed, voices on foreign policy matters, Tyrrell advocated a more efficient rationalisation of the Foreign Office's press arrangements. He wrote:

> The main attraction we can offer journalists is the accuracy of the news which we furnish, but for sensationalism and substantive rewards we cannot outbid the other establishment. I would therefore suggest that we should refrain from trying to inspire and guide those representatives of the press who are merely touts and reporters, but we should endeavour to persuade some of the morning papers to send down occasionally a serious member of their staff for the purpose of obtaining information of a general character as to the trend of our policy. The papers I have in mind are the 'Daily Telegraph', 'The Times' and the 'Morning Post'.[26]

In accordance with Lord Curzon's wishes, Sir Eyre Crowe, permanent under secretary from 1920 to 1925, discussed the entire question with Tyrrell, Vansittart and Leeper. Their primary concern was to introduce a system of contact designed to prevent possible future indiscretions in the press and to 'curtail the facilities at

The Foreign Office and the press

present afforded to all who call, while at the same time endeavouring to maintain the friendly relations existing between the greater part of the press and this Office, and the influence which can be exercised from here on their views'.[27] A careful distinction was drawn between, on the one hand, 'the average journalist or reporter who calls here daily to enquire into matters of fact' and, on the other hand, 'the editors or responsible representatives of important papers with whom from time to time questions of policy might be discreetly discussed'.[28] Crowe considered that only material of a non-controversial nature should be issued to the former. The prestige press was, however, to be carefully cultivated; influential journalists were to be given direct access to the private secretaries, in whose offices 'from time to time, meetings might take place and information be supplied on the distinct understanding that such information was never to be directly used in the press, nor its source given away'.[29]

Until 1925, J. D. Gregory was charged with responsibility for this task. Gregory recorded that he found it 'superfluous for me to try and convey anything original or anything really worth conveying to men so well versed in international affairs' but nonetheless recognised the value of maintaining intimate contact in order to create an atmosphere of mutual trust and confidence.[30] It was believed that through a frank exchange of information and opinions, the press would come to a more sympathetic understanding of the problems facing British foreign policy-makers. Because Fleet Street tended to provide a mirror of British life for foreign observers, the image thus reflected abroad would generally be more favourable. Ideally, government and press would speak with one voice in order to project an image of domestic harmony, but although this was greatly facilitated by the departure of Lloyd George from office and by the death of Northcliffe, this rarely proved to be the case in a democratic society which cherished the tradition of a free press. All that the Foreign Office could really hope to achieve was the supply of accurate information and reliable comment to journalists on the basis that an informed critic was preferable to a misinformed sycophant.

This was the assumption behind the Foreign Office's dealings with Fleet Street. In so far as the foreign press was concerned, the News Department employed three methods of supplying news: (1)

to foreign journalists residing and working in London; (2) direct to foreign newspaper offices and news agencies through the British Official News Service; (3) through the appointment of press attachés at various overseas missions.

Percy Koppel succeeded Tyrrell as head of the News Department early in 1921. Koppel had won his propaganda spurs while serving in Wellington House and later in the PID during the war. He was fully aware of the propagandist value of supplying news to the foreign press corps in London, particularly as, he wrote, 'in some cases this is the only method by which the British point of view can be given prominence in the press abroad, and the eagerness with which correspondents take advantage of the opportunity of obtaining British political news and information is shown by the large number of callers dealt with by the Department'.[31]

An alternative method of securing good copy in the foreign press for the British point of view was through the News Department's overseas representatives, the press attachés. During the war, official agents abroad had formed an integral part of the propaganda distribution process, and they now became equally important in peacetime. In 1919, Sir Ronald Graham, assistant under secretary at the Foreign Office, had informed the Treasury that 'an essential feature' of the News Department's work would be 'the existence in each foreign country of a representative in charge, under the Ambassador or Minister, of all forms of propaganda there'.[32] Proposals were accordingly submitted for the appointment of seven such attachés, who would 'avoid the appearance of conducting British propaganda in the narrower sense of the word' but who would provide a local information service 'on all subjects, internal and external, political and commercial, relating to the British Empire' for people connected with government, the press and the native trading community.[33] In 1920, there existed a total of ten press attachés overseas, three of whom were employed on a part-time basis.[34] However, by 1922, following instructions from the Treasury to effect economies, only four remained – in Paris, Rome, Berlin and Sofia (although the latter was soon transferred to Brussels). Their role was defined as keeping their respective ambassadors fully informed 'with regard to personalities, tendencies, articles etc. in the local press, to prepare resumés for the information of the [Foreign] Office, and by their influence, local knowledge and information prevent the local press

The Foreign Office and the press

from going wrong on subjects about which it may be misinformed'.³⁵

Perhaps the best-known press attaché between the wars was Sir Charles Mendl in Paris. One of his colleagues had written that it was Mendl, more than any other official, who helped to develop the post into the important position it later became.³⁶ Essentially, the press attaché was held responsible for meeting representatives of the local press and, on occasion, foreign correspondents from Britain. A man such as Mendl, with his seemingly endless supply of contacts and influence in the political and newspaper communities of Paris, was an invaluable asset to any programme of British overseas publicity.³⁷ He would also produce a daily summary containing a detailed appraisal of domestic and world events as seen through the columns of the French press.³⁸ Nevertheless, as one official later recalled of the 1920s, 'at that time the apparatus of British political publicity was negligible, and these Press Attachés were thus more receptive than productive'.³⁹

In 1919, Lord Burnham, the owner of *The Daily Telegraph*, had taken the trouble to congratulate the Foreign Office on its decision to establish machinery for the regular supply of news and information to the press. He wrote:

I have always believed that newspapers offer the best means of propaganda, especially when it is directed to the intellectual classes; but I admit that the cinema is of great value in its appeal to the masses. Newspaper propaganda must depend upon newspaper standards and ideas; it is therefore necessary to rule out what is sometimes, I dare say, called with prejudice 'officialism', and to be guided by those who have practical knowledge of the idiosyncrasies and tastes of the newspaper public, not only in the various countries but in the provinces of the various countries. This means a close acquaintance with different types of newspapers, their circulation, and with what is called in the trade their 'pulling power'.⁴⁰

This was sound advice to a department of state with a reputation for secrecy and indifference to the changing moods of public opinion. But, despite the efforts of first Tyrrell and then Koppel while serving as successive heads of the News Department, the Foreign Office was until 1921 unable to employ a man with the necessary qualifications. That man was Arthur Willert, who was appointed, to borrow Maurice Hankey's phrase, to enter 'the lions' den of the press'.⁴¹

Publicity and diplomacy, 1919–1939

'A permanently going concern'

Willert joined the News Department of the Foreign Office in the spring of 1921 following a distinguished career as Washington correspondent of *The Times*. During the war he had gained some experience of propaganda while serving in the British official organisation in the United States. His journalistic experience, combined with his extensive contacts in influential American political circles, was immediately put to good use by the Foreign Office when he was despatched to the Washington Conference to take charge of press publicity on behalf of the British delegation.[42] This was, in fact, the first time that an officially accredited representative of the Foreign Office was made responsible for public relations at a major international conference. At Paris in 1919, no such official had been appointed at first, although Lloyd George had been forced under pressure to invite Lord Riddell to undertake the task.[43] On arriving in Washington, Willert discovered that Riddell was again being utilised by the Prime Minister.[44] Although the Foreign Office 'disapproved' of Riddell's presence, Willert admitted that he liked him a great deal, 'against my better judgement'.[45] After some initial confusion concerning the role of each man, Willert decided to 'make the best' of Riddell's considerable experience, and an arrangement was reached whereby Riddell, Fleet Street's representative, supervised the daily press conferences until his departure in December 1921, when Willert took over.[46]

Willert considered that he generally received a good response from the newspapermen who chose to attend his press conferences: 'They seem to like mine all right and flock to it in great numbers. The cross-questioning usually lasts for 20–30 minutes. It is rather fun. One is quoted in the press as being "a British spokesman".'[47] However, once the novelty had worn off, Willert began to find the work mentally and physically exhausting. Before long, he was to be found describing the harsh realities of his task: 'I never want to see a journalist again. I marvel at people's patience with me when I was one. Every morning I have to go and be heckled by the correspondents. At first it amused me. Now it fills me with nausea aggravated by fear of saying the wrong things.'[48] But despite his occasional bouts of depression, the British publicity arrangements were widely praised as a great triumph.[49] 'If so', Willert concluded, 'it shows

The Foreign Office and the press

what can be done by telling nothing but the truth and not trying to have propaganda.'[50] Indeed, such was considered to have been the success of the Washington experiment in supplying official news and comment relating to the daily progress of the conference that the diplomatic tradition was henceforth established whereby a News Department official was attached to the British delegation at every major international gathering.

On his return in 1922, Willert assumed responsibility for the News Department's press work with the British and foreign newspaper correspondents in London. His job involved the issue of daily communiqués to journalists 'seeking background as much as hot news'.[51] Important editors and representatives from the so-called prestige press were usually handled by the private secretaries. Following the departure of Lloyd George, Willert also advised the Prime Minister's office at 10 Downing Street on all press matters relating to foreign affairs.[52] A further duty, which began during the Chanak crisis, was the compilation of news telegrams on important foreign policy issues for the benefit of the Colonial Office, which in turn transmitted them to the governments of the Dominions.[53] Willert continued this work only until 1926 when Dominion susceptibilities led to the creation of a Dominions Information Office with responsibility for handling all information between the British government and the Dominions.[54] Percy Koppel was transferred from the News Department to supervise this work, while Willert himself became head of the News Department in 1925.

Willert was fortunate in that his promotion broadly coincided with the appointment of Sir William Tyrrell as permanent under secretary at the Foreign Office following the death of Sir Eyre Crowe. Crowe had not been particularly enthusiastic about the News Department's press work. Willert has described how Crowe once informed him that 'he could not see why I was necessary, why diplomacy had to hold the press in such consideration. But Tyrrell, who knew about these things, said it was. Therefore, he Crowe, would always be at my disposal.'[55] J. D. Gregory has confirmed this, stating that Crowe considered it 'quite unnecessary to bother about public opinion: he ignored the influence of the press which he hardly read'.[56] One suspects that Willert and Tyrrell were the exceptions; most officials would undoubtedly have been more sympathetic towards Crowe's attitude. Austen Chamberlain, who became

Foreign Secretary in 1924, certainly leaned towards traditionalism. Willert's first consideration in his new capacity as head of the News Department was to make the publicity arrangements for the signature of the Locarno Treaties in London in December 1925. Willert quickly discovered that his chief was 'anything but news-conscious', and he was forced to enlist the aid of Tyrrell in persuading the Foreign Secretary to permit the world's press to witness the ceremony. Willert described Chamberlain's desire to perform the ceremony 'in dignified privacy' as 'an outstanding example of his ignorance of the needs of those who deal with the news of international politics'.[57] Indeed, it was only through the intervention of Tyrrell, who appealed to Prime Minister Baldwin, with whom Tyrrell enjoyed a close relationship of confidentiality,[58] that Willert was able to secure the admission of journalists and photographers into the conference room.[59]

The conditions under which Willert's staff laboured proved extremely difficult. As Willert complained in June 1925, 'It might be just possible to carry on with the present staff were holidays unnecessary, if one could work continually under high tension, and if there were no League of Nations Meetings, no crises, no Conferences and no other emergencies.' But, he continued,

> we should be carrying on only under the constant menace of disaster. One of our greatest difficulties has been the lack of time for adequate consultation with Members of the Office, for quiet thought, for the cultivation of confidential relations with the more important members of the press and the development of our liaison with the Prime Minister's Office, the Treasury, etc. Unless we can keep in well-informed touch with those whose affairs we have to discuss we are obviously living on a volcano.[60]

Willert maintained that the press work would not become 'a permanently going concern' until 'it is established upon a basis sufficiently broad and elastic to permit it to work methodically and smoothly'.[61]

In view of these fears, it was perhaps fortunate that the Locarno Treaties which Willert had sought to publicise heralded a new period of relative calm in international affairs. Willert described life in the Foreign Office during the Locarno era as quiet and uneventful,[62] a statement which is reflected in the files of the News Department. But it was during this period that the press work on the News Department was placed upon a smooth and efficient basis. The propaganda side of the work was, however, reduced. In 1925, the

The Foreign Office and the press

staff of the News Department had totalled fourteen – more than any of the political departments.[63] This was halved during the following two years. The expenditure of the department, which had been £80,000 in 1920, was also steadily reduced during the course of the 1920s, and in 1927 a mere £17,550 was sanctioned.[64] A further illustration of the Treasury's policy of retrenchment in so far as the News Department's expenditure was concerned was the discontinuation of the post of press attaché at Brussels. It was decided to employ instead a part-time official on similar lines to those already existing in Sofia, Tokyo and Buenos Aires.[65]

The various other forms of propaganda conducted by the News Department since the end of the war were also gradually reduced to a position of secondary importance, the main emphasis being placed upon press publicity. The general administrative supervision of the News Department was undertaken by those officials who were also responsible for the collection and distribution of news to the British and foreign press. In the late 1920s those officials were Willert, Clifford Norton (later private secretary to Sir Robert Vansittart, 1930–7), E. M. B. Ingram (later diplomatic adviser to the Ministry of Economic Warfare, 1939–41) and George Steward, who was, more usually, supervising press publicity for the British delegation to the League of Nations in Geneva. In 1929, Steward was joined by Norton following complaints that there was 'an absence of touch between the British delegation and the press'.[66] These officials were also responsible after 1925 for interviewing editors, foreign editors, leader-writers, diplomatic correspondents and representatives from the news agencies. Information was issued orally, unless there was an official communiqué, and often on the understanding that it should be regarded as unofficial, with instructions not to disclose its source.

This proved to be a far more satisfactory and workable method than had existed since the war. Indiscretions and leaks were, of course, inevitable. But when a confidence was broken, as in December 1926 when the *Daily Chronicle* published a series of articles attacking Mussolini, Willert would suggest to the guilty journalist that 'We did not wish to curtail anybody's liberty of criticism, but that we did feel that it was unfair to the Italians, and against our own interests, that such obvious libels should be allowed to appear in a British newspaper of standing.'[67] In fact, there was little that the

Publicity and diplomacy, 1919–1939

News Department or indeed anybody could do in the event of indiscretions other than express wisdom after the event. There was no desire to return to the mutual antipathy of the immediate post-war years. Rather, an atmosphere of mutual trust and confidence was sought in an attempt to avoid similar embarrassments. But as Norton pointed out, 'the papers most prone to scandal-mongering are precisely those over which we have least influence'.[68]

On occasion, the News Department would receive a request from a foreign government or minister to 'lecture or even control the British press on their behalf'. Willert would reply in such cases:

> We always explain to them (1) that HMG have no power of censorship over the press; (2) that if a foreign government wants to approach the British press, it must do so itself. The only concession which we ever make is to promise to try unofficially, as occasion offers, to prevail upon our press to use the right spectacles.[69]

It was this gentle art of persuasion and friendly advice that Willert sought to introduce to the Foreign Office's dealings with the press. As a former journalist himself, he was aware of the limits to which he could go without causing alienation; yet he was equally aware of the limited nature of his department's work when dealing with recalcitrant newspapers.

The procedures for receiving the press, as introduced by Willert and continued by his successors, remained largely unchanged until the outbreak of the Second World War. At 12.30 pm each day, a member of the News Department's staff or, in the event of a crisis, the head, would conduct a meeting principally for the benefit of the news agencies and the evening papers, at which routine news was given out and any questions answered. The information thus released was of an elementary nature, 'the sort of stuff that you are apt to see on the tape-machines at lunchtime', as one official put it.[70] Other newspapermen were welcome to attend the midday meetings if they so wished, but views and guidance were not normally a feature of them. The bulk of the work tended to be conducted during the course of the afternoon when the staff made themselves available for interviews with foreign editors, diplomatic correspondents and important foreign journalists either collectively or, if preferred, individually. Willert personally concentrated upon seeing 'as much as possible ... the foreign editors of the big newspapers and the

The Foreign Office and the press

more important newspapers, British and foreign' to discuss international affairs in private.[71] The staff would meet together twice daily to exchange information 'and to get a definite uniform line as to what is to be given out, and what views and guidance is advisable on important questions'.[72] If specific issues were raised, the staff would consult with the relevant political departments of the Foreign Office. Although it was maintained that there were 'no discrimination and no favours to anybody', Willert's assertion that 'there is really no difference in our treatment of the Foreign Press and the British Press'[73] must be treated with some scepticism.

In marked contrast to Austen Chamberlain, Willert discovered that his successor, Arthur Henderson, was fully receptive to his ideas concerning publicity in diplomacy. Willert later recalled that 'during my fourteen years at the Foreign Office, I worked with only one Secretary of State, Arthur Henderson, and with one Permanent Under Secretary, Lord Tyrrell, who really understood publicity'.[74] Immediately after taking office, Henderson emphasised to Willert the importance of the News Department's work.[75] There was the additional bonus of the new Prime Minister, Ramsay MacDonald, who also proved enthusiastic, and the cordial relationship which existed between the Foreign Office and 10 Downing Street was clearly evident in the successful publicity arrangements at the 1930 London Naval Conference.[76] Co-operation with the Prime Minister's office was not, in itself, unusual, because, since Lloyd George's departure, the News Department had advised No 10 on all press matters connected with foreign affairs, and had even on occasions organised prime ministerial press conferences.[77] However, what was unusual was that the publicity arrangements, which involved press, radio and newsreel coverage, were an unqualified success. Shortly afterwards, George Steward was transferred from the News Department to help establish a press office at the Prime Minister's office. He remained at No 10 throughout the 1930s.

Following the enlightened paternalism of Henderson towards the work of the News Department, Willert experienced almost a complete reversal of attitudes under Sir John Simon. Willert had first experienced Simon's lack of tact during the Manchurian crisis when the Foreign Secretary made an off-the-record comment expressing sympathy for the Japanese in the presence of American correspondents.[78] Mutual antipathy between the two men was to develop further during the proceedings of the World Disarmament Conference, because Willert, who spent most of his time in Geneva supervising the publicity for the British delegation, believed that Simon's speeches did much to undo the impression he had striven to create with the press.[79] Tension came to a head in November 1934 when, following certain indiscretions by Simon in the lobby of the House of Commons, Willert reminded the Foreign Secretary: 'I have more than once ventured to warn you that in speaking to the British press you are, in effect, also speaking to the foreigner.'[80] Simon retorted by accusing Willert of failing to secure a favourable image for him in the press. Willert recalled that the Foreign Secretary then told him that 'I was too old for the job. What he wanted was some young man who could interpret his mind and pass it on to the press in the right way.'[81] It appears, however, that Willert had not been happy at the Foreign Office for some time. Uncertainty concerning his future position and pension (he had remained a temporary counsellor since his appointment) was aggravated by illness, and the rows with Simon had forced him into an impossible position. He resigned in December 1934 to the general regret of the press, who presented him with a silver rose-bowl as a tribute to the man who had placed their relations with the Foreign Office on a sound footing and, indeed, had made them 'a permanently going concern'.

Rex Leeper

During the course of the 1930s, the Foreign Office became increasingly preoccupied with alternative methods of securing publicity for the British point of view. Although the News Department's press work continued to occupy an integral position within its overall propaganda programme and even, between 1935 and 1939, became the centre of much controversy, the changing emphasis was symbolised by the replacement of Willert by Reginald (Rex) Leeper.

Rex Leeper had joined the News Department in 1929 as Willert's second-in-command. He and his talented brother, Allen, were Australian by birth, and both were devout Anglo-Catholics. Both had served in the wartime propaganda machinery: Rex had been in charge of the Russian section of the Political Intelligence Department, and Allen, the elder by one year, held the corresponding position in the Balkan section. Rex's offices in Victoria Street were

The Foreign Office and the press

directly below those used by Maxim Litvinov, the Russian Bolshevik Party's first 'ambassador' abroad, and he was, in fact, the only British official then allowed to see Litvinov.[82] Rex wrote extensively on Russian affairs for *The New Europe*, as did Allen on Central European affairs, and their linguistic expertise was to prove invaluable in their writing of PID memoranda during the Paris Peace Conference.[83] It was at this time that they first came into contact with William Tyrrell. After the war, Allen became assistant private secretary to Lord Curzon and began a close personal friendship with Robert Vansittart. In 1933, he was appointed head of the League of Nations and Western Department of the Foreign Office, but a promising career was tragically cut short when he died suddenly in 1935 at the age of forty-eight.[84]

Rex Leeper had remained in the diplomatic service during the 1920s, serving at Riga, Constantinople and Warsaw before joining the News Department in 1929. He embarked upon this latest stage of his career with a passion and enthusiasm rarely equalled, and, before long, Willert considered him 'by far the best First Secretary I have ever had'.[85] Leeper shared Willert's attitude towards Sir John Simon, considering him 'slow, indecisive and afraid',[86] but he did not have to endure him for very long; six months after his appointment as head of the News Department, Simon was replaced by the ill-fated Sir Samuel Hoare.

During the early 1930s, while Willert was busy in Geneva, Leeper deputised for him in meeting the press in London, and the invaluable experience which he gained at this time proved to be his apprenticeship before succeeding Willert in January 1935. Leeper's experience of the press left him somewhat cynical. In October 1932, he felt that the British press was 'showing itself quite incompetent to deal with foreign affairs' and was not exercising its proper influence.[87] In contrast to those views which had been current at the end of the First World War, Leeper was more realistic in recognising that foreign affairs remained the interest of a very limited section of the population. The press was thus potentially in a strong position to guide, rather than follow or reflect, public opinion on a larger scale. Part of the problem, he felt, derived from the decline of the journalistic profession; the emphasis was no longer on quality but on circulation, finance and business. As a result, diplomatic correspondents who called at the News Department as one source of their information were not receiving the support of their editors, particularly in the popular press, who did not think that the public was interested in foreign affairs. Yet even the journalists themselves did not escape criticism. Leeper wrote that 'the tendency of the diplomatic correspondents is to employ a phraseology even more diplomatic than that of diplomacy with the result that their contributions are both dull and obscure and are probably ignored by the average reader'.[88] He further considered that the journalists who attended the daily meetings at the News Department only when it suited them to pick up or to confirm snippets of information did not fully appreciate that 'the main function of the Foreign Office is to discuss the important questions of the day and to preserve continuity of policy so that an intelligent public opinion may be formed on foreign affairs'.[89] Leeper therefore proposed that Fleet Street should be reminded of the facilities available to them in this respect, because, he continued,

the muddled-headedness and inconsistency of English public opinion as expressed in the newspapers causes difficulties to our own Government and accentuates differences in Europe. If newspapers would really maintain close and serious contact with the Foreign Office, they would not always agree with official policy, but they would at any rate have a much clearer picture as to what it was they disagreed with. Their criticisms might then be better informed and more useful.[90]

It was upon these assumptions that Leeper based his techniques of supplying news and information to the press when he took charge of the News Department. By then, he had already established valuable contacts with several journalists who were quite prepared to take advantage of the facilities provided for them by the Foreign Office.[91]

However justified Leeper's conception of the Foreign Office's role in the education of British public opinion may have been, he was to become a controversial figure between 1935 and 1939, because his interpretation of the policy which he believed the government should adopt often differed radically from that of his political masters. Leeper was on close personal terms with Sir Robert Vansittart, the permanent under secretary until 1937, and with Anthony Eden, Foreign Secretary until February 1938, and, as the official responsible for revealing the 'Foreign Office view' to the press, he was in a unique position. Never before had the liaison between these three key positions within the Foreign Office been so close. Unfortunately, because Leeper's transactions with the press were usually

The Foreign Office and the press

conducted orally, there remains little record of what was said on either side.[92] But there is some evidence to suggest that Leeper did on occasion — if not more often — utilise, perhaps even abuse, his position to give public expression to his own personal views, views which generally tended to coincide with those of Vansittart or, less frequently, with those of Eden.

A passionate advocate of rearmament, Leeper saw the work of the News Department as an extension of that programme which he termed 'psychological rearmament'. Like Vansittart, he saw a resurgent Germany under Hitler as posing the main threat to European peace, a belief which was central to his political ideology. On 28 April 1935, Leeper wrote to his sister:

Germany continues to commit every act of folly and is rapidly alienating opinion here. The Times has steadily continued a pro-German campagn in the face of our contrary advice and are only slowly beginning to realise the magnitude of their error. There is only one thing the Germans understand and that is force. The only way to preserve peace is to stand up to them.

Again, on 14 May 1935, he wrote:

My main preoccupation is of course the position in Germany. It is difficult to educate public opinion here as to the danger that threatens us. The English prefer not to face unpleasant facts and to put off the evil day for as long as possible. If you point out the danger at all forcibly they describe you as an alarmist. Many people are saying this of me at present, but one has to put up with it.

Leeper believed that British rearmament would serve as a deterrent to possible German aggression, and although he did not exclude the possibility of concessions, he did consider that wholesale concessions would only serve to jeopardise Anglo-French relations without setting a limit to future German expansion. It was for these reasons that he opposed the Anglo-German Naval Agreement signed in June 1935.

Leeper's views concerning Italy were less consistent. During the months leading up to the Italian invasion of Abyssinia in October 1935, he was initially inclined towards the appeasement of Mussolini in order to preserve the solidarity of the Stresa 'front' against Germany, but, in August 1935, he began to urge a pro-League policy. However, he feared that the British government 'will simply let events take their course with Italy and Abyssinia' which, as he informed his sister on 7 August, would be 'to my mind the most dangerous thing that could happen. When you refuse to take small risks you are generally confronted with greater ones later on. In the present case this will certainly be true ... I can merely say that I regard it as vital to risk a war with Italy in defence of the Covenant.' Hence, when Hoare's speech in Geneva early in September appeared to provide the League with the full force of British support, Leeper was optimistic. On 11 September, he wrote:

> The British Government by remaining absolutely firm have rallied steady and increasing support to their side. The Italians are now completely isolated... The most important thing is that our own Govt. should act firmly but not violently and retain the limited support of our own people. Then they must have an election as soon as possible and immediately put through a big programme of general rearmament. Until we become really strong there is no security for Europe. If we do so quickly and on an adequate scale, it will be possible we hope to prevent a European war.

However, his optimism was short-lived. Following the Italian invasion of Abyssinia on 3 October and the imposition of, albeit limited, economic sanctions, Leeper wrote (on 22 October):

> Watching events from here I am impressed more than anything by the fact that neither this country (in spite of speeches and resolutions) nor any other is prepared to fight for the League. These weeks have made me extremely sceptical. The main desire here is to get out of this imbroglio as quickly as possible and have peace. Once the Election is over I think the Govt. will be more active in trying to come to terms with Italy. The League will have to be preserved and then transformed, but never again will we go through with the League in its present form.

Instead, Leeper now began to urge a non-commital policy, preferring to avoid commitments until rearmament was in a more advanced stage. By November 1937, Leeper again began to urge a pro-Italian policy over the question of 'volunteers' in the Spanish Civil War in order to prevent Mussolini from being driven irretrievably into the German camp.[93] Oliver Harvey, Eden's private secretary, noted: 'Rex and Van[sittart] are now quite frantic on this subject – how they change!'[94]

It proved to be only a momentary change of heart. Leeper soon became opposed to the notion of concessions to Mussolini during the negotiations for an Anglo-Italian rapprochement at the close of 1937. Bruce Lockhart, a close friend since their wartime association

The Foreign Office and the press

with Litvinov, recorded that Leeper saw no need to yield to 'bluff and bluster', because, despite outward appearances, Britain had much hidden strength.[95] However, the vigorous anti-British propaganda campaign in the state-subsidised German and Italian press had been posing a serious threat to Britain's search for an agreement with the dictators. Many Foreign Office officials had become increasingly alarmed at the apparent failure of the British press to exercise restraint and ignore the challenge. Diplomacy was forced to operate under extremely difficult conditions. During Lord Halifax's visit to Germany in November 1937, Hitler had suggested that 'nine-tenths of all tension was produced simply and solely' by the press.[96] This, albeit exaggerated, view was not entirely without substance; only a few days before the Hitler–Halifax talks, a statement had been issued to the press by Leeper emphasising the informal and limited nature of the meeting, but it had not been published by British newspapers.[97] Indeed, propaganda had become such a live issue by the winter of 1937–8 that Eden informed Count Grandi, the Italian ambassador in London, that unless anti-British propaganda ceased during the negotiations for a rapprochement, 'it would be impossible to create an atmosphere which was necessary for these conversations. In our view, therefore, the cessation of propaganda ... was an essential preliminary to successful conversations.'[98]

Because the British press was not entirely without guilt in creating such a heated international atmosphere, Leeper decided to review the methods employed by the News Department in its dealings with Fleet Street. In January 1938, he returned to his theme about the continuing 'deterioration' in the quality of British journalistic standards. The blame for 'the present irresponsible and sensational tendency of the British press in treating foreign affairs' lay, he believed, with the editors and proprietors, who 'must be made to realise that this country cannot afford to let foreign affairs be treated with the same irresponsible freedom as home affairs. In the event of war they would not dream of doing so.'[99] Leeper therefore proposed increased ministerial contact with leading editors and with the Newspaper Proprietors' Association rather than confining their contact to answering questions in the lobby of the House of Commons. Of course, Baldwin had seen much of Geoffrey Dawson, editor of *The Times*, and his successor, Neville Chamberlain, had regular contacts with *The Sunday Times*.[100] But Leeper wished to see greater ministerial contact with the press as a whole rather than individual contacts. He concluded: 'We can only hope to induce the press to exercise restraint in foreign affairs by taking those irresponsible persons into our confidence. A free press is an enormous asset to the country provided that freedom does not degenerate into irresponsible licence. At present we are not tackling the heart of the problem.'[101] Such were the views of a man whose own conduct was becoming the subject of increasing concern, particularly at 10 Downing Street, where many people might have termed Leeper's behaviour as having 'degenerated into irresponsible licence'.

The activities of the Prime Minister's press office had been the subject of considerable anxiety within the Foreign Office since the advent of Neville Chamberlain as premier. Initially, during the early 1930s, relations had been cordial and co-operative. In the final three years of peace, however, those relations deteriorated rapidly. No 10 was suspicious of the press releases issued by the News Department. For example, in November 1937, Maurice Hankey wrote to Vansittart on the problems confronting Anglo-Italian relations:

> Perhaps I am wrong to say what follows, and I only do so because I know that some other people feel the same, namely, a doubt as to whether the Foreign Office are really convinced from the bottom of their hearts that we ought to make friends with Italy or that we can do so. It would obviously require a greater effort on the part of the whole Office, including especially the Press Department.[102]

Yet suspicion was mutual. Eden suspected that the exaggerated press reports which had appeared prior to the Hitler–Halifax meeting were the result of inspiration by No 10.[103] Tension came to a head early in January 1938 following the publication of an article in *The Times* describing the harsh conditions of Italian rule in Abyssinia which closely resembled an official despatch received in the Foreign Office from Addis Ababa a few months earlier.[104] This appeared to confirm the belief of many Downing Street officials that the News Department under Leeper was attempting to undermine the government's Italian policy and was conducting 'a deliberate anti-Italian campaign'.[105] Moreover, as the rift between Chamberlain and Eden appeared to be broadening in February 1938, Oliver Harvey noted:

> Fleet Street is full of rumours of the division of the Cabinet between the PM and AE. This is, of course, the inevitable result of Whitehall speaking with

The Foreign Office and the press

two voices – i.e. recent accounts of our negotiations with Italy (whether put out by No 10 or by some other Cabinet Minister) independently of, and in conflict with those of the FO News Department. I can't believe the PM can have put them out, though Rex has very circumstantial evidence from journalists that they did come from No 10 at any rate.[106]

Whatever the real truth of the matter, one thing is clear. Following the 'promotion' of Vansittart in December 1937, and the resignation of Eden two months later, Leeper's own position was in jeopardy. Within six months he had been removed from the public limelight by being taken off press work and placed in charge of the purely propaganda activities of the Foreign Office.

Leeper's relationship with Vansittart's successor, Alexander Cadogan, had not been as cordial. Similarly, Eden's successor, Lord Halifax, proved less enthusiastic about the News Department's work, though no immediate changes were made. Bruce Lockhart noted that Leeper did not like these changes in personnel and that Cadogan in particular did not take the 'same interest in the News Department and all the propaganda work which Rex has built up'.[107] Although Leeper informed his sister that, although Halifax was 'very charming to deal with', he did not have much confidence in him as a Foreign Secretary because 'he doesn't throw himself into it in anything like the way that Eden did'. Indeed, in May 1938, Cadogan noted that Leeper was 'still hypnotised by A[nthony Eden] and very anti-Chamberlain'.[108] Leeper himself made no secret of his views concerning the Prime Minister's policies, particularly with regard to Germany. He informed his sister on 13 May 1938: 'I am no upholder whatever of our present regime here and I regard the PM as a disaster. I favoured an agreement with Italy, but I do not favour negotiations with Germany, as there is nothing to negotiate but our own surrender.' Three weeks earlier, he had written (20 April):

I regard Germany as the one dangerous enemy and everything is subordinate to that. At the same time I don't want to exaggerate what can be got out of it [i.e. an Anglo-Italian agreement]. We are not going to separate Italy from Germany, as we are not strong or impressive enough for Mussolini to take any such risk. It does however reduce our own troubles in the Mediterranean and does to a certain extent make Italy less dependent on Germany. It is a very good thing that France is now going to make a similar arrangement with Italy. We and France must keep in line in everything we do. I don't like the terms of the settlement with Italy, but we are not in a position in which we can stand too much on our dignity.

As the Czechoslovakian crisis threatened to come to a head in the summer of 1938, Leeper informed his sister (on 29 June):

> 1938 is going to be, I think, a year not of war, but of a great retreat on our part. We have rearmed much too slowly and are now caught. We are likely therefore to go on giving way to Germany. That seems to me to be the real meaning of the Chamberlain policy for which I have no enthusiasm, but which officially I have to support with the press.

Even so, before long, Barrington-Ward, the assistant editor of *The Times*, gained the impression that 'the news department of the Foreign Office is really a centre of anti-Government propaganda'.[109] Although this statement must be treated with some caution, it does appear to confirm the suspicion that the News Department's press office was releasing information to journalists which supporters of Chamberlain would have preferred not to see published. It was perhaps for this reason that under Leeper's direction, assisted by his second-in-command, Charles Peake, the News Department earned the affectionate nickname from journalists of 'Leak and Peeper'.[110]

Leeper's behaviour during the crisis of September 1938 sealed his fate. On 26 September, Leeper was responsible for the release of the press communiqué which stated that, in the event of a German attack, Britain and the Soviet Union would 'certainly stand by France' in defence of Czechoslovakia.[111] Neither the French nor the Russians knew anything about it. A repudiation was issued immediately, but the damage had been done. Leeper had succeeded in embarrassing the government by trying to force its hand. His action did not go unnoticed among Chamberlain's 'inner circle'. As one of its members, Samuel Hoare, recalled, 'the incident warned us of the need for improving relations with the press, and it was for this purpose that I held daily meetings with the representatives of the leading papers'.[112] The increased ministerial contact which Leeper had advocated earlier in the year had finally materialised, but only at great expense to his own career.

However, Leeper's position was not quite decided. At the end of September 1938, he re-examined the procedures employed by the News Department in its dealings with the press in light of the recent crisis. In an unusually subdued, almost repentant, mood, he wrote:

The Foreign Office and the press

'I am not sure whether the methods we have always adopted and are still adopting are the best in the circumstances.'[113] He suggested that the existing arrangements whereby representatives from the news agencies were received shortly after midday, and diplomatic correspondents throughout the afternoon, worked well enough under normal circumstances but, he continued,

> I am doubtful whether it is wise to continue this method in the present critical circumstances when we have to be extremely careful what we say and when it is important to eliminate the risk of being misinterpreted. It is essential for the News Department to act and speak in the closest understanding with No 10 and to avoid being led into discussions on matters of foreign policy beyond what is necessary to explain the official view.[114]

In a remarkable reversal of his previous attitude, Leeper then went on to advocate the complete discontinuation of individual interviews, preferring instead to meet the entire press collectively at 5 pm daily, and the foreign press immediately afterwards. He continued: 'By doing so we should avoid being drawn into discussions and should confine ourselves to giving official news and views and answering legitimate questions ... I am most anxious that the News Department should do its best for the Government during these times and that No 10 should understand our practice and approve it.'[115] Whether or not Leeper made this sudden *volte-face* in a fit of depression – it was the day of Chamberlain's visit to Munich – or because he was trying to salvage his career, or even because he had become disillusioned with certain journalists for misinterpreting his views or abusing his confidences, is impossible to ascertain from the available archives. Whatever the real reason, this latest memorandum constituted a damaging admission of guilt. Leeper was to pay the price of a permanent official involving himself too deeply in the affairs of his political masters early in October 1938 when he was taken off press work and placed in charge of the News Department's purely propaganda work. Charles Peake replaced him as the Foreign Office's press officer.

Peake continued to conduct the News Department's relations with the press along the lines drawn up by Willert and developed (some might say abused) by Leeper. But this might not have been the case had various proposals put forward by Peake been implemented. Peake took over the press office at a time when the Foreign Office News Department's relations with 10 Downing Street were at a low ebb. He attempted to improve matters by working in cooperation with, rather than against or parallel to, George Steward's press office at No 10. He suggested a 'tacit agreement' whereby the News Department's press work would be much reduced and 'guidance on the major questions' relating to foreign affairs would be the responsibility of the Prime Minister's office, while the Foreign Office would limit itself to 'guidance and information on routine questions'.[116] Had these proposals come into force, they would effectively have heralded a return to the situation which had existed during the period of the Lloyd George government. That they did not was largely due to the rapid unfolding of events during the final year of peace, when the number of visiting journalists, particularly from the foreign press, increased steadily. In July 1938, an average number of forty correspondents were calling at the Foreign Office every day; a year later, the number had risen to over fifty.[117] By the outbreak of war, the News Department's press officer was considered to be 'one of the hardest working men in the Foreign Office' and among the demands of the job included being on call around the clock and seemingly endless luncheon appointments.[118]

In the aftermath of Munich, the press continued to disappoint Leeper. On 23 October 1938, he informed his sister that 'the amount of stupid or dishonest articles that I read in the English press is almost incredible'. Even as late as April 1939 his lack of respect for the British press as a whole was still evident. He particularly disapproved of proprietors who, in his opinion, continued to ignore the hard facts of life in Germany, despite the efforts of the News Department to enlighten them. He wrote: 'The German press are simply telling lies about us on instructions. Our press are not telling lies about Germany. In fact they say very very little about the horrible things being done in Germany. There is no misunderstanding here to be cleared up ... it is definite misrepresentation.'[119] The implication was that, if British public opinion was not fully aware of the issues at stake in the Europe of 1939, particularly after the rape of Prague in March, this was not due to any lack of effort on the part of the News Department.[120] If the British press could not always be relied upon to provide a reliable medium of official publicity, then the fault lay not with the governmental machinery created specifically to inform that medium, but rather with the existence of a free and independent

The Foreign Office and the press

press in a democratic society which cherished the traditions of free speech and freedom to publish what it liked. War would create a quite different set of criteria.

Under normal peacetime conditions, the policies of a newspaper were determined by such factors as the political views of the proprietor and his editor, and even to some extent of the correspondents themselves. Their views were in turn affected by commercial considerations. The Foreign Office created and maintained its press office to ensure that newspaper coverage of foreign affairs would be based upon accurate information and intelligent comment. Yet what became of that information once it had left the News Department was dependent upon factors largely beyond the control of the Foreign Office, or indeed of any British department of state, unless, of course, publication jeopardised the defence of the realm. It was because of this somewhat limited function that the News Department sought to cultivate an atmosphere of mutual trust and respect with journalists in an attempt to exert the subtle influence inherent in personal contacts.

This is well illustrated by one episode in particular. In 1937, Leeper made a special arrangement with Printing House Square whereby special privileges would be granted to the diplomatic correspondent of *The Times*.[121] At first, Arthur Barker enjoyed the benefits of this arrangement, such as the ability to telephone the News Department – a facility denied other newspapers. But when Iverach McDonald replaced Barker in 1938, Leeper discovered an ideological ally in his distaste for the policies of the Chamberlain government. It has been suggested that Leeper 'doubtless hoped that by feeding *The Times* with official view-points in the form of news, it would become possible for foreigners and others to distinguish clearly between the paper's policy as declared in the leading articles and that of the government as reported in the news columns'.[122] If so, the arrangement almost certainly failed to achieve the desired result. Leeper would discuss the latest developments in the international situation with McDonald in private for about an hour, for his 'innermost guidance, not for repetition in any form'.[123] Only about a quarter of the material divulged in this manner was intended for publication. McDonald, after gathering information from his various other sources, would thus be in a position to write up his pieces from a much more knowledgeable standpoint than would have been the case without Leeper's confidential briefings. Whether or not his pieces were published in the newspaper depended upon the editor, Geoffrey Dawson, or his assistant, Barrington-Ward. Knowing their particular views, however, McDonald recognised that he would have to exercise great caution in the style and content of his articles so as to avoid revealing his own, and Leeper's, anti-appeasement views. But, as McDonald has claimed, 'several correspondents worked on the assumption that a wrapped-up truth in *The Times* was more effective than a stark truth in another paper with less influence. Some good ... was done in that way, but not enough to counter the harm done by the leaders.'[124] In other words, *The Times* may have served as an instrument of British overseas publicity because it tended to be regarded abroad as the house magazine of the establishment or even as the mouthpiece of the British government, but its views were not those of its diplomatic correspondent or of the News Department under Leeper.

The News Department's press work may thus be described as preventative rather than propagandist in the real sense. It was designed to prevent misinformed or misguided reports from appearing in the press which might react unfavourably upon the government of the day. Nevertheless, any appraisal of the News Department's work in the 1930s is complicated by the fact that Rex Leeper was its head between 1935 and 1939. Leeper was often suspected of attempting to use his position as press officer to secure publicity for his personal views. Evidence on this matter is thin, and, unfortunately, Leeper appears to have left no detailed record of his activities in the 1930s,[125] while his transactions with the press were usually conducted orally. Much of the controversy about his position undoubtedly derived from his close personal association with Sir Robert Vansittart, who was said to be 'one of Rex's heroes'[126] and whose views concerning the threat to peace posed by a resurgent Germany under Hitler were largely shared by Leeper. It is known that both men had worked together with Ralph Wigram in March 1935 to secure publicity for certain information relating to the alarming progress of German rearmament.[127] The utilisation of the press as an aid to their personal cause did not go unnoticed in Fleet Street. Two months later, in May 1935, Leo Kennedy of *The Times* claimed to have 'proof of rather outrageous attempts' by the Foreign Office, under Vansittart's direction, 'to rush the public into forming un-

The Foreign Office and the press

favourable opinions of German official utterances'.[128] Exactly what 'proof' Kennedy possessed is unknown, but it is not beyond the imagination to suspect Leeper of periodically leaking information to suit his own, or Vansittart's, purposes.

Between 1935 and 1938, Leeper became a prominent member of that admiring group of permanent officials who flocked around Anthony Eden during his tenure as Foreign Secretary. In March 1937 it appears that he was even offered the post of Eden's private secretary, but declined, preferring to stay at the News Department.[129] Leeper regarded Eden as the only member of the Baldwin and Chamberlain cabinets 'with any "guts"',[130] and he soon became one of the Foreign Secretary's closest advisers.[131] It is surely no coincidence, therefore, that Leeper, who became an outspoken opponent of appeasement following the departure of first Vansittart and then Eden from influential positions within the Foreign Office, was himself taken off press work within months of the loss of his two most powerful patrons. The precise reasons for his move sideways to take charge of the purely propaganda side of the News Department's work remain vague, but it was not due solely to the unfortunate episode of the Leeper communiqué of 26 September. As Cadogan noted,

> Since Anthony's departure (and before) I have had constant complaints from No 10 of the handling of the press by our News Department. Blame has been particularly attached to Leeper, not, I am bound to say, without some reason. But he has tried to do his best – if he has failed, I attribute it to no base motives.[132]

Regardless of his motives, however, Leeper had overstepped the mark on too many occasions to render his position secure.

Leeper's influence upon the development of Britain's overseas publicity and propaganda activities during the 1930s will constitute a major recurring theme of subsequent chapters, but, at this point, a brief résumé of those achievements may throw some further light on this extraordinary civil servant. It was on his initiative that the British Council was founded in 1934, and he was largely responsible for persuading the BBC to inaugurate broadcasts in foreign languages for the first time in 1938. A year earlier, he had been appointed assistant director-general designate (news division) of the shadow Ministry of Information, although he had been deeply

Publicity and diplomacy, 1919–1939

involved in the planning from the outset in 1935. In 1938, Leeper was charged with the task of reconstituting the Political Intelligence Department of the Foreign Office, and he also became involved in the preparations then under way for 'black' propaganda in wartime. It thus comes as no surprise to see him emerge in 1940 as the head of the Political Warfare Executive housed at Woburn Abbey. In 1943, he became British ambassador to the Greek government first in Cairo and then in Athens, a period which he recalled in his only book, *When Greek Meets Greek*.[133] From Greece he went on to the Argentine before retiring in 1948.

Despite his innovations in the controversial area of peacetime propaganda during the 1930s, it was his dealings with the press which were to excite immediate hostility. The position of Foreign Office press officer was undoubtedly a difficult task. Arthur Willert had also experienced problems with Sir John Simon. Although, once again, evidence concerning the row which resulted in Willert's resignation in 1934 is thin, Willert did leave a voluminous collection of personal papers as well as his published memoirs, several books and numerous articles. From these various sources, it is evident that Willert laboured constantly to convince some of his seniors of the importance of press publicity in modern British diplomacy. Eyre Crowe, Austen Chamberlain and Simon emerge as representatives of the older school which could see neither the point nor the value of taking the press into the confidence of the Foreign Office. After his resignation, Willert devoted much of his time to writing and lecturing on the greater need for increased activity in this direction. In 1939, for example, he wrote:

> Our public men still lag behind those of other countries in matters of organised publicity... In London it is an event for the Prime Minister or Foreign Minister to see the press either *en masse* or separately. And when they see the press they are as likely as not to help neither themselves nor the journalists... That same British modesty which renders self-advertisement so rare among our politicians can doubtless be made to account for our carelessness in regard to the organisation and inspiration of state publicity. It is also obviously difficult for a school of statesmanship so long inculcated with the idea of the inevitable and automatic supremacy of Great Britain in world affairs to realise how things have changed in that respect and how thoroughly the present precariousness of our position, both political and economic, justifies the growing demand for an adequate system of national advertisement.[134]

The Foreign Office and the press

There was unquestionably a great deal of truth in this statement, and it reveals a further example of the obstacles which faced the News Department between the wars. Had it not been for the support of men such as William Tyrrell, Arthur Henderson, Vansittart and Eden, British overseas publicity in peacetime might have fallen greater victim to prejudice and tradition.

It is certainly ironic that the Foreign Office, traditionally the most difficult of government departments to penetrate in the nineteenth century, should prove to be the first to open its doors to the press on a regular and systematic basis at the end of the First World War. In 1919, when the Cabinet presented Whitehall with the opportunity to create some machinery for the conduct of publicity,[135] only the Foreign Office chose to do so. Other government departments gradually recognised the need for such equipment,[136] but the News Department was the pioneer of what may be termed official public relations. Its wartime experience of propaganda had shown many Foreign Office officials the potential value of publicity in time of peace. It was felt that diplomacy had much to gain from a properly handled system of releasing official information to the press, both at home and abroad. Despite Northcliffe's opinion that the first generation of press and public relations officers were merely 'official excuse-makers',[137] the Foreign Office News Department was largely designed to correct misstatements and misconceptions about the nature of British foreign policy. The British image abroad would, it was believed, benefit as a result. The British press did, after all, provide foreigners with an important source of information about events in Britain, and if Fleet Street was reasonably well informed, then so, it was hoped, would the foreign observer be. But in an age when propaganda was increasingly being exploited by foreign governments to further their national interests in a forceful and competitive manner, means other than press publicity were required if Britain was to ensure that her own interests did not fall victim to the aggressive propaganda of her rivals.

2

The Foreign Office and propaganda abroad

Although the exact nature of the contribution made by British propaganda towards the achievement of victory in 1918 must necessarily remain the subject of historical debate,[1] the value of propaganda as an effective instrument of warfare was nonetheless widely appreciated by contemporaries. Regardless of whether the reputation for success either in helping to attract the United States into the war on the Allied side or in bringing the Central Powers to their knees is an undeserved myth or an undervalued reality, the fact remains that many people believed (or chose to believe) that these decisive events were not unrelated to the British government's skilful employment of propaganda between 1914 and 1918. There was, after all, much profit to be made from praising the work of Wellington House or that of Crewe House. In the United States, for example, the belief that the American people had somehow been duped into involvement in 1917 by propaganda merely served to reinforce the arguments of those isolationists who advocated withdrawal from the devious machinations of the Old World. And in Germany, the testimonies of prominent enemy personalities such as Hindenburg and Ludendorff ('we were hypnotised by the enemy propaganda as a rabbit by a snake')[2] were seized upon by Adolf Hitler to perpetuate the legend that the German army had not been defeated on the field of battle but had been betrayed from within following the collapse of morale at home caused by Lord Northcliffe's propaganda from Crewe House. Northcliffe was himself more modest about his achievement, being content merely to claim: 'We have to some extent hastened the end.'[3]

The British propaganda experiment had certainly proved an impressive lesson in improvisation. As J. D. Squires has written, 'Great Britain entered the World War with nothing that could even remotely be termed an official propaganda department. She finished the struggle with the best developed and probably the most effective

The Foreign Office and propaganda abroad

organisation devoted to propaganda of any of the belligerent nations.'[4] Having emerged from being something of a side-show at the start of the war, propaganda became a fully integrated wartime activity of the British government with the creation of a full Ministry of Information and the enemy propaganda department at Crewe House in 1918, although even by the time of the Armistice there was no single unified organisation to conduct propaganda from under one roof. Domestic propaganda, for example, remained the preserve of the National War Aims Committee. Inter-Allied coordination of propaganda policy had never really gone beyond the planning stages. And the older-established Whitehall departments had to a considerable degree closed ranks in order to preserve their traditional duties when Beaverbrook and Northcliffe appeared to be encroaching upon them.[5] Nevertheless, despite these deficiencies, the role of propaganda in any future war seemed guaranteed. It was the value of propaganda as an effective instrument of peacetime diplomacy which remained open to considerable doubt.

From wartime expedient to peacetime commitment

During the closing stages of the First World War it became necessary to consider the possible future role – if any – of propaganda in the context of Britain's peacetime foreign policy. The automatic reaction of most politicians and officials was to abandon altogether the system for propaganda in foreign countries. The intense secrecy which had surrounded the work during the first two and a half years of the war, combined with the storm of indignation which had erupted over Lloyd George's appointment of Beaverbrook and Northcliffe in February 1918,[6] had served to reinforce the prejudices of those who already disliked the idea of official propaganda as a matter of principle. During the only major wartime debate on the subject, in August 1918, therefore, the attitude of the House of Commons was predictably hostile.[7] However, the testimonies of leading enemy personalities could not simply be ignored, and the apparent success of the wartime propaganda experiment was considered to be such that a few farsighted officials were prepared to give the subject careful and dispassionate examination.

On 16 October 1918, Lord Beaverbrook drew up a memorandum for the benefit of the War Cabinet in which he argued the need for considering the role of the Ministry of Information on the return of peace. While recognising that the aims, content and style of his ministry's propaganda would necessarily have to be modified to meet peacetime conditions, Beaverbrook nonetheless considered that it would be advisable to continue to work, at least until a peace treaty was signed, 'for public opinion will be a vital object to His Majesty's Government during the intervening period'.[8] He felt that the policy of the British government at the peace conference 'will have to be explained to the world day by day if the solidarity of Allied opinion is to be maintained' and that it might also be necessary 'to dwell on the efforts Great Britain has made during the war'.[9] He accordingly sought Cabinet authority to continue his work in order to secure 'public support in all foreign countries for the view of the Imperial Government and to give the reason why the Imperial Government is justified in adopting a certain attitude towards the problems before the Conference. In this way Allied opinion will be kept solid and neutral opinion friendly.'[10] Beaverbrook's scheme was not to materialise. The Minister of Information was forced to resign for reasons of ill health within a week of writing his memorandum, which was anyway not considered by the Cabinet until two days after the Armistice. It then lacked a sufficiently powerful champion, despite the support of John Buchan, who was appointed the official liquidator of the ministry.[11]

Similar schemes to that of Beaverbrook's were formulated in Crewe House. Campbell Stuart, Northcliffe's assistant, believed that 'the maintenance of British prestige demanded that our position in regard to the peace should be explained and justified by the widespread dissemination of news and views, both before and during the Peace Conference'.[12] Wickham Steed, then foreign editor of *The Times* as well as a senior official in Crewe House, was another who envisaged a peacetime role for propaganda, believing that it could serve a valuable purpose in particular with regard to future Anglo-German relations. Steed argued that by the promotion of international understanding through the free exchange of news and information, propaganda could enable the people of one nation to better understand the actions and policies of another. He felt that Crewe House could accordingly be converted into 'an agency of enlightenment on both sides, and might help to find a "common denominator"'. Otherwise, he continued, 'the conclusion of peace

The Foreign Office and propaganda abroad

would be followed by a dangerous period of ignorance and misunderstanding'.[13] Steed secured the support of his chief, but the scheme became less ambitious in the process, Northcliffe preferring instead to transform the work into a means of 'enabling the German people gradually to see why Germany had lost the war, and, to understand the force of the moral ideals which had ranged practically the whole world against her'.[14]

Northcliffe approached the Prime Minister on 3 November with a request to undertake 'peace terms propaganda in the closest collaboration with the various departments of state until the final peace settlement has been concluded'.[15] It was an inopportune moment. Relations between Northcliffe and Lloyd George, always erratic, were fast deteriorating, and the question of the future role of propaganda became inevitably submerged beneath more immediate issues.[16] Northcliffe, like Beaverbrook, had not been in the best of health. The question of peacetime propaganda and the future role of the press lords was a highly delicate political issue, and few seemed prepared to tackle the issues with the kind of commitment required to see through schemes for the re-education of Germany or for the propagation of the British point of view. Northcliffe was broadly correct when he wrote: 'As a people, we do not understand propaganda ways.'[17] Lloyd George was an exception in this respect, although, as A. J. P. Taylor has pointed out, if anything, he rated the importance of the press and propaganda too highly.[18] It was perhaps for this reason that many of his contemporaries disliked propaganda not only on principle but also for political reasons; it was not beyond the imagination of his critics to envisage official propaganda being utilised as a means of sustaining political power. With an impending general election, the maintenance of the wartime propaganda machinery might have caused a political outcry.

Northcliffe resigned his post as director of propaganda in enemy countries on 12 November 1918. The Crewe House machinery ground laboriously to a halt by the end of the year. Buchan, in his role as official liquidator, chose to dismantle the wartime machinery almost in its entirety. Most of the work was terminated completely, or, where this did not prove immediately possible, he issued instructions for its gradual cessation. Buchan further decided to return the responsibility for any remaining work, about which he was either uncertain or which he considered desirable to maintain, back into the hands of the Foreign Office for that department's deliberation and decision. This was not an unusual move. The Foreign Office had been effectively in control of propaganda from 1914 to 1917.[19] The Ministry of Information and Crewe House were officially closed down on 31 December 1918, although the process of liquidation did in fact take less time than originally anticipated, the Foreign Office having inherited the remnants some weeks earlier.[20] Writing in 1924, Wickham Steed lamented the discontinuation of British overseas propaganda at a time 'when I thought, and still think, it might have been constructively useful. With it disappeared also the chance of carrying out the plan for the enlightenment of the German people.'[21]

Steed was not entirely correct in his assumption that British official propaganda ended with the First World War. Having inherited the remnants of the wartime propaganda machinery, it remained for the Foreign Office to decide what to do with them. It turned out that Lloyd George was not the only representative of his generation who valued the importance of propaganda. Victor Wellesley, for example, who was at this time a member of the Commercial and Consular Department of the Foreign Office and who was to become a deputy under secretary from 1925 to 1936, was one official who did feel that there was room for a 'Propaganda Department' in the post-war Foreign Office. Writing essentially from his usual economic standpoint, he believed that the peacetime character of British overseas propaganda should fall into three categories:

1. Political. To maintain and develop British prestige in all parts of the world and to encourage smaller states to direct their political orientation towards this country.
2. Commercial. To develop British commerce in all available directions and by all legitimate means, e.g. by disseminating knowledge of British institutions, manufactures and produce, and trade facilities.
3. Cultural. To render available to foreign countries all that is best in British life and education, using that term in the widest possible sense, so as to include book learning, art, literature, methods of training youth, athletics, etc. This in reality forms part of the economic policy.[22]

Wellesley's latter comment provides an early illustration of the recognition that cultural and commercial propaganda were dependent for their success upon each other. However it took another ten years before this vital point became more widely accepted.

The Foreign Office and propaganda abroad

During the winter of 1918–19 there existed much confusion within the Foreign Office with regard to the question of propaganda. In January 1919, it was estimated that the total staff of the News Department numbered 223, including 44 messengers and 19 charwomen, of whom 118 seem to have been inherited from the Ministry of Information.[23] Foreign Secretary Balfour had already decided to reconstruct a smaller version of the original News Department in order to carry on such work of the ministry as it had been considered desirable to maintain.[24] This provided the signal to begin a salvage operation on the wreckage of the wartime machinery in order to construct what was called 'a skeleton organisation at home and abroad which can be clothed with flesh and blood at short notice in case of need'.[25]

Opinions within Whitehall varied considerably as to the desirability of continuing propaganda in peacetime. Lord Robert Cecil, for example, probably spoke for many when he wrote that, in peace, he 'disliked the idea of propaganda in foreign countries on general principles, apart from commercial propaganda which was the real line to follow'.[26] On the other hand, there was within the Foreign Office a small group of articulate officials with experience of propaganda work who argued strongly for continuation. George Beak had played a key role in distributing British propaganda material into Germany through neutral Switzerland while serving as consul-general in Zurich. In December 1918, Beak gave his reasons for supporting continuation, which centered on his belief that because the war had served to increase the level of popular interest in foreign affairs it had now become necessary to ensure the maximum publicity for the British point of view over that of other governments. But, he added,

> It need hardly be said ... that the spirit of British propaganda would differ wholly and entirely from the German, in that it would not be aggressive in character. Germany's aim was to secure an Empire and dominate Europe; our aim is, presumably, to preserve and develop what we already have. The object of our propaganda, therefore, would be chiefly to make our institutions, mode of Government, arts and sciences known and understood.[27]

Another official with experience dating back to the early part of the war, S. A. Guest, considered that peacetime propaganda was not simply desirable but essential, like it or not. He wrote:

> One of the chief lessons to be drawn from the experience of the war, and the

Publicity and diplomacy, 1919–1939

events leading up to it, is that Diplomacy by itself is not enough for the maintenance of satisfactory international relations... The fault lies in our lack of foresight in having to provide something further than Diplomacy. Now that nations are taking a much larger share than hitherto in their own government and international relations are being influenced by interests other than those of dynasties, we should be living in a Fools' Paradise if we were to expect that we should be able to maintain international equilibrium by means of a service which was originally designed to work under conditions which no longer exist. Commercial, financial, labour organisations and the press, to which the officially accredited diplomat, as such, cannot obtain direct access may, at any given moment, exercise a far more powerful influence on international politics than that which can be exerted by any Foreign Office, and unless we have means of directly observing and affecting these and other agencies, we shall not be in a position either to obtain knowledge of the drift of affairs, or to intervene in time to forestall injurious tendencies. For this purpose we require a permanent organisation for Political intelligence and 'Propaganda'.[28]

Quite apart from his plea to modernise the Foreign Office in such a way as to make it more capable of dealing with the new requirements of the twentieth century, Guest also maintained that because the return of peace had been accompanied by an escalation of the use of propaganda by foreign governments to further their national interests – often at the expense of British prestige – it had become essential for Britain to counter the false and malevolent claims of others. There was, in other words, a need to project a more balanced and representative picture of British aims and policies to combat the anti-British propaganda of foreign governments. He continued:

It would be the most puerile folly on our part to expect that henceforth a true version as to the policy, either internal or external, or the resources of the British Empire, will permeate everywhere and be maintained intact, and erroneous and dangerous misconceptions will be obviated, without continuous effort on our part... The scheme for establishing a League of Nations, to which our Government is now fully committed, even if we succeed in carrying it through its preliminary stages, cannot work successfully in practice in an atmosphere of unnecessary suspicion and misunderstanding between nations, whether within or without it.[29]

Such views were representative of a growing body of opinion – both within the Foreign Office and beyond – which considered that the News Department was a necessary institutional response to the new demands of post-war diplomacy.

The Foreign Office and propaganda abroad

It was because of these, and similar, views that Cecil Harmsworth, the acting minister of blockade and parliamentary under secretary for foreign affairs 1919–22, proposed a departmental conference to examine the entire question of propaganda with a view to clarifying the confusion. 'We are', he minuted, 'apparently going to be held responsible for "information" and we ought to formulate a policy or arrive at a decision of some kind without delay.'[30]

The proposed meeting took place on 20 March 1919 with Lord Curzon, acting foreign secretary during Balfour's absence at the Paris Peace Conference, in the chair. Such was the degree of confusion which existed within the Foreign Office concerning the future of propaganda that Curzon found it necessary to begin the meeting by establishing two fundamental axioms: '(1) that propaganda should continue, and; (2) that it should continue strictly in connexion with, or under the control of, the Foreign Office'.[31] It was estimated that a minimum figure of £100,000 would be required to carry on the necessary work satisfactorily. Sir William Tyrrell considered that special attention was 'desirable in the new countries, probably with a commercial "window dressing"'.[32] Little more is known about this important meeting. The rest of the discussion was concerned with the type of man who should be chosen to supervise propaganda. There was no suggestion that an outsider be appointed to head the News Department. Instead, it was decided to accept Lord Curzon's suggestion to appoint a permanent official – a decision which was to remain in force until the services of Sir Arthur Willert were recruited from *The Times* in 1921.

For the moment, Tyrrell emerged as the natural choice, and, on 26 March 1919, Curzon appointed him head of the News Department, it being decided between them to revive the old title in favour of the suggested 'Propaganda Department'.[33] Together they worked out the basic structure of the new body. Because of the importance of intelligence to the efficient conduct of propaganda, it was decided to amalgamate the Political Intelligence Department (of which Tyrrell was already head) with the News Department, an association which was to last only until 1920 when the PID was abolished. Tyrrell was to take his instructions 'on matters of high policy' directly from the Foreign Secretary, to whom he would be granted free access. The parliamentary under secretary of state for foreign affairs would serve as public spokesman for the department, and he would also be responsible for interviewing prominent journalists. Moreover, with regard to the position of the News Department's representatives abroad, it was laid down 'as a general principle' that

> the representative abroad should be a member of the British Embassy or Legation, selected for the purpose, and acting under orders of his chief. He might or might not be a member of the Foreign Service. The representative might require to be in touch with independent and unofficial organisations outside the Embassy or Legation.[34]

The organisation in the Foreign Office itself was to be divided into three broad sections: (1) a Cables and Wireless Division; (2) a Nationals or Administrative Division with seven geographical sub-sections, modelled on the PID's wartime system, and responsible for collecting and collating information from the various foreign sources for the benefit of the overseas agents 'on the spot'; (3) a Facilities Division, which would also be responsible for receiving the press.[35]

It was estimated that the News Department would require at least £100,000 for its work in the year 1919–20 – a reduction, in fact, of 95 per cent on the £2 million spent on all forms of propaganda during the final year of the war.[36] Mindful of the need for financial retrenchment, the Foreign Office worked hard to keep the estimate as low as possible, but still feared that 'in some cases the efficiency of British propaganda abroad may be gravely impaired' and trusted that, in reducing its staff and costs, the News Department's estimate did not fall below 'the level of prudence required by the prestige, political and commercial, of the British Empire abroad'.[37]

It was at this stage that the Foreign Office proposals, which had hitherto enjoyed a relatively uninterrupted passage, began to encounter severe opposition. There began a series of protracted negotiations with the Treasury chiefly over the question of finance, finally resulting in severe limitations on the range and scope of the News Department's post-war work. The estimates were submitted to the Treasury on 2 April, only to be queried, the main objection being to a figure of £25,000 which had been reserved for 'miscellaneous propaganda expenditure'. Under this heading, the News Department intended to extract the maximum propaganda value from, say, sending a Union Jack to an anglophile society or subscrib-

The Foreign Office and propaganda abroad

ing to boy-scout movements abroad modelled along British lines or even from presenting a challenge trophy to foreign amateur soccer teams.[38] Small wonder that the Treasury, with its keen eye for financial extravagance, should prove sceptical.

Accordingly, on 14 May, Tyrrell, Harmsworth and Stephen Gaselee presented their case at a Treasury conference summoned to discuss the News Department's estimates. The Financial Secretary, Stanley Baldwin, presided. It was generally agreed that the proposed propaganda programme 'must be regarded as tentative and experimental and that for the present the Foreign Office must to a great extent feel their way'.[39] The Foreign Office delegation explained their definition of what they meant by propaganda. They disclaimed 'all intention of conducting propaganda of the "Corpse Factory" type' but considered it essential 'to have some machinery for calling attention at once to statements relating to foreign affairs which required contradition or correction'.[40]

While the Treasury considered the Foreign Office case, a circular despatch signed by Curzon was transmitted to all diplomatic missions abroad, with the single exception of the embassy in Washington (see p. 71 below), informing them of their new peacetime responsibilities regarding propaganda. Since it marked, in effect, a major departure from established peacetime tradition, it merits extended quotation:

British propaganda in Foreign Countries shall, in future, be regarded as part of the regular work of His Majesty's Missions Abroad... [During the war] it became necessary to appoint a special officer to carry on British propaganda in conjunction with the Embassy or Legation. In a few countries it may still be possible to preserve some such arrangement, but in the majority of cases, His Majesty's Diplomatic Missions must themselves undertake the task, assisted by His Majesty's Consular Officers, and by Committees of local British subjects; or, in small centres, by individual British subjects.

I do not doubt that, from the experience of the past four years, you will have learned what forms of propaganda to encourage and what to avoid... British interests would be ill-served by a blatant publicity of the kind associated with German agents abroad, official and unofficial, before and during the war. On the other hand, a complete and contemptuous silence, however gratifying to our self-respect, is no longer a profitable policy in times when advertisement – whether of past achievement or future aims – is, perhaps unfortunately, almost a universal practice of nations as of individuals.[41]

Publicity and diplomacy, 1919–1939

Curzon's final remark is a telling one. However much British officials may have disliked propaganda, they could no longer afford to ignore the point that it had become a fact of modern diplomatic life. The British may have blamed the activities of other governments for this unfortunate development, but the real irony was that it had been the British government itself which had demonstrated the great power of propaganda between 1914 and 1918. Pandora's box proved easier to open than to close.

At the end of May, the Treasury replied on the question of the News Department's estimates. While recognising that it was not 'at the present moment practicable to terminate altogether the [remaining] system of propaganda', the Treasury did expect the Foreign Office to 'discontinue any particular type of propaganda as soon as experience shews that it is not productive of valuable results'.[42] The estimates were reduced by £20,000, the cuts mainly falling on the 'miscellaneous expenses', and the Treasury took note of the Foreign Office's policy of 'gradually converting British propaganda from a purely political aspect to largely commercial lines and assume that, as a corollary, the work will pass to a great extent to the Department of Overseas Trade'.[43] The proposed Facilities Division of the News Department was to be absorbed into the Government Hospitality Fund, leaving the two remaining sections for Administration and for Cables and Wireless.

No sooner had this battle ended than the PID came under Treasury attack. The policy of retrenchment was to continue, and propaganda was a natural victim. J. W. Headlam-Morley, a member of the Paris Peace Delegation who was to become historical adviser to the Foreign Office in the 1920s, expressed his frustration at the proposed further cuts. He wrote in defence of the News and Political Intelligence Department: 'It would perhaps be more agreeable if the whole work were stopped and we went back to the original system by which the Government divested itself of any responsibility for the immediate control of foreign opinion.' But, he continued,

> This is now impossible. In a condition of things when the foreign policy of each nation is no longer determined by a small group of men at the head of affairs often in close connection with a court, but is becoming more and more the immediate concern of peoples and parliaments, we cannot ignore the importance of using legitimate means for influencing this opinion.[44]

The Foreign Office and propaganda abroad

Headlam-Morley secured the influential support of Hardinge, the permanent under secretary, and of Curzon,[45] now Foreign Secretary, but despite protracted negotiations with the Treasury throughout the first half of 1920, the Foreign Office was instructed to re-examine the entire position of the News Department with a view to effecting economies. It seemed that in the post-war administrative reforms there was to be little room in the Foreign Office for such expensive activities as propaganda and political intelligence.[46]

Percy Koppel, shortly to succeed Tyrrell as head of the News Department, undertook the unenviable task of administrative reform during the late summer of 1920.[47] His recommendations included the closure of the PID. Tyrrell and Hardinge reluctantly agreed,[48] and Curzon's endorsement sealed its fate.[49] The PID's staff was disbanded in September. Many of its members returned to academic life or found employment elsewhere in the diplomatic service, and some were instrumental in the early development of the newly founded Institute of International Affairs at Chatham House, a body which continued privately many of those functions which it had been found impossible to continue under official auspices in the PID.[50] The News Department itself survived, although in much reduced form, and continued to conduct propaganda chiefly through the British and foreign press. When, therefore, Koppel succeeded Tyrrell early in 1921, he inherited a truncated and demoralised body, for the reduction of which he had personally been largely responsible.

Arthur Willert was recruited in 1921 to deal with the press work in London. Koppel, the News Department's head until 1925, handled administration and the various overseas propaganda activities of the department. These involved: the compilation of the British Official News Service for dissemination by the Cables and Wireless branch; the imparting of official information on political and commercial questions to journalists and leader-writers abroad, often in the form of the *Weekly London Letter*; the transmission of articles and cuttings to countries beyond the range of the wireless service; the supervision of the work of the press attachés; the occasional provision of British books, newspapers and cinematographic films to overseas libraries, societies and clubs.[51]

Koppel and Willert worked towards the same aim, but their activities appear to have been conducted quite separately from each other. Before long, the system was proving unworkable. While the demarcation of duties was essentially quite distinct, there was little flexibility, and various anomalies arose. There was also an element of rivalry between the two men. While Koppel's work continued to be the victim of post-war retrenchment, Willert's work with the press was gaining in importance. In February 1925, J. D. Gregory proposed a reorganisation of the News Department in favour of Willert's press section. Gregory pointed out that, whereas the press work had initially developed as an offshoot of the News Department's propaganda work and had functioned as part of, but subordinate to, Koppel's activities, 'in the course of time and as an obvious consequence of the greater demand for publicity it has naturally tended not only to overshadow and even outgrow its parent but to chafe under the restrictions inherent in its position'.[52] Gregory believed that Willert's direct press work was now 'by far the most important of the activities', because, he wrote,

It conducts *immediate* propaganda both inwardly and outwardly, and of these it is difficult to say which is the most essential in days when public opinion at home is as difficult to educate as public opinion abroad, and when there is not a pin to choose between native and foreign recalcitrants. The era when it was possible either to lead opinion in foreign politics by mere authority or tradition, or to ignore it from Olympian heights, has long since vanished, and once modern contact, however vulgar, has been established, it is not possible to confine it to an intermittent dispensation of tit-bits of news at the will of one or two minor officials or as a subsidiary function of an unspecialised department. It has become, and must be, practically a never-ceasing intercourse with the publicity world.[53]

Gregory accordingly suggested that the press work should be completely severed from the main News Department and reconstituted as a separate unit. He added: 'Both Departments would doubtless have the same object, and there is thus a prima facie argument for maintaining the old order and keeping them in one. But in the course of time the functions of propaganda have become gradually differentiated, and two distinct kinds of machinery for carrying them out have accordingly become necessary.'[54] Willert did not agree. Indeed, he considered that the work should be more closely integrated, not separated, although he did wish to see a readjustment in favour of the press work.[55]

There is little record of the views taken at the higher levels of the

The Foreign Office and propaganda abroad

Foreign Office on this question. On 28 October 1925, a meeting was held to examine the situation, at which Tyrrell (who had replaced Eyre Crowe as permanent under secretary earlier in the year), Montgomery, Gregory and Wellesley were all present. These men decided that the work of the News Department was 'one and indivisible and that it would be fundamentally wrong to continue to maintain it in two sections'. It was also agreed that Willert's work was 'the dominant factor', and it was decided to readjust the structure of the News Department in favour of the press section, which would also henceforth constitute the main branch of the department. Willert was promoted to the position of counsellor and also made head of the News Department, a post he was to hold for nearly ten years. Koppel was transferred to the newly created Dominions Information Department, whether or not of his own volition is not known.

The British Official News Service

The 1925 reorganisation of the News Department laid greater emphasis upon press publicity than on other forms of propaganda. One facet of press publicity which was not discussed in chapter 1 was the British Official News Service, which was the responsibility of the Cables and Wireless section of the News Department. This service provided a regular stream of official news exclusively for the benefit of the foreign press. It was initially designed and maintained to supplement the other methods of securing publicity conducted by the Foreign Office, although, in many countries, it provided the only method whereby British news and views could secure adequate publicity. In a sense, the news distributed abroad by cables and by wireless was merely an extension of the press work conducted by the News Department in London. There was, however, one significant difference. The British Official News Service by-passed the system of direct personal contact with foreign journalists who called at the Foreign Office. It concentrated upon the written rather than the spoken word. Ultimately, both services depended upon the co-operation of the journalists themselves to provide the desired publicity for British news once it had left the News Department. But the British Official News Service was a direct method of securing indirect publicity through the medium of the press.

Publicity and diplomacy, 1919–1939

The importance of wireless as an instrument of national propaganda was, of course, related to technological development. Whereas during the First World War, with wireless still in its infancy, cabled messages were more widely employed, broadcasting proved a vital, and perhaps the most effective, instrument of propaganda between 1939 and 1945. During the 1930s, a period which Asa Briggs has described as 'the Golden Age of broadcasting', technological advances in such areas as short-wave radio transmission led to the increased significance of propaganda through the ether and helped to complement the methods of news distribution by cables. The implications for international politics were far-reaching; broadcast propaganda became a powerful weapon in the national armouries of the world.

On the outbreak of war in 1914, Britain's domination of the international cable network provided her with a considerable advantage in the war of words. This advantage manifested itself in two ways. In the first place, Britain's control over the transatlantic cables enabled her to monitor and regulate the output of all telegraphic news sent from Germany to the United States. Secondly, this same control enabled British propagandists to utilise the cable network for the presentation of the British point of view. During the war, the News Department had conducted a great deal of its work by direct official telegram. Every important item of news that was considered likely to be of interest in allied and neutral countries was telegraphed to overseas representatives, who had instructions to make use of it for such purposes of publication as they thought desirable.[56]

In October 1914, George Mair, then head of the Neutral Press Committee, inaugurated a wireless service to transmit news messages in Morse code to neutral countries. The service rapidly expanded, and an arrangement with the Marconi Company was reached whereby official news messages were transmitted from the station at Poldhu in Cornwall. This arrangement lasted until 1917, when the Admiralty station at Horsea Island was used in preference to that of Marconi. A similar arrangement was reached with Reuters, who were contracted to disseminate cabled news messages and official communiqués under the title Agence Service Reuter. Thus began the Foreign Office's traditional preference for conducting official propaganda through intermediary organisations in order to protect

The Foreign Office and propaganda abroad

the credibility of the material put out. Official propaganda known to be such is almost useless.

On the return of peace and the dissolution of the wartime propaganda machinery, there arose the question of the future of the cables and wireless services in the context of international communications as well as in the context of a reconstituted News Department. The contract for the Agence Service Reuter, which had been handed over to the Ministry of Information, once again became the responsibility of the Foreign Office. It was due to expire on 31 March 1919. In February, Sir Roderick Jones, the managing director of Reuters, warned the Foreign Office that the return of peace had not been accompanied by a decline in the use of propaganda, but rather by its escalation. While admitting to being more concerned with 'pence and not with policy', he observed that the contract for the Agence Service Reuter looked like being terminated simply because 'the Ministry which controlled it ceased to be'. This, he felt, would be a grave mistake, and he argued forcefully for renewal.[57]

The arrangement with Reuters was, in fact, more in the nature of a mutual understanding. There had never existed a written contract as such. The Foreign Office, followed by the Ministry of Information, had met the cost of transmission by Reuters 'of material which has a "propaganda" rather than a "news" value' – that is, messages which would not otherwise have been sent abroad by Reuters on commercial grounds.[58] Stephen Gaselee was opposed to renewal of the arrangement, not least because it would serve to excite parliamentary hostility. Moreover, he argued, 'As to the future, news is a commodity like any other, and I see no reason to subsidise its purveyance unless we are very directly involved. News proceeding from Great Britain will ordinarily be favourable to us, and in ordinary times this industry, like others, should stand on its own legs.'[59] On the other hand, Hubert Montgomery pointed to the advantages of renewal: 'Reuters is a normal press channel for getting sound British news into papers all over the world which would not otherwise be possible, and Reuters telegrams sent direct from British Government sources most certainly will not.'[60] Curzon agreed with Montgomery and suggested that the Treasury be invited to negotiate a new short-term arrangement between Reuters and the Foreign Office.[61] The outcome of the resultant talks was not entirely that desired by Reuters. An agreement was reached whereby the

Foreign Office would occasionally instruct Reuters to send specific messages abroad on behalf of the News Department. Payment would be made 'on the basis of the difference between the wordage so sent on Foreign Office instruction and the wordage which they would have sent in the ordinary commercial way of business'.[62] This somewhat clumsy arrangement was anything but a continuation of the old, and the semi-official Agence Service Reuter was terminated as a result. The new arrangement merely enabled the Foreign Office to utilise the cables and facilities of Reuters whenever the normal diplomatic channels of communications were overburdened. It was not an official subsidy, but rather a normal business arrangement which proved to be useful only in emergencies. Indeed, by 1928 C. J. Norton was complaining that the arrangement was 'not altogether satisfactory since we have to accept their word as to how much they would normally have sent'.[63] Other than this arrangement, Reuters had to content itself with disseminating news abroad in the normal course of its work on a commercial basis.

Although the semi-official news service therefore came to an end in 1919, the Foreign Office did decide to continue its own British Official News Service.[64] The format laid down shortly after the war varied only slightly throughout the ensuing twenty years. The Cables and Wireless branch of the News Department was made responsible for the compilation of news messages likely to secure favourable publicity overseas. The wireless messages transmitted from Horsea Island contained brief summaries of political, commercial and general information and were broadcast at midday, 8 pm and midnight with the aim of 'expressing generally the British standpoint on international questions and [of] keeping other countries informed on British industrial and economic developments'.[65] The Marconi station at Caenarvon in Wales was also utilised to transmit longer messages which contained a more comprehensive account of events in Britain, including parliamentary debates and ministerial speeches.[66] The emphasis from the outset was upon news content. As one official explained,

There seems to be some misunderstanding regarding the nature of our work. In no way is it 'propaganda' so-called. 'Propaganda', as such, has long been dead. We present our case by records of facts, figures and authoritative statements. We give news of the kind that it is advantageous to us to be known, and the rapidity of wireless enables us to get in first with sober

The Foreign Office and propaganda abroad

accounts of events to which, on the other hand, many foreign newspaper correspondents in England look for their sensation.[67]

This seemingly contradictory statement about the nature of the News Department's cables and wireless services does illustrate two important points: first, it shows the sensitivity of officials towards the use of the word 'propaganda', with its sinister wartime connotations and its association with lies – the News Department was constantly trying to point out that its work was a propaganda 'with facts'; secondly, it reveals a preference for sending the official version of events directly abroad rather than relying upon the whims of journalists in London to interpret the news handed to them by the Foreign Office in the manner desired by the source. The wireless messages were transmitted to Europe, Scandinavia and the Middle East, where they were received either by diplomatic and consular missions for distribution to the local press or by direct reception in the offices of foreign newspapers and news agencies.

Although at the end of the war the News Department also decided to continue the transmission of cabled news telegrams, their number and volume were greatly reduced in 1919 owing to their high cost at a time of financial retrenchment.[68] As with the wireless messages, they were distributed abroad by diplomatic representatives overseas such as press attachés or other agents 'on the spot' if they were not sent direct to foreign newspapers. The cabled news telegrams, which varied in length from seventy-five words for Addis Ababa to a thousand words for South American countries, were sent twice weekly and contained reliable news plus comment. In South America, which after the war became 'a happy hunting ground for the propagandist of any nation who wishes to push its trade there',[69] the cabled messages were particularly important until technology brought that continent within range of radio telegraphy. They usually took the form of a biweekly *London Letter* which contained commentary upon political, commercial and general news. The *Letter* was received and translated into Spanish and Portuguese by the various embassies and legations, whereupon it was distributed free of charge to the South American press, which was said to give the *Letter* 'great prominence'.[70]

The propaganda value of these messages increased as other countries began to utilise state-subsidised propaganda as part of

Publicity and diplomacy, 1919–1939

their commercial drive in Latin America. Yet as one News Department official maintained, the messages

are not intended to be merely commercial propaganda – to boost British trade – but are rather to keep South American countries supplied with reliable British news in order that this country may not be relegated entirely to the background in consequence of the efforts of self-advertisement carried on by other important powers, efforts which sometimes take the form of deriding British policy and achievements.[71]

In the early years of the service, however, numerous complaints were received from diplomatic representatives abroad stating that the news messages were dull and uninteresting and evoked little interest among the foreign press.[72] Percy Koppel wrote in 1920 that 'our past experience has led us to accept the necessity for mixing in some journalistic "jam" with the powder, which must in itself be somewhat tasteless, and we can only endeavour to make the "jam" as unobjectionable as possible without decreasing its savour'.[73]

Yet it was not simply a question of injecting lively news items. The official news service utilised two direct media, cables and wireless, to secure publicity through the indirect medium of the press. Once the messages had been compiled in the Foreign Office and distributed by overseas representatives to the foreign press, the News Department had little control over whether the messages were actually published or indeed over the form they took. Moreover, as it was recognised,

No two journalists regard news from the same standpoint. Whereas many countries like bright and brief telegrams, others – Holland, for example, prefer their information to be more detailed... From a purely newspaper standpoint, our messages are hampered by the purpose they are designed to serve. Nevertheless, the items we particularly want published abroad will stand a better chance of publicity when included among general items of a more diverse and 'newsy' character. It must, however, also be remembered that the brief facts of news are covered by the agencies, whereas we, in our messages, strive to convey, not too ostentatiously, a point of view.[74]

Apart from projecting this pro-British interpretation of the news, it also remained important for the British Official News Service to continue its constant struggle to correct misstatements and misunderstandings held abroad as to the nature and implications of Britain's foreign policy.

In November 1921, the range and efficiency of the wireless service were vastly improved with the transfer of the broadcasts from

The Foreign Office and propaganda abroad

Horsea to the new high-powered GPO station at Leafield, near Oxford.[75] The change brought beneficial results almost immediately, while the messages themselves became 'more efficient politically' through daily consultation between the Cables and Wireless branch and Allen Leeper, Curzon's assistant private secretary.[76] The service was considered to be particularly important in countries which did not receive a regular supply of British news through other channels. This unfortunate situation had arisen because of various agreements made by the leading international news agencies such as Reuters, Havas and Wolff to divide the world into spheres of news influence.[77] In South America, for example, Havas and the American United Press held the exclusive right to distribute news on that continent. Added to this was the fact that many of the continental news agencies were heavily subsidised by their governments. The result was that Reuters found itself in a disadvantageous position. Any of its news sent to Germany had first, because of its agreement with Havas, to pass through Paris, where it was subjected, as one official believed, 'to a drastic fining process'.[78] Koppel stated that Germany was almost entirely dependent for its foreign news upon Havas, 'which does not go to any particular pains in the adequate or accurate presentation of British policy'.[79] British news sent under normal commercial conditions was subjected not only to severe competition from state-subsidised agencies but also to manipulation and arbitrary selection by journalists who may or may not have been sympathetic to Britain's cause. It was this situation which the direct messages of the British Official News Service sought to rectify.

Between 1919 and 1936, the Cables and Wireless branch of the News Department was under the direction of William Ridsdale. Assisted by two officials with journalistic experience, N. E. Nash and E. W. Gilbey, Ridsdale worked in close co-operation with the private secretaries to the Secretary of State for Foreign Affairs in compiling the news messages. The procedure by which the messages were made available to the foreign press varied slightly from country to country. In Greece, Austria, Poland, Czechoslovakia and Bulgaria they were received by government wireless stations and forwarded to the national press bureaux, where they were translated and distributed to local news agencies and newspapers. In Scandinavia, there existed reciprocal arrangements whereby, in return for the circulation of official British news, the GPO received short wireless signals for distribution to British news agencies. In Madrid, the Spanish Marconi Company was paid a small fee for distributing the messages, although local subscribers were charged for the news. In Holland and Denmark, news agencies received the messages in their offices and incorporated them into their own news releases. The broadcasts were also received by ships at sea.[80] And in 1922, the range of the service was further extended with the completion of the GPO wireless chain station at Cairo.[81]

The British Official News Service increased in importance as the 1920s unfolded because of the increasing foreign demand for information about Britain and the inability of Reuters to meet that demand. Only the wealthier foreign newspapers could afford to maintain a foreign correspondent in London. For those which could not afford such a luxury, but whose circulation requirements necessitated the inclusion of news about Britain, alternative sources of information had to be found. Reuters news was expensive, especially when compared with the favourable rates offered by other news agencies which enjoyed governmental support. And because those foreign news agencies were being increasingly utilised as instruments of national propaganda, often with an anti-British slant, the British case was in danger of gross misrepresentation. This the News Department sought to combat through the free distribution of the official news messages. The apparent success seemed to justify the cost involved. In 1922 Koppel observed that the official messages secured a wider degree of publicity than those broadcast by foreign stations. He attributed this to three factors: '(a) the absence of a good supply of British news from other sources; (b) a strict adherence to facts, and; (c) an adequate understanding of the needs of the foreign newspaper sub-editors who ultimately deal with the news'.[82] Moreover, with the extension of the range of wireless transmission, it became possible to reduce still further the amount of expensive cabled telegram traffic to Europe, although detailed cable messages continued to be sent on important occasions. However, under constant Treasury pressure to reduce its overheads, the News Department was gradually forced to limit the number of words in the more expensive cables, with the result that the cabled messages were mainly sent to South America, still beyond the effective range of wireless in the 1920s but remaining 'a hot-bed of anti-British propaganda'.[83]

The Foreign Office and propaganda abroad

These reductions alarmed not only the News Department but also Reuters. At intermittent periods throughout the inter-war period, representations were made by Reuters to the Foreign Office in an attempt to increase the supply. The inability of Reuters to compete successfully with the state-subsidised propaganda of foreign news agencies was, it was argued, a matter of national concern. Yet the Foreign Office remained opposed to the idea of a direct government subsidy to Reuters. As Stephen Gaselee wrote, 'News is like any other commodity – good news will be taken, and paid for, because it helps to sell the newspapers in which it appears; while no amount of artificial support will ensure the reception of bad news (i.e. late, uninteresting material).'[84] Tyrrell agreed,[85] but the problem remained a difficult one for Reuters, whose self-denying arrangement with Havas continued to hamper the satisfactory representation of the British point of view in such vital areas (that is commercially) as South America. Roderick Jones recorded that there was some tension between Reuters and the Foreign Office over the role of the British Official News Service,[86] although the News Department was always keen to avoid direct competition with the news agencies. The official service was designed to complement the work of Reuters and to meet a demand which Reuters could not.

By the late 1920s, the problem had grown to such proportions that it demanded greater attention by the Foreign Office. A subsidy to Reuters remained out of the question; a combination of Treasury reluctance to sanction expenditure on anything that might have been construed as propaganda and the prevailing assumption of the time concerning governmental interference in private bodies preempted such an idea. C. J. Norton believed that the only possible solution, at least with regard to South America, was for Reuters to end its arrangement with Havas.[87] In fact, the arrangement had come up for renewal in 1927, and Reuters had decided not to continue with it, thereby leaving the company free to enter the South American field.[88] Only the problem of finance remained. Roderick Jones, however, could not imagine a serious challenge to the lead already developed by Havas and the United Press without sufficient financial resources.[89] Once again, he approached the Foreign Office. Although the News Department welcomed the idea of Reuters operating in South America,[90] the request for an annual subsidy of £20,000 had to be turned down.[91]

Publicity and diplomacy, 1919–1939

The question of increasing the amount of British news to South America, and to foreign countries in general, must be viewed in the context of the growing conviction in the late 1920s and early 1930s that Britain must begin to take more positive steps to make herself known and understood abroad. This will be discussed in greater detail in the following chapters. But it is important to remember that, regardless of the other forms British propaganda was to take, news continued to constitute an integral part of what became known as 'the projection of England'. In December 1929, Ridsdale commented upon the increasing significance of the official wireless messages:

> The original conception of the British Official Wireless as a means of supplementing British news and correcting misstatements about ourselves in the European press has grown out of all knowledge. The extension of the range of wireless transmission, partly by the employment of the short-wave to supplement the long-wave system, places our messages, broadly speaking, within reach of every inhabited part of the globe. Reception has been organised not only in foreign countries and British Dominions hitherto outside the range of the messages but also – and with an eagerness with which it required little imagination to understand – in the smaller isolated communities on the outskirts of the Empire.[92]

The potential power of radio as an instrument of communication and a purveyor of news abroad, as will be seen, was fully appreciated by the BBC and led to the inauguration in 1932 of its Empire Service and, six years later, of its Foreign Language Service. These broadcasts injected a new dimension into the conduct of British overseas propaganda in peacetime in that they were directed towards foreign audiences on a large scale. The British Official Wireless Service, however, served an entirely different purpose, because it was, at least at the initial stage, directed towards a much more limited and exclusive audience, namely the opinion-makers in the offices of foreign newspapers and news agencies. The BBC conducted direct publicity; the Cables and Wireless branch of the New Department aimed at a larger audience only through the intermediary medium of the press. In other words, the British Official News Service was conducted in accordance with the Foreign Office principle of attempting to influence those foreigners who were in a position to influence much larger numbers of people.

In 1935, Rex Leeper was keen to develop this approach further

The Foreign Office and propaganda abroad

partly by extending the British Official News Service. The completion of the GPO's new high-powered short-wave transmitter at Rugby provided an opportunity to transmit official news to any part of the globe and would thus help to combat the aggressive anti-British propaganda disseminated by Italy, Germany and Japan. Leeper therefore appealed to the Treasury for increased expenditure on the official news messages, particularly in view of a recent decision to reject a subsidy to Reuters as 'financially and politically objectionable'.[93] He wrote:

> Sir John Simon, impressed by the immense return which is already received from the modest expenditure incurred by the maintenance of the British Official Wireless Service, is strongly of the opinion not only that this well-tried system should be continued but that its development is essential in view of the present trend of world events. The British Official Wireless Service is, in effect, not only an integral part of any scheme for the defence of British interests in time of crisis, but is a sound investment which in normal conditions gives an extremely high return for the money spent upon it.[94]

The appeal proved successful.[95] The British Official News Service was expanded in 1936 to meet the increased demand.

Because, however, the service was 'official', and at no time masqueraded as anything but 'official', its credibility in the eyes of the foreign press tended to be somewhat limited. Foreign journalists undoubtedly regarded the news contained in the official messages with a greater degree of scepticism than they did Reuters news. It was largely for this reason that the Foreign Office began in the late 1930s to turn its attention towards means of increasing the supply of British news abroad through private channels of distribution in order to aid the cause of national projection. In December 1937, the Foreign Secretary, Anthony Eden, submitted a proposal to the Cabinet for governmental assistance to Reuters. Eden maintained that the GPO could provide reduced rates of wireless transmission for Reuters to send its news from Rugby. This proposal, he admitted, was 'practically equivalent to the grant of a subsidy' but was necessary if Reuters was to effectively compete with the state-subsidised propaganda agencies of foreign states.[96] If accepted, Eden proposed that it would become essential for Reuters and the Foreign Office to reach an informal agreement designed to establish 'the closest possible contact' in order to ensure 'a more definitely British presentation of news'.[97] The Cabinet was sufficiently impressed with Eden's argument to hand the question over to a committee for further investigation.[98] This was the Kingsley Wood committee, which will be discussed in chapter 5.

The British Library of Information at New York

Throughout the inter-war period, the Foreign Office was extremely careful to avoid the appearance of conducting official propaganda, whether direct or indirect, in the United States. Even in the late 1930s, when few countries of political commercial or strategic significance escaped the attention of Britain's expanding peacetime propaganda machinery, the United States remained the exception to the rule. This was so despite certain obvious advantages, such as common language and culture and the so-called 'special relationship', which would ordinarily have greatly facilitated the sympathetic reception of British propaganda. However, guided by the advice of consecutive British ambassadors in Washington, the Foreign Office continued to regard the Americans as something of a special case in so far as propaganda was concerned.

The reason for this cautious approach was essentially quite simple. During the First World War, Britain had conducted an intensive and highly organised propaganda campaign in the United States, many of the details of which only came to light on the return of peace. This not only convinced many Americans that their country had been duped into intervening on the Allied side in 1917 but also that they must be careful to avoid any repetition in a future European war – a view which was especially popular among the 'isolationist' elements. British officials were conscious of the fact that, as a result of these beliefs, American opinion had become highly sensitive, almost to the point of obsession, to any activity by a foreign government in the United States which might be interpreted as propaganda.

It was between 1914 and 1917, when the United States had been regarded as the most important of neutral countries, that the Foreign Office in conjunction with Wellington House had begun its tradition of treating the Americans as a special case with regard to propaganda. The American journalists who had flocked to London following the severance of the transatlantic German cables had received preferential treatment and special facilities from the

The Foreign Office and propaganda abroad

Foreign Office. In the United States itself, great care was taken from an early stage to avoid the appearance of a propaganda campaign in an attempt to avoid offending American sensitivities any further than the blatant propaganda of the Germans was believed to be doing.[99] This naturally became less important with the entry of the United States into the war. Accordingly, when Foreign Secretary Balfour visited America at the head of a large official mission in April 1917, it was decided to set up the British Bureau of Information on New York's Fifth Avenue. Arthur Willert, then serving as Washington correspondent of *The Times* but also involved in the official propaganda work, believed that the bureau was 'one of the most tangible administrative achievements of the Balfour Mission. It represented a reversal of British policy.'[100] However, it was not until June 1917 and the arrival of Northcliffe to take charge of the British War Mission that the bureau was placed upon a sound footing.[101] By the end of the war, the bureau had opened branch offices in Washington, Chicago and San Francisco, employing a total of ninety-six officials.[102]

When, on the return of peace, there arose the question of the future role of British overseas propaganda, the United States occupied a great deal of Foreign Office time and consideration. As Sir Eric Drummond (later Lord Perth) wrote in January 1919, 'The question of propaganda in the United States is causing us some anxiety. We are receiving information from all sides that it would be a grave mistake to abandon altogether the machinery now set up there. At the same time, it is clearly desirable to reduce it considerably.'[103] While the Foreign Office went ahead in early 1919 with its reconstruction of the News Department, William Tyrrell decided to ascertain the views of Sir William Wiseman, the head of British intelligence in the United States. Wiseman replied:

I understand propaganda to be any method of putting our case before the public, and its purpose to promote good relations between the two peoples. The activities should be twofold. A careful tracing to its source of malicious anti-British propaganda, and a study of the genuine misunderstandings which exist or may arise from time to time; and secondly, our efforts should be directed to exposing the malicious propaganda and removing the genuine misunderstandings by whatever means appear most effective at the time. We should also encourage anything which may tend to bring our peoples closer together, and find means of explaining to the Americans the meaning of the British Empire.[104]

Publicity and diplomacy, 1919–1939

Wiseman went on to suggest that any British activity should adopt one of two methods: 'The first might be called the method of aggressive and the second the method of unobtrusive propaganda.' The latter, he considered, was more appropriate to American conditions:

> Many people ... believe the aggressive method is the only effective one and would like to see Anglo-American societies organised all over the United States, with public demonstrations and meetings, and even go so far as to recommend a big advertising campaign, through the press, posters and leaflets ... I can only say that I consider such a method would be disastrous and produce exactly the reverse effect to that which its advocates contemplate. I am sure that any kind of artificial demonstrations must have a corresponding reaction, apart from the fact that this method is undignified and offends good taste in both countries.[105]

He also warned against British propaganda becoming involved in American party politics. Instead, he advocated a broadly cultural approach involving educational exchanges, lecture tours, visits by influential personalities, an interchange of literature and a better exchange of news. He nonetheless suspected that such methods would evoke a limited appeal and that his own personal concept of propaganda as an instrument of uniting the 'peoples' of the two countries was illusory. Moreover, he wrote, 'I am afraid too that the existing Anglo-American societies are mostly drawn from one class, and from one small sector of the Unites States ... British propaganda supported by those who live on Fifth Avenue will always be regarded with deep suspicion by the mass of the American public.'[106] Such sound advice was favourably received within the Foreign Office, although the question did produce a divergence of opinion.

There emerged two clear schools of thought. On the one hand, it was considered inadvisable for any News Department official to be associated with the British embassy in Washington in order not to offend American sensitivities that might arise over the presence of foreign propagandists. The appointment of a press attaché in Washington was thus opposed, although the possibility of appointing an official with equivalent duties in a disguised position was not excluded. On the other hand, it was suggested that such secrecy would merely serve to increase still further American suspicions and

The Foreign Office and propaganda abroad

that it would therefore be more sensible to admit openly the existence of a News Department official at the Washington embassy, thereby precluding any possible misunderstanding.[107] Lord Reading, the British ambassador to the United States, favoured the latter approach.[108]

In the event, a compromise solution was found. In 1920 the wartime bureau was rechristened the British Library of Information at New York and placed under the joint direction of Angus Fletcher and Robert Wilberforce. The library was to be regarded as experimental at first and was maintained on a temporary basis in order to meet the demand for official information on economic and political questions affecting the United Kingdom and the British empire. It was not a true propaganda organisation in the real sense, and it survived as a mere shadow of its wartime predecessor. The New York headquarters was the only office to survive, the various branches being closed down. The library was maintained chiefly as a repository for official documentary material – Blue Books, White Papers and other government publications – and thus served 'as a means whereby the American public can inform itself on British affairs, not through statements prepared especially for American consumption, but through such information and documents as are prepared for and consulted by the various peoples of the British Empire in the ordinary course of government'.[109] Indeed, the library continued to function throughout the inter-war years on the basic assumption that 'British policy and British responsibilities become an object of interest to the whole world, the understanding of which is necessary for peaceful and friendly relations among the nations'.[110]

The British Library of Information at New York was a rather unusual experiment in British governmental publicity for two reasons in particular. In the first place, it confined itself solely to the provision of information about Britain and the British empire; it generally abstained from making any comment on the affairs of actions of other nations. Secondly, the information was purely official in character and depended almost entirely upon the written word. Moreover, it was purely a reference library and not a distributing centre. The documents, newspapers and other material available in the reading room could be consulted on the premises free of charge, although, if requested, material could be obtained from the Stationery Office for purchase by American writers, historians, commentators and so on. Inter-library loan facilities were also available. The impetus to acquire information about Britain was left entirely to the Americans. Any enquiries received by letter or telephone were answered whenever official information on the subject in question was available. In short, the library was a publicity centre in New York, financed by the British government and supervised by the News Department of the Foreign Office for the supply of official information to American citizens who sought it voluntarily for their own purposes.

Such an approach was particularly well suited to the Anglo-American relationship between the wars. Following the failure of the American Senate to ratify the Treaty of Versailles, the United States entered a period of relative isolation in foreign, although less so in economic, affairs. Just as it was important for British statesmen to avoid offending the principles which lay behind that policy, so also was the News Department careful to avoid the appearance of conducting blatant propaganda in the United States. For example, in 1927 Foreign Secretary Austen Chamberlain warned of the dangers of attempting to persuade the United States to join the League of Nations with the help of propaganda. He wrote:

I have no idea of making propaganda in the United States and that for two reasons: first, that if any such propaganda is to be successful, it must be done by Americans and be native to the soil, and secondly, because I am by no means persuaded that, in the present stage of their constitutional development, the accession of the United States to the League would be of advantage to the latter.[111]

It is, however, doubtful whether the Americans would have accepted the presence of British propaganda at a time when the publication of Harold Lasswell's *Propaganda Technique in the World War*,[112] George Viereck's *Spreading Germs of Hate*,[113] and J. D. Squires's *British Propaganda at Home and in the United States from 1914 to 1917*[114] was reminding people of the impact British propaganda had had during the war.

This particular problem occupied a great deal of Angus Fletcher's time. He was constantly at pains to convince many critics that the work of the library was not, strictly speaking, propaganda. In 1928 he informed Willert that

From the beginning this Library has had to fight against the charge of propagandist activities, and we have stated categorically that it is not engaged

The Foreign Office and propaganda abroad

in propaganda. There has never been any doubt in my mind as to what was meant by that statement. It meant that the Library is not engaged in special pleadings – that is to say, it is not trying to convince the American public on particular questions by calling attention to whatever makes for, and diverting it from whatever makes against, the conclusion that might be most favourable to British interests and prestige. We meant that the Library's procedure was not argumentative. Indeed, if the American public did not choose to come for information we would have expected the Library to languish and decay.[115]

Fletcher maintained that his main problem derived from the 'debased meaning of a sinister activity'. Propaganda was, he claimed, 'a good word gone wrong – debauched by the late Lord Northcliffe'. To the American public, it not only meant 'special pleading' but also implied 'the falsification or distortion of facts'.[116] This misconception of the British use of the word required correction; otherwise, Fletcher appealed, the British should avoid using the word altogether.

By 'propaganda', the Foreign Office meant the honest and open dissemination of accurate news and information which would reflect favourably upon the foreigner's image of Britain. The truth, nothing but the truth, and as near as possible the whole truth would, it was believed, create the desired propaganda effect. During Arthur Willert's ten-year period as head of the News Department, great care was taken to avoid the appearance of overt or blatant propaganda, particularly in his dealings with American journalists in London. Given that the main emphasis under Willert was upon press activities, the Foreign Office News Department could quite easily assume the role of a news source without appearing to be conducting propaganda; what journalists decided to do with information received from this particular official source was theoretically beyond the control of diplomats. Nevertheless, the official news was released to create a deliberate effect, and it was this element of calculated premeditation which made the work 'propagandist'. The advance of technology provided a new dimension for this approach. For example, during the 1930 London Naval Conference, Willert recognised the value of the newsreels in this connection:

Especially in the United States, the publicity value of the news film in cinematograph theatres is rapidly approaching that of the press... What would really suit the moving-picture world, especially in America, and

Publicity and diplomacy, 1919–1939

what would give us the best 'propaganda' results, would be an opportunity at the first possible moment of taking both sound and silent moving pictures of the Prime Minister and of the principal foreign delegates.[117]

In so far as the United States was particularly concerned, the temptation to indulge in interpretation of the news was to be avoided. The American public must be left free to draw its own conclusions from the news presented to it.

It was for this reason that in 1933, when the News Department was informed of a proposal for certain prominent individuals to visit America on a lecture tour, Leeper considered the plan 'dangerous', believing instead that 'the only useful propaganda for us must be done by Americans'.[118] Similarly, when in 1934 the BBC proposed a series of broadcast commentaries on British affairs for the benefit of American audiences, as part of a reciprocal arrangement with an American radio company, which would be 'aimed at fostering a better understanding between the two peoples', the News Department again became alarmed. Both the British Library of Information and the Washington embassy considered that the BBC already publicised itself 'rather too energetically and ill-advisably' in the United States, and 'thereby provoke criticism on the ground that HMG is attempting to influence American opinion by broadcast propaganda. To the American public, the BBC are HMG'[119] From New York, Fletcher warned that the proposed broadcasts 'would immediately be construed as propaganda':

> We know from past experience that this sort of 'hands across the sea' propaganda is extremely disliked by an important section of the American public. The real danger is that, although officials, and a fair number of more intelligent journalists, know that the BBC is an organisation quasi-independent of His Majesty's Government, the majority of people in the United States believe that it is HMG. Hence there is a possibility of an outcry against what may be regarded as *direct* propaganda by His Majesty's Government and an attempt thereby to influence public opinion in the United States.[120]

Having said this, it is rather amusing to note the opinion of Ronald Lindsay, the British ambassador in Washington, who had suggested that it was high time for the Foreign Office 'to step in and put a severe bit in the teeth' of the BBC.[121] This was, in fact, what happened in February 1935 when Sir Robert Vansittart issued a polite

The Foreign Office and propaganda abroad

but firm warning to Sir John Reith not to conduct propaganda in the United States:

> Our view is that the important thing, from the point of view of our relations with the United States of America, is to avoid talks put on by the BBC having the appearance of being directed expressly 'at' the United States... The question of Anglo-American relations is so important and the BBC can play a considerable part in them.[122]

An indignant Reith was forced to comply with Foreign Office wishes, and the proposal for reciprocal broadcasts was dropped.[123]

The middle and late 1930s was a period which witnessed the massive exploitation of propaganda by the great powers. Despite the relatively cautious approach adopted by the Foreign Office in this activity, many Americans remained suspicious of British propaganda. As one critic wrote in December 1937, 'the Union would be in a much more presentable state just now if it were not so infested and itchy with foreign propagandists, especially those of the British persuasion. The self-respecting American is down on all propagandists, as the self-respecting housewife is down on vermin.'[124] Such passionate views were, at least in part, to contribute to the passing in 1938 of a law by the American Senate (the Foreign Agents Registration Act) which required the registration with the U.S. government of all foreign propaganda organisations operating on American soil.[125]

The cautious approach of the Foreign Office did, however, appear to reap the desired effect during the Munich crisis of 1938. Basing their conclusions upon observations made during the crisis, the directors of the British Library of Information at New York reported:

> While the Library does not dispense day to day news its role in time of emergency could be an exceedingly active one, with appropriate provision in terms of staff and material. During the critical weeks of September and October we were called upon most for information to explain press despatches. Since then, as the news began to enter upon the stage of argument and discussion, the White Papers and Parliamentary Debates have been frequently consulted and our assistance has been sought by writers, speakers, students and others.[126]

The policy of what may be termed passive publicity thus appeared to be vindicated, although the directors did admit that

> The principal evidence of progress in such an organisation as the British Library of Information is the extent to which use is made of it by the public

it is intended to serve. This is difficult to assess. We can only say that the indices used to measure progress hitherto continue to show an increasing demand for the Library's services.[127]

Accordingly, when, in the winter of 1938–9, the question was raised whether or not to embark upon a more active propaganda campaign in the United States, all the available evidence pointed to a continuation of the existing policy.[128] Yet the success of the library appeared to have been such that several News Department officials advocated its expansion and, more significantly, the establishment of branch offices in other important American cities.

Christopher Warner, for example, suggested that, 'at this juncture, there was a good case for duplicating or triplicating' the library, although he was quick to point out that the actual function of the information bureaux should remain as before. Sir Ronald Lindsay, whose opinion was immediately sought, replied:

It seems to me that as regards public opinion the work in this country of the British Library of Information, of the Consulates, of the Embassy, and of His Majesty's Government, has now been almost accomplished, and it makes no difference whether this is the result of British restraint and honesty or of German activity and immorality. The fact remains that today the United States has arrived at a pitch of unneutral thought which even a short time ago we should hardly have dared to hope for.[129]

This was a fascinating observation made only a week after Hitler's occupation of Prague. It may well have been that American opinion had moved satisfyingly in the direction of sympathy and cooperation with Great Britain (although clearly not enough to produce much practical effect in terms of policy), but Lindsay's implication was that this had not been ostensibly due to any programme of propaganda. Hitler's actions had spoken much louder than British words. Indeed, Lindsay's opinion was that, by deliberately keeping British propaganda in the United States to a minimum when other countries were increasing theirs, American opinion, with its antipathy towards foreign propaganda, had favoured the country which was appearing to do the least. It was for this reason that he opposed any expansion of the British organisation in America. As one News Department official minuted, 'No one could have foreseen the extremely rapid development of "unneutral" thought in the United States: but, as things are, I think

The Foreign Office and propaganda abroad

it is fair to say that an extension of the BLI facilities would be gilding the lily.'[130] And in April 1939, Lindsay added:

America is so thoroughly inoculated against anything faintly resembling propaganda that our attitude must be one of extreme caution. It is for the Americans to educate themselves about international issues. With their feelings generally as friendly as they are, they ought to be able to do this all right. Our own role must be subsidiary and secondary only – a readiness to give help when it is asked for. I think it is far more important for us to avoid mistakes than to go out for new or extended successes... Our policy as regards publicity and information should tend to lag behind American demand for it.[131]

Indeed, it was this supply-on-demand policy, combined with letting the British cause speak for itself, that constituted the guiding principle of the work of the British Library of Information at New York between the wars. That principle was based upon the assumption that Americans did not wish to be told about the merits of British policy or British achievements but that, if they did choose to discover Britain of their own accord, the facilities for enlightenment should be made available to them. Those facilities were designed to provide a British, as distinct from a foreign and possibly hostile, point of view. But even then, great care was taken to let the Americans believe that they were making up their own minds.

British overseas propaganda, therefore, did not end with the First World War only to begin again with the outbreak of the second in 1939. However, its conduct in peacetime did take place on a much reduced scale, far below either the wartime levels or indeed the level desired by the Foreign Office. The News Department laboured constantly to expand its work in the face of, at times, overwhelming opposition – even, one suspects, from within the Foreign Office itself. Propaganda was, quite simply, an unpopular activity. At the close of the First World War, the general reluctance of the Treasury in its role as keeper of the public purse and the official conscience stemmed, it was maintained, from an inability to justify or defend the large-scale continuation of a distasteful activity to a Parliament mindful of the need for financial economies and sensitive to the widespread suspicions concerning the use of official propaganda.[132] All propaganda, irrespective of the form it took or the difference among its political, cultural or, if to a lesser degree, economic variations, was viewed with distaste and suspicion. It was considered 'un-English', a wartime expedient which had served a valuable purpose but which had no place in peacetime. As one observer noted,

> That the State should advertise itself was an idea which occurred to few before the war and which, had it been brought before the notice of the general public, would have seemed to them repellent: advertisement, apart from commercial advertisement, which through lapse of time had acquired respectability, was thought to be the work of the vulgarian; it was also thought useless.[133]

The Times in 1918 reported Robert Donald, editor of the *Daily Chronicle* and deeply involved in wartime propaganda, as saying that the work was 'utterly repugnant to our feelings and contrary to our traditions',[134] an attitude which was undoubtedly widely shared.

The post-war opposition to propaganda originated during 1918 when the work of the Ministry of Information and of Crewe House had been publicly discussed. From a political point of view, the ministry had been disliked because of its direct accountability to the Prime Minister rather than to Parliament or the Treasury. It was even accused of putting out propaganda based upon policy which had not previously been discussed in the House of Commons.[135] Hence, 'the manner of its creation, the appearance of an extra-parliamentary power, and the fear that its propaganda activities on behalf of the Government might survive the war, had obviously combined to inspire a mood of deep suspicion'.[136]

There were, of course, other arguments against the continuation of propaganda. Britain had emerged from the war with the prestige that came with victory. As Lord Curzon observed in November 1918, 'The British flag has never flown over a more powerful or a more united Empire... Never did our voice count for more in the councils of nations; or in determining the future destinies of mankind.'[137] The British cause had proved a worthy one; it had been vindicated on the field of battle. The British point of view was evident before the eyes of the world at the Paris Peace Conference. A lasting peace, safeguarded by the League of Nations, would remain as a more than adequate testimony to the merits and achievements of British ideals and civilisation. After all, before the war, official propaganda on behalf of Britain had not been found necessary:

The Foreign Office and propaganda abroad

'Thanks to her comfortable position in the world, the British people, far from feeling any need to blow their own trumpet, had acquired the habit of understatement as an unconscious but effective form of self-advertisement. Why not now return to this pleasant way of being?'[138] If propaganda was to continue, it should do so only on an experimental basis and, the Treasury maintained, with a commercial emphasis. It was far more acceptable to undertake, in effect, an advertising campaign on behalf of British trade and commerce than an uncharacteristic form of national self-glorification. Although, with the benefit of hindsight, it is possible to question the wisdom of such assumptions, they were nonetheless perfectly understandable in the context of the immediate post-war years. As Rex Leeper wrote in 1935,

> When the war ended, the establishment of the League of Nations with the enthusiastic support of Great Britain seemed to many of us the outward and visible sign that we had ceased to be insular in our habits of thought and that we really desired to understand and to be understood by others. It is true that during the brief period of peace and apparent prosperity which followed, we cherished the comfortable illusion that through the League of Nations we could maintain European peace without involving ourselves in too many responsibilities.[139]

The result was that British propaganda was drastically reduced and the reconstructed News Department was forced to work under the constant threat of reductions and, on occasion, closure. It meant that the British case went largely unstated, or else left to others to state, invariably laying it open to misinterpretation and misrepresentation. Although the News Department worked to correct such false impressions as may have been created by aggressive foreign propaganda, it had neither the financial resources nor the staff necessary for continuous and effective effort. For example, on receiving a request in 1919 from Lord Allenby for permission to inaugurate propaganda in Egypt, the News Department was unable to support the scheme on financial grounds, and John Tilley was prompted to reflect: 'We shall have to rely on successful administration for propaganda in Egypt.'[140] That this was applicable to most areas of the world was a sad reflection on the limited scope of the News Department's work in the 1920s.

Despite the limited work being done, however – and it must be remembered that, although the work was severely restricted, it was nonetheless an innovative peacetime activity for the British government — the arguments and ideals which had played a major share in reducing the work after the war were soon to be exposed as hollow and illusory. If, on the return to peace, it was widely believed that British overseas propaganda was unnecessary, the subsequent growth in its use by rival governments made a reappraisal inevitable.

PART TWO

The projection of Britain, 1919–1939

Foreign policy alone, however wisely conceived, cannot remove misunderstandings unless it can work on a background of knowledge. Some form of national publicity, if wisely directed, with the Government, education and industry in a working partnership, can do much to provide a fruitful ground for policy.

(*The Times*, 20 March 1935)

3
Commercial propaganda and the concept of national projection

If, on the return of peace in 1918, the British government proved reluctant to embark upon a programme of national propaganda overseas, it was, paradoxically, more prepared to undertake official propaganda at home. During the post-war period of social and economic dislocation, with its widespread strikes and disillusionment, it appeared to many officials and politicians that there existed a very real danger of insurrection and possibly even of revolution. Accordingly, during the 1919 railway strike, the Cabinet was prepared to authorise the use of posters, leaflets and press advertisements in an attempt to explain and clarify the government's position.[1] As the number of strikes continued to increase, the Cabinet agreed, in April 1921, that it was of the utmost importance to take greater steps 'to deal with the Government propaganda on a more elaborate scale than was at present in force' to ensure that the public was being 'correctly informed' with regard to the main political issues.[2] The Conservative Party was quick to learn the lessons of this experience, and by the mid 1920s it began experimenting with a small fleet of cinema vans which toured the country showing political films and cartoons.[3] *The Times* noted in 1926: 'The Conservative Party are now making use of the cinematograph regularly in propaganda work. Political propaganda seems to be the thin edge of the wedge, the other end of which may be national propaganda.'[4] And so it proved. In January 1935, Ramsay MacDonald's National Government established the National Publicity Bureau, which has been said to have 'carried through the first modern, large-scale propaganda campaign on a national basis in the history of British politics'.[5]

Before public attention began to focus upon the increasingly aggressive policies of Mussolini's Italy and Hitler's Germany, the British government's chief anxiety had been with the problem of Moscow-inspired communist propaganda.[6] In 1920, William

The projection of Britain, 1919–1939

Tyrrell had warned that the internal affairs of one country were no longer the sole concern of the domestic government. He wrote: 'The connection between labour and foreign policy is increasing daily. The study of labour questions has therefore become essential to the administration of foreign affairs.'[7] This was particularly pertinent in view of the activities of the Third International, and it was partly to curb those activities that the following clause was inserted into the 1921 Anglo-Soviet Trade Agreement:

That each party refrains from hostile action or undertakings against the other and from conducting outside of its own borders any official propaganda direct or indirect against the institutions of the British Empire or the Russian Soviet Government respectively, and more particularly that the Russian Soviet Government refrains from any attempt by military or diplomatic or any other form of action or propaganda to encourage the peoples of Asia in any form of hostile action against British interests or the British Empire, especially in India and in the independent State of Afghanistan.[8]

The British undertaking was entirely in accord with the post-war policy of reducing her propaganda activities abroad, and adherence to these terms was thus more palatable. Although there is no evidence to indicate that the Foreign Office, as the department of state primarily responsible for overseas propaganda, broke the terms of the agreement, the problem of Soviet propaganda in Britain continued to cause alarm throughout the 1920s, particularly during the period between the Zinoviev letter and the general strike. As a result, similar clauses were inserted into the Temporary Commercial Agreement with Russia in April 1930, but their complete disregard by the Soviets, combined with the additional tension created by hostile propaganda broadcasts from Moscow, served to keep this subject very much alive during the early 1930s.[9]

The growth of totalitarianism in Europe, accompanied as it was by the dramatic employment of state-subsidised propaganda to further national aims and prestige, presented its rivals with a new set of problems in international affairs. Until some form of democratic response to the problem of hostile propaganda became unavoidable in the 1930s, Britain was ironically to remain a disarmed bystander while her opponents utilised the lessons of the British wartime experience and combined them with technological advancements in such areas as broadcasting and the cinema in order to mould propaganda into a powerful weapon of nationalistic expansion and ideo-

Commercial propaganda and national projection

logical penetration. However much British officials and politicians would have preferred otherwise, it soon became apparent that there was to be no return to the pre-1914 period when propaganda had been regarded as a relatively harmless factor in international politics.

Trade, the flag and flagging trade

The Foreign Office contained some of the few people in Britain who recognised this at an early stage. However, through a combination of prejudice, short-sightedness and illusion, they had been forced to watch the loss of an important British initiative as the wartime propaganda machinery was dismantled on the return of peace. The years that followed witnessed an increase in the use of national propaganda rather than a decline, with the result that there began to emerge a body of opinion, whose members were not confined solely to the Foreign Office, which began to advocate increased British involvement in propaganda abroad. Their arguments gathered increasing weight with the disintegration of the victorious wartime coalition, worsening Anglo-French tension in Europe and the disappointing progress of economic recovery, but, thanks to the easing of tension during the so-called Locarno era, they were not to succeed in their goal until the early 1930s. In the meantime, they argued that British interests, both political and commercial, were suffering from a lack of adequate representation and explanation abroad and that consequently British prestige in its widest sense was in the process of decline.

The detrimental effects of aggressive foreign propaganda upon British interests might not have been so marked had the original Foreign Office proposals for peacetime propaganda been accepted at the end of the war. Those effects first became most visible in the field of trade and commerce. In 1919, when the Foreign Office had first considered the future role of the News Department, it had been generally assumed that commercial propaganda would constitute one, albeit crucial, component of the programme of national propaganda overseas, along with cultural and (if to a lesser extent) political advertisement. Even so, this was a significant assumption. It was partly a reflection of changing official attitudes towards the role of commerce in the context of British diplomacy. 'The great flaw' in the pre-war system, Vansittart wrote, 'was that economics had no place in it.'[10] But the First World War had dealt a violent blow to traditional attitudes regarding the value of *laissez-faire* and the role of private enterprise, with increased official involvement in commercial affairs and a greater use of the economic weapon with the imposition of the blockade. Apart from the Ministry of Blockade itself, the expanding wartime responsibilities of the government had necessitated the creation of two temporary wartime departments: the Board of Trade's Commercial Intelligence Department and the Foreign Office's Foreign Trade Department. On the return of peace, and the lifting of the blockade, it became important to ensure that the economic and commercial determinants of British foreign policy should henceforth receive as much consideration as that already afforded to military and strategic factors if financial recovery was to be achieved. A major problem centered on which department should be responsible for the formulation and supervision of commercial policy abroad, the Foreign Office or the Board of Trade. Because the new work fell broadly between the responsibilities of the two, the Department of Overseas Trade (DOT) was created as a compromise solution, being made jointly responsible to both.

The challenge to Britain's domination of world markets, begun in earnest during the final decades of the nineteenth century, had continued to an ever increasing extent with the rapid economic growth of Europe and America, and the unprecedented expansion of overseas trade. At the end of the war, it became essential for Britain, with her dependence for survival upon imports and exports, to try to recapture her former markets and expand into new trading areas if she was to maintain her proportionate share of world trade. Propaganda offered one method of securing this end. Other governments recognised this much earlier than in Britain. Indeed, it was from this commercial factor that concepts of national projection were eventually to emerge.

For the moment, however, blinkered vision prevailed. The Foreign Office argued in vain that commercial and cultural propaganda were mutually complementary and must be conducted side by side. In other words, the success of one was dependent upon the successful conduct of the other. This was essentially a long-term strategy, designed to create an atmosphere of mutual respect and understanding which would in turn benefit not only Britain's commer-

Commercial propaganda and national projection

cial interests and prosperity but would also serve to lubricate the wheels of British diplomatic procedure. To a more critical Treasury, such innovative ideas appeared to be an expensive substitute for good government and efficient business management. If propaganda was considered to be at all necessary, the Treasury was naturally more inclined to authorise expenditure for commercial advertisement because of the prospect of immediate, short-term and, above all, visible returns. It was for this reason that the conduct of cultural propaganda was completely forbidden, while the Foreign Office was instructed gradually to transfer its responsibility for commercial propaganda to the DOT, although it was recognised that 'the application of this principle might not altogether be an easy matter in practice'.[11]

To the Foreign Office, this was an error of the first order. In the News Department it was recognised that the old maxim that 'trade follows the flag' was rapidly changing to a situation where trade followed the newspaper, the book, the schoolteacher and the language of a country. It was simply no longer possible to separate trade from other forms of commercial intercourse in a highly competitive world. Nevertheless, having been debarred from conducting any form of cultural activity, the Foreign Office was forced to concentrate upon its only remaining weapon: news. The News Department was reduced to supplying a regular stream of accurate news and reliable information, chiefly through the medium of the press, in an effort to publicise Britain abroad. This might have proved sufficient to promote commercial relations had it not been for the energetic activities of other governments, which were busily harnessing propaganda to national economic policy in an attempt to expand into commercial markets at the expense of rival competitors. As one official wrote of the situation in South America shortly after the war,

> We have evidence that this propaganda sometimes takes the form of sneering at England. In these circumstances it seems essential, if we are to remain on an equal trade footing with our trade rivals in the country, that South America should be kept continuously supplied with news about England and that this should make a good show in the press.[12]

British prestige, he continued, was clearly suffering as a result of the intense propaganda programmes of rival countries in a continent which offered expanding trade opportunities and a wealth of natural resources to any power that could offer the most attractive inducements. The same official warned: 'we should try to prevent England being lost sight of or relegated to the position of a second-rate power in South American opinion – as she might be if the papers were flooded with news about the United States or Germany'.[13] The British Official News Service thus assumed added significance, particularly as Reuters was a party to the self-denying ordinance of the agreements among the international news agencies which made South America the special sphere of influence of Havas and the American agencies. The problem was, however, not solely confined to South America, and it soon became apparent that news, by itself, was an inadequate counter to the comprehensive propaganda activities of rival states.

Alternative methods of securing increased publicity for the British point of view in foreign countries were considered at various times throughout the 1920s. As early as 1920 there was a proposal to establish a Foreign Office Film Unit to produce propaganda films, chiefly for commercial purposes, but the scheme was pre-empted by Percy Koppel, who was probably correct in assuming that 'the Treasury would never allow it'.[14] Thereafter, the News Department endeavoured to encourage individual film-producers to send their own films abroad or, where this proved impossible, to itself provide films 'of an influential character' for exhibition at overseas film festivals or other such gatherings.[15] In accordance with this practice, the News Department arranged for the Imperial War Museum to lend several British war films to the Argentine government for purposes of military instruction and training,[16] although such transactions became less frequent with the progressive erosion of funds during the 1920s. Nevertheless, both the Foreign Office and the DOT remained acutely aware of the importance of film for trade propaganda purposes, but had to rely upon the initiative of individual concerns to publicise their achievements abroad. This was the case with a film made by the British motor industry[17] and another about making matches produced by Bryant and May.[18]

The discontinuation of the successful official wartime periodical *America Latina* created a further vacuum which proved difficult to fill. In May 1919, this deficiency was temporarily rectified when the Foreign Office secured 3,000 free copies of the newly created 'Latin American Supplement' of *The Times*. Because of the 'valuable

Commercial propaganda and national projection

propaganda material' contained in this publication, the News Department attempted to capitalise upon the high regard which existed abroad for *The Times*, particularly after December 1919, when the supplement was printed in Spanish.[19] However, Printing House Square was reluctant to supply any further free copies, and one News Department official wrote that unless the necessary expenditure could be found to enable it to subscribe to the publication,

> this would be a great loss to the country, for The Times Spanish Supplement is the only publication of its kind which deals with all branches of British trade. There are numbers of other trade journals published in Spanish, but they each deal with some particular trade and not with British interests as a whole.[20]

The money was simply not available. An alternative and somewhat desperate solution, namely that *The Times* should itself meet the costs of overseas distribution, was considered out of the question by the newspaper, because, 'after all, we as a business institution could not undertake what would be tantamount to Government propaganda'.[21]

Instead, the News Department had to rely upon compiling its own publicity articles for insertion in the foreign press. There were four different types of article: (1) a weekly *London Letter* of about 200–250 words covering a wide range of topics; (2) a special weekly article of about 800–900 words on general subjects relating to commerce, industry, science, sport and literature; (3) a fortnightly article on finance and commerce of about 800 words; (4) a monthly commercial news letter, usually containing extracts from the Overseas Trade Bulletin. The articles were generally written under pseudonyms or by free-lance journalists.[22] Whereas the first two categories included material which could loosely be described as 'cultural', the latter two were more specifically commercial in content. The articles were compiled either in the News Department or in the DOT and translated prior to their distribution by cables, wireless or diplomatic bag to press attachés, consuls or ministers abroad, whence they were circulated to the local press free of charge.

Despite the supposed gradual transfer of responsibility for commercial propaganda to the DOT, the compilation of these articles remained an integral part of the News Department's work, evidently because the Foreign Office did not consider its newer and less experienced partner as being capable of performing the task discreetly and efficiently. Of the methods adopted by the DOT in its press publicity, Victor Wellesley complained in 1921:

> It is in my opinion altogether wrong that the Consular Officers should be utilised, under cover of the official sanction of the Department of Overseas Trade, for supplying the press with articles on any subject relating to foreign affairs. When it comes to writing on economic subjects, the practice is particularly dangerous because it is often difficult to keep off political ground, or abstain from political bias... It is obviously objectionable, and the DOT must be told so, but in any case I should have thought that the DOT should be ordered to stop the practice altogether.[23]

Tyrrell agreed,[24] and, following suitable chastisement of the little brother, it was decided that the Foreign Office should for the moment continue to be responsible for the compilation and supply of articles, commercial or otherwise, to the foreign press.

Whereas the DOT did not possess any propaganda section as such, there were two divisions which retained an active interest in the subject. The first of these, the press sub-section of the Central Section, was responsible for the compilation of the DOT's *Monthly Bulletin* and for the insertion of commercial news items in the British and foreign press. In such matters, the press sub-section worked very closely with its counterpart in the Foreign Office, the press section of the News Department. But it was further responsible for deciding which items of overseas commercial information were suitable for communication to the press, for selecting the recipients, for securing publicity for the DOT's annual reports, and for ministerial and departmental publicity through the publication of leaflets and booklets.[25] It was also in charge of advertising and maintained close contact with advertising associations and individual business firms, supplying them with such items of overseas commercial information as might prove of interest.[26]

The second section of the DOT concerned with publicity was the Exhibitions Division, which conducted its own propaganda on behalf of the British Industries Fair (BIF). This proved to be a consistently effective form of commercial publicity: because 'BIF propaganda carries with it paid advertising, an opportunity frequently occurs to combine it with some propaganda on behalf of British

Commercial propaganda and national projection

industry generally'.[27] It was not the concern of the DOT to advertise on behalf of individual industries or business firms, which was left to private initiative and imagination, but rather to promote the interests of British industry as a whole. Hence the need to remain in contact with the Federation of British Industries and with the Association of British Chambers of Commerce. The latter organisation in particular appreciated that a wider knowledge and appreciation of the British way of life abroad was a necessary prerequisite to the expansion of commercial interests in the modern world.[28]

Greater official participation in international exhibitions was advantageous not only to individual firms and British industry in general but also to British prestige. This question began to assume added significance in view of the considerable attention devoted by foreign governments to their image abroad. In Britain prior to 1912, any official involvement in overseas exhibitions was the responsibility of specially appointed Royal Commissions, but in that year all such work was placed in the care of the newly formed Exhibitions branch of the Board of Trade. The DOT inherited this task in 1918, although official British involvement in overseas exhibitions tended to remain somewhat limited. As one official later recalled,

Unlike the practice of certain other nations, no regular sum was ever set aside for this type of propaganda. Britain has never actually offered an official show to another power. For reasons of national economy, a 'wait and see' policy has always been practised, each application being considered on its merits and a good case had to be made out for it in order to make participation possible.[29]

Indeed, where the British had participated, as in 1922 at the Brazilian Centenary Exhibition or in the 1925 Paris Decorative Arts Exhibition, it had been regarded as highly successful. The British pavilion at the 1927 Brussels Exhibition proved no exception, attracting some 300,000 visitors.[30] There nonetheless remained a need to integrate the commercial and cultural aspects of Britain's entries more efficiently, because, it was argued,

Acquaintance with British art through the medium of such exhibitions cannot fail ... to evoke curiosity as regards Great Britain and interest in her life, with the result that foreigners will be inclined to visit the United Kingdom, thus promoting commercial and social intercourse, and the study of the English language, which latter study is the best of mediums for the enhancement of national prestige and advertisement of national products.[31]

Pressure in this direction was beginning to mount to such a degree

The projection of Britain, 1919–1939

by the late 1920s, both within Whitehall and beyond, that the issue could no longer be swept under the Treasury's carpet, as it had effectively been in 1919.

John Bull at home

In 1928, the News Department announced that it was ready to implement the Treasury ruling of 1919 and transfer any remaining responsibility for commercial propaganda into the care of the DOT. Arthur Willert informed E. F. Crowe, the comptroller-general of the DOT, that

> A development of the purely commercial, industrial and financial side of this form of publicity could probably be better effected in the hands of your department than of ours, while the continuance of the cultural propaganda on the existing lines could not, we feel sure, suffer from any transfer such as we are tentatively contemplating.[32]

There is some evidence to suggest that the News Department was finding its partial dependence upon the goodwill of individual commercial secretaries and consular officers in distributing the press articles an unsatisfactory arrangement. Some were reported as being genuinely interested in the work and quite willing to extend their full co-operation to the Foreign Office in this matter. However, 'there are others who cannot be moved to anything but criticism of everything we do; and there is no hope in them'.[33] By handing over responsibility for compiling the articles to the DOT, it was assumed that a greater degree of control and efficiency would result, but the proposal, coming as it did after nearly a decade of Foreign Office involvement in the work, aroused DOT suspicions and prompted much internal debate concerning the desirability of setting up a specific propaganda section, comparable to the News Department, within the DOT.

One official, L. A. de L. Meredith, who had himself recently proposed just such an idea, welcomed Willert's suggestion: 'I said then, and I still say, that insufficient attention is paid to this matter, which is of considerable importance.'[34] On the other hand, C. M. Pickthall, another senior DOT official, was less enthusiastic:

> I have misgivings about the DOT assuming the function of a Government

Commercial propaganda and national projection

propaganda department on behalf of industry collectively or individually. If we take on this work we may expose ourselves to a good deal of criticism, or even risk some discredit. The work might have political merits, but from the official point of view, it does not seem to me to be the Department's job, or one that it should take on.[35]

At this point, Pickthall's view had more support. Another official insisted that the DOT should be concerned with 'facts not propaganda', and he warned of the consequent loss of credibility as a source of commercial information should a propaganda section be created. He continued: 'This, of course, does not mean that propaganda is not useful. But it should be kept where there is no danger of those whose business is to ascertain and disseminate facts becoming mixed up in their own minds as to which is fact and which is speculation.'[36] It was further pointed out that the Foreign Office News Department already had the experience, the trained staff, and the goodwill of visiting journalists, which merely made it more important for the DOT 'to keep the News Department supplied with material from which the News Department can cull information suitable for publicity'.[37] The overwhelming weight of DOT opinion favoured closer liaison with, rather than distinct separation from, the work of the News Department. Crowe accordingly informed Willert that the existing arrangements for the dissemination of commercial news abroad would best be left as they were.[38]

The DOT looked to the newly formed Travel Association of Great Britain and Northern Ireland for help in rectifying the deficiencies in commercial propaganda overseas. The Travel Association, which had evolved from the privately sponsored 'Come to Britain Movement', was created in December 1928 on the initiative of several leading businessmen who among them had decided that their collective interests required promotion abroad. A meeting was held at the Mansion House on 20 December, presided over by Lord Derby, at which two resolutions had been passed. The first was that an association be formed, under the presidency of Lord Derby, of persons and institutions interested in the encouragement of foreign visitors to Britain. The second resolution called for the creation of a provisional committee to take the necessary steps in setting up the association, raising subscriptions, ascertaining terms of reference and appointing an executive committee.[39] Also present at this meeting were the president of the Board of Trade, Sir Philip Cunliffe-Lister, and Douglas Hacking, representing the DOT, both of whom promised official support for the work of new body.[40] Following a joint appeal by the Foreign Office and the Board of Trade to the Treasury,[41] a small grant-in-aid of £5,000 was awarded to the Travel Association, to be borne on the DOT's vote.[42] This sum supplemented a figure of £11,000 already raised from private sources for work in 1929.[43]

At the Mansion House meeting, Lord Derby spoke of the dual purpose of the Travel Association: 'Our ultimate aims are twofold, the promotion of international understanding through personal contacts and – let us be honest about it – business.'[44] It was this latter aim which attracted the support of many prominent businessmen who had a vested interest in attracting more tourists to Britain. The type of concern which was prepared to back this new venture is illustrated by the composition of the provisional committee, which included: Lord Ashfield, chairman of the Underground Railways and Omnibus Companies; Alderman F. Britain, chairman of the Conference of Health and Pleasure Resorts; F. H. Cooke, chairman of Thomas Cook and Son, Ltd; S. J. Lister, manager of the Cunard Steamship Company; Sir Felix Pole, general manager of the Great Western Railway; Gordon Selfridge, chairman of the department store.

However, it was the first aim which attracted Lord Derby's interest and the support of government. In a speech which epitomised the mood of those early pioneers of national self-advertisement, Derby stated:

We believe that people who visit these islands and see John Bull at home will discover that he is really a good natured person of simple tastes, who never harbours malice and only wishes to be friends with all the world. Having discovered this they will be slow to believe that John Bull is actuated by base motives such as are imputed to him, sometimes by his enemies and sometimes through ignorance of his character. Similarly, it cannot but be good for John Bull at home to learn that there may be another point of view than his own, and that the stranger is a fellow much like himself. If at the same time the country is benefited by the expenditure of our visitors – well, John Bull is a practical person and business is business.[45]

Not only did the Foreign Office and the DOT view this aim as one means of countering the effects of hostile foreign propaganda upon

Commercial propaganda and national projection

Britain's image abroad, but it also attracted the support of certain private individuals concerned with the problem, such as Sir Harry Brittain, founder of the Imperial Press Conference and currently vice-president of the Pilgrims, Lord Riddell, president of the Newspaper Proprietors' Association, and Sir Gilbert Vyle, a past president of the Association of the British Chambers of Commerce.[46]

In February 1929, the Travel Association's provisional committee decided that the new body should be incorporated under the Companies Acts as a company limited by guarantee. The idea was that the association would operate as a non-trading organisation, working independently of government control, with its own staff, offices and finances. The DOT would provide as much assistance as possible, 'whether through the overseas services of the Department or by bringing pressure to bear on bodies, corporations, and, if necessary, other departments to remove hindrances and obstructions'.[47] The links with the DOT were in fact to prove much closer. Louis Beale, former trade commissioner in New Zealand, was made director of the Travel Association, and Meredith was seconded by the DOT to act as his secretary. An extremely close liaison between the two bodies was established from the outset, this work being undertaken at first by Pickthall and then, from 1930, by E. L. Mercier.[48]

In May 1929 a circular despatch was distributed to all overseas commercial and diplomatic representatives informing them of the existence of the new organisation with instructions to do 'everything in their power to forward its aims and objects in their district'. Those aims were listed as being:

To increase the number of visitors from overseas to Great Britain and Ireland; to stimulate the demand for British goods and services and to promote international understanding by every means, and in particular:–
(1) by the stimulation abroad of interest in Great Britain and Ireland;
(2) by the promotion of voluntary co-ordination in advertising;
(3) by the collection from official and other sources abroad of information useful to members;
(4) by the examination of customs and passport facilities, etc.;
(5) by the examination of laws affecting the overseas visitor;
(6) by the provision of information useful to members.[49]

Because, however, the Travel Association had been created too late to begin its work in anticipation of the summer of 1929, this proved to be a blessing in disguise in that more time was available to develop its future strategy.

The Travel Association operated on two, albeit related, levels. The first may be generally described as tourist information and publicity, involving the provision of details and advice concerning the various beauty spots and holiday resorts in the British Isles. By utilising publicity to promote the interests of tourism, the Travel Association hoped to capture a proportion of the world's growing tourist market and thereby exert 'what may be called a human tidal pull towards these shores'.[50] It was argued that 'It is accepted on all hands that the people of most nations, as if stirred by a common impulse, and doubtless assisted by the tremendous increase in facilities for travel, are today taking a new keen interest in each other. Travel is world-wide, a great common idea.'[51] The founders of the association, representing as they did a wide range of trade and business interests, 'whose prosperity or depression are matters of vital concern to the nation as a whole, recognise in the beauty and history of Great Britain and Ireland an asset of immense possibilities for the general welfare'.[52]

On the second level was the political and international aspect of the association's work. As Lord Derby pointed out, the publicity employed was not solely designed to promote tourism, 'but has set out to develop through travel a greater knowledge of, and interest in, British culture and British goods, thus bringing about, we are confident, an increase in our export trade, visible as well as invisible'.[53] It was further argued that 'The visitor who comes over here reads our newspapers, shares our recreations, talks with our people and makes friends, with many of whom he keeps in touch afterwards. Such a person recognises the common interests of nations... In fact, he becomes an ambassador for this country.'[54] It was towards these aims that, at the close of 1929, the Travel Association embarked upon an ambitious publicity campaign abroad. Information likely to be of interest to potential visitors, including leaflets and photographs, was distributed free to the foreign press. Similarly, articles on the British Isles were also released for publication, and travel posters were donated to foreign hotels and clubs.[55] *The Times*, which had been following these developments with some interest, noted in August 1929:

Commercial propaganda and national projection

While the Travel Association is, perhaps, of too recent origin to suggest that the increased bookings of the leading steamship companies are directly due to the efforts of the Association, there can be no doubt that the dissemination of literature by the Association in the United States, together with the steady pursuit, in other directions, of its policy of advertising the attractions of this country, has not been without its psychological effect.[56]

That effect was said to be visible in the increase of foreign visitors from 266,000 in 1928 to 280,000 in 1929: 'the number would have been larger still but for the smallpox scare and, curiously enough, the General Election, which some foreigners who did not know the British thought could cause upheaval'.[57]

Although, initially, the co-operation of diplomatic and commercial representatives abroad was considered essential in helping to distribute publicity material and in determining the areas in which to operate, the Travel Association quickly decided that its work would receive greater consideration and supervision if it was conducted by specially appointed officers or advisory committees in the various regions. The first such committee was appointed in 1929 at Buenos Aires – again a reflection of the priority afforded to South America by British propagandists in the 1920s – under the chairmanship of Sir Herbert Gibson and with the full support of the British embassy. The News Department of the Foreign Office fully endorsed this development and even entered into collaborative arrangements with the Travel Association in order to avoid overlapping and to reduce costs.[58]

A proposal to establish a similar committee in New York was treated with greater official reserve. Meredith considered that there was a considerable field for the association's activities in the United States, particularly in the direction of broadcast talks on Britain from various American radio stations, the distribution of photographs of 'well-known Americans enjoying themselves in this country', and the provision of news to the American press.[59] The Foreign Office, which had since the end of the war been advocating extreme caution in so far as British propaganda in the United States was concerned, considered that it would be more acceptable for 'propaganda of this sort' to be conducted unofficially, i.e. by the British financial and business communities in America. It was essential for the association to avoid 'too much of a "hands across the sea" tendency'.[60] The DOT concurred,[61] and thereafter all publicity emanating from the association's New York office was more obviously concerned with tourist and travel information than with any overt form of national self-advertisement.

The creation of the Travel Association was significant for three reasons. In the first place, it provided the first real recognition in peacetime of the importance of conducting a national, permanently active publicity campaign to make Britain more widely known and understood abroad. Secondly, it provided testimony to the growing conviction of the importance of bringing the peoples of different nations closer together in order to promote the interests of international peace and understanding. As Prime Minister Ramsay MacDonald wrote in a foreword to an association booklet, 'enmities are born of ignorance and prejudice; friendships of personal contacts and understanding. The best way that peoples of different nations can get to know each other is by travel.'[62] Third was the fact 'that the trade and commerce of any nation are enormously helped if potential customers can be persuaded to see and get to know that nation'.[63] In other words, commercial propaganda was dependent for its success upon supplementary methods of persuasion.

Nevertheless, although a beginning had been made to counter the prejudicial effects of hostile foreign propaganda upon British interests and prestige, it was on a relatively small scale and barely adequate to combat the intensive programmes of rival powers. By the late 1920s, both the Foreign Office and the DOT were becoming increasingly alarmed at the frequency of disquieting reports received from their overseas representatives which generally made it clear that the image of Britain abroad was suffering from a lack of adequate proselytisation. The limited nature of British efforts to dispel images such as 'perfidious Albion' was becoming more and more apparent. One observer, who stated that 'it is usually taken as a bad sign when an old firm saves money on advertisement', posed the following question: 'The teaching of its language in a foreign country is the soundest advertisement that any nation as a whole can make. Can Britain afford to save money on any form of advertisement on which her commercial rivals are spending so much?'[64] The Foreign Office and the DOT began to insist that it had now, perhaps more than ever before, become important to utilise publicity as a means of promoting peace and trade. South America remained at the forefront of their attention, for reasons which partly derived from the

Commercial propaganda and national projection

lack of British news on that continent. The high costs of the transatlantic cables made it cheaper to send news there via New York rather than direct to Buenos Aires. One official wrote:

> British trade with Latin America suffers accordingly, and will, I think, continue to suffer in an age of advertisement, unless a remedy is found. In large areas of Latin America the only items of British news and views that ever appear in the press are the News Department articles. They are published with fair regularity in about 116 newspapers in 15 countries. In Brazil, the British Official Wireless helps, but in no other country is it even moderately successful.[65]

Not until the problem of cable costs was resolved could Reuters or any other British news agency successfully enter the field dominated by Havas, the United Press, the Associated Press and Wolff, but despite periodical attempts by Reuters to secure an official subsidy and despite the appointment in 1938 of a government committee of enquiry into this question, a remedy was never really found during the inter-war years.

A similar problem existed with regard to film propaganda. The 1926 Imperial Conference had devoted some attention to this question,[66] and in 1928 the DOT launched an enquiry into the use of industrial films for purposes of overseas propaganda. G. E. C. Hatton felt that, in view of the shortage of official money, local councils or Chambers of Commerce might be encouraged to produce films of general interest for foreign audiences. He wrote:

> Can it be doubted that any audience anywhere would welcome a good picture of life and business in the largest city of the world [i.e. London]? Its size could be shown from the air, views could be given of its tubes, its docks, its shopping centres, and its commercial quarters. If the world at large could see the workers pouring out of the railway termini of a morning, would England still be thought decadent?[67]

The commercial benefits of such films would, he believed, be considerable, but there was a problem with regard to cultural propaganda:

> There is likely to be more difficulty in obtaining new interest films dealing with English life and national customs. Such films are likely to be acceptable overseas because they savour more of entertainment and less of propaganda. It is however difficult to see who could be asked to make them,

except the Government. This form of propaganda, which again can hardly fail to bring commercial results, has hardly been touched.[68]

The Foreign Office agreed that there was much commercial credit to be drawn from films depicting British scenery, institutions and sporting and current events, and even from entertainment films 'featuring episodes in which the Britisher, whether man or woman, plays a heroic role or featuring famous British film actors'. However, the Foreign Office was quick to emphasise its 'function of "prevention", that is of criticism'. In other words, it was only concerned with preventing: '(a) the production and showing of films in this country which react unfavourably on foreign political relations... (b) the showing of a foreign-produced film of the nature of ... Cruiser Potemkin'.[69] The problem was compounded by the existence of very few British films which were suitable for overseas audiences, especially in view of Hollywood's domination. Hatton argued:

Pictures with human interest are needed; there must be touches that audiences can appreciate, even though the subjects of films do not appeal from a trade point of view, and the industrial or national propaganda must be kept in the background... In general, I cannot imagine that foreign audiences, particularly Latin American ones, would tolerate the average existing British Industrial picture at full length, especially if there had been a charge for admission.[70]

Yet some solution had to be found, particularly as, in the words of one expert, 'one foot of film equals one dollar of trade'.[71]

The mounting pressure for some form of determined official response to the intensive anti-British propaganda of state-subsidised agencies received a welcome stimulus with the publication of the report of the British Economic Mission to South America in January 1930. This four-man mission had toured various Latin American countries in late 1929 under the distinguished leadership of Lord D'Abernon, formerly British ambassador to Germany.[72] Their findings reinforced the view that commercial and cultural relations were inextricably related. An entire chapter, entitled 'The Commercial Importance of Cultural Influence', was devoted to this subject and pointed to the failure of successive governments to capitalise upon the reservoir of pro-British feeling which had existed in South America since the time of Canning. In view of the propaganda now

Commercial propaganda and national projection

being conducted by rival competitors such as France, Italy, Germany and the United States, the report urged the British government to recognise that 'the feeling for us in South America is an important commercial fact'.[73] It therefore recommended official support for the work of the Argentine Association of English Culture (founded in 1928) and an increase in the supply of British books, newspapers, films and theatrical productions and of English teaching facilities to the continent as a whole. The report concluded: 'To those who say that this extension in influence has no connection with commerce, we reply that they are totally wrong; the reaction of trade to the more deliberate inculcation of British culture which we advocate is definitely certain and will be swift.'[74] The report was favourably received not only in the Foreign Office and the DOT[75] but also in the House of Commons.[76] When, therefore, the Foreign Office submitted its appeal for the 1919 embargo on cultural propaganda to be lifted, the Treasury found it extremely difficult to resist the demand.

The economic crisis which reverberated around the world in the wake of the Wall Street crash of 1929 gave rise to renewed efforts on the part of those who advocated increased British trade propaganda overseas. The response of the DOT was to establish an interdepartmental Trade Propaganda Committee in April 1930 with the following terms of reference:

To consider and report whether in general it is proper and desirable for the Government to participate in trade advertisement and propaganda overseas and, if so, what form or forms such participation may usefully take.

Further, to report whether any existing departmental organisation or organisations are fitted to put into effect the recommendations of the Committee, and, if a new organisation is found necessary, to make recommendations as to its constitution and control.[77]

The Trade Propaganda Committee first met in April 1930 under the chairmanship of G. M. Gillett, parliamentary secretary to the DOT, who was assisted by Sir Oswald Mosley, chancellor of the Duchy of Lancaster, although the latter's connection with the committee ended in May with his resignation from the Labour government.

Several months earlier, a Committee on Trade and Industry under the chairmanship of Sir Arthur Balfour had argued against increased commercial propaganda on the grounds that any such step would involve His Majesty's Government in undesirable responsibilities and would probably be regarded by foreign countries as involving a direct subsidy to export. If, as is probable, our example should find imitators, the result would be to foster a new and insidious form of State bounties on foreign trade, which it was the desire of the Geneva Economic Conference to bring to an end.[78]

The Trade Propaganda Committee, however, felt that events had overtaken this conclusion, 'and the state of our export trade is growing so critical during the continuing depression, that any objections to Government participation in trade advertisement and propaganda are far outweighed by the urgent need for everything possible to be done to restore and stimulate our vital export trade'.[79] It was pointed out that the British would be the imitators, as foreign governments already conducted trade propaganda on a large scale.

The Trade Propaganda Committee therefore proposed that the DOT should be enabled to assist empire 'Shopping Weeks' in overseas countries by the provision of posters, cards, shop-window display material and the offer of trophies. It was also suggested that the DOT could distribute trade journals free of charge to selected persons abroad. Moreover, 'we have considered the question of propaganda by the use of films, and are impressed by the demonstration given to us of what Russia, in particular, is doing in this direction'.[80] A films sub-committee was appointed to examine this question further, but in the meantime it was urged that any requests for British films 'which offer an advantageous opportunity of propaganda' should be met by the DOT. The committee also endorsed the belief of the Foreign Office in the importance to commerce of cultural propaganda. But these would be expensive projects. True to form, the Treasury representative on the committee, E. N. R. Trentham, 'while agreeing that propaganda overseas at the present time, if carefully directed, should be of assistance to the export industries', did not wish to commit the Exchequer to meeting the cost.[81] Once again, this proved to be the major stumbling-block to any further progress – at least for the moment.

The economic crisis posed a double-edged problem in so far as national propaganda overseas was concerned. The need, on the one hand, to implement cutbacks in government spending threatened to jeopardise the promising initiatives made thus far. Propaganda might be regarded as a necessary evil, but it was, as yet, a relatively

Commercial propaganda and national projection

untried and unproven activity of British government and was thus an automatic candidate for financial retrenchment. On the other hand, both the Foreign Office and the DOT argued that propaganda offered one means of salvaging something of benefit from the decline in world trade. In other words, the economic crisis had merely made it even more essential for Britain to utilise propaganda as a means of promoting British interests. The early 1930s is the history of the triumph of the latter view over the former. It was during this period that the advocates of national self-advertisement redoubled their efforts to persuade the government that increased effort in this direction was a necessary instrument of the modern state. The visit of the Prince of Wales to South America in February 1931, during which he opened the British Empire Trade Exhibition at Buenos Aires, helped to keep the issues raised by the D'Abernon report very much alive.[82] So did Sir Ernest Thompson's Economic Mission to the Far East in 1930–1, which reported that 'if we are to fight a winning battle in the China trade, we must educate China to our methods and our products by educating young Chinese in Great Britain'.[83] Similarly, the general report of Sir Alan Anderson's Trade Mission to Scandinavia in 1933 warned that because Germany still attracted young trainee engineers from Norway, Sweden and Finland, once qualified they tended to adopt German standards and send their orders to Germany. For this reason, the report stated, 'it is very necessary for us to encourage the rising generation to learn our language, adopt our techniques and assimilate our culture'.[84] It was this need to extend intellectual and cultural relations to the rest of the world in order to promote the peaceful and profitable development of British commerce and diplomacy that was the subject of repeated emphasis by the Foreign Office and the DOT during the late 1920s and early 1930s. However, perhaps the most famous exponent of the entire school of thought was Sir Stephen Tallents, who first coined the phrase 'the projection of England' in an influential pamphlet published under that title in 1932.

Wonderful Britain

Tallents derived his views largely from his experience as secretary of the Empire Marketing Board (EMB) which, in the wake of the 1923 and 1926 Imperial Conferences, had been established under the aegis of the Dominions Office with the object of 'furthering the marketing in the United Kingdom of Empire products, including home agricultural produce'.[85] This ambitious and innovative organisation began its work in 1926 chiefly in the areas of marketing and research, but it also devoted a substantial proportion of its considerable government grant towards publicity on behalf of imperial produce in general. Leo Amery, Secretary of State for the Dominions at the time of the board's creation, recalled:

> What we wanted to sell was the idea of Empire production and purchase, of the Empire as a co-operative venture. Above all as a co-operative venture between living persons interested in each other's work and in each other's welfare. Our task was, not to glorify the power or the wealth of the Empire, but to make it live as a society for mutual help, a picture of vivid human interest as well as of practical promise.[86]

Under the driving force and inspiration of Tallents, the EMB embarked upon an imaginative publicity campaign, using public relations techniques to a large degree imported from the United States, involving press advertisements, posters, lectures, exhibitions, display material, leaflets, broadcast talks and film. The board was responsible for the first 'Buy British' campaign, and it was under its patronage that the British documentary film movement was to flourish.[87] Indeed, it was largely due to the success of the board's imperial commercial propaganda that subsequent organisations, such as the Travel Association and the British Council, were able and willing to adopt similar techniques for their own work beyond the empire.

Initially, the EMB's publicity was directed exclusively towards the British public. In 1930, however, a special sub-committee, appointed by the Committee on Economic Co-operation of the Imperial Conference, proposed that

> While the Board should continue to concentrate its main publicity on the United Kingdom market – the one in which all countries can at present derive benefit from such propaganda – it should not be debarred, subject always to the concurrence of the Government concerned, from taking advantage of such opportunities as may present themselves in co-operating in publicity in overseas countries.[88]

J. H. Thomas, the Dominions Secretary, responded by summoning a meeting on 3 March 1931 to discuss how the EMB's terms of refer-

Commercial propaganda and national projection

ence could be broadened to accommodate this resolution. He began by saying that whereas in the past Parliament had tended to belittle the idea of trade propaganda by Whitehall departments, it had now come to recognise that something more positive had to be done. The meeting was in general agreement that 'more use should be made of the weapon of propaganda ... as a means of pushing UK trade than had been the case in the past', and it was eventually decided to resuscitate the DOT's Trade Propaganda Committee (which had been abandoned in late 1930 through shortage of funds) in order to re-examine the entire question.[89]

The new body, known as the Oversea Propaganda Committee, first met on 24 March 1931 under the chairmanship of William Lunn, the parliamentary under secretary for the Dominions Office and vice-chairman of the EMB. Representatives from the DOT and EMB and from the Foreign Office News Department explained the publicity work currently being undertaken by their respective organisations,[90] and at a second meeting three days later representatives from the Travel Association and other interested government departments repeated the exercise. It appeared to the committee that, 'while a considerable amount of work was being done, there was clearly some confusion and lack of co-ordination. Although there might well be a large measure of unofficial contact, there was no official co-ordination between the activities of the various Departments in this field.'[91]

At this point, the DOT shifted on to the defensive. One official wrote that 'The Committee is ... imbued with the idea that trade propaganda is the most needful activity, and it appears to me that there is a fairly general feeling that the DOT is not doing its job in regard to this.'[92] He challenged this view on the grounds that it was not the role of the DOT to advertise individual products but to conduct publicity on behalf of British industry as a whole. He continued:

we could not ask Consuls to stamp their local correspondence 'Bovril is best for babies' or other specific appeals; we could hardly ourselves use photographs of the Prince of Wales driving at Buenos Aires in Humber cars if we emphasised the make of the car. Official propaganda to a very large extent must be a matter of creating an appreciative *background* for the seller of concrete goods, and it is I suppose for this reason that sporting records and stories of national prosperity and efficiency, the Boat Race and the Grand National are influential. Almost any topic which magnifies British institutions comes within this sphere.[93]

This kind of 'background' work, effectively cultural propaganda, could not, however, be undertaken by a government department, in the author's opinion. Rather, it would need to be undertaken by an unofficial or semi-official body, working on a reciprocal basis. 'This is not at present in sight; EMB is official, the Travel Association is concerned with one way traffic only.'[94]

Another DOT official reiterated the point that 'our primary duty in this respect is not publication but dissemination of information, and our publicity methods are merely utilised as the best means to this end'.[95] The DOT could not be criticised for inefficient handling of propaganda for British goods because that was not one of the department's functions. In anticipation of a proposal that the DOT should now enter this field, he wrote:

Any scheme of propaganda must have for its object the inculcation of a central idea in the minds of those to whom it is directed. Before we proceed with schemes it appears necessary to examine precisely what idea we wish to promulgate. The idea, or attitude of mind rather, to which our efforts should be directed is not perhaps easily crystallised into a phrase, but, so far as I can see, it would run somewhat on these lines: 'Britain is still a virile, cultured nation with immense manufacturing resources and technical ability, and is still in the forefront of scientific research and material progress. It is a country harbouring friendly feelings to other nationals and the world's most important customer for their products. For these reasons you should buy British products'. Any scheme of propaganda with a more narrow object than this appears to me to be likely to fail as being based on false premises, or on premises which one cannot drive home.[96]

Stated in these terms, the DOT did not feel that it should accept the main responsibility for such work.

In May 1931 the Oversea Propaganda Committee produced its report. It was secret, written on the assumption that its contents would not be published, and is therefore a full and frank exposition of the issues involved. Because this important document provides clear evidence of official appreciation of the need to project Britain abroad at an earlier date than is often assumed (it was written a year before Tallents's *The Projection of England* appeared), it merits detailed examination.

The report began by pointing to the increase in the use of

Commercial propaganda and national projection

propaganda by foreign governments as an instrument of commercial expansion since the end of the First World War. Although the DOT and the Foreign Office News Department were said to have made 'an important contribution to the projection of British prestige overseas', their work was hardly comparable to that conducted by France or the Soviet Union. The committee had been impressed by 'the facts':

(a) that the idea is spreading in all oversea countries, and not least in the Dominions, that Great Britain is a failing force in the economic field;
(b) that the United Kingdom Government has ready to its hand suitable material which, by the skilful and continuing co-operation of the departments now concerned, could be effectively employed to create background prestige propaganda designed to demonstrate overseas the powerful industrial resources of the United Kingdom, the high quality of United Kingdom goods and the up-to-date methods of their manufacture.[97]

The Travel Association and the EMB had also recently entered the field, and it was urged that all efforts to avoid overlapping should be taken. However, the committee felt that the field was by no means being completely covered, 'nor is full advantage being taken of much of the ready-made material for propaganda that exists'. For example, it was suggested that

the Faraday Centenary offers unique opportunities for indirect propaganda calculated to stimulate the export of United Kingdom electrical products ... as do ... such widely diverse subjects as the achievements of our doctors in the field of tropical medicine and the speed records we have established on land, sea and air ... The technical quality of the British optical glass industry has, since the War, surpassed all foreign competitors, but, through lack of suitable propaganda, the general impression still exists that German optical instruments are technically the best.[98]

Undoubtedly conscious of the likely opposition that would greet any announcement of increased official propaganda, the committee added an important footnote to these observations: 'We consider that any propaganda undertaken will be doubly valuable if it not only advances our trade overseas, but also heartens our industry here. Propaganda overseas should, wherever possible, be capable of being brought alive to the minds of our people at home.'[99] This was something which was to hound British propagandists throughout the 1930s. Despite steadily increasing support for their work as the decade unfolded, they were never really able to dispel fears or sus-

suspicions about their work or to escape either the wartime or totalitarian connotations which the word 'propaganda' evoked.[100]

The report proposed increased co-ordination between the existing propaganda organisations and an expansion of their activities in the fields of press publicity, posters, films, exhibitions and shopping weeks. The EMB, under its new terms of reference, was considered to be the most likely instrument for this purpose, although the specialist activities of the other interested bodies were to be further developed. The report concluded with the following statement:

> In submitting the foregoing recommendations, we have felt compelled to confine ourselves to such as might be adopted without unduly stretching the financial resources now available. We wish to emphasise, however, that we do not regard our recommendations as more than laying out a modest foundation on which propaganda for United Kingdom trade overseas can begin to be built up. We submit them in the hope that they may lead in the future to an expansion of the work on a scale commensurate with the importance of the subject and with the potentialities which, we are convinced, exist for its profitable development.[101]

In light of subsequent developments, these appear to be prophetic words. In the early 1930s, however, not everybody agreed with them.

The DOT was among the first to take exception to the report, in particular the proposal to utilise the EMB as the main central organisation for trade propaganda abroad. One official doubted the capacity of the board, with its many imperial representatives, to devote its attention to the claims of a single country.[102] He also warned that the DOT 'must not be pushed out of things by the EMB', adding, 'I am sure they will if they can!'[103] Another official advocated caution in replying to the Dominions Office, which fully endorsed the proposals to expand and develop its offspring,[104] with the following words of wisdom: 'Attack the child ... and the mother will fight on its behalf.'[105] The secretary of the DOT, G. M. Gillett, who had led his department's investigations into the subject during the previous year in his capacity as chairman of the Trade Propaganda Committee and was thus sympathetic to the cause of national projection, was equally unenthusiastic about the report. He replied to J. H. Thomas:

> No Government, so far as I am aware, has ever envisaged doing for UK trade

Commercial propaganda and national projection

the kind of propaganda work which the EMB is doing for Empire trade ... I hope, none-the-less, that the day will come when the Government, whatever its political colouring, will realise how much the 'cutting edge' of the Department of Overseas Trade might be improved if that Department were empowered to undertake this kind of work in the interests of the country's export trade. I am fully convinced that neither the EMB nor any other Department can perform for us the work which I feel we should be doing in this direction.[106]

Moreover, he added, 'the diluted brew of Empire-managed propaganda can never properly take the place of the stronger brew of United Kingdom propaganda which is so essential'.[107]

As it turned out, the debate over the report proved to be academic. The DOT, it seemed, was not the only opponent. In August 1931, Thomas informed Gillett that the report of the Committee on National Expenditure had recommended the abolition of the EMB and that all discussion of the board's possible future role in propaganda beyond the empire would therefore have to be placed in abeyance until its fate had been decided.[108] Although a final decision on the EMB was deferred for the moment, the impact of the economic crisis was felt immediately in the form of financial cutbacks, as reflected in the drastic reduction of the board's allocation on publicity from £213,000 in 1929 to £92,000 in 1931,[109] and to just under £63,000 in 1932.[110] As a result, the proposals of the Oversea Propaganda Committee were never put into effect. The only real outcome was an increased level of co-ordination between the various existing propaganda organisations.[111] When, in the summer of 1933, the EMB was finally dissolved, it was perhaps one of the major casualties of the economic crisis, and it was certainly the unfortunate victim of increasing determination on the part of the dominions to emphasise their autonomy by not co-operating in a joint imperial venture in the wake of the 1931 Statute of Westminster. The board's closure was widely lamented,[112] but, as *The Times* noted, 'A successful experiment cannot be obliterated. The Empire Marketing Board, like Marley's ghost, will continue to exert a lively influence, though its corporeal existence has come to an end.'[113] This was indeed to be the case. The DOT, for example, which had not lifted a finger to help save the board,[114] eagerly awaited an opportunity to fill the vacuum created by the board's inability to conduct trade propaganda abroad. 'Under modern conditions', it was argued, '"it pays to advertise", whether the advertising be on behalf of individual firms or whole industries, or even national in its scope.'[115] Nevertheless, the DOT had to wait until 1939 before it was permitted by the Treasury to enter the field, although in the meantime it was forced to rely upon the efforts of its foster child, the Travel Association, whose terms of reference were broadened in 1932 to encompass industrial propaganda overseas and whose name was altered to 'The Travel and Industrial Development Association of Great Britain and Northern Ireland'. In so far as propaganda in the empire was concerned, the board's demise was more significant, because despite the efforts of the BBC's Empire Service from 1932 and despite the work of the Colonial Empire Marketing Board from 1937, the projection of the British empire went largely unpractised until the Second World War.

Prior to its closure, the EMB had been the subject of a considerable campaign conducted in the press, influential journals and elsewhere to save it from extinction.[116] Tallents's pamphlet *The Projection of England*[117] must not simply be seen as merely another contribution to this debate but rather as the focal point in the campaign for increased national propaganda overseas. His published views closely resemble the arguments which had been expressed in the Foreign Office, the DOT, the Travel Association and the Oversea Propaganda Committee (of which Tallents had been a member) for some time. Moreover, his arguments were subsequently adopted and developed by a wide variety of individuals, while Tallents's personal influence in the field of public relations and propaganda was reflected by his later appointments as public relations officer at the GPO in 1933 and at the BBC in 1935, a post which he held simultaneously with that of director-general designate of the nucleus Ministry of Information.

Among the many fascinating idiosyncrasies of this unusual man was his skill in bookbinding in ratskin, and he was renowned for his cultivation of willows for cricket bats as well as for his expertise in cooking squirrels for his dinner guests. Tallents's background was essentially diplomatic. He had served in the Baltic and as imperial secretary for Northern Ireland before taking up his post as secretary of the EMB. During this period he had witnessed the growth of state-subsidised propaganda by foreign governments and had been alarmed by its impact upon British interests and prestige. In essence

Commercial propaganda and national projection

his argument was that Britain had always remained aloof from, and indifferent to, world opinion. This she could no longer afford to do. He wrote: 'No civilised country can today afford to neglect the projection of its national personality or to resign its projection to others.' England's world-wide responsibilities, both as a European partner and as head of a great empire, made it essential for her to project an accurate and representative picture of herself to the peoples of foreign countries. He continued:

> Today, as a result of scientific discovery, a people is known to its fellows by the impression which it makes upon them through the cable and the printing press, on the air and on the screen. If a nation would be truly known and understood in the world, it must set itself actively to master and to employ the new, difficult and swiftly developing modes which science has provided for the projection of national personality.[118]

His argument was that if England was to maintain her commercial prosperity and prestige, it was essential to inaugurate the serious study and practice of what he called 'the new art of national projection'.

Tallents believed that the widespread use of the English language, the numerous British communities abroad, the immeasurable influence of commercial and personal contacts, the global cable network and the position of British news agencies, and the dominance of British shipping companies provided conditions 'very favourable to the effective projection and sympathetic receipt of England's image'.[119] In this respect, he also pointed to the 'incalculable moral and emotional influence of the cinema'. For these reasons he believed that England must,

> In the first place, project upon the screen of world opinion such a picture of herself as will create a belief in her ability to serve the world under the new order as she had served it under the old. This role implies neither self-advertisement, as distinct from honest self-expression, nor self-righteousness, as distinct from honest confidence.[120]

He did warn of the dangers of appearing to patronise foreign audiences, preferring instead to encourage sympathy and to arouse interest and admiration for the British way of life. 'Reticence and modesty are still attractive', he wrote, 'and we must adopt and retain a complete willingness to learn from the successful methods of other countries.'

The projection of Britain, 1919–1939

Tallents believed that by taking Britain to the rest of the world, and by providing the necessary educational facilities for foreigners to come to know and appreciate Britain, national projection could serve a constructive peacetime purpose:

In the cause of good international understanding, within the Empire and without it; for the sake of our export trade; in the interests of our tourist traffic; above all, perhaps, in the discharge of our great responsibilities to the other countries of the Commonwealth of British peoples, we must master the art of national projection and must set ourselves to throw a fitting presentation of England upon the world's screen.[121]

Not only would Britain's commercial prosperity and national prestige benefit from such a programme, but also, he continued, 'peace itself may at any time depend upon a clear understanding abroad of her actions and her motives'. In order to succeed in these goals, 'the English people must be seen for what it is [sic] – a great nation still anxious to serve the world and to secure the world's peace'.[122] It was important to dispel the myth, fostered by foreign propaganda, that England was 'down and out' and to substitute for this impression a more favourable image of British society and culture.

Tallents did praise the work already begun in this direction by such organisations as the Travel Association and the Pilgrims, but where he differed from his fellow protagonists in the DOT and in the Foreign Office, who called for increased effort by existing organisations, was in his proposal that

We need, I suggest, to create, in the borderland which lies between Government and private enterprise, a school of national projection... Here is an enterprise which, in spite of its national importance, in spite of the immense 'invisible export' which it might well create, is not suitable for complete Government maintenance and control. Still less can it be entrusted to private commercial enterprise. The project is such that, once the necessary methods have been worked out, the Government and private interests can very happily and very profitably combine for its advancement.[123]

Tallents did not feel that his 'school of national projection' would benefit from direct government control, because, as 'a correspondent' (in fact, Tallents) wrote in *The Times*, 'There is still a feeling among the controllers of the Civil Service that publicity is

Commercial propaganda and national projection

disreputable and to be avoided. In general, too, the allocation of resources to Departments for publicity purposes seems haphazard and to depend on the energy of the particular Minister rather than on the needs of the State.'[124] Similarly, the proposed organisation must not be allowed to fall under the complete domination of industrialists and businessmen, because 'it must not be subjected to the demand for immediate tangible results which dogs the undertakings of commercial enterprise'.[125] Rather, the new body must provide a central nucleus which would maintain close contact with existing publicity organisations and also with the press, the BBC, the news agencies and the film industry. Its members would be drawn from industrial, commercial, cultural, educational, scientific and political walks of British life. Its policy should be long term, designed to create an atmosphere of goodwill and mutual understanding in which trade and diplomacy could flourish.

Two particular aspects of Tallents's pamphlet are worthy of further comment. In the first place, the organisation proposed by him resembled in almost too many ways to be mere coincidence that established in 1934 which came to be known as the British Council. This development will be discussed in greater detail in the following chapter, but here it is necessary to say that the council, founded under the auspices of the Foreign Office, owed its existence to the imagination and determination of Rex Leeper. As will be seen, it was created following attempts by Leeper first to co-ordinate the publicity activities of existing organisations and then after the failure to establish something akin to 'a school of national projection' under the aegis of the All Peoples Association. Had this latter scheme proved successful, its position would undoubtedly have been more clearly established 'in the borderland which lies between Government and private enterprise'. Indeed, the British Council, as a semi-official body dependent for its income upon an annual government grant and from private subscriptions, may be said to have occupied this twilight area.

The second aspect of *The Projection of England* which merits some further comment is more immediately apparent from the pamphlet itself. Throughout the essay, Tallents steered away from using the word 'propaganda'. He clearly went to great lengths to avoid using it, creating a wide range of euphemisms, of which the most common is 'national projection'. This reflected the widespread

The projection of Britain, 1919–1939

dislike and suspicion of the word, with all its unpleasant wartime and totalitarian connotations. Nevertheless, 'national projection' to Stephen Tallents was not to be merely the British equivalent of disreputable foreign propaganda. Rather, it was intended to be 'educational' in the broadest sense. The projection of England was to be neither aggressive in tone nor derogatory in content. It was to be 'pro-British' rather than 'anti-foreign'. However, it must be pointed out that the word 'propaganda' continued to be widely used in official circles, and any objections to the use of the word were to decrease with a wider appreciation of its meaning in the British context. Certainly, neither Leeper nor the permanent staff of the British Council (whose views were admittedly not usually written for publication) were to prove so reluctant to call a spade 'cultural propaganda'.

Making Britain known

The need to embark upon 'background' propaganda occupied much of Leeper's attention between 1932 and 1934. The idea of creating an entirely new organisation to undertake the task of national projection emerged during the period immediately after the closure of the EMB and the disappointing progress being made by the Travel Association. The association was heavily dependent for its income upon private subscriptions, and although this source of income increased steadily from 1929 onwards, it nonetheless remained insufficient to meet the demands for its work, despite the provisions of the Local Authorities (Publicity) Act of 1931, which enabled individual town councils and municipal boroughs to subscribe to the association.[126] By 1934, one-third of the association's total income derived from local authorities, which recognised in travel publicity an ideal opportunity for increasing tourism, thereby benefiting local business.[127] On the other hand, the government grant remained at the level of £5,000 until 1939.[128]

In 1932, the Travel Association had not only extended its work into the field of commercial and industrial propaganda but had also created its own film unit. A number of films were produced for non-theatrical distribution to foreign schools and societies, for which it was said 'the demand is always greater than the supply'.[129] Several short documentary films and travelogues were produced,

Commercial propaganda and national projection

including *So This Is London, So This Is Lancashire, The Heart of an Empire, For All Eternity* (a film about British cathedrals), *Beside the Sea* and *Around the Village Green*. The association also used broadcasting as a means of making Britain more widely known, supplying 'a large number' of news items, chiefly of domestic industrial interest, to the BBC for inclusion in the Empire Service bulletins.[130]

Apart from the co-operation of diplomatic and commercial representatives abroad, the Travel Association also employed correspondents in Belgrade, Brussels, Copenhagen, Lyons, Oslo, Ottawa, Vienna and Tokyo to distribute travel and other material to the local press and tourist agencies. The aim was to establish a world-wide network of offices, similar to those which had already been established in New York, Buenos Aires and, more recently, Paris. The association's New York office, housed in the British Empire Building at the Rockefeller Center, proved highly successful in supplying weekly broadcast talks 'on some aspect of life in Great Britain' to over 250 radio stations in North America between 1932 and 1934.[131] The association's office in Buenos Aires was instrumental in the publication of *Las Islas Britanicas*, a Spanish edition of the Travel Association's British Isles booklet, and it also secured the distribution of other publicity material to the national and provincial press of the various Latin American countries.[132]

The work of the Travel Association towards the projection of Britain was best illustrated by H. Noble Hall, the head of the Paris office, in a speech made at the London Publicity Club in November 1934. Evidently much influenced by Tallents, Noble Hall stated:

> My job is to project upon the screen of France a true picture of England. My work is national propaganda in all its forms: travel, industrial, cultural propaganda, but always in general terms... It is no use advertising abroad to attract visitors or to sell goods unless the people of the country where you advertise are in a receptive mood, and I am creating in France an atmosphere favourable to England by giving the people and especially the youth a knowledge of and liking for things English.[133]

He referred to the enthusiasm of the previous ambassador, Lord Tyrrell, for his work and described the recent opening of the new office by Tyrrell's successor, Sir George Clerk. He also commented upon the general support extended to him by the embassy staff, by the British Institute in Paris, and by the Association France–Grande

Bretagne. The French press had also proved amenable: 'It is an understatement to say that the amount of space that the French newspapers devote to non-political news about England has trebled since the Travel Association came upon the scene and this is also true of the number of photographs the French press publishes.'[134] Working largely on the basis of personal contacts with editors and political friends, Noble Hall summarised his work as 'inspiration, information and communiqués', with particular emphasis on the younger generation: 'there I was not only getting immediate results, but I was also building for the future'. He described his tours of French schools and universities where he delivered lectures with visual aids and organised courses for the study of English.[135] He also emphasised the importance of film in his work: the recent showing of Alexander Korda's celebrated film *The Private Life of Henry VIII*, made in 1933 starring Charles Laughton in the title role, was said to have been 'an enormous success' in Paris. Noble Hall concluded by placing these efforts in their proper and somewhat limited perspective by drawing attention to the enormous sums of money devoted to similar work by foreign governments. Italy, he said, was spending 17 million francs in France, Spain nearly 10 million, and Germany 6 million, whereas the association's expenditure in France amounted to a little over £2,000.

This speech was reported in the *World's Press News* under the headline 'Britain's "Widow's Mite" for Foreign Propaganda' and provoked some excitement in the Foreign Office News Department.[136] For the past two years, Rex Leeper had been devoting much of his time to the creation of a 'cultural relations committee' which, by the end of 1934, resulted in the foundation of the British Council. The Travel Association, however, was unaware of this development and was thus not in a position to realise that, by extending its travel and commercial publicity more and more into the field of cultural 'projection', it was infringing upon territory already cornered by the Foreign Office for its own offspring. Roland Kenney, the News Department's film expert, warned that 'if matters go on in the present way, then it seems to me that we are certain to have trouble with the Travel Association'.[137] Leeper agreed, adding: 'The Travel Association is first and foremost a tourist agency. They are now trying to extend their activities to cover all fields of cultural propaganda. This is clearly wrong.'[138]

Commercial propaganda and national projection

Accordingly, in December 1934, Leeper and Kenney met with the association's secretary, L. A. de L. Meredith, and informed him of the existence and aims of the British Council. Kenney noted that Meredith was 'obviously quite oblivious of the fact that the T. Ass. is overstepping the line of demarcation between tourist and cultural propaganda, but when Mr. Leeper explained that there must be a more strict delimitation of frontiers he was quite agreeable'.[139] However, the association continued to see itself as something more than a tourist board and maintained its aspirations to conduct cultural and background propaganda for the benefit of Britain's commercial interests. Even as late as August 1937, when the British Council was just beginning to find its feet, its secretary-general was alarmed at the manner in which the Travel Association was regarded in some quarters as 'the only, or at any rate, the most important organisation for cultural propaganda in existence'.[140]

The DOT and the Travel Association were generally forced to stand in the shadows of the Foreign Office and the British Council during the 1930s. Despite their pioneering role in initiating the projection of Britain, they had to play second fiddle in an orchestrated movement of self-advertisement which was becoming louder as the decade unfolded. An ideal opportunity to steal at least some of the thunder presented itself with the opening of the New York World Fair in 1939. The theme of the fair, 'Building the World of Tomorrow', not only afforded the DOT and Travel Association a chance to conduct trade and tourist propaganda in a country where the British Council did not operate, but it also enabled them to initiate a policy of national projection in the United States essentially for the first time. From the moment the British government accepted the invitation to participate in May 1937, the DOT was made responsible for planning the British official entry. It was decided that this would be designed

To foster friendship and goodwill between the United Kingdom (and Empire) and the USA by shewing as much as we can – in the relatively limited space available – of these islands and the Empire; our adaptability to a changing world and the non-rigid character of our Empire Commonwealth partnership; in short, to present the beauty and greatness of our life and country (or countries) with dignity and charm, and thus to enable the millions of Americans who will visit the Fair to know and appreciate us and in due course to visit us.[141]

The projection of Britain, 1919–1939

The British entry, noted one official, was to be 'distinctively British' in order to provide a background of sympathy and respect beneficial to political opportunities; 'the commercial purpose, excluding the tourist trade, is secondary'.[142]

As it was, the DOT and Travel Association had to share the limelight in New York with the British Council. Following a DOT enquiry into the inadequate distribution overseas of British documentary films during 1936–7, it was decided that film should constitute an essential part of the British entry, and the DOT had invited the Joint Films Committee of the British Council and the Travel Association to select suitable candidates in which 'specific advertising is subordinated to the general interest'.[143] This did not prove to be a straightforward task. There were very few existing films which were suitable for overseas audiences, at least from the point of view of national propaganda. There were even fewer suited to the theme of the fair. Nor was the situation helped by differences of opinion within the Joint Films Committee itself. As one British Council official wrote in March 1938,

The Travel Association do not know much about foreign countries and are therefore not really qualified to select the most suitable films to be shown in each country. Anybody could have told them that as there are no railways in Albania it was hopeless to send that country *Night Mail*, and that a church film, *For All Eternity*, would probably cause offence in modern Germany.[144]

Nevertheless, the British Council's dependence upon the Travel Association's film unit meant that the DOT faction tended to dominate the Joint Films Committee. The British Council representative noted that 'they like to see an impressive piece of machinery at the end of a film and do not seem to take account of other forms of British culture'.[145] In fact, the DOT was gradually coming round to appreciating the importance of general prestige films, although this commercial versus cultural debate was periodically to hamper the planning for the British entry in New York, particularly when an ill-informed press campaign was launched against the authorities in 1938.[146]

By 1939, however, the Joint Films Committee was in general agreement as to the type of film to be shown in New York, namely those which would show 'the pageantry of English life'.[147] An arrangement was also made with the Newsreel Association of Great

Commercial propaganda and national projection

Britain whereby the five leading newsreel companies would take it in turn to produce a special edition for the fair, *British News*, which turned out to be one of the major successes of the British exhibition.[148] Several documentary films were also commissioned for the fair, including *Spare Time* and *British Made*, both of which were made by the Post Office's film unit. Indeed, the official British entry was a triumph for the projection of England. Within two weeks of the formal opening in April, almost eight million people had visited the site, over half of whom had entered the British pavilion. The most popular exhibits were replicas of the Crown Jewels, Magna Carta, the pedigree of George Washington and a film depicting the coronation.[149] Following a royal visit in June, it was estimated that 2,000 people were passing through the cinema in the British pavilion every day.[150] Although it is impossible to measure in any exact terms, the amount of pro-British feeling generated at the fair at a time when the threat of war was looming over the European horizon may have been a significant – and perhaps even a vital – factor in the shaping of American sympathies towards Britain between 1939 and 1941.

The British contribution to the New York World Fair may have been a triumph for the concept of national projection in terms of the number of people reached, but it was an uncharacteristic performance, because, unlike its totalitarian counterparts, British propaganda was not a 'mass' movement. An analysis of the subject matter quite clearly demonstrates this. It also reveals a great deal about the image which British propagandists sought to foster abroad about Britain and the British way of life while, at the same time, providing an insight into their image of themselves.

In his 1932 pamphlet, Tallents had drawn up a list of subjects which he considered suitable candidates for national projection. These included: the monarchy, parliamentary institutions, the Royal Navy, the English Bible and the works of Dickens and Shakespeare. Other elements of 'the standing raw material of England's esteem in the world' included: the Derby and the Grand National; Henley and the Boat Race; Test Matches; the Trooping of the Colour; the Lord Mayor of London; Piccadilly; Bond Street; Big Ben; Oxford and Edinburgh; the Metropolitan Police; London omnibuses and underground railways; *The Times*, *Punch* and the

The projection of Britain, 1919–1939

Manchester Guardian; English countryside and villages; foxhunting; English servants; English bloodstock and pedigree stock; the arts of gardening and tailoring. He also considered it desirable to take advantage of certain images of Britain which he felt already existed abroad, namely: 'In international affairs – a reputation for disinterestedness; in national affairs – a tradition of justice, law and order; in national character – a reputation for coolness; in commerce – a reputation for fair dealing; in manufacture – a reputation for quality; in sport – a reputation for fair play.'[151] In short, this was the England of a romantic, civilised and cultured man who would have been more suited to the role of an eighteenth-century country squire than that of a senior civil servant. This is not to suggest that Tallents did not prove an efficient and capable administrator, for he unquestionably was, despite his idiosyncrasies and rather atypical flair for public relations. His list represented his idea of what many people abroad would be interested in. He believed that Britain's cultural heritage and present level of civilisation could play a constructive role in international affairs. He therefore wished to stress all that was best and noble, as he saw it, in the British way of life, and to illustrate through the use of modern technology how those great historical achievements and peculiar traditions had helped to mould the character and behaviour of the contemporary Englishman.

His argument proceeded from the assumption that Britain could no longer afford to remain aloof from world opinion as she had done for long periods in the past. This, however, raised a paradox. Whereas Tallents had advocated the use of the mass media, such as radio and film, many of the subjects which he sought to project, such as foxhunting and Savile Row suits, were arguably not of the nature required to arouse the interest of foreign opinion on a mass scale. At the risk of overgeneralisation, it would appear that such facets of English life would provoke fascination and perhaps even appreciation, but to the majority of foreigners they would remain imagery rather than become reality. Tallents did, after all, warn of the dangers of appearing to patronise. But then again, bearing in mind the Hollywood phenomenon and the massive number of people who flocked to see the latest manifestation of the American dream in order to escape the harsh realities of the depression, perhaps Tallents's image might have had more mass appeal than one

Commercial propaganda and national projection

might assume. If this was the case, the British film industry, despite attempts to protect it from being swamped by American films in the form of the 1927 and 1938 Cinematograph Acts, was rarely in a position to fulfil this role. In 1930, it was argued:

> It is horrible to think that the British Empire is receiving its education from a place called Hollywood. The Dominions would rather have a picture with a wholesome, honest British background, something that gives British sentiment, something that is honest to our traditions, than the abortions which we get from Hollywood... The American film is everywhere, and is the best advertisement of American trade and commerce. Trade follows the film not the flag.[152]

This may well have been true, but if Tallents was relying upon his own experience of film while serving at the EMB, he was thinking more in terms of documentaries than of entertainment 'escapist' films. And these were hardly likely to have a mass appeal, whether at home or abroad.

The point was that British overseas propaganda was not directed to a mass audience, at least not directly, but rather to the opinion-makers in foreign societies who were in a position to influence much larger numbers of people. Hence the emphasis upon personal contacts with such people as newspaper editors and journalists, intellectuals, authors, influential professional men and fellow diplomats. It was towards this educated and selected audience that the British Council devoted the majority of its attention. So did the Travel Association. Noble Hall, in his November 1934 speech describing his work in France, referred to his activities as an 'appeal to the "elite" in the great cities'. With this aim in view, he had organised lecture tours in which his audiences had comprised local municipal officials, mayors, district military commanders and professional businessmen. 'In many cases', he said, 'an audience of the very highest quality [attended] to which I was able to make an appeal that, I was told, was most effective.'[153]

This approach had its critics, particularly during the late 1930s when the more blatant excesses of the totalitarian powers excited much attention concerning their 'mass' impact. Kingsley Martin, for example, recalled that during a visit he had made to the 1937 Paris Exhibition he had been struck by the sharp contrast in style between the British pavilion and the vigorous and dynamic portrayals of Nazi Germany and the Soviet Union. He wrote:

The projection of Britain, 1919–1939

When you went in, the first thing you saw was a cardboard Chamberlain fishing in rubber waders and, beyond, an elegant pattern of golf balls, a frieze of tennis rackets, polo sets, riding equipment, natty dinner jackets and, by a pleasant transition, agreeable pottery and textiles, books finely printed and photographs of the English countryside. I stared in bewilderment. Could this be England?[154]

Even accounting for Martin's political disposition, and his chagrin at not finding 'a sign anywhere of a proletariat', his embarrassment was caused by the stark contrast of two military powers competing against each other on the battlefields of Spain with the non-aggressive approach of Britain. It may not have been the England of Kingsley Martin, but it was the England idealised by Stephen Tallents and projected by the British Council, which organised the pavilion in Paris. Besides, Martin had missed the point of the British exhibition. Britain's peacetime propaganda was attempting an entirely different function from that of its more aggressive continental rivals. It was an attempt to represent an England at peace with herself, a stable, civilised country in an increasingly unstable, uncivilised world.

Tallents was the most articulate exponent of this concept, and his influence is evident in several subsequent published articles on the subject. In an essay by Rex Leeper, which was unusual because it was written for publication by a serving permanent official, the importance of national projection was emphasised still further. He wrote:

There is a widespread feeling that in an age of instability England alone is stable, and that the secret of this stability deserves careful study and attention... It is time that this nation of shop-keepers did a little stocktaking to see how far our contribution to civilization is understood elsewhere and to decide how best we can satisfy this new demand for fuller information about almost every aspect of our national life, character and institutions.[155]

Leeper proved less reluctant than Tallents had been to use the word 'propaganda'. After referring to the recent creation of the British Council to conduct cultural propaganda on lines similar to the Alliance Française, he qualified his terms:

Many people are suspicious of the word propaganda, which they connect with the control and manufacture of information for political and military purposes during the war. Certainly the word itself suggests the diffusion

Commercial propaganda and national projection

rather of what it is wished that others shall believe than of unbiased fact. Yet the French example shows that there is a legitimate form of propaganda, which benefits directly those who receive it and directly those who conduct it, and that this kind of propaganda is a most valuable contribution to international relations.[156]

Leeper thus stressed the importance of educational work abroad and of encouraging the wider use of the English language.

Lord Eustace Percy, who became chairman of the British Council in 1936, developed this educational theme still further. In an article entitled 'The Projection of Britain: Intellectual Co-operation', he referred to the work begun 'under the impulse of a few of the younger men in the Foreign Office and with the encouragement of their chiefs', and explained of the council:

National self-revelation is our primary business... [but] a nation's cultural exports cannot be controlled; they must respond to a foreign demand which is beyond the reach of the exporting government. What really limits the effectiveness of government intervention in international cultural exchanges is the general suspicion of 'propaganda'. Our own government is particularly sensitive to this suspicion, and rightly so. As science multiplies the instruments of world propaganda, the fear of such propaganda may well become a chief cause of war.[157]

Percy therefore warned of the dangers of national projection becoming an activity similar to the nationalistic propaganda of other governments, and he appealed for greater co-operation in cultural and educational exchanges as a means of promoting greater international understanding in the cause of peace.

Although the need for Britain to embark upon a programme of national propaganda overseas was initially recognised as a response to the anti-British activities of rival countries, by the mid 1930s the work began to assume a more constructive role. Once the interaction of commercial and cultural propaganda came to be recognised, the projection of England became a political activity, as Sir Samuel Hoare, then Foreign Secretary, appreciated:

The commercial arguments in favour of intensifying the work of British cultural propaganda are no less strong than the political arguments. In all, the danger of German cultural and commercial penetration, which may be expected to increase as the power and wealth of Germany revive, makes it particularly desirable for British cultural propaganda to secure as firm a hold as possible on the minds and interests of the population, and particularly on the younger generation, before the counter attraction becomes too strong.[158]

This was the uphill task facing the British Council and British propaganda in general. The methods adopted to achieve this end often came under attack, particularly with the growing conviction that Britain might have to face another war in the near future. John Grierson, for example, considered that the image of Britain as a 'functioning democracy' was more appropriate to the conditions of 1938 than that envisaged by Tallents in 1932.[159] He wrote:

When Britain appears in its international role as a pillar of democracy, the picture they expect from here is a somewhat detailed picture of just those personal freedoms and social goods the pillar upholds... We have a great deal to tell about our contribution to constructive democracy for we have as fine a record in matters of housing and health, education and the public welfare as any country. If we don't tell it, it is because we are, as a nation, still very diffident about appearing in our working clothes.[160]

4
Cultural propaganda and the British Council

Prior to the establishment of the British Council under the auspices of the Foreign Office in 1934, British overseas propaganda was characterised largely by its strict adherence to news and factual comment. Ever since the close of the First World War, the Foreign Office News Department, as the main nerve-centre of official peacetime propaganda abroad, had worked on the assumption that the rapid and continuous dissemination of reliable information and sensible comment would provide some form of antidote to the aggressive foreign propaganda being directed against British interests and prestige. In view of the shortage of funds, it could do little else. By the early 1930s, however, the somewhat limited nature of this response was becoming increasingly apparent in influential circles beyond the Foreign Office and the DOT. It was essentially short term and political in approach, while being primarily counter-propagandist in effect. But anti-British propaganda had for some time been assuming various non-political disguises. In the economic sphere, the Empire Marketing Board and the Travel Association had begun, albeit on a small scale, to combat the detrimental effects of foreign trade propaganda upon Britain's commercial interests. Yet propaganda remained merely one of their many self-appointed tasks. Moreover, with the growing appreciation that commercial and political advertisement was largely dependent for its success upon supplementary techniques of persuasion, there developed an increasing demand for a more constructive long-term approach to the problem of foreign cultural propaganda. It was in this respect that the British Council was to provide the most imaginative response to that concept which Stephen Tallents had labelled 'the projection of England'.

Cultural propaganda may be broadly defined as the promotion and dissemination of national aims and achievements in a general rather than specifically economic or political form, although it is

The projection of Britain, 1919–1939

ultimately designed to promote economic and political interests. The decision in late 1934 to establish an organisation designed purely to undertake cultural propaganda injected a new dimension into the traditional conduct of British diplomacy. It was believed that cultural propaganda – or, as many officials preferred to describe it, cultural diplomacy – would not only serve to enhance national influence and prestige abroad through the promotion of British interests but would also effectively further the broader ideals of international peace and understanding. How successful was the British Council in achieving these goals during the first five years of its existence? How did its founders conceive their role in the context of British foreign policy in the 1930s? Above all, why did the British government decide in the first place to sanction such a marked departure from established peacetime diplomatic tradition?

Antecedents

Characteristically, the necessity for some form of British overseas propaganda was initially recognised as a response to the activities of other governments. It has been noted that 'when British officials utter the words "cultural diplomacy" they usually have the French in mind'.[1] It is an association which dates from the late nineteenth century, when the French government was the first to recognise the value of international cultural exchanges. The Quai d'Orsay had embarked upon a comprehensive programme of cultural propaganda with the establishment of the Service des Oeuvres des Françaises à l'Etranger, which operated chiefly through the Alliance Française (founded 1880) and the French missionary schools scattered about the world. This innovative approach to international affairs continued thereafter to occupy an increasing proportion of the French national budget.[2] Although the main emphasis was placed upon educational or what was sometimes described as 'intellectual' propaganda, the cultural programme was not simply designed to spread the use of the French language or to perpetuate the glories of French civilisation, for, as one minister realised, 'ideas and sentiments are effective tools' which, in the service of diplomacy, 'become useful instruments of propaganda'.[3] In fact, the Third Republic regarded cultural relations as an effective method of creating an atmosphere favourable to the extension of

Cultural propaganda and the British Council

political and commercial interests by bringing the full weight of the national cultural heritage to bear in support of its foreign and economic policies and of its political prestige abroad.[4] In other words, it was believed that cultural propaganda could provide a favourable backdrop to the stage upon which diplomacy and commerce were conducted.

Not far behind the French initiative came that of the German government. In the years following the Franco-Prussian War and the unification of Germany, cultural propaganda was utilised not only as an instrument for strengthening the spirit of Pan-Germanism beyond national frontiers but also as a weapon for the extension of national interests and prestige abroad. As one German writer observed, 'As long as Germany was merely a political conception, not a political power, Germanism abroad was considered as neutral and harmless; now it is considered aggressive and threatening.'[5] Small wonder that this was so when, here again, there were underlying political and economic motives in the disguise of international philanthropy. As the Imperial Chancellor stated in 1913: 'Our place in the heart of Continental Europe will forever lead us to devote all the physical and moral powers of the nation to the complete maintenance of our continental position of power... But these same forces make imperative a further expansion in the field of world economy and world culture.'[6] It was towards these goals that the Verein für das Deutschtum im Ausland had been directing its efforts to spread German *Kultur* abroad since the 1880s, working primarily through the *Auslandsschulen*.[7]

In Great Britain, by way of contrast, the need to embark upon a policy of cultural relations overseas was only recognised as a direct result of the First World War. Before 1914, Britain's prestige in the world was thought to have been so readily apparent that there was felt to be little, if any, need for a policy of self-glorification or national advertisement. One glance at the areas painted red on any map of the world was all the foreigner needed to remind himself of British achievements. Unlike France or Germany, Britain's chief concern was for the consolidation and defence of existing interests rather than the extension of her commitments or responsibilities. The necessary atmosphere in which concepts of cultural or intellectual expansion overseas were conceived was thus generally absent. Accordingly, Britain earned a reputation abroad for aloofness and indifference to the affairs of Europe, choosing only to emerge from what was seen as her complacent self-satisfaction when her national interests were directly threatened. Indeed, British achievements were generally left to speak for themselves, although it must be said that the conversation was greatly facilitated by the predominant position of the English language. But in the face of increasing political, commercial and cultural competition, British actions were left open to misinterpretation and misrepresentation, while the British case went largely unstated. Rex Leeper, analysing in the 1930s the reasons for what he described as the enigmatic attitude of people in the 'unknown island', wrote:

> We are perhaps dimly aware that our habits of thought and action are often extremely irritating to foreigners, but our equanimity is hardly ruffled when they show their irritation, and for that very reason to make little effort to correct its cause... As for taking positive steps to explain our aims and achievements, that we regard as undignified and unnecessary. Good wine, we optimistically feel, needs no bush.[8]

Although this attitude prevailed until 1934, a growing awareness of the need to state the British point of view and to explain those foundations upon which British attitudes rested emerged as a result of the First World War.

Between 1914 and 1918, the conduct of cultural propaganda occupied a position of secondary importance in the war of words. Only in the third year of the war did the question receive serious consideration. In August 1917, the failing Department of Information appointed Sir Henry Newbolt as chairman of a committee set up to enquire into the circulation of British books and periodicals abroad. After twenty-four meetings, the committee produced a report which focused upon the grave inadequacies of existing distribution methods. Consequently, the report stated, this had 'seriously affected the foreign appreciation of British thought, ideals and efficiency; and ... the results of this lack of appreciation have operated in many directions to the detriment of British policy and of British trade'.[9] The scarcity of British literature abroad was largely attributed to the refusal of the Post Office in 1911 to accept subscriptions for British newspapers and periodicals from overseas readers. This refusal had resulted in the establishment of British distribution centres in Liège and Cologne rather than in London.

Cultural propaganda and the British Council

Thus, 'even before the beginning of the war, the whole machinery was in the hands of the enemy'.[10]

Despite the seriousness of this problem from the point of view of the wartime propagandists, the Newbolt committee was more immediately concerned for the future, pointing to the German cultural programmes already in existence for the post-war period. Moreover, the report continued,

Apart from the inadequate methods of distribution, we have been impressed by other causes of the general depreciation of the intellectual impulse which British thought can claim to have given the world at large, and of the general misapprehension of the facilities which British invention and enterprise can offer to the trade and manufacture of foreign countries.[11]

Not only did the report conclude with a plea for increased reciprocal cultural exchanges, but it also provides one of the earliest examples of the recognition that cultural and commercial propaganda were mutually complementary. It was believed that, by increasing cultural intercourse with foreign societies, whether by the interchange of books and periodicals or through student exchanges, the opportunities for British trade would directly increase as a result. The report therefore proposed the appointment of a special committee to examine the arrangements for the reception and education of foreign students at British universities and technical schools and to investigate the opportunities for 'extending the distribution of British thought by aiding educational institutions in foreign countries'.[12]

On the return of peace, however, with the dissolution of the wartime propaganda machinery and the transference of remaining duties into the care of the Foreign Office, the question of cultural propaganda was destined to remain a point of discussion rather than action. Victor Wellesley's scheme for a reconstructed Foreign Office, drawn up in November 1918, did envisage a positive role for propaganda, particularly cultural propaganda, in the conduct of post-war diplomacy. The cultural aspect was the widest of all forms of propaganda, 'because its sphere of operations is unlimited'.[13] Wellesley continued:

Every activity of the human race ... comes within its scope. Every class of society is open to it, and each needs its own instrument or medium; for the more or less illiterate – the cinema film, the daily newspaper, the night school; for the middle classes – the theatre, the illustrated magazine; for the cultivated classes – the monthly review, the educational and especially the technical book, the good concert; for the young – the boy scout and girl guide movement; for the adolescent – the grammar school, the college, the Chair of English in the University, and so on.[14]

This attempt to break down the various strands of cultural activity into media, class structure and age groups is notable because it stands out of character to other Foreign Office concepts, which dictated that British interests would be best served by directing propaganda abroad to those foreigners in a position to influence others. The categories are, of course, stereotypes, but Wellesley's attempt does illustrate the degree to which various officials were prepared to give the subject of propaganda in peacetime considerable thought.

But for the moment, the process of transferring the remaining duties of the Ministry of Information into the hands of the Foreign Office during December 1918 gave rise to some confusion concerning the position of Sir Henry Newbolt, formerly chairman of the departmental committee on the distribution of British books abroad. Following a conversation with William Tyrrell, Newbolt appears to have gained the impression that he was to be appointed head of a reconstructed News Department. Working from this assumption, Newbolt submitted a scheme to the Foreign Office for the reorganisation of propaganda in which great emphasis was placed upon cultural work.[15] It seems, however, that Newbolt was merely being considered as a possible head of one branch of the News Department which would be designed to deal with the kind of work recommended by his committee.[16] Whatever the cause of the misunderstanding, the proposed cultural section was not to materialise, and it is open to speculation whether cultural propaganda would have received greater official consideration sooner than 1934 had the News Department not encountered such severe opposition on this issue in 1919.

There had, in fact, been several early indications that such strong opposition would emerge. On 31 January 1919, for example, Cecil Harmsworth received a deputation from the Royal Society of Literature (RSL), which proposed to establish institutes in various Allied cities 'for the purpose of promoting by every cultural means good relations between the peoples'.[17] The News Department, though prevented by previous wartime arrangements with the

Cultural propaganda and the British Council

Treasury from subsidising work of this nature,[18] was nonetheless in favour of the RSL promoting cultural activity privately. As Stephen Gaselee minuted,

> I would much rather entrust an endowment for the purpose – with proper safeguards – to a body such as the R.S.L. than attempt to conduct the Institutes ourselves... We know that the Institutes of this kind founded by the Crewe House Committee in Italy did a great deal of good – Sir R. Rodd [British ambassador in Italy 1908–19] speaks most highly of them; and it is with very great regret that we now find ourselves forced to bring our support of them to an end.[19]

Even so, the Foreign Office had always expressed a preference, wherever possible, for conducting propaganda through an intermediary organisation with no direct governmental link, and it now offered to support any RSL application for finance from the Treasury. That support, however, turned out to be of no avail. The RSL's application proved unsuccessful, and it was left to conduct its cultural work without official support, leaving Newbolt greatly embittered in the process.[20]

When the News Department's financial estimates for the first year of peace were eventually submitted to the Treasury in April 1919, they encountered severe opposition on the question of cultural propaganda. The Treasury's view was quite simply that any programme designed to disseminate British culture abroad 'must be regarded as too wide'.[21] While claiming to recognise the need for correcting inaccurate statements and misconceptions about the nature of British policies in the domestic and foreign press, it was nonetheless feared that

> there is some danger that this object may be imperceptibly transformed into a general desire to spread British culture throughout the world; and ... [we] do not think it would be possible to defend in Parliament or its Committee expenditure for such a purpose – to which it would not be easy to assign definite limits.[22]

Wellesley had made exactly the same point about broad terms of reference, but where he had seen the advantages of such ambiguity, the Treasury proved understandably more sceptical, particularly at a time of financial retrenchment. The Foreign Office, with the French example in mind, saw cultural propaganda as a long-term policy which, by promoting an atmosphere of international understanding and co-operation, would ultimately benefit both the political and economic climate in which British interests could flourish. To the Treasury, however, cultural propaganda appeared to be a vague, indefinable and somewhat nebulous activity which did not hold out any promise of immediate or visible returns. Commercial propaganda, on the other hand, did offer short-term benefits and was thus financially more justifiable. It was to take another decade before the Treasury was to admit that the conduct of cultural relations was a profitable prerequisite of commercial relations. But in the meantime, an embargo was placed upon the News Department preventing it from initiating cultural propaganda of any kind.

This remained Treasury policy despite the recommendations of the Foreign Office Committee on British Communities Abroad. This committee was appointed in 1920 with Sir Charles Eliot as its initial chairman, although it completed its investigations under the direction of Sir John Tilley following Eliot's departure to take up the Tokyo embassy. The Tilley committee, as it became known, continued its enquiries where the Newbolt committee had left off in 1918 with regard to books and periodicals. Its terms of reference, however, were much more extensive.

Tilley encountered two distinct schools of thought concerning the extent to which state intervention in the various British communities abroad was considered desirable. On the one hand, there were those who strongly advocated governmental assistance in helping the communities to preserve that spirit of patriotism which had been generated by the war. Some communities, particularly those which were currently being subjected to intense anti-British propaganda, were considered to be in danger of losing their sense of identity with Britain, while all constituted pockets of British culture within foreign societies. It was argued that these communities should be encouraged to generate a wider appreciation and knowledge of the English language, national culture, ideals and values. On the other hand, the opposing view deprecated state intervention on the grounds that it would merely hinder the natural development of gradual integration of the communities, and also argued that unnecessary interference would only serve to antagonise rather than endear.[23]

Although the committee expressed itself as 'firmly opposed to any

Cultural propaganda and the British Council

form of political propaganda', it nonetheless felt that the British government had a 'moral obligation' to assist in the educational and cultural welfare of its overseas residents and their children, and 'to make British ideals known to, and appreciated by, foreign nations'.[24] This objective, it was argued, could best be achieved by the distribution of technical and 'representative' literature to British schools abroad, by assisting in the education of British children and by the establishment of cultural centres and libraries in the more important foreign towns and cities. The committee also urged the government to stimulate and encourage the foundation of patriotic societies. Anglo-foreign associations and such groups as boy scout and girl guide movements modelled on British lines. To implement these proposals, it was further suggested that a standing inter-departmental committee be permanently established to consider the extension of facilities for the reception and education of foreign students at English schools and universities. Finally, the Tilley report advocated increased governmental participation in international exhibitions and a strengthening of the commercial branches in overseas missions.[25]

The Treasury decided to reject these far-sighted proposals outright. One official stated that he was unable 'to understand the "moral obligation" on the Govt. to which the Ctee. refer', pointing out that the overseas residents were voluntary exiles.[26] Another opponent noted that the recommendations involved considerable expense 'in spite of the protested regard for economy', and anyway the proposals went beyond the committee's original terms of reference.[27] It was also pointed out that, 'even if otherwise unobjectionable, the present is not the time to impose further burdens on the British taxpayer on behalf of communities which do not pay tax'.[28] There were, moreover, strong political objections to such a policy:

Continental conscriptionist countries which are afraid of losing their potential soldiers by absorption in the countries of their residence may find the expenditure advantageous for military reasons, and notoriously this was the German practice, but (a) this country is not permanently conscriptionist; (b) it has not found such nursing of nationalism necessary and there seems no reason for thinking its recent victory has caused it to become so... The propaganda side of the proposals, taken alone, is thought to be (a) of doubtful success; (b) of doubtful validity, and (c) anyhow insufficient justification for the expenditure.[29]

In short, the report was considered to be, as another official put it, 'a wild-cat scheme for wasting money'.[30] The weight of Treasury opposition to the recommendations was overwhelming, and the report was rejected in its entirety in July 1920.[31]

Foreign Office disappointment quickly turned to apprehension when, later that year, the French government announced its budget. In sharp contrast to the British policy of retrenchment with regard to propaganda abroad, the French sanctioned an increase in the expenditure for its 'propaganda programme' of intellectual expansion and penetration overseas. An examination of the figures involved revealed that the money was divided among objects which were 'precisely similar to those on which the expenditure of public funds by His Majesty's Government has been repeatedly recommended either by the Foreign Office Committee on British Communities Abroad, or by the different departments of the Foreign Office, in almost every case without success'.[32] Why was it, it was asked, that France, with serious economic problems of her own, considered this type of work to be so important whereas Britain did not? Such questions were posed as a direct challenge to those Treasury arguments which had hitherto prevented any serious action: '... if France in her present state can afford to undertake this varied programme for the extension of her interests abroad, and the maintenance of her prestige, both political and commercial, can this country under the stress of severe competition which has followed the conclusion of peace, afford to neglect the use of similar means?'[33] The answer was that apparently it could, although not without a considerable struggle from the Foreign Office.

Such was the depth of conviction existing within the Foreign Office concerning the importance to Britain of entering the cultural propaganda field that the Foreign Secretary, Lord Curzon, decided to take the issue to the Cabinet. In February 1921, he urged the immediate acceptance of the Tilley report and also the provision of £100,000 annually to support British Institutes abroad.[34] But when the Treasury re-examined the proposals, its officials remained unconvinced. The furthest one was prepared to go was 'to refuse any responsibility – other than actual protection of life and property under the doctrine of Lord Palmerston – for persons who voluntarily leave the United Kingdom for their own purposes'.[35] Such antiquated views proved incompatible with the forward-looking attitude of the Foreign Office. Treasury opposition to the proposals persisted on the grounds that they were 'so vague and so meagrely supported by specific instances as to the evils alleged to result in the lack of British education of persons abroad'.[36] This was indeed so, but Curzon nonetheless managed to impress the Cabinet with the principles underlying the proposals, and the matter was referred to the Parliamentary Finance Committee for further consideration.[37] This decision proved to be the death-knell of the Tilley report. In the wake of the Geddes Inquiry into Government spending, few politicians were prepared to champion a cause for which parliamentary and Treasury opposition was almost certainly guaranteed.

The implications of this disappointing anticlimax became almost immediately apparent in the Foreign Office following requests from certain Baltic governments for aid in extending the use of English in Lithuania and Latvia. 'We are helpless', lamented Koppel,[38] and the requests were reluctantly turned down. This situation prevailed throughout the 1920s, a period in which the News Department found itself repeatedly debarred from conducting cultural propaganda.

While Britain remained a passive observer in the field of cultural relations, other governments continued to increase their activities. In Weimar Germany, for example, the republican government carried on the cultural diplomacy inaugurated by the imperial regime, and in 1920 created a Directorate for Germanism Abroad and Cultural Relations. This was a direct response to the territorial clauses of the Versailles treaty, which had increased the number of Germans living outside the Reich. Cultural propaganda provided an ideal instrument for preserving their sense of national identity. As Chancellor Bauer stated in 1919,

> The thing which no peace treaty can take from us is the feeling of national unity, and what no one can forbid us is the fostering of this feeling. Our German racial comrades who are and who in the future will be separated from us, shall know what we think of them and that we provide for them in all ways which the peace treaty allows. Not politically, but linguistically and humanly all these relations will be even warmer.[39]

This cultural approach to the problem of the *Auslandsdeutsche* was to assume a much more sinister dimension with the advent of Hitler.

The projection of Britain, 1919–1939

There is some evidence to suggest that the large sums expended by the French government throughout the 1920s were, at least in part, a direct response to the escalation of German activities in this direction.[40] Prompted also, perhaps, by the additional factor that, at the Paris Peace Conference, the English language had become a recognised medium of diplomatic communication, the French redoubled their efforts. The Quai d'Orsay reorganised its Service des Oeuvres des Françaises à l'Etranger in 1920 and allocated an annual sum of 17 million francs to it. As one spokesman explained, 'Propaganda is nothing but intellectual and moral influence and yet it is the most immediate and most valuable means for seconding the efforts made by this country to establish and develop her material prosperity.'[41] Indeed, it was the French who provided the model for other nations. 'Look at the French Republic', said Stresemann in 1929. 'She has never spared funds for this: she knows exactly how she has won over the Orient intellectually, with her French schools, with her French influence.'[42]

The continuing struggle to recapture economic markets during the post-war years was marked by a dramatic increase in the use of state-subsidised propaganda to achieve this end. With the French example as a precedent, Germany, Italy and the Soviet Union embarked upon a campaign of commercial and cultural penetration abroad for the extension of national personality and ideology. In 1925 the Soviet Union created the All Union Society for Cultural Relations with Foreign Countries (VOKS) which declared as one of its motives for popularising Soviet culture 'the necessity for mobilising foreign intellectuals against alleged plans for military attack on Soviet Russia'.[43] In Italy, the Dante Alighieri Society had been working since its foundation in 1889 for the active propagation of Italian culture, and in 1926 Mussolini began to establish Italian cultural institutes abroad, although it was not until 1938 that the Institute for Cultural Relations with Foreign Countries (IRCE) was created to co-ordinate the work abroad. By fusing cultural propaganda with more conventional methods of diplomacy, such work evolved into a powerful weapon of nationalistic expansion in the hands of the totalitarian regimes. It is clearly ironic that these regimes utilised the lessons of the British wartime experiment in propaganda and combined them with technological advancements in communications in order to seize the

Cultural propaganda and the British Council

initiative in an escalating war of international propaganda, whose effects were feared from the Third international to the Fifth Column. It was a war in which Britain remained a helpless bystander until 1934.

Nevertheless, there were in Britain during the 1920s some important developments, particularly in the sphere of education, significant for the future conduct of British cultural propaganda. Eustace Percy, president of the Board of Education in the second Baldwin administration, subsequently wrote that

> after the war a hardly noticed revolution took place in British policy. For the first time in her history Britain became obscurely conscious that she had created not only an Empire but a civilisation. In 1923–25, she formulated an educational policy for her African colonies. In 1926 she remembered that a whole network of British schools had grown up in Argentina neglected and unorganised, and sent out there one of His Majesty's inspectors. About the same time she began to realise that, during fifty years of occupation, she had left a mark on Egyptian finance and irrigation but none on Egyptian education. She began to send out English teachers to the new University at Cairo.[44]

It must be said, however, that this 'hardly noticed revolution' manifested itself more in the minds of a few imaginative Whitehall officials than in any consistent policy of education abroad.

Meanwhile, the Foreign Office continued to correct misunderstandings on specific issues in the foreign press through the distribution of accurate news, but there remained no machinery for the correction of misrepresentative opinions concerning the British character. The work of various private organisations such as the All Peoples Association and the English-Speaking Union was undertaken without official assistance and was hampered by a continuous shortage of funds. Both the Foreign Office and the Department of Overseas Trade gradually became increasingly alarmed at the large number of anxious reports received from their overseas representatives concerning the absence of any British cultural propaganda. It was argued that British interests were suffering at the hands of foreign propagandists, who were becoming not so much pro-French or pro-German as anti-British. When, therefore, the appropriate occasion presented itself, the News Department seized the opportunity to reopen the debate on cultural propaganda.

The projection of Britain, 1919–1939

Following a request in 1928 from a small Central American state for a token gift of English books, it was discovered that the necessary funds to support deserving institutions abroad were exhausted.⁴⁵ Although the Treasury ruling of May 1919 prevented the News Department from conducting any form of cultural activity, it had been the practice to meet small requests for books from foreign institutions and libraries in exceptional circumstances. Provided that the amount requested was minimal, funds had been deducted from the News Department's incidental expenses, an arrangement which normally involved the curtailment of expenditure on other activities.⁴⁶ The sum now in question was indeed minute – £10 per annum – and the applicant, Guatemala, insignificant in terms of British interests, but this proved to be a question of principle. What little funding had been allocated in the past was decided on the basis of 'first come, first served'.⁴⁷ The News Department was, therefore, strictly speaking, exceeding its authorised duties. One of its officials remained in favour of continuing what he described as 'our haphazard, spasmodic and (I regret the term) surreptitious method of dealing with stray requests for books, until such time as a carefully worked-out scheme of cultural propaganda can be evolved with some chance of obtaining Treasury sanction for it – a chance which in view of the present regime of economy, seems to me to be remote'.⁴⁸ The department's head, Arthur Willert, agreed, adding: 'So far as it is possible to judge, we get good value for the small sums we spend in this way.'⁴⁹

Not all the News Department staff were prepared to accept this. One official, for example, considered the distribution of books a legitimate propaganda activity; 'If, however, it is decided that it is "surreptitious", we cannot, in any circumstances, accede to any further requests.'⁵⁰ Clifford Norton, with an appalling pun, observed that the foreign student 'may read Dumas, Goethe, or Cervantes in the original, but not Milton, except possibly in the American edition. We may tell foreigners about our aeroplanes and our coal strikes, but not about our poets and painters. We may, in fact, export bacon but not Bacon.'⁵¹ Accordingly, Willert decided to make a tentative approach to the Treasury with a view to reversing the ruling of 1919. It was, he wrote, important to clarify the existing position so that

Cultural propaganda and the British Council

first, we may be able to continue our present homoeopathic use of 'cultural propaganda'; second, that we may be clear, when and if we think the change advisable, for a diversion of a larger proportion of the News Department funds to a method of national advertisement which nearly all other governments, I believe, practise to a considerable extent.[52]

The moment for a fundamental reappraisal of British policy was fast approaching.

Foundation

In 1929 the Foreign Office estimated that the French government was devoting the equivalent of £500,000 to cultural propaganda, the Germans £300,000 and the Italians only slightly less.[53] These figures, combined with the numerous requests which poured in from overseas sources for some form of British cultural initiative, finally served to convince many officials that the moment for a renewed approach to the Treasury had arrived. Two particular events provided the final conviction. The first was the advent of Rex Leeper, who entered the News Department at this time. Leeper immediately began to take an active interest in cultural propaganda, and he was soon to emerge as the foremost Foreign Office exponent of its value and importance. More significant in the short term, however, were the recommendations of the D'Abernon trade mission to South America which repeatedly emphasised the inter-dependence of commercial and cultural propaganda.

Perhaps of equal importance was the receptivity of the Foreign Secretary, Arthur Henderson, to the News Department's view that some form of answer to the aggressive propaganda of other countries was urgently required. On 23 June 1930 he informed the Treasury that he was no longer able to ignore the advice and warnings which had reached him from innumerable sources on this issue, and he asked for a small sum of £10,000 annually 'for the purpose of extending as far as possible a knowledge of this country and of its culture'.[54] While awaiting a reply, an urgent request was received by the News Department in November for £300 to purchase books for foreign libraries, which was immediately granted.[55] Then, on 16 December, the Treasury informed the Foreign Office that henceforth an annual grant of £2,500 would be made available for British cultural activities abroad.[56] This was a decision of the utmost significance and marked the real departure from previous government policy towards cultural relations in peacetime.

The Treasury ruling of 1919 thus reversed, it remained for the News Department to ascertain which areas required immediate attention. In the spring of 1931, Angus Fletcher and Stephen Gaselee visited South America on behalf of the Foreign Office with the object of investigating the possibilities of initiating cultural propaganda in accordance with the recommendations of the D'Abernon mission. Their proposals involved a total estimated cost of £6,000.[57] However, the economic crisis in which Britain now found herself necessitated retrenchment in government spending. The News Department's recent award for cultural propaganda was an obvious target, and the expenditure was duly suspended. Of the £2,500 awarded for work in 1931, one-third had already been spent on broadcast talks, lectures fees and expenses, photographs and lantern slides, and gifts of books and periodicals.[58]

But despite this temporary suspension of the cultural programme, the significant factor was that, following a decade of virtual inactivity, the principle had been accepted by the Treasury. Indeed, such was the general conviction concerning the real necessity for cultural propaganda that expenditure was soon renewed despite the financial crisis. Ten years earlier, during a period of similar economic retrenchment, this conviction had not been present within official circles. The News Department was permitted to embark upon a programme of cultural relations in 1932 because the evidence pointing to the detrimental effects of foreign propaganda upon British interests and prestige was now overwhelming and irrefutable. That the evidence provoked the action it invited was due, in no small part, to the pioneering efforts of Sir Henry Newbolt, Sir John Tilley, Stephen Tallents and Rex Leeper.

In April 1931 Robert Vansittart, the permanent under secretary of state at the Foreign Office, informed the Prime Minister, Ramsay MacDonald of 'a new line of work which we have recently been enabled to undertake by the removal of the Treasury embargo on what, for want of a better term, is called cultural propaganda'.[59] He invited MacDonald to compile a short article, on any appropriate subject, for distribution abroad. Vansittart explained the importance of 'doing something to promote a better knowledge of

Cultural propaganda and the British Council

English manners and customs and of the ideals on which our particular culture is based'. He continued:

> Hitherto, in comparison with other countries, we have done remarkably little, but now, after mature reflection, we have decided that there are some things we can and ought to do. For instance, we are trying to extend the knowledge of English literature both by presents of books to institutions abroad and in other ways. We are encouraging outstanding Englishmen to lecture abroad on English literature, music and science, and some recent lectures by the Poet Laureate in Angora and Athens were a great success. Our experience is that any offers we make will meet with a very warm welcome abroad. The sum of money at our disposal is still, of course, limited, but we are doing our best to make it go a long way, and I am sure you will agree the work is both important and interesting.[60]

MacDonald did agree. He replied that he had 'been keen about this ever since the visit I paid to Berlin some years ago, when I found French influence in full blast'.[61] He even added his own advice, claiming that 'what the foreigner wants to know is Great Britain itself – not its political policy, not its work in the world, but the modes it has adopted to express its own being', but he was forced regretfully to decline the invitation to write an article because of pressure of work with an impending general election.[62]

Meanwhile, the News Department continued with its preparations for a cultural programme beginning in 1931–2. The allocated sum of £2,500 had been sanctioned primarily for work in Europe (with the exception of Russia), and in an explanatory memorandum Leeper subdivided the work into four categories: books, lectures, films and broadcasting. At the heart of the programme lay an emphasis on the spread of the English language which was to provide the vehicle for all consequent activity. On 30 April 1931, Leeper's memorandum was circulated abroad together with a circular despatch instructing that 'in future ... it will be for each Mission to regard the promotion of cultural relations on the lines indicated in this memorandum as a regular feature of its work'.[63] Thus, from the outset, it was recognised that the ultimate success of the work depended upon the personal initiative of the heads of overseas missions both in suggesting schemes for possible action and in supervising the work in their respective countries 'on the spot'. And it was to be through these traditional diplomatic channels that the bulk of the funds for this new activity was to be distributed to foreign libraries and Anglo-foreign societies abroad, mainly in the form of published literature.[64]

The election of the National Government in August 1931, and the appointment of Lord Reading as Foreign Secretary, did not result in any fundamental change of policy with regard to cultural propaganda. Nevertheless, 'owing to the urgent need for economy', the News Department did suffer a temporary setback with the suspension of its cultural expenditure.[65] Missions were instructed to continue the work wherever it was found possible to do so without financial assistance but were warned against giving the impression of 'panic economy', which might prove harmful to national prestige.[66] Existing commitments were, however, to be fulfilled, and the continued foundation of anglophile societies was to be encouraged. As Lord Reading appreciated, the work had now, perhaps more than ever before, assumed significant responsibilities:

> At the present time, it is of great importance that this country's affairs should be presented to foreign peoples in the most favourable light possible. Close relations with the local press should be cultivated and maintained... If material affecting the affairs of this country is sought by the foreign press, such requests should be forwarded by Missions in order that an attempt may be made to provide what is required. It is important to bear this in mind during the present period of economic and financial depression, when misunderstanding and misinterpretation of this country's position is likely to be frequent.[67]

The suspension of funds lasted for just nine months. Following an informal discussion between Vansittart and Sir Warren Fisher, the permanent under secretary at the Treasury, a formal letter was addressed to the Chancellor on 8 June 1932 explaining that Foreign Office attempts to conduct cultural propaganda without financial assistance had not proved successful. A request was submitted for the urgent provision of £1,000 in order to renew the cultural programme in 1932–3, and a few days later, on 11 June, the Treasury wrote to authorise the expenditure.[68] In the following November, the News Department succeeded in gaining a supplementary figure, thereby bringing the total sum for cultural propaganda back to £2,500.[69]

Although the allocation of these sums constituted a significant de-

Cultural propaganda and the British Council

parture from previous official policy, the somewhat limited nature of Britain's cultural activities abroad becomes blatantly apparent when contrasted with the expenditure incurred by foreign governments. In 1934, the figures for German and French cultural propaganda were estimated at over one million pounds each. The Italian counterpart of the Alliance Française, the Dante Alighieri Society, was granted a Royal Statute in 1933, and within two years it was calculated that 0.3 per cent of the total Italian budget was being devoted to cultural propaganda. The Japanese had also entered the field in April 1934 with the foundation of the Kokusai Bunkwa Shinko Kwai (Society for the Promotion of International Cultural Relations) aided by a government subsidy of £60,000. Even the smaller countries, such as Switzerland and Czechoslovakia, were devoting something in the region of £40–50,000 yearly to cultural work.[70] By comparison, British efforts appear small and inconsequential. 'If only we could do as much for English', lamented one official,[71] but the Foreign Office was shortly to console itself with the belief that quantity was no substitute for quality.

During the brief period in 1932 when expenditure had been temporarily suspended, the News Department began to consider the possibility of conducting cultural activity through an intermediary organisation which might more readily attract private support. There was anyway a need to co-ordinate the work of the growing number of organisations engaged in British overseas propaganda, whether official, semi-official or private, such as the Foreign Office, the Boards of Trade and Education, the Empire Marketing Board, the Travel Association, the Ibero-American Institute of Great Britain, and the British National Council of the All Peoples Association. Insufficient evidence leaves the early proposals somewhat vague, but during 1934 a distinguishable pattern begins to emerge. In the spring of that year, Leeper formulated several ideas which were ultimately to become the guiding principles upon which British cultural propaganda was initially conducted. In the first place, he believed in the value of qualitative rather than quantitative propaganda, because, he argued,

propaganda defeats its own end unless you propagate what is really worth propagating. It is a delusion to think that you are doing well simply because you are doing a great deal. Ill-considered enthusiasm can do nearly as much harm as indifference. It is not only a waste of money and effort, but it lowers rather than raises our prestige. For this reason, the Foreign Office should keep a close eye on what is being done, and only give its blessing to what is well done.[72]

Leeper advocated official support for the work of the British Institutes in Paris and Florence, the Ibero-American Institute and the All Peoples Association (APA), believing that the work of the latter body in Europe and Egypt merited 'a special effort to help this organisation'. Moreover, Leeper continued,

> In conducting cultural propaganda, we should avoid the idea that it is directed against any other country or indeed that it is competitive. Cultural relations will only improve political relations if they are maintained on a basis of strict reciprocity. It is just as good propaganda for this country to bring distinguished foreigners to lecture and meet people here as it is to send our own speakers abroad. We shall obtain better publicity for our own culture in other countries if we take an equal interest in their culture. The Ibero-American Institute appreciates this, while it is the very basis of the APA's activities. It is more subtle and very much more fruitful than the one-sided propaganda which French, Germans and Italians are apt to pursue so vigorously. In the long run, we shall be the gainers by this method. Not only we, but Europe in general.[73]

Leeper believed that because the APA had introduced 'a new spirit in propaganda' it deserved the moral support of the Foreign Office and some official financial assistance to help pay the expenses of visiting lecturers.[74]

In June 1934, Leeper further developed these views in an imaginative memorandum which proposed the establishment of an unofficial Cultural Relations Committee, financed by private sources, but which was to be assisted by liaison officers from the various interested government departments. In effect, Leeper was reviving the recommendation of the 1920 Tilley report for a standing committee to examine and implement proposals for the extension of British culture and education abroad. He began his argument with the observation that 'cultural propaganda has been recognised of late years as an effective and necessary instrument of national policy'.[75] Basing his views on a close examination of the techniques employed by foreign governments, he repeated his warning that 'excessive propaganda is not only a waste of money and effort, but may do positive harm'. He then went on to advocate caution at first, concentrating on already proven techniques and

Cultural propaganda and the British Council

careful scrutiny of any new proposals before the work was extended. Moreover, he believed that, whereas the direction of policy should remain firmly in the hands of the Foreign Office, the actual propaganda itself 'should so far as possible be conducted through private organisations, which should be encouraged to stand on their own feet, and not be entirely dependent on official assistance'.[76] The proposed work was divided into five main categories: (1) the provision of prizes and scholarships to foreign schools and universities in order to increase the study of the English language; (2) the establishment of British libraries abroad; (3) the arrangement of lecture tours by distinguished British speakers; (4) sponsored visits to England of prominent journalists and professional men; (5) films. Leeper was all too aware of the immense propaganda potential of film, but he was alarmed at the serious shortage of existing cultural films which were suitable for overseas distribution, adding: 'what can be supplied from the GPO Film Unit and Travel Association is very meagre'.[77]

In order to keep a watchful eye on foreign propaganda and to supervise any British activity under these headings, Leeper placed great emphasis upon the role of the various diplomatic missions abroad. He also expected them to provide encouragement to existing anglophile societies and clubs or, where none existed, to help stimulate their foundation. Vansittart, who responded favourably to Leeper's scheme, added:

The value of members of our missions abroad is now in some degree tested by their economic ability (or utility?). The old test was purely political (and wholly insufficient in practice). In future there will be a third criterion which links up with the other two, and that criterion will be energy and capacity in this cultural direction.[78]

Indeed, as subsequent developments were to prove, the success or failure of Britain's cultural diplomacy was to a large degree dependent upon the varying degrees of enthusiasm, or otherwise, generated by overseas missions for this type of activity, the level of enthusiasm in turn being directly proportional to the intensity of foreign anti-British propaganda within the different geographical areas.

Having secured the support of Vansittart for his views, Leeper soon discovered that other government departments were also receptive to his proposal for some sort of cultural relations committee. The findings of the D'Abernon Economic Mission to South America had been confirmed by Sir Ernest Thompson, who led the British Economic Mission to the Far East in 1930–1, and by Sir Alan Anderson's Trade Mission to Scandinavia in 1933. As a direct result of their findings, following a meeting of the Overseas Trade Development Council on 11 April 1933, at which politicians, officials and industrialists were present, it was decided to recommend the establishment of a committee to examine the training of foreign students in British industry 'and thereafter to consider the general question of cultural relations with foreign countries'.[79] The Boards of Trade and Education accepted this proposal and in June 1933 appointed the Committee on the Education and Training in the United Kingdom of Overseas Students under the chairmanship of Sir Eugene Ramsden, the chairman of the Trade and Industry Committee of the House of Commons.[80] Ramsden was invited 'to consider what further steps could usefully be taken to encourage students to come to the United Kingdom for education and training – general, commercial and technical'.[81] After detailed examination lasting for nearly a year, an interim report was produced in 1934 which confirmed that the question of overseas students was merely part of the overall problem caused through ignorance abroad concerning British educational, scientific, technical and cultural achievements.[82] Moreover, growing anxiety for the implications of this situation was increasingly discernible within industrial and business circles.[83] Sir Robert Vansittart discovered that ICI for example were prepared to donate £1,000 towards any cultural programme initiated by the government.[84]

Encouraged by these developments, Leeper decided to approach Sir Evelyn Wrench, the chairman of the All Peoples Association, for support in setting up a central co-ordinating body to supervise British cultural propaganda overseas. Wrench, who was then proprietor of the *Spectator*, had been instrumental in the foundation of the Overseas League in 1910 and of the English-Speaking Union in 1918 before extending his activities in the cause of international friendship during the 1930s with the foundation of the APA. At the end of June 1934, the Committee of International Understanding and Co-operation came into being with Wrench as its chairman and

Cultural propaganda and the British Council

with the object of 'making the national life and institutions of Great Britain and the British Empire better known abroad'.[85] Industrial and educational interests on the committee were represented by Ramsden, William Rootes (vice-president of the Society of Motor Manufacturers and Traders), Sir Edwin Deller (principal of London University) and J. W. Ramsbottom (director of the City of London College), although no official from any government department was initially represented. Further information relating to this body, the forerunner of the British Council, is rare, but it does seem that several meetings were held throughout the summer of 1934 with a view to raising financial support from the private sector. On 11 July, Leeper explained to the Overseas Trade Development Council that the new cultural relations committee had been created to meet a real demand:

Europe was suffering from an excess of nationalism, politically, economically and psychologically. It was clearly necessary, however, to accept things as they were and to see how national sentiments could be brought into closer sympathy with each other. Very little could be done politically, perhaps more could be achieved economically, and certainly a great deal more psychologically or culturally.[86]

Moreover, Leeper continued,

Ignorance, misunderstanding and suspicion were serious impediments to trade, and the main objects of the Cultural Relations Committee would be to remove these impediments by spreading knowledge of other countries in the United Kingdom... The British nation has made, and was still making, an immense contribution to the common stock of ideas. The task of the Cultural Relations Committee was to see that that contribution was better known and understood overseas. It was an asset which it was legitimate properly to exploit. It was time that we should rid ourselves of our traditional aloofness and insularity not only because it would pay to do so, but because we should lose heavily if we did not.[87]

The Overseas Trade Development Council agreed, and expressed its wholehearted support for Wrench and his committee.[88] An appeal to industry was launched in the weeks that followed, backed by both the Foreign Office and the Department of Overseas Trade.

It was at this point that serious differences of opinion began to emerge between the industrial and various other interests involved in the project. Although the precise details remain vague, a power struggle seems to have developed over the question of who controlled the cultural relations committee. The principle of conducting national propaganda was not in dispute. It was unanimously agreed that

> The lesson that the War has taught the nations of the world is that they cannot live and prosper in isolation. It follows that no nation can afford to remain aloof and misunderstood. Both the larger and the smaller states have recognised this and have engaged in active national propaganda. Of all the Great Powers, Britain has done least.[89]

However, now that this position was beginning to be resolved, there was a need to decide exactly what form British activity should take. On this issue, there were two distinct schools of thought. The Foreign Office wanted to follow the French example and utilise cultural propaganda as a means of promoting national prestige in the broadest sense. Britain's commercial position would, it was argued, improve as a result. On the other hand, the industrial element, backed by the DOT and its offspring, the Travel Association, considered that if it was expected to bear the brunt of the financial cost involved, then it should retain the right to determine the direction of the committee's work. In effect, that would have meant that the major emphasis of the work would be on commercial propaganda. Meredith, the secretary of the Travel Association, remains the sole source of information for the curious sequence of events which followed. Leeper is said to have asked Wrench to organise a luncheon, at which Vansittart was present along with 'one or two rich men of the kind who want titles', for the purpose of raising funds. Meredith continued:

> At the same time, with the assurance, which Wrench has in writing, of Foreign Office support, he went to the considerable expense of taking the All People's Association house in Arlington Street. A certain amount of work was done, and it was suggested then by Leeper that they should have an additional official to help Wrench's staff, and Leeper strongly recommended a Colonel Bridge, to which Wrench said he agreed in a hurry on the eve of going abroad.[90]

It is likely that Leeper saw the appointment of Charles Bridge, a close friend and ally, as a means of checking Wrench's growing preference for industrial and private support over that of the Foreign Office. Bridge shared Leeper's distinctive views of the cultural role of the new committee. Perhaps this was why he began to argue with the staff at the APA. Whatever the real reason, on 5

Cultural propaganda and the British Council

November 1934, Leeper informed Wrench that his co-operation was no longer required. Claiming to speak on Vansittart's behalf, Leeper wrote that 'since the idea was first put forward, difficulties have arisen with other societies and he [Vansittart] has therefore decided to dissolve the Committee and to start afresh on different lines in consultation with other departments concerned'.[91] Wrench's polite but terse reply, in which he stated that 'I myself thought that the APA was being forced into a false position',[92] does not appear to have fully revealed the real extent of his personal indignation at the way he had been treated, particularly as the replacement committee was believed by him to have been launched with the aid of funds raised by his earlier efforts. Meredith's account concluded: 'Wrench, I may say, was exceedingly angry about the way he had been treated and would welcome an opportunity of telling Van. about it. He went so far as to say that he thought there ought to be a public enquiry, when he would like to brief leading counsel.'[93]

Meredith's version of the whole affair, which was based largely upon a conversation he had with Wrench twelve months after the event, is admittedly biased against the Foreign Office; the Travel Association deeply resented the News Department's efforts to create a new cultural propaganda body at a time when it saw itself as filling the bill. Wrench undoubtedly had good cause to feel bitter also. But to the Foreign Office, and particularly to Leeper as the official most directly involved, it was essential that the conduct of cultural propaganda should benefit the national rather than specific industrial or business interests. The APA proved to be as unacceptable as the Travel Association was considered to be in this respect. Although, in the absence of further evidence, it is difficult to paint a much clearer picture, the subsequent dispute which was to emerge during the British Council's first year of existence would seem to confirm that this was essentially a struggle over emphasis. Cultural propaganda would, the Foreign Office argued, benefit industrial and commercial interests in an indirect manner as the direct consequence of an increase in British prestige abroad. The Department of Overseas Trade, to name but one opponent, considered that national prestige would result from a direct increase in British trade. Ironically, after more than a decade of unanimity in advocating that cultural and commercial propaganda were mutually complementary, the various interested parties now found themselves locked in a type of chicken-and-egg debate.

Meanwhile, in order to ensure closer Foreign Office control over the second version of the cultural relations committee, Leeper had invited William Tyrrell, the recently retired ambassador to France, to take charge of the project. In November 1934, Tyrrell accepted the invitation to become chairman of what was originally called the 'Advisory Committee for the Promotion of International Relations' with Bridge acting as his secretary, and with an office in Shell-Mex house in the Strand.[94] When informing the Foreign Secretary, Sir John Simon, of this latest development, Leeper failed to mention the tension with Wrench, and he also advised Bridge to remain silent on this issue until he had clarified everything with Vansittart, adding, 'until then I must walk warily and not commit the FO to anything that E [velyn] W [rench] could say was personal on my part'.[95] Indeed, had the Foreign Secretary been in possession of the whole story, he might not have been so readily prepared to 'heartily' congratulate Leeper on his achievement.[96]

The first meeting of 'Lord Tyrrell's Committee' took place on 5 December 1934. Representatives from four government departments were joined by members of the original committee – Rootes, Deller, Ramsden and Ramsbottom. Leeper, the natural Foreign Office representative, suggested the title 'The British Committee for Relations with Other Countries', which was accepted.[97] The composition of this committee, which before long became known as the British Council, was not only more acceptable to Leeper personally, being more in line with his original conception, but also to the Foreign Office in general, because it would retain a greater measure of influence in the formulation of policy. This was why Tyrrell, who had spent most of his distinguished career in the diplomatic service, was preferable to Wrench as chairman. However, because the council's initial concern was almost inevitably with finance, the continued presence of representatives from trade and industry was necessary if the new organisation was to attract confidence and financial support from the private sector. And this factor was to cause Leeper a constant headache during the early years of the council's life.

The Treasury's decision in January 1935 to award a £5,000 grant-in-aid, to be borne on the Foreign Office Vote, did serve to alleviate the acute initial shortage of funds and to enable the British

Cultural propaganda and the British Council

Council to begin its 1935–6 programme on a small scale in Scandinavia.[98] But it was originally intended that the bulk of the council's income was to derive from non-official sources. The industrial representatives on the council's governing board, who were soon reinforced by the inclusion of the Sheffield steel magnate Sir Arthur Balfour (later Lord Riverdale), who became vice-chairman, continued to feel that, in return for their money, the emphasis should be on commercial propaganda. Leeper remained adamant in his belief that the council should conduct national rather than sectional propaganda. As he informed Vansittart,

> For my own part I have very little faith in the vision or imagination of our industrialists. They will be influenced mainly by the desire for commercial rather than political results and I am convinced that our aim should be political rather than commercial and that the Foreign Office should have the major say in the policy of the Council.[99]

He became particularly irritated with C. M. Pickthall, the DOT's official representative on the governing board, whom Leeper suspected of manipulating potential industrial sponsors against the views of the Foreign Office.[100] The resultant tension was temporarily eased by the personal intervention of Vansittart,[101] although it was to reappear spasmodically over the next few years and only finally subsided as a result of the failure of successive financial appeals to industry, which forced the British Council to rely increasingly upon its government grant.[102]

During the first year of its existence, the council was thus more preoccupied with financial survival and in constructing a working administrative machinery than with the formulation of a coherent policy or with the inauguration of much cultural activity abroad. Only by the summer of 1935, 'with Pickthall ousted and the money in sight', did Leeper feel that he was beginning to see daylight over the whole question. Regardless of his treatment of Wrench, his personal role in the inauguration of such a marked departure from established peacetime tradition had been such that he might be forgiven the following expression of self-satisfaction when he wrote to Bridge in July 1935:

> You and I started this thing together and you and I have really done the whole job. I have done the touting outside and the lubricating inside while you have been steadily building up the whole structure from within ... I believe that this is going to grow into something really big, and you and I

are going to have the chief say in it ... I think we can look forward to an interesting time ahead... There is no better work than in constructing something from nothing.[103]

Administration

In its early formative years, the British Council in effect functioned as an annex of the Foreign Office News Department. Despite the early efforts of the industrialists to increase their influence, the Foreign Office retained ultimate control over council policy. There did not exist any delegated lines of responsibility between the two offices, but an atmosphere of friendly and mutual co-operation developed around the personal friendship of Leeper and Bridge, at that time the only permanent council official. Moreover, because finances were extremely limited, and requests for cultural activity exceeded available resources, the British Council was forced to rely heavily upon the co-operation of diplomatic representatives abroad for the conduct of any work in foreign countries. Missions were informed of this additional responsibility in December 1934 with a reminder that 'at a time when the flow of international trade is checked by the growth of economic nationalism, it is all the more important that intercourse between this and other countries should be maintained and promoted through those channels most likely to assist in creating a better mutual understanding'.[104] A further strengthening of the links occurred in 1936 when Kenneth Johnstone of the News Department was seconded to work with the council as liaison officer, a post which he held until 1939. It was both council policy and preference to work through the normal diplomatic channels in order to retain the initial interest of the overseas missions,[105] and it was not until the close of 1938 that sufficient funds were available to appoint its first overseas representative, C. A. F. Dundas, to supervise cultural propaganda 'on the spot' in the Middle East from an office in Cairo. Undoubtedly, there were some officials serving abroad who were cynical, if not apathetic or even hostile, towards their new ally in the representation of British overseas. As one observer has noted, 'to those few it seemed that it would be altogether too embarrassing and even dangerous to have an organisation sponsored by Government operating on behalf of Britain and yet not directly subject to the ambassadors' control... But on

Cultural propaganda and the British Council

the whole the Missions accepted their new burden with a good grace.'[106]

On its creation, the British Council inherited the cultural activities and existing commitments previously conducted by the News Department. In return, the Foreign Office provided the council with access to the normal diplomatic channels and facilities. But although the council relied heavily upon those facilities, it would not be entirely correct to assume, as many foreign observers did, that the council was a purely official propaganda organisation. Rather it was, following the analogy of the BBC, a semi-autonomous body, ultimately responsible to its paymaster, but with control over its own administration and activities. It was an arrangement entirely in accord with the Foreign Office preference for conducting propaganda through private or semi-official organisations, thereby preserving a greater degree of credibility for its work.

In 1935, a comprehensive statement of the British Council's aims was drawn up, and, as it continues to reflect generally the aspirations of the council, it merits extended quotation:

To make the life and thought of the British peoples more widely known abroad; and to promote a mutual interchange of knowledge and ideas with other peoples. To encourage the study and use of the English language, both in foreign countries and the Crown Colonies and Dependencies; to assist overseas schools in equipping themselves for this purpose; to enable students from overseas to undertake courses of education or industrial training in the United Kingdom. To bring other peoples into closer touch with British ideals and practice in education, industry and Government; to make available to them the benefits of current British contributions to the sciences and technology; and to afford them opportunities of appreciating contemporary British work in literature, the fine arts, drama and music. To co-operate with the self-governing Dominions in strengthening the common cultural tradition of the British Commonwealth.[107]

The Prince of Wales, who became patron of the British Council, neatly summarised these aims in a speech which captured the mood of the early pioneers when he said: 'Of all the great Powers this country is the last in the field in setting up a proper organisation to spread a knowledge and appreciation of its language, literature, art, science and education – that is to say, to let the world know what it owes to British achievements in these spheres.'[108] To achieve these aims it was decided to adopt a long-term policy 'and to strive for lasting results in the future rather than for small, immediate successes'.[109] In other words, there was no question of entering into competition with the larger (and richer) state-subsidised propaganda agencies of foreign governments. There were neither the financial resources nor the inclination to do so. Rather, the British Council was to continue the News Department's traditional preference for 'pro-British' rather than 'anti-foreign' propaganda. It was to be neither provocative in tone nor critical in content. Success was to be achieved in spite of foreign aggressive propaganda rather than in competition with it. As Leeper put it, 'the work of the British Council is therefore educational in the widest sense'.[110] It was towards these aspirations that the council began to construct its administrative machinery during 1935.

Ultimate control over council affairs lay in the hands of a small executive committee, known originally as the 'Governing Board', which met periodically and comprised representatives from all the major interests concerned. The day-to-day administration, however, was performed by a small permanent staff led by the secretary-general, Charles Bridge. A number of specialist committees were further established to consider and suggest activity on specific aspects of cultural work. It was following the publication of the full Ramsden report in January 1935 that the first of these committees, the Students Committee was created. Ramsden had recommended to the Boards of Trade and Education that they should take full steps to encourage the flow of 'carefully selected students from overseas and that reciprocal relations with overseas countries should be established whenever possible in regard to the education and training of students; and that a central organisation should be set up for this purpose'.[111] Because the question of students was considered to be an integral part of the overall task of cultural propaganda, the Students Committee of the British Council was set up under Ramsden's chairmanship to carry out the report's proposals. Of all the specialist committees subsequently created by the British Council, the Students Committee was the only one directly involved in bringing foreigners to Britain; the rest were concerned with cultural dissemination in the opposite direction.

A Lectures Committee was appointed to arrange lecture tours abroad by prominent Englishmen and recognised experts to speak on various aspects of literary, artistic, cultural and scientific themes.

Cultural propaganda and the British Council

The Fine Arts Committee was established to help arrange the exhibition of British art overseas, a task which it took over from the DOT.[112] The British entries at the Empire Exhibition in Johannesburg in 1936 and the exhibitions in Paris and Venice in 1938 were arranged by this committee. In July 1935, the Music Committee was created to arrange concert tours by British musicians and orchestras. Arthur Bliss and Ralph Vaughan Williams were among those who provided their advice on this committee. Another body was required to continue the News Department's commitments in the supply of 'representative British literature' to foreign libraries and anglophile societies. According to a list drawn up by the Foreign Office in 1933, 'representative literature' seems to have meant just about everything published by famous British authors including works by Conrad, Hardy, Joyce, Strachey, H. G. Wells and Rider Haggard, as well as the standard works of Defoe, Dickens, Dryden, Chaucer, Milton, Pope, Shakespeare, Wordsworth and so on.[113] For this purpose, a Books and Periodicals Committee was set up initially under the chairmanship of the poet laureate, John Masefield, and from 1936 of the publisher Stanley Unwin. Their committee also arranged for the publication of book reviews in the foreign press, but, despite the commercial advantages which this scheme extended to British publishers, the establishment of this and other purely cultural committees helped to loosen the initial grip of the industrial element upon the early development of the council's work.

Owing to the shortage of funds and the dangers of overlapping and duplication of effort, it was essential for the British Council to establish and maintain close contact with other organisations working in the same field. The absence of any British cultural propaganda in Latin America had been a source of anxiety in the Foreign Office for some time. The problem had received considerable publicity in the wake of the D'Aberbon trade mission and the official visit of the Prince of Wales. Indeed, Latin America had been the first target of the News Department when cultural propaganda was resumed in 1930. Meanwhile, the Ibero-American Institute of Great Britain, under the direction of Philip Guedalla, embarked upon its own privately financed programme of cultural relations and was instrumental in the foundation of the Brazilian Society of English Culture at Rio de Janeiro and of the Paulista

The projection of Britain, 1919–1939

Society for Cultural Relations with England at São Paulo in 1934. The institute also organised lecture tours and student exchanges.[114] During the summer of 1934, following a lecture tour by Guedalla and Compton MacKenzie, the News Department had received glowing reports of their success. Leeper concluded from these reports that the institute's work 'has been most effective in attracting the attention of the public in Latin American countries to Great Britain's cultural heritage'.[115] Once the British Council had been created, the Prince of Wales, who, as patron of both organisations, provided a distinguished point of contact, took the initiative in advocating close collaboration between the institute and the council. He said of the institute:

> To my mind, the work which it has been doing exactly corresponds to that which we wish to do all around the world, and I sincerely trust that means will be found, by affiliation or otherwise, to ensure its immediate co-operation with the Council, of which it would be something in the nature of a local offshoot.[116]

Shortly after this speech was made in July 1935, the British Council entered into negotiations with the Ibero-American Institute with a view to collaborative action in attempting to combat the detrimental effects of anti-British propaganda in South America.[117]

The outcome of these negotiations was an arrangement whereby the institute would in future serve as the Ibero-American Committee of the British Council.[118] Guedalla, director of the institute, became chairman of this new body, thereby becoming an *ex-officio* member of the council's executive committee (which had by now replaced the governing board) in the process. The task of the Ibero-American Committee was to make recommendations for cultural activity in each South American country and, if approved by the executive committee, the work would be carried out by the institute on behalf of the council, which would foot the bill. This rather unusual arrangement proved, however, to be the source of occasional friction. In 1938, for example, Bridge complained of 'Guedalla's habit of presenting us with *faits accomplis*',[119] and in January 1939, following the distribution of Professor C. K. Webster's council-sponsored book *Britain and the Independence of Latin America, 1812–30: Select Documents from the Foreign Office Archives*,[120] he wrote:

Cultural propaganda and the British Council

It is quite clear ... that the position as regards the Ibero-American Institute and the Ibero-American Committee of the British Council is not clearly established. Guedalla seems to have dealt with this matter as though it were an Ibero-American Institute matter, and only concerned the Council when the question of payment arose.[121]

Despite such occasional friction, the arrangement nevertheless generally worked quite efficiently, and a marked improvement in British cultural propaganda to South America was discernible to those who had observed the demand before the council's foundation.

It also became equally, if not more, important for the British Council to establish a close liaison with the Travel Association. Relations were, however, severely strained from the council's inception. Essentially, the problem was that the Travel Association, which had been campaigning for a higher government grant since 1932, resented the council's more immediate success on this score. The association also had aspirations to becoming a cultural body, and the council was seen as a threat to its own integrity and capacity. As Meredith complained,

The whole question is exceedingly difficult for us because, in my view, Leeper, with excellent intentions, has made a first-class muddle, has committed Vansittart and the Foreign Office to this Council, and is now using all resources open to him – and they are pretty considerable – to keep it going, regardless of the effect on other organisations.[122]

He was also irritated by the fact that the association had not been formally consulted at the time of the council's inception and that it had, in effect, been presented with a *fait accompli*. A brief period of mutual consultation ensued, but Meredith remained unhappy, believing that the council,

with the full force of Foreign Office backing, which they have through Leeper, and what I call 'snob appeal' to people who want titles, might get fairly considerable sums of money, and their method of procedure has shown that they endeavour not, as they were set up to do, to help existing organisations, but to displace them ... We have tried to work with them, but whether of ineptitude or malice – I think a bit of both – we have found it difficult to do so.[123]

This element of jealousy in the association's attitude towards the council was to characterise relations between the two bodies until the outbreak of the Second World War. Meanwhile, an interim arrangement was made in an attempt to avoid further tension and overlapping, although the relationship between them remained ill defined despite the appointment of Lord Derby, the president of the Travel Association, to the council's executive committee in February 1936.

Consequently, in the months that followed, two collaborative committees were established within the council's administrative apparatus. The first of these, the Joint Broadcasting Committee of the British Council and Travel Association, held its first meeting in June under the chairmanship of Sir Alan Dawnay, then controller of programmes at the BBC.[124] Cecil Graves, shortly to replace Dawnay at the BBC, was also a member, and the presence of both men on the joint committee ensured a close liaison with Broadcasting House. The Travel Association had, some years before, embarked upon a policy of distributing gramophone recordings of talks about the English countryside and other tourist attractions to foreign radio stations such as Radio Luxembourg, primarily with the object of attracting more visitors to Britain. The Joint Broadcasting Committee enabled the British Council to utilise this experience in order to secure the distribution of recorded music and talks on a wide range of artistic and cultural themes. The BBC, which first had to be reassured that such work was 'not propaganda in the accepted sense of the term' but rather was 'the spreading of information regarding this country', decided to place its full experience and assistance at the disposal of the committee.[125] This aid manifested itself chiefly in the selection and advising of speakers on the methods of delivery and presentation in recording the talks. However, despite its early aspirations, the committee's progress turned out to be slow and undramatic. It met only infrequently, and, by the end of 1937, it even began to question the need for its own existence, especially at a time when the BBC was about to launch its own broadcast programme in foreign languages. Yet the committee survived and provided occasional advice and material in the hope that it might be needed for more important work at some future date. Its main achievement before the Second World War was to serve as the normal channel of communication among the BBC, the British Council, the Travel Association and the Foreign Office.

The second, and more effective, collaborative committee was the Joint Committee on Films, which held its first meeting in April 1936

Cultural propaganda and the British Council

under the chairmanship of Philip Guedalla. Because the council did not possess, nor could it afford, its own film unit, the Joint Films Committee was partly formed to examine the means by which the Travel Association's existing film unit could be efficiently utilised in the production and distribution overseas of cultural films.[126] The committee also assumed responsibility for the distribution abroad of British newsreel and documentary films as a form of national propaganda. Strengthened by the support and expert advice of men such as John Grierson, the effective founder of the British documentary film movement, and Oliver Bell, the director of the British Film Institute, the Joint Films Committee provided the first constructive peacetime attempt to rectify the serious deficiencies and innumerable problems which had hitherto prevented the effective utilisation of this potentially powerful medium in the projection of Britain abroad.

The mass propagandist value of film had been widely appreciated since the closing years of the First World War when Sir William Jury had been appointed head of the Cinema Propaganda Department of the Ministry of Information.[127] During the 1920s there had developed an increasing sensitivity to, and a greater understanding of, film as propaganda, notably under the aegis of the Empire Marketing Board. In 1934 the GPO created its own film unit and, continuing the traditions of the EMB, produced some highly successful documentaries such as the deservedly acclaimed *Night Mail*.[128] Several other government departments began to take an active interest in the production of films by the GPO film unit, although they were in the main more concerned with domestic audiences. The question of publicity films for overseas distribution, which was raised periodically by the Foreign Office News Department, generally received less consideration in Whitehall. The same could not be said in the private and industrial sectors, where bodies such as the British Commercial Gas Association, Shell-Mex and British Petroleum were busy sponsoring the production of publicity and documentary films. 'Government agencies such as the Travel Association, the British Council and the Imperial Relations Trust, responsible for overseas national publicity, gave some assistance. But the main work of establishing contacts abroad, particularly in the United States of America, was carried out by the documentary producers and by Film Centre.'[129] Film Centre was established in 1937 by a group of film-makers led by Grierson to act as a central advisory body to the film industry.[130]

The Joint Films Committee of the British Council and Travel Association began its work by compiling a census of the available British films suitable for overseas distribution,[131] which not only exposed the serious shortage of such films but also their poor condition.[132] It was therefore suggested that a film library be set up, but this proposal was rejected by the council on the grounds of expense.[133] However, the dearth of suitable films which could serve a definite propaganda purpose was to some extent relieved in October 1937 by an offer of the British Film Institute to place its own library at the joint committee's disposal,[134] although progress was achieved at only a slow pace and was hampered by factors largely beyond the control and influence of the committee. Several films were distributed in Latin America and the Middle East with some measure of success,[135] although it did not compare with the later acclaim accorded a film depicting the coronation of King George VI.

Such was the nature of the films distributed abroad that they were hardly likely to attract mass foreign audiences. Instead, the Joint Films Committee chose initially to concentrate upon non-theatrical distribution. British films were mainly shown by anglophile societies and clubs, film societies and international film congresses or in foreign schools. This did not particularly bother the British Council; the smaller, educated audiences were exactly those it was trying to influence. The films would have had to be expensively dubbed with a foreign-language soundtrack and injected with a greater degree of entertainment content if they were to reach larger audiences. But after 1937 there developed a greater demand among British publicists for increased theatrical distribution. The Travel Association, prompted, no doubt, by its master, the DOT,[136] advocated the increased circulation of industrial and engineering films such as *Steel* and *Wedgwood*. One council official, commenting upon the influential weight of the DOT on the Joint Films Committee in the selection of films, warned that 'we must be careful that people do not look upon us as being... "just a smokescreen for British trade penetration"'.[137] This was not simply a question of the old industrial-versus-cultural interpretation of the council's work. It was a question of policy and the type of foreigners whom the council

Cultural propaganda and the British Council

wished to influence. As H. P. Croom-Johnson, an early council official, explained,

> I feel that the Committee is apt to underestimate the mentality of the foreign films audiences. Guedalla remarked that 'we are trying to place ourselves in the position of a low-class Maltese tobacconist'. Admittedly this was flippantly meant, and the Committee was right in remembering that to many film audiences abroad, the sound commentary will be incomprehensible and must largely be discarded. Against this, however, should be remembered the verdict of the Finnish–British society which roundly condemned as very poor two films sent to them recently by the Travel Association. By 'playing down' to film audiences we shall not gain the interest of the unintelligent (who do not matter to us anyway) and we shall lose the sympathy and interest of intelligent anglophil societies and the moderately intelligent newspaper readers at whom we should presumably aim.[138]

Rarely was the different propaganda approach of the Foreign Office and the British Council on the one hand, and of the Travel Association and the DOT on the other, more clearly illustrated. But because the Joint Films Committee continued to be dominated by the Travel Association's purse, which was in turn supplied by the DOT, the overseas distribution of purely cultural films remained wholly inadequate, despite the occasional individual success.[139] Indeed, of the various different aspects of national projection abroad, film remained the most seriously deficient until the outbreak of war.

Personalities and policies

During the council's first year, little time was devoted to questions of general policy; the major preoccupation had been with finance and the establishment of a working machinery. Once these issues had been largely settled, the council began to develop a more precise conception of its own role in the context of British diplomacy during a period of worsening international tension. Leeper believed that 'Never in our long history have our help and leadership been more earnestly sought, never has there been so great a curiosity and desire to know what we stand for. This being so, we are clearly bound not only to inform ourselves better about other countries, but equally to see that they are better informed about us.'[140] Similar views were shared by the council's first chairman, William Tyrrell, who regarded cultural diplomacy as 'work of real importance ... not only in the national interest, but also in that of a return to sanity in international relations'.[141] Tyrrell conceived a long-term role for the council's activities:

> I do not hesitate to say that with a large part of the world in its present bewildered and excited state there never was a greater opportunity and need for us to present our own outlook on life to other countries, so that it may be thrown into the common pool as a definite contribution to whatever ideas the present and coming generations are to bring forth.[142]

This was written in March 1935. Following the British Defence White Paper and Hitler's reintroduction of conscription in Germany that month, many were preoccupied with the question of armaments and the possibility of a future military explosion. Tyrrell maintained that 'we must regard our educational and cultural forces with as much care as our armed forces'.[143] He reiterated this novel line of argument in January 1936 when he launched the British Council's appeal to the Chancellor of the Exchequer, Neville Chamberlain, for an increased grant. He wrote:

> We have much to learn from others, but we also have much to teach them. If we do not do the teaching ourselves, we shall be misunderstood and misinterpreted. If you will regard us as a body able and willing to do this educational work abroad, may I ask you also to regard us as people who are assisting practically in our national defence. Modern defence consists not only in arms but in removing misunderstanding and promoting understanding.[144]

The line of argument proved successful. A government grant of £15,000 was awarded for the year 1936–7, an increase of 200 per cent.

Tyrrell resigned the chairmanship in May 1936 to become the council's first president, a post he held until 1947. He was succeeded by Lord Eustace Percy, a former Minister of Education and recently retired minister without portfolio. Percy's appointment as chairman was in fact a reflection of the increasing 'educational' emphasis of the British Council's work. Although Percy mentioned only briefly his period at the council in his memoirs, stating that his business was 'simply to bring the Council out of its initial obscurity and win for it a respectable Treasury grant',[145] he was doing himself an injustice. During his short career at the council he succeeded in placing the

Cultural propaganda and the British Council

London headquarters on a sound administrative basis, which included a move into larger quarters in Chesham Place. He played an active role in the daily running of the work and was not content to play the role of a distinguished figurehead – 'so different from Tyrrell', observed Leeper.[146]

Percy was fully aware of the great task which lay before him, because, he wrote, 'what we have to do immediately in many of these countries is not so much to enhance British prestige as to rescue that prestige from the consequences of past neglect'. This could only be achieved, in his opinion, by a concentration on the extended use of the English language, by improving the facilities offered by British schools and libraries abroad, and by increasing the standard of English teaching and the general projection of British cultural achievements. 'There is no question of propaganda', he insisted; 'we aim at no one-sided indoctrination of other countries, but at an interchange.'[147] The aim was peace, as he explained in a council pamphlet issued in January 1937: 'the Council's policy is inspired by their belief in the decisive contribution which the character, ideals and achievements of the British people can make to the cause of peace and peaceful trade; and by the desire that the nature of this contribution shall be understood and appreciated by the rest of the world'.[148] This almost missionary conviction in the decisive role of British culture in the cause of peace is reflected throughout Percy's writings. It had become, he believed, 'a matter of life and death, not only to ourselves but to other nations, that we should be reasonably ready to wear our heart, not on our sleeve perhaps but on the other hand, not up it – at least peeping out of our shirt cuff'.[149]

Nevertheless, Percy was fully aware in 1937 that the original conception of the council's work had changed radically since its foundation. Partially attributing the change to the failure of successive financial appeals to the private and industrial sectors, and a corresponding increase in the dependency upon government funding, he observed: 'The Council is no longer expected merely to rescue British prestige from neglect; it has now to defend that prestige from deliberate attack. The political motive has become overwhelming; the "bread and butter" motive, always more shadowy, has receded into the background.' Given the worsening international situation, he continued,

The projection of Britain, 1919–1939

the effect of this change on the Council's position is almost ludicrous. It is supposed (to mention only one aspect of its work) to be doing at least something towards making good the ground of British influence in Egypt, in the Eastern Mediterranean, and in Portugal against Fascist cultural penetration; and it has to perform these tasks with resources no more than sufficient to enable it to conduct pleasant Sunday afternoons for Anglophils in Gothenburg and Helsingfors.[150]

Though the Treasury grant to the British Council had been doubled to £30,000 for 1937–8, it nonetheless remained inadequate to defend Britain against 'the moral attack which is now being directed against this country from abroad'.[151]

It can hardly be denied that the political importance of cultural propaganda had assumed greater significance with the increasing hostility of Hitler and Mussolini towards Britain. The collapse of the Stresa 'front' and the alienation of Mussolini during the Abyssinian crisis, followed by Hitler's remilitarisation of the Rhineland and the outbreak of the Spanish Civil War in 1936 were all accompanied by an intensification of anti-British propaganda. As Kenneth Johnstone, the Foreign Office's liaison officer with the British Council, argued,

> The emergence of the totalitarian state in Europe has presented us with new and urgent problems. To deal with them a new outlook is required. We are faced with competition on a formidable scale in many parts of the world, and that competition is taking new forms to which this country has hitherto been unaccustomed. One of these forms is what is commonly known as propaganda, powerfully and deliberately directed, to promote the political and commercial influence of the national state. It has during the last few years been forged into a political weapon which is already exercising a potent influence in certain areas where British interests are directly concerned, and where they are visibly suffering as a result of this new impact.[152]

Following a review of the effects of the propaganda conducted by Germany and Italy in Europe, the Middle East and South America, Johnstone concluded with a plea for a much enlarged cultural programme:

> It is particularly important to spend now, before the danger has grown to unmanageable proportions, and we must row against the tide. It is no exaggeration to say that unless we are prepared to show our concern for the world to which modern development is binding us continually closer we shall, when the need of them arises, find our present and potential friends

the unwilling but helpless allies of those who have shown their intention of making every encroachment on our power that we can be forced, or deluded, into allowing.[153]

This view, that cultural propaganda could serve as a means of retaining the friendship and trust of potential future allies, was to reappear continually during the remaining years of peace. It did not suggest any fundamental reappraisal of the council's policy — at least, not yet — but merely the provision of more funds to intensify established activities. Johnstone was 'more convinced than ever' that Britain should conduct counter-propaganda, but he believed that, ultimately, 'our best propaganda would be to govern the country well and to answer impertinences and untruths as immediately and as firmly as we can'.[154]

Whether it was because of the overwhelming evidence which suggested that Britain could no longer afford to neglect propaganda as an instrument of national policy in peacetime, or because of the growing conviction in many circles that Britain might have to face another war in the near future, and one in which she would be ill equipped to engage in psychological warfare, arguments similar to those of Johnstone were beginning to make an impact. Leeper, who considered that the only possible explanation for the continued reluctance of the Treasury to subsidise an increase in overseas propaganda was that 'new ideas are anathema to the official mind', urged that the entire question be taken from the realms of inter-departmental debate and be placed before the Cabinet 'as a matter of major policy'.[155] Vansittart agreed, adding:

It is still possible to make considerable use of our beaux yeux but they will no longer shine as they did in a naughty world, and in the business, strict business, of 'making eyes at' lesser but serviceable people, we have now very keen and efficient rivals who are already getting the better of us and will do so further if we are not prepared to help ourselves more liberally than by little departmental dollops.[156]

Anthony Eden, the Foreign Secretary, had already lodged an appeal with the Treasury for an increased British Council grant.[157] Although the Chancellor had replied advocating cautious expansion because a sudden substantial increase in the grant would involve 'a complete change in the traditional British attitude towards propaganda abroad', Chamberlain did not completely discount the possibility of such an increase.[158]

Eden and Vansittart therefore decided to redouble their efforts. The Foreign Secretary believed that a change in government policy was now 'justifiable and indeed necessary ... in view of the way the totalitarian States are undermining our position and in view of the way we are suffering in consequence of our own neglect'.[159] Vansittart appealed to Warren Fisher for closer co-operation on the whole question: 'You and I have worked so closely on rearmament questions that I ask you now to treat this other form of rearmament with the same sympathy and interest that you have always shown for our problems of defence.'[160] When, in May 1937, Chamberlain became Prime Minister and was replaced as Chancellor by Sir John Simon, who had been Foreign Secretary at the time of the council's foundation, Eden persisted in his appeals to the Exchequer. He explained: 'This work has now become of real political importance and we cannot afford to neglect it... We cannot afford to wait until the public slowly awaken to the importance of doing this work and I am not at all sure whether, when they do so awake, they will not insist that this is, as I have already said, a Government responsibility.'[161] Simon proved 'not unsympathetic' to Eden's anxiety, but although he was prepared to award a supplementary grant of £30,000 to the council, bringing its total government income to £60,000 for 1937–8, he raised the same old Treasury argument that

> Cultural propaganda seems to me to be a field in which the law of diminishing returns applies, and while a moderate expenditure carefully applied can do good, there is no better propaganda than the bad and extravagant propaganda of our rivals... In my view we should no more regard the scale of Italian propaganda as something to be equalled than we should regard its manner as a suitable model for our own.[162]

Eden reassured Simon that the Foreign Office had no intention of imitating the methods of others but would rather base its approach 'on a reasonable estimate of what our own permanent methods require us to do in the way of making ourselves understood abroad'.[163]

Eustace Percy resigned the chairmanship of the British Council in July 1937 in order to take up his appointment as rector of King's College, Newcastle. It fell to the Foreign Office to nominate his successor. The names of Sir Horace Rumbold[164] and Earl de la

Cultural propaganda and the British Council

Warr[165] were initially considered. Rumbold was an obvious candidate. As ambassador to Germany during Hitler's rise to power he had been able to witness at first hand Nazi propaganda techniques, and his more recent work on the Royal Commission of Enquiry in Palestine had enabled him to study Italian propaganda in the Middle East. He may, however, have been regarded in some quarters as too much of a diplomat in the mould of Tyrrell. On the other hand, de la Warr, lord privy seal in Chamberlain's new Cabinet, would have given the council some form of top-level representation, but it seems that the council's desire to remain apolitical ruled him out as a possibility. Instead, the appointment of Lord Lloyd of Dolobran was accepted, an event which proved to be a significant development in the early history of the British Council.

Lord Lloyd had been serving as chairman of the council's Near East Committee since 1935, and he had toured the Mediterranean in that capacity during the spring of 1937. The Near East Committee had originally been formed as an offshoot of the council's Committee on Education Abroad but had, since June 1936, been functioning as a full committee in its own right to deal with the wider problems of cultural propaganda in the Mediterranean. Lloyd was, of course, already well acquainted with the area. As a distinguished former high commissioner in Egypt, he had encountered the full force of Arab and Turkish nationalism. Prior to his tenure in Egypt, he had been an admired governor of Bombay; indeed, until 1935, Lloyd had proved to be one of the government's main opponents over India. He was regarded as a most vigorous and unbending defender of the British empire in its old form, an impression which his association with Churchill in opposition to the Government of India Bill merely served to confirm. Moreover, considering the strained nature of his relationship with the second Baldwin administration during the later part of his tenure in Egypt, combined with the fact that he was for all practical purposes dismissed by the Labour government in 1929, his appointment as chairman of the British Council may have come as a surprise to many of his contemporaries. Furthermore, he was also a passionate advocate of rearmament, having served as president of the Navy League since 1930, and there is no doubt that he saw the work of the British Council as an extension of the more conventional forms of rearmament. Despite his reputation for being abrasive, he was a man of legendary energy and a scholar of considerable distinction who had moved in influential circles for most of his political life, and he was accordingly a most valuable asset to the council in his dealings with the government, particularly as he enjoyed the friendship of the new Prime Minister, Chamberlain.

On his appointment, Lloyd immediately began to throw his immense energy and enthusiasm into the cause of cultural diplomacy and to secure for the council a still higher government grant. His first success was to obtain Chamberlain's support in backing a council appeal for funds from the private and business sectors. Chamberlain declared himself not to exaggerate 'when I say that I regard the prosecution and development of the Council's activities as of urgent national importance'.[166] The Prime Minister repeated this conviction in a parliamentary debate on foreign affairs in the Commons on 21 December 1937.[167] On the following day, Lloyd invited Eden's support in the council's forthcoming campaign for a still higher government grant and took the opportunity of 'placing on record my conviction of the vital significance of the Council's work'. He wrote:

In the fierce war of ideas to which we are inevitably, if defensively committed, we have to face, with very slender resources, expenditure by foreign countries on a vastly larger scale... If we fail to tackle the situation on a scale commensurate with its urgency, not only shall we find that all our peoples will suffer grave hurt, but serious and perhaps irreparable damage will be done to our position among the greater nations of the world.[168]

Eden forwarded Lloyd's views to the Treasury with a covering note expressing his complete agreement. He reaffirmed his belief that the work of the council was 'a vital necessity, and not merely a useful ally, in our dealings with foreign countries', and he further maintained:

It is perfectly true, of course, that good cultural propaganda cannot remedy the damage done by a bad foreign policy, but it is no exaggeration to say that even the best of diplomatic policies may fail, if it neglects the task of interpretation and persuasion which modern conditions impose. We have daily experience of what we may expect to suffer if we leave the field of foreign public opinion to our antagonists, and we must face the fact that these misrepresentation can only be countered by equally energetic actions on our part on behalf of the truth.[169]

The need for speed was only too apparent 'if we are not to find that our efforts come too late'.[170]

Cultural propaganda and the British Council

The proposal nearly to double the council's grant, bringing its government income for 1938–9 up to £110,000, was greeted by the Treasury with some alarm. One official commented that 'the rapid growth of expenditure on this service cannot but give rise to anxiety, since ... there is practically no limit to the amount that might be spent'. Moreover, he continued, the development of Britain's overseas propaganda activities 'must cause anxiety to all those who mistrust the process of casting out devils by Beelzebub. As long as it is controlled by people of moderation, our propaganda may remain harmless, though expensive; but the organisation which is being built up might be a most dangerous weapon in the wrong hands.'[171] The British Council was, he believed, 'a horribly vigorous sapling' whose rapid growth should be checked. Such objections were to no avail. Following a meeting between Lord Lloyd and Sir John Simon on 12 January 1938, at which Lloyd impressed the Chancellor with the 'strategic' importance of cultural propaganda,[172] the way was made clear for an increase in the council's grant to £130,000 for work in 1938–9.

The area which demanded the council's greatest consideration during the late 1930s was the Middle East and Mediterranean, where the problem of Italian anti-British propaganda had become acute since Mussolini's attack on Abyssinia in October 1935. However, the problem of British cultural penetration in the area had its roots in historical developments well before that time, as Sir Percy Loraine, Lloyd's successor as high commissioner in Egypt, recognised in 1933. He wrote:

> The failure of England to make use of the forty years from 1882 to 1922 to create for herself a strong cultural position in Egypt is one of the most extraordinary phenomena of our illogical Imperial story. It was partly due to Lord Cromer's inability to recognise the importance of the educational factor and to the uninspired direction of Mr. Dunlop who, for twenty years, was maintained as adviser to the Ministry of Education. It was, however, mainly due to a fundamental English inability to understand the force of ideas and the danger of leaving their shaping in the hands of others.[173]

Whereas Britain had devoted little effort to cultural activities generally – in part, perhaps, because of Loraine's latter sentiment – her rivals, chiefly France and Italy, had spent large sums of money in an attempt to establish their cultural predominance in Egypt. As a result, one American observer noted, 'In Egypt, England had an army, France an idea. England had educational control – France, a clear educational philosophy. Because the French did have such an organised philosophy, and the British did not, the French pen has proved mightier than the English sword.'[174] The intensified French efforts of the 1920s and 1930s were accentuated by the Italian injection of fascist propaganda which, particularly during the Abyssinian crisis, assumed an increasingly hostile flavour to both France and Britain. The resultant threat to Britain's strategic, political and commercial interests hardly needs labouring.[175]

Kenneth Johnstone observed that the Italians had pressed their national culture 'into political service, and cultural propaganda, exceeding its legitimate and useful function of interpreting one people to another, has become a weapon of aggression'.[176] The main themes of Italian propaganda centred on the imperial past and the future glories of Rome in the Mediterranean basin, glories which were to be achieved at the expense of rival powers. Concerned for the maintenance of Britain's strategic position, Johnstone was alarmed at the ascendancy of Italian influence in Egypt, Palestine, Malta and Cyprus. Whereas the French remained the predominant cultural influence in Egypt, at least according to Sir Miles Lampson, the ambassador in Cairo,[177] this provoked little concern so long as Anglo-French relations remained reasonably friendly. But, as will be illustrated in the following chapter, the problems caused by intensive Italian anti-British propaganda were considered to be so great that they threatened to jeopardise the success of a possible Anglo-Italian rapprochment in the winter of 1937–8.

The British Council's Near Eastern Committee attempted to tackle these problems by adopting a long-term approach with a concentration upon educational facilities for British, Maltese and Cypriot children living in troubled areas. In the absence of a sufficient number of British schools, such children had in the past been forced to attend French and Italian establishments. It was equally important to encourage the Egyptians, who, caught between French and Italian inducements, were nonetheless believed to have retained their 'foundation of goodwill' towards Britain. And yet, as Johnstone observed,

While we are admired we are not understood, and our failure to take steps to make ourselves understood is put down to weakness or indifference...

Cultural propaganda and the British Council

We cannot rely indefinitely on our general political prestige. Prestige is a matter of reputation, and reputation is founded upon such knowledge as the public can acquire. If its only source of knowledge is the distorted picture presented to it by foreign cultural propaganda from its earliest years, in the school and in the club, then our reputation will gradually dwindle until it is merely a synonym for our physical power.[178]

Although Johnstone recognised that, in the last resort, 'like can only be met with like and propaganda with propaganda', he insisted that 'there is no need for us to be aggressive'.[179] With adequate financial support, the British Council felt that it could ensure that the English language would be as widely taught as possible, which, in turn, would be the preliminary to introducing the foreigner to the British way of life through books, lectures and a broad educational framework.

It was to investigate these possible remedies that Lord Lloyd toured the Near East in 1937, 1938 and 1939. Johnstone, who accompanied him in 1937, believed that the council needed to base its work 'upon a positive rather than a negative basis', meaning that it must not be confined to counter-propaganda but must take a constructive initiative in promoting a sense of respect for Britain amongst foreigners.[180] Charles Bridge initially believed that this approach would only serve to 'cramp its effect and misinterpret its aims'.[181] But the continuing anti-British bombast of Italian propaganda demanded immediate action. The BBC entered the field by initiating the first of its foreign-language broadcasts, in Arabic, in January 1938. Meanwhile, Lord Lloyd set to work with the aid of a large anonymous donation of £50,000, intended specifically for cultural work in the Near East.

Under Lloyd's direction, the council was able to assist in the foundation of British schools in Cairo, Alexandria, Port Said and Suez catering for the children of various nationalities. Existing schools in Palestine and Transjordan also received aid. British Institutes with library and reading-room facilities were set up in many Middle Eastern towns, and in Cairo adult English classes were started. A report of Lloyd's 1938 tour maintained that the situation was 'less deplorable than it was' but that there still existed everywhere an appetite for more: 'what the Council has up to now been able to do has merely whetted the appetite for more'.[182] By September 1938 the council could claim some minor individual

The projection of Britain, 1919–1939

successes in the various parts of the world in which it operated, most notably in the Middle East and in South America. Yet it considered that its main achievement had been to recognise the areas in which there existed a genuine demand for its services:

> We have ... acted just in time to preserve our influence ... but there is always the possibility that the favourable position which we have won may be turned, from the political flank and all our gains lost. This possibility applies, of course, the whole world over... However, the outlook, from the limited and special point of view of the British Council, is for the moment, promising.[183]

The British Council may well have felt that it had good cause to feel optimistic about its future role from its own 'limited and special point of view', but the reasons are not readily apparent. The comments above were, after all, written in September 1938 when the crisis over Czechoslovakia was threatening to engulf Europe in another major war. Despite its minor successes, the council could hardly claim to have made a discernible impact on the increasingly oppressive atmosphere of the late 1930s.

In 1935, Rex Leeper had written:

> I am convinced, as most of us are, that if this country does not play its proper part in Europe, the latter will drift into war, or else into a position in which Germany is all powerful, but I do definitely cherish the hope that the influence of this country may avert war... If we could strengthen our influence very considerably ... with adequate sums at our disposal we could use our cultural work as a very definite political instrument. This work should go hand in hand with our foreign policy.[184]

This latter point was an important one. Cultural diplomacy was designed from the outset to provide a lubricant to the everyday workings of British foreign policy. If that policy failed, then so would the British Council. For, as E. H. Carr has written, 'the success of propaganda in international politics cannot be separated from the successful use of other instruments of power... It is an illusion to suppose that if Great Britain (or Germany or Soviet Russia) was disarmed and militarily weak, British (or German or Soviet) propaganda might be effective in virtue of the inherent excellence of its content.'[185] In other words, propaganda, as the servant rather than the master of diplomacy, was dependent for its success upon the realities of power from which such factors as 'influence' and 'prestige' derived.

Cultural propaganda and the British Council

Views such as Leeper's were based upon the fundamental assumption that Britain still possessed a large measure of influence in international affairs. This may well have been true, but the fact remains that, during the inter-war years, Britain was both relatively and absolutely in the process of decline. Commitments were fast becoming liabilities in the face of increasingly hostile actions on the part of Japan, Germany and Italy. The broadening gap between Britain's world-wide responsibilities and her capacity to defend the very source of her strength was repeatedly being driven home by anti-British propaganda. Moreover, Britain was vulnerable to attack, particularly from the air, in a way that she had not been before. Britain simply no longer enjoyed that position of supremacy which had enabled her to remain aloof for long periods in the past. The British Council was created partly to perpetuate the appearance of power in the minds of foreigners at a time when hostile propaganda was beginning to expose the harsh realities of Britain's decline. Although the council would not have considered itself to be in the business of mythmaking, the very fact that there was felt to be a need to project British achievements abroad was in itself symptomatic of Britain's declining influence in international affairs.

The growth of totalitarianism in Europe presented Britain with a new set of problems, not least of which was the large-scale employment of state-subsidised propaganda to further national interests and prestige. Although the effects of this development first became visible in the field of trade and commerce, it soon became apparent that democracy itself was under attack. The British Council was, in this respect, a democratic response to totalitarianism. It was for this reason that the council placed so much emphasis upon the projection of British institutions and traditions and, indeed, upon the British way of life. Nevertheless, the Europe of the dictators tended to be more apprehensive about the future, and the British Council was constantly being called upon to generate a sense of calm and stability in an apprehensive and unstable world. The areas which required special attention were self-evident by the late 1930s, and special efforts were made in central and south-eastern Europe and in the Mediterranean. The sums of money spent in those areas were admittedly slight when compared to the vast expenditure being incurred by countries such as Germany and Italy, but the council consoled itself with the belief that quality and goodwill were more than a match for quantity and aggression. It was a financially expedient argument.

In the 1930s the council did not operate in either the United States or Soviet Russia, two powers of enormous potential strength which, for different reasons, played a relatively minor role in international relations between the wars. The Americans were considered to be something of a special case by British propagandists and, given that the teaching of the English language was one of the council's cardinal aims, there was obviously less demand for such work in the United States (as in the white Dominions). The Soviet Union, on the other hand, was a difficult regime to penetrate. The same problem applied, if to a slightly lesser extent, to Nazi Germany and Fascist Italy or indeed to any totalitarian regime which exercised a rigorous system of censorship. How could the British Council tell the German or Russian or Italian people about all that was best in Britain when Nazi or communist or fascist propaganda was telling them something quite different? Besides, the British Council preferred to operate on a basis of reciprocity. The Soviet and Nazi ideologies were anathema to the British sense of democracy. The Third International and the Fifth Column were not to be presented with a legitimate basis to operate behind the cloak of reciprocal cultural relations.

Early in 1936 Leeper had considered the possibility of embarking upon a campaign of cultural relations with Germany. In seeking the advice of Sir Eric Phipps, the British ambassador in Berlin, he explained:

There are two considerations which have hitherto caused the Council to abandon any idea of systematic action and to confine themselves to arranging a few isolated events, such as lectures or concerts at Hamburg or Bonn. In the first place, it may be doubted whether, under the present system of Government in Germany, the German public would be, or would be allowed to be, sufficiently receptive to foreign cultural propaganda, even of the friendliest and least political kind. Secondly, in a country like Germany, which is geographically large and culturally among the leading powers of the world, any scheme of cultural propaganda must be widespread and of the very highest quality, and in consequence expensive, in order to have any favourable effect at all.[186]

Nevertheless, he had no desire to ostracise Germany by excluding her from a world-wide programme, and 'still less do I wish to leave

Cultural propaganda and the British Council

anything undone which might help to maintain a civilised and friendly intercourse between British and Germans, particularly if the latter sincerely desire closer contact with this country and better opportunities for making its acquaintance'.[187] Phipps, however, was opposed to an extensive propaganda campaign in Germany on the grounds that the German government would expect reciprocal facilities and, because of the German censorship, this would place the British Council at a serious disadvantage.[188]

The question was not seriously considered again until after Munich. One council official suggested that

> The recent Peace Agreement at Munich must be capitalised. England must take a positive view. While feeling between the two countries is friendly it is essential to take advantage of the situation, and to place the English point of view before the Germans. If the two countries are to live at peace, Germany must learn to appreciate British freedom (freedom of press, of speech and of institutions).[189]

It was argued that the British Council must try to provide an intellectual outlet for spiritually isolated Germans and, while appreciating that 'if the two countries are to entertain lasting sympathy for each other, their forms of Government, without necessarily being similar, must tend to approximate', he nonetheless remained optimistic that cultural propaganda could play a valuable role in promoting greater mutual understanding. He continued:

> It should be emphasised that the hands of the true friends of England in Germany, i.e. the territorial nobility and the professional middle-class, will be strengthened by methods of indirect propaganda. But speed is essential. The generation which knew liberty is growing older, and the young are in the grip of a new Nazi education. Now is the time, when friendship between these countries has burst out afresh.[190]

However, time was not on the council's side, and little was achieved in the remaining year of peace. Germany, like the Soviet Union, had little faith or respect for what the British had to offer, whether it be democracy or the guarantee to Poland.

Instead, British cultural propaganda concentrated upon those countries threatened by more powerful and aggressive neighbours. If those countries could somehow be reassured of Britain's goodwill towards them, it was believed that the smaller threatened states would not succumb to political, economic or ideological pressure. Far from criticising the British Council for not operating in the more 'important' countries,[191] the alternative thesis might be suggested that it was attempting to create a cultural ring of buffer states designed to check the further spread of ideologies and political systems which were anathema to the British point of view.

The real value of cultural relations was considered to be long term. Five years of activity, from 1934 to 1939, is thus an unfair basis on which to make a valid judgement of the council's success or otherwise.[192] Much of the council's attention was directed towards the youth of foreign societies, and educational work figured prominently in everything it undertook. It was believed that the results, often invisible, would ultimately manifest themselves, both directly and indirectly, in various forms of goodwill beneficial to Britain's national interests and prestige. This was the underlying political purpose of cultural propaganda. But Lord Lloyd's biographer, Colin Forbes Adam, was probably correct when he wrote that 'the important and melancholy fact was that the Council started far too late in the day in a race where the competitors, Germany and Italy, had several laps start and infinitely greater resources'.[193] Given that the race had started for Germany and Italy well before their totalitarian experience, in the long-term work of cultural relations their initiative was almost certainly of critical importance.

It would not be too ungenerous to suggest that the council's main achievement prior to the outbreak of the Second World War was that of survival. This was especially true of its early years when its critics had quite clearly outnumbered its supporters. Having emerged from its initial teething pains over finance and the debate over cultural or commercial emphasis, the council became a more respectable body under the direction of Lord Lloyd. This was due partly to Lloyd himself, who was the council's best possible public relations officer, partly to the growing recognition that there was a genuine demand for British cultural activity and that something had to be done to satisfy the demand or else give offence, and partly to the recruitment of political figures from the three major political parties on to the council's executive committee: Sir John Power and Sir Eugene Ramsden from the Conservative Party; Attlee and Alexander from Labour; and Sinclair from the Liberals. This all-party formula helped to dispel fears, often voiced in Labour circles, that on the one hand Lloyd was a political reactionary and,

Cultural propaganda and the British Council

on the other, the council might be used as a propaganda instrument by an unscrupulous government to sustain political power.

One of Lloyd's most lasting achievements was his ability to place the London headquarters of the council upon a sound organisational footing prior to the award of the royal charter. In 1938, he strengthened the administration by creating two posts of deputy secretary-general to assist Bridge, posts which were filled by Johnstone (whose services were made available full time by the Foreign Office) and A. J. S. White (who was transferred from the Indian Civil Service). A regional structure was designed in order to secure a more efficient concentration of effort in the various parts of the world in which the council operated. The permanent staff, which had numbered only two in 1934, totalled over forty by 1939, and new quarters were opened at Hanover Street to accommodate them. E. D. O'Brien, a journalist formerly with *The Daily Telegraph*, was appointed press officer early in 1938. His duties included the attempt to secure favourable publicity for the council and its activities and the provision of articles and photographs for insertion in the foreign press. In 1939 the council launched its own periodical, *Britain Today*, with the historian E. L. Woodward, as its editor 'to deal in a factual manner with recent events in Britain for free distribution abroad to people important in finance, commerce, industry, administration and politics'.[194] Moreover, under Lloyd's direction, the council's work not only began to gather momentum but also began to develop a life and ethos of its own, with a distinctive personality. Links with the Foreign Office remained close, but the appointment of the first of many council overseas representatives in 1938 was indicative of its growing independence.

Lloyd's influence was to remain for many years beyond his untimely death in 1941. In a speech delivered two years earlier, Lloyd summarised the principle on which the British Council's work was based in the years before the war. He said:

Our cultural influence is in fact the effect of our personality on the outside world. As a race we have too long been content to remain aloof and misunderstood. Our strength and our wealth have in the past won us respect; we have never sought sympathy or understanding... We have in many places a critical audience to convert, but our opponents' lack of discretion has worked largely in our favour. Everywhere we find people turning in relief from the harshly dominant tones of totalitarian propaganda to the less insistent but more responsible cadences of Britain.

The projection of Britain, 1919–1939

We do not force them to 'think British'; we offer them the opportunity to learn what the British think.[195]

It was Lloyd who moulded the British Council into the embodiment of those ideas conceived in the minds of Rex Leeper and Stephen Tallents, and it was his dynamism which inspired the council's work in such a way as to inject a sense of real purpose and direction into the concept of national projection. Under his guidance, cultural propaganda came to be accepted as a necessary and legitimate responsibility of the British government. That, in itself, was a most remarkable achievement.

PART THREE
Psychological rearmament, 1935–1939

Having been old fashioned for many years, I find myself unable to show enthusiasm for propaganda by this country and I still cannot bring myself to believe that it is a good substitute for calmly getting on with the business of Government, including a rational foreign policy.

(Horace Wilson, 18 January 1938. PREM 1/272)

Our politicians must realise that the days are over when publicity could be pushed into the background as an inevitable, but luckily subordinate, nuisance. They must realise that, if only on account of what other countries are doing, national publicity must be taken really seriously as an integral part of national policy.

Propaganda ... has become an essential part of military preparedness. It helped us to win the last war. In another war it would be even more important.

(Arthur Willert, 'National Advertisement', *The Fortnightly*, January 1939)

5
The BBC foreign-language broadcasts

The inadequacies and shortcomings of Britain's somewhat limited conduct of national projection overseas during the 1920s and early 1930s, which were made all the more conspicuous by the progressive escalation of totalitarian propaganda, had resulted in the establishment of the British Council in 1934. This development was significant not simply because of the attempt to rectify some of the deficiencies which had existed in the representation of Britain abroad since the dissolution of the Ministry of Information and Crewe House at the end of the First World War. The British Council was the first genuinely constructive institutional response in Britain to the increasing importance of propaganda as a factor in peacetime international affairs. Moreover, the evidence and arguments which had led to such a development continued to gather force and wider currency during the remaining five years of peace. The subject of propaganda received a measure of consideration, both within official circles and beyond, unprecedented since 1918. The issue was kept alive not only by the continuation of anti-British propaganda but also by repeated questions and debates in the House of Commons, regular attention in the press, numerous articles published in learned journals and the appearance of several books.[1] Nor was it a question of concern merely confined to the lower and middle levels of government administration. Quite the contrary, in fact, for, between 1935 and 1939, propaganda became a recurring topic of high-level and even Cabinet consideration.

Things to come

The political importance of cultural propaganda derived from its long-term aim to make Britain more widely known, understood and appreciated abroad in order to promote British interests and the cause of international peace and co-operation. However, once the

Psychological rearmament, 1935–1939

British Council had assumed responsibility from the Foreign Office for the conduct of such 'background' work, there remained an urgent need to rectify the serious deficiencies which continued to hamper the wider dissemination of British news and views for the more immediate short-term propagandist task. The British case with regard to specific issues was still not being adequately explained, with the result that British foreign policy was left open to misinterpretation by malevolant propaganda. It was towards finding a solution to this problem that Rex Leeper next turned his attention.

Readiness for war is not simply a question of armaments. It rests also upon psychological conviction. In the wake of Hitler's reintroduction of conscription in March 1935, Leeper became more convinced than ever of the threat posed to peace by Nazi Germany. In his memoirs, Anthony Eden described Leeper as 'an early prophet of the Nazi menace',[2] and the head of the News Department certainly became closely associated with the views of Vansittart in this respect. But whereas Vansittart advocated military rearmament as a means of strengthening Britain's bargaining position in the government's dealings with Hitler, Leeper urged greater official commitment to the conduct of propaganda abroad as a means of strengthening British influence in those areas which were vulnerable to German political and economic penetration. This he termed 'psychological rearmament'. By this he meant preparing the public, both at home and abroad, for the issues which he believed lay ahead.

Psychological rearmament really operated on two distinct, albeit related, levels. In the first place, Leeper recognised that he would have to persuade people at home, particularly those responsible for sanctioning expenditure on propaganda, that such work was worthwhile and indeed necessary to reinforce the more conventional forms of rearmament and to lubricate the mechanics of British diplomacy. Secondly, it meant the utilisation of propaganda to bolster British interests and the cause of democracy in foreign countries which might be called upon to act as future allies in the event of war. The former condition was a prerequisite of the latter, and Leeper was fortunate in that he enjoyed the support of both Vansittart and Eden.

It was because Leeper and Vansittart regarded Germany as the principal threat to European peace that they initially supported the appeasement of Italy over Abyssinia in an attempt to prevent Mussolini from being driven into Hitler's camp. In May 1935 Leeper wrote:

> Politics are getting very complicated. Hitler's new peace proposals will cause differences of opinion here and I shall have to show a certain native cunning in dealing with them. It is no use the F.O. being defeatist in advance, however sceptical we may feel. But the gravest complication of all is Mussolini's determination to go to war with Abyssinia. English opinion will go against Italy, and in that case Italy will leave the League. A pretty complication, all to the advantage of Germany.[3]

Britain's treatment of Italy during the Abyssinian crisis was therefore critical in their eyes. Following the departure of Sir John Simon in June 1935, and his replacement as Foreign Secretary by the unfortunate Sir Samuel Hoare, Vansittart even considered bringing the force of British opinion to bear in support of an alternative policy to League sanctions against Italy. Prior to his visit to Paris with Hoare to discuss what became known as the Hoare–Laval proposals in December 1935, he asked Leeper: 'How long will it take to alter public opinion on the Abyssinian issue?' Leeper replied that, given the prominence of the collective security issue at the recent general election, it would take at least three weeks to prepare the public mind for a negotiated settlement in place of the imposition of sanctions.[4] Although Vansittart appreciated that this was insufficient time, the public outcry which followed the premature disclosure of the Hoare–Laval proposals would seem to indicate that even Leeper's estimate was somewhat optimistic.[5]

The severity of Fleet Street's reaction to the proposals convinced Leeper that increased official guidance to the press on the issues at stake during the crisis was essential. On New Year's Day 1936, he wrote a fascinating memorandum in which he set out his views concerning the lessons to be drawn from the events of the previous year. After commenting upon the 'overwhelming body of opinion' which expected the British government to devote its wholehearted support to the League, Leeper recognised that although 'aggression must not be allowed to succeed and will therefore be opposed' it was nonetheless important 'to try to get the situation in its proper perspective'.[6] The press had not fully appreciated the implications of a hostile Italy. Leeper therefore advocated 'give and take on both sides' and argued for the 'slow and tentative' application of sanctions if the

Psychological rearmament, 1935–1939

League was to 'eliminate further acts of aggression in the future in the disputed area' of Africa. 'We must', he wrote, 'find a middle way between not rewarding and not punishing the aggressor.' He continued:

> Our main objective must be to avoid being involved in a first-class European war. It is therefore in our interest to do everything in our power to eliminate the danger of war. It is not enough to say, as do our hot-heads here, 'Back the League'; we must be certain that through our influence the League may become the proper instrument for guiding Europe from war to peace. For that reason the present Italo-Abyssinian crisis cannot be considered as something in a water-tight compartment apart from the general European or indeed the world situation.[7]

Leeper did not share the view that a League victory over Italy would deter future German aggression. Instead, he believed that British foreign policy could more profitably concentrate upon the maintenance of unity between those member states upon whom the League depended for its success while simultaneously strengthening the position of individual countries as quickly as possible in order to add weight to their support for collective security. Accordingly, a breach with France was to be avoided at all costs, while the German menace must form a major consideration in Britain's dealings with Mussolini. Leeper did not consider that this meant giving in to Italy over Abyssinia, but

> It does mean every legitimate caution to avoid war with Italy which, even if it did not spread to Europe, might so weaken England and France as to leave Germany free to dictate to the rest of Europe. Our support of the League surely cannot require us for the sake of punishing, or as some put it, not rewarding the Italian aggressor, to drive Italy into a course suicidal to herself but also dangerous to ourselves and to the rest of Europe. We can only avoid such a course by educating our own public and Geneva to accept the idea that a peace by negotiation and conciliation is the right and proper solution.[8]

While accepting that Germany did have legitimate grievances and that to keep Germany 'in a prison without attempting to remove her discontents is so negative a policy that it is bound to fail', Leeper nonetheless felt that 'it is equally foolish to hope that Germany's discontents can be peacefully allayed unless those who make the attempt are sufficiently strong to see that a proper settlement can be agreed'.[9] It was important, Leeper concluded, to make these issues clear to the press in order for them 'to sink gradually into the minds of the public so that they will accept it without propaganda or compulsion'. Reason rather than emotion must govern public opinion, while negotiation rather than aggression must govern the League's dealings with Italy and Germany.

Vansittart was 'in full agreement' with the majority of Leeper's memorandum. He minuted:

> I do not think that the public has yet begun to realise how far we now go *in theory*; nor will they until the aggressor is Germany – unless we set about things now. One will be to educate our own people, and one to educate the other non-contributive states (non-contributary in force). For, if we are to succeed, we must *all* be ready to the best of our ability not only in word but deed; and we must be ready to go eventually *in practice* as far as we at present go *in theory*. Otherwise we must fail. And we have only a very little while ahead of us to re-educate the man in many streets.[10]

Vansittart further endorsed Leeper's view that Germany would judge her own future policy not against any League victory over Italy but 'purely by the strength of the League members measured, in most material and detailed terms, against her own'. Moreover, because the League looked to Britain for its lead, British rearmament constituted an example for others to follow. It was thus essential for Britain to emphasise her determination to resist German aggression, particularly in the smaller countries most susceptible of Nazi influence, first through the process of private persuasion and, once this had been achieved, 'by something more public and impressive'. 'There is no time to lose', he continued. 'Once we have got some courage into these minor but essential races, they have got to spend their money on defence. And as *we* unfortunately know now, that can't be done in a hurry, even when the will has been pumped in.'[11] It was this combined policy of rearmament and conciliation that would eliminate the danger of future German aggression, provided, in the opinion of Leeper and Vansittart, that it was accompanied by psychological rearmament.

Leeper submitted his proposals to his new Foreign Secretary, and although there is no surviving record of Eden's reaction, there is some indication that he generally concurred at least with the spirit of Leeper's memorandum. This is illustrated by the record of a meeting held a fortnight later, on 14 January, between Leeper and Barrington-Ward, the assistant editor of *The Times*. The head of the

Psychological rearmament, 1935–1939

News Department, 'speaking for Eden and with his approval', explained that the government had recently been getting its foreign policy 'on to a basis of principle' and that the policy now favoured was 'simultaneously to rearm and to push the League principle forward in the hope of reaching a political settlement in Europe (which they believe will be possible if the Italian affair goes well) and thus to get back to arms limitation'. This, in turn, would help to restore British prestige in the Far East. Leeper added that such a policy was in general accord with public opinion, 'and that it will chime with the sentiments both of the Dominions and of the United States'.[12] Barrington-Ward observed: 'They [the Foreign Office] want to get these principles settled, though not necessarily specified in public, as to the lines of British action, and have the informed and conscious collaboration of the press in London and the provinces.'[13] The process of psychological rearmament had seemingly begun, at least at home, with the apparent support of both Vansittart and Eden.

On 27 January 1936, Leeper developed his views and set out in greater detail his proposals for the 'education' (he chose the word in deliberate preference to 'propaganda' – 'with its evil connotations') of public opinion at home and abroad. He began:

We are approaching a stage in international relations when the people of this country will have to be brought face to face with realities in a way that has not happened since the last war. We have to rearm our people not only materially, but morally. The easy-going post-war period came to an end openly and dramatically when Italy attacked Abyssinia. It really ended when Japan entered Manchuria, although Europe shut its eyes to the danger because it was far away. But when Hitler came to power in Germany and began to destroy the Versailles system, only those who were wilfully blind failed to see what was happening. Mussolini's action is but the prologue to the European drama which will be enacted in the near future. Can we prevent this drama ending in a tragedy far greater than that of 1914?[14]

Leeper noted that the Nazi Party was utilising propaganda to prepare the German people so that 'it may speak with one voice when the time for action arrives'. In Britain, by way of contrast, the public was receiving little or no guidance on the issues which it might be forced to defend. Moreover, he continued,

We must ... concentrate not only on our own rearmament, but on bringing other nations to our side and by instilling in them such confidence in our leadership and determination that they too will rearm and abandon an atti-

The BBC foreign-language broadcasts

tude of defeatism vis-à-vis Germany. But if we are to inspire them with this confidence, education must begin at home. We have no time to lose. We must be swift, bold and persistent.[15]

This was the essence of psychological rearmament. The News Department and the British Council both had a critical role to play in this context. But the time had now arrived for the government to review its position in relation to propaganda and to consider a programme fully integrated with policy requirements 'if it is to bear fruit and to bear fruit quickly'.

Leeper proposed that the News Department should serve as a nucleus for the various official, semi-official and private organisations engaged in national publicity, namely the BBC, the League of Nations Union, the British Council, the press and 'perhaps the churches', which should be mobilised to work in the cause of 'instilling a greater sense of realism' into the public. It was not his concern, he claimed, to suggest the direction which he believed the government should pursue (he had already done that in his earlier memorandum), but he maintained that 'we should proceed in order to ensure that the policy, once established, should be understood by and should penetrate as widely as possible into all classes of our own people'. 'At present', he concluded, 'there is a great deal of news available on foreign affairs, but insufficient guidance; while visibility increases, vision lags behind.'[16]

Once again, Vansittart was prepared to endorse Leeper's arguments in their entirety. He added:

What is really and ultimately at issue in the world is dictatorship or democracy, liberty or the man-machine. I am not sure that there will ultimately be room in the world for both, possibly not without a struggle of some kind, though it need not necessarily be a world-war again, or a war at all if democracy will show plainly that it can and will look after itself in the League... Meanwhile the people of this country are receiving no adequate education – indeed practically no concerted education at all – against the impending tests.[17]

It was because of this latter deficiency that Leeper and Vansittart were quite prepared to utilise the services of people who shared similar views concerning the Nazi threat – men such as Winston Churchill.[18]

Meanwhile, the Foreign Office continued its search for an agree-

Psychological rearmament, 1935–1939

ment with Germany and, on 14 February 1936, Eden proposed the acceptance of German remilitarisation of the Rhineland as part of a more comprehensive settlement.[19] Two days later, when Leo Kennedy of *The Times* called at the News Department, Leeper admitted to him that the British government did not wish to keep Germany in an indefinite position 'of inequality anywhere' and that this principle applied to the demilitarised zone.[20] Leeper further stated that the government was not pleased with the Franco-Soviet Treaty even if it did not contravene the terms of Locarno. Even so, the Berlin embassy was not anticipating a German attempt to 'jump the Rhineland'. However, when Hitler did decide to reoccupy the demilitarised zone three weeks later, the British government was again deprived of an invaluable bargaining card in its attempt to deal with a revisionist Germany from a position of equality, let alone from a position of strength.

Radio propaganda

With the effective destruction of the League's credibility following the failure of economic sanctions, and the further estrangement of Italy from the Stresa Front following the outbreak of the Spanish Civil War, the realisation that Britain might have to face another major war in the near future began to gain wider currency. Leeper fully appreciated that the disappointing progress of British rearmament transferred the diplomatic initiative into Hitler's hands, and he saw in psychological rearmament a means of checking the growth of German influence in Europe. As Hitler moved from strength to strength, each success being driven home by an ebullient propaganda machine, the inadequacies of British attempts to explain and justify her cause in the name of democracy became increasingly apparent. Although the British Council worked towards the projection of British civilisation for the promotion of international co-operation in the long term, there was still no concerted British attempt to secure publicity for issues of immediate concern, despite the work of the Foreign Office News Department. If Britain's actions were to be understood, they had first to become known.

Of particular concern was the increased use of radio as an instrument of international propaganda. The potential of radio as an

The BBC foreign-language broadcasts

instrument of communication between different peoples had long been appreciated; Marconi had considered it 'the greatest weapon against the evils of misunderstanding and jealousy'.[21] This might well have been true, but Marconi's opinion was based upon an optimistic view of human nature. In the twentieth century, the age of the politicised masses, radio provided an ideal instrument of political propaganda, particularly in the hands of the dictatorships. During the inter-war years, the lofty BBC ideal that 'Nation shall speak peace unto Nation' gradually gave way to the exploitation of broadcasting as an instrument of nationalistic expansion and aggressive diplomacy. At first, in the 1920s, radio was used only periodically in international disputes. During the Franco-Belgian invasion of the Ruhr in 1923, for example, a 'radio war' did develop between Berlin and the Eiffel Tower station. The German government again used radio during its dispute with Poland over the Upper Silesian question, which finally resulted in 1931 in a broadcasting 'non-aggression pact' between the two countries.[22] By the 1930s, however, broadcast propaganda became a regular feature of international relations, greatly facilitated in the process by the advent of short-wave transmission, which served to extend the range of radio to a world-wide arena.

The new Nazi regime in Germany was largely responsible for developing radio as a political instrument, capitalising upon the lessons and techniques already pioneered by the Soviet Union. Not only was radio used to foster the spirit of Pan-Germanism among the *Auslandsdeutsche* while at the same time spreading the doctrine of national socialism, but it was also employed in helping to make the nascent regime more acceptable abroad before it embarked upon a more ambitious foreign policy.[23] Prior to the Saar plebiscite in January 1935, radio propaganda transmitted from the Zeesen station was used to great effect.[24] It was a characteristic feature of Austro-German relations between 1934 and 1938.[25] The successful alliance of radio propaganda and totalitarian ideology in the name of the new *Weltanschauung* was a lesson quickly learned by Fascist Italy.

The special qualities which made radio such an effective instrument of national propaganda were essentially quite simple. It relied upon the spoken word and was thus more direct in approach and personal in tone than any other available medium. It was also immediate and extremely difficult to prevent. It was capable of reaching large numbers of people, regardless of their geography, literacy, political and ideological affiliation, or social status. Furthermore, because there were no territorial limitations to its range, radio enabled the propagandist of one nation to speak to large numbers of people abroad *from the outside* – a quality which was of critical importance in any attempt to influence the audience of a closed society, as in a dictatorship. These peculiar characteristics were clearly illustrated during the Spanish Civil War, an experience which provided an illuminating insight into the future role of broadcasting in wartime.[26]

Whereas the totalitarian regimes utilised radio in the cause of nationalistic expansion, the League of Nations, conversely, was more concerned with the value of broadcasting in the cause of peace. E. H. Carr has pointed out that propaganda 'was first raised to the dignity of a universal issue when the Polish Government made proposals to the Disarmament Conference for a convention on "moral disarmament"'.[27] As a result of this initiative, on 24 September 1931, the League Assembly requested member states to encourage the use of radio to 'create better mutual understanding between peoples'.[28] In the meantime, the Assembly requested the International Institute for Intellectual Co-operation to investigate 'all the international questions raised by the use of broadcasting in regard to good international relations'.[29] Throughout 1932 and 1933, a committee of experts worked on drafting an international broadcasting convention and, after several amendments, a special League of Nations conference was convened at Geneva in September 1936 to consider the final document. The outcome was the League's International Convention concerning the Use of Broadcasting in the Cause of Peace. This convention bound the signatories to prevent the transmission of material, 'which to the detriment of good international understanding, is of such a character as to incite the population of any territory to acts incompatible with the internal order or the security of a territory of a High Contracting Party'.[30] The convention also attempted to outlaw the transmission of aggressive propaganda, deliberate misstatements, and incitements to war or insurrection. Instead, radio was to be used 'to promote a better knowledge of the civilisation and the conditions of life in one country, as well as of the essential features of the development of its relations with other peoples and of its contribution to the organisation of peace'.[31]

The importance of the convention lay more in the spirit of its intent than in its effect. The articles were framed in such a way as to prohibit only manifestly serious offences; there remained sufficient room for manoeuvre by any signatory wishing to broadcast propaganda. Moreover, Britain, France and the Soviet Union were the only Great Power signatories.[32] The absence of the two countries whose propaganda was at that time causing the most serious concern, Germany and Italy, rendered the convention virtually meaningless. Because, by 1936, the success of the League was seen to be determined by the degree to which its professed aims coincided with the national interests of its most powerful members, the success of the Broadcasting Convention depended on the degree to which those interests were suffering at the hands of hostile propaganda. In this respect, even the British government was forced to reappraise its attitude towards broadcast propaganda with the dramatic escalation of anti-British Italian propaganda during the Abyssinian crisis.

Sir John (later Lord) Reith, the director-general of the BBC, had long been aware of the potential value of overseas broadcasting, but although experiments had been conducted as early as 1927, the BBC was unable to inaugurate its Empire Service until December 1932. The service, which was transmitted in English, was designed to keep the scattered Dominions and expatriates in constant touch with the mother country and to ensure that British overseas communities were kept reliably and regularly informed of events in Britain.[33] Reith also appreciated that the new service was a valuable addition to the projection of Britain abroad, not least because the transmission could be received in almost any part of the world.[34] It therefore became important for the BBC to establish a close liaison with the Foreign Office, although this was hampered during the early 1930s by a series of clashes concerning the BBC's coverage of foreign affairs.[35] Despite the establishment of a liaison in 1930 for the purpose of the News Department supplying information to the corporation on lines similar to those which already existed for the press,[36] a degree of tension remained, and it was not until 1934 that relations between the two bodies were improved.[37] An American observer considered that the effect of this latest arrangement had been to convert the BBC's news coverage into 'a constant flow of

Psychological rearmament, 1935–1939

reports from government departments [which] amounts to gentle propaganda in favour of things as they are'.[38] Whatever the validity of this statement, the consequent easing of tension undoubtedly made greater co-operation possible when the question of foreign-language broadcasts was first raised in 1935 and 1936.

The development of the German short-wave propaganda broadcasts over the previous few years had provided a point of common concern for the BBC and the Foreign Office. When, to this, was added the problem of Italian medium-wave broadcasts from the Bari station during the Abyssinian crisis, the inadequacy of the Empire Service to disseminate British news and views in order to combat the effects of anti-British propaganda became all too apparent. Even Reith admitted that the service 'was efficient, but nothing like sufficient'.[39] Much of this was due, as one writer had observed, to the fact that 'the Imperialist function, the upper-class bias and tone of the Empire Service narrowed down its appeal to those that shared that same patriotic confidence in Britain's role'.[40] Accordingly, both the Foreign Office and the Dominions Office were quite prepared to support the BBC's appeal to expand and extend the service when the Ullswater Committee on Broadcasting convened in October 1935.[41]

The Ullswater committee's report, published in February 1936, provided the main stimulus to the increasing demand for some form of British response to the foreign-language services of rival powers. It stated in part:

> We attach great importance to the maintenance and development of the Empire Service. The world-wide transmissions of broadcasts by His Majesty the King George V at Christmas and the Jubilee celebrations have been outstanding examples of the importance of linking the Empire by broadcasting, and interest in the day-to-day programmes is constantly growing. There has been a conspicuous development of broadcasting in English by certain foreign countries, and these services are received in all parts of the British Empire. It is all the more important that what has been called 'the projection of England' should be effectively carried out by a steadily developing Empire service of our own... In the interests of British prestige and influence in world affairs, we think that the appropriate use of languages other than English should be encouraged.[42]

As Asa Briggs has observed, talk of empire broadcasting as an extension of 'sentimental ties' was gradually giving way to talk of the need to project England.[43]

The BBC foreign-language broadcasts

The problem of Italian propaganda in the Near East and Mediterranean region was one which occupied much of the British Council's attention between 1935 and 1938. The Bari broadcasts, combined with short-wave transmissions from the 2 RO 4 station at Rome, exploited existing tensions and grievances in this vital area of British interests, such as in Palestine, by portraying Britain as the imperialistic oppressor while the Duce was held up as the protector of Islam.[44] The British empire was portrayed as 'decadent' and the Royal Navy as 'a museum piece' while special emphasis was placed upon the past and future glories of Rome. Broadcasting in seven languages, including English, Greek and Arabic, the Italian radio programmes were carefully structured and presented by Arab employees with a command of local dialects. Music by Verdi alternated with stories of British atrocities. Receiving sets locked on to Italian frequencies were distributed among the Arabs free of charge, thereby ensuring a captive audience.[45] 'Never before in times of peace', wrote one observer, 'had such a sustained campaign of invective and abuse been launched by one country against a supposedly friendly power.'[46] The need for countermeasures was apparent and urgent.

In June 1936, a BBC memorandum entitled 'The Use of Languages, other than English, in the Empire Broadcasting Service', was distributed by the Foreign Office to its overseas representatives in an attempt to ascertain their views concerning the desirability of foreign-language broadcasts in their respective areas.[47] The replies indicated strong support for the idea of broadcasts in Arabic for the Near East and in Spanish and Portuguese for South and Central America.[48] As a result, the Foreign Office began to formulate its proposals for the inauguration of the foreign-language broadcasts, supported by the Colonial and India Offices and, of course, by the BBC. The Dominions Office proved more cautious. Sir Harry Batterbee, the assistant under secretary of state for Dominions affairs, warned that, with the single exception of the official in New Zealand, Britain's high commissioners feared that the introduction of foreign-language broadcasts into the Empire Service would impair the confidence and credibility of Dominion listeners in that service.[49] The BBC agreed. A report of March 1937 stated:

> To introduce foreign languages into the Empire Service would ... inevitably prejudice the integrity of the Service. The Service would be addressing

part of its programmes specifically to foreign countries: it would, *pro tanto*, be indulging in propaganda: and in doing so, it would lose its present indisputable title to be called an Empire Service.[50]

Accordingly, this question was discussed at an inter-departmental conference held at the BBC on 13 April 1937. Leeper stated that he would prefer to keep the proposed broadcasts separate from the Empire Service, but the Foreign Office felt that foreign languages '*should* be introduced, by whatever method might be necessary'.[51] He was more concerned at this stage that something should be done urgently before the impending publication of the Palestine report than with haggling with the BBC over technical details, which he considered 'foolish... One would think from the BBC attitude that there was no international crisis at all.'[52] Vansittart agreed that 'the thing has *got* to be done and done quickly'.[53] The success of the broadcasts would, in Leeper's opinion, depend upon the quality and accuracy of the news, which, he felt confident, 'would be such as to allay any suspicion of propaganda'.[54] The BBC eventually decided that the foreign-language broadcasts must be kept separate from the Empire Service and appointed a special sub-committee to determine how this could be done.

While the BBC worked out the details of separate broadcasts during the summer of 1937,[55] the Foreign Office decided to push ahead with its own scheme – one which excluded the BBC from its plans. Prompted by the urgency of the situation in the Mediterranean, and by the continued concern of Parliament in the subject of Italian anti-British propaganda,[56] the Foreign Secretary prepared a memorandum on the question of Arabic broadcasts for consideration by the Cabinet. Eden pointed out that the Bari broadcasts, 'even if they are not taken at their face value and occasionally even excite ridicule by their exaggeration, do by their very persistence end by creating, if not a feeling in favour of Italy, at least a prejudice against Great Britain'. He continued:

> The time has now come when some more positive steps should be taken than that of asking the Italians to desist. Without attempting to imitate the tone or the methods of Bari, it is essential for His Majesty's Government to ensure the full and forcible presentation of the British view of events in a region of such vital importance.[57]

He therefore made a formal request for the immediate inauguration of medium-wave broadcasts in Arabic. The reasons for proposing

The BBC foreign-language broadcasts

medium-wave transmissions were that, although the number of private listeners in the Middle East remained small, the size of the potential audience to be reached was immeasurable because most cafés (the usual communal centres for the exchange of news in nomadic societies) possessed medium-wave receiving sets capable of tuning in to Bari but incapable of receiving the BBC's short-wave empire signals from Daventry. Moreover, medium-wave sets were less expensive, and the only two radio stations in the Arabic world capable of undertaking the task, at Cairo and Jerusalem, possessed only medium-wave transmitters. But because, for political reasons, it would be unpractical to utilise Cairo, and because Jerusalem was in mandated territory, Eden proposed the construction of a government medium-wave station in Cyprus at a cost of £50,000. During the nine-month period needed to build the official station, Jerusalem would be asked to undertake the counter-propagandist broadcasts prepared in the Foreign Office by a specially appointed Arabic expert. There was no mention of the possibility of requesting the BBC to perform the task, although the BBC appears to have been unaware that its services would no longer be required.

The Cabinet considered Eden's proposals at its meeting on 31 July 1937. The appointment of an Arabic expert to the News Department was approved, and it was further decided to set up a special Cabinet committee to examine the viability of a government station in Cyprus.[58] In the meantime, the temporary scheme for the transmission of Arabic news bulletins from Jerusalem was authorised to begin from the end of August.[59] These decisions marked a major, if hardly noticed, departure from traditional government policy with regard to political propaganda overseas. They were certainly unnoticed by the BBC, which continued to work out the technical details of its own foreign-language service.

The Kingsley Wood committee

Such was the sheer volume of evidence in favour of Britain embarking upon radio propaganda in the Near and Middle East that it now outweighed any possible – and indeed probable – criticism. Nevertheless, in anticipation of such criticism, the Foreign Office had already prepared its case to allay the fears of critics. One statement in particular is worthy of extended quotation for the insight it gives into the direction of official thinking during the summer of 1937:

> Some anxiety has been expressed at our engaging on a wireless war with Italy in the Near East. This appears to misunderstand the object we have in view. It is the considered view of His Majesty's Government that British material rearmament is the best guarantee for European peace during the next few years. Our weakness is a temptation to the aggressor not only to attack us but to attack others. In the same way any failure on our part to present our case properly in the Near East is not only a temptation to Italy to exploit our difficulties among peoples who have little or no access to the real facts of the situation, but also tends to undo the effect of our rearmament in a part of the world where our interests are very vitally concerned. We have no intention of imitating the methods of the Bari broadcasts by abusing or misrepresenting Italy or any other country. Our object is solely to maintain a reliable service of British news and see to it that false or malicious reports are not left unchallenged. There is no more reason to suggest that this policy will lead to a War on the Air than that our rearmament will lead to a war in Europe. If the contemplated news service in Arabic is properly conducted, it should have a steadying effect and on the principle that good news drives out bad should diminish rather than increase the tension in the Middle East.[60]

Having accepted the principle of foreign-language broadcasts, it remained to determine whether the government or the BBC should conduct them. Despite the avowed uncontroversial tone of the broadcasts, the Foreign Office suggested that the very fact that such broadcasts were taking place 'automatically discredits those who employ them' and, consequently, 'the only result of this departure will be to cast doubt on the veracity of His Majesty's Government or the British Broadcasting Corporation, whichever is responsible'.[61] On this point, the Foreign Office considered that there was both a positive and a negative response:

> The negative answer is that, if we keep silence, the result is not that we are respected for our integrity and reserve, but that we are ignored in favour of those who take the trouble to express their views. The positive answer is that good news drives out bad. We must assume ... that the news service which we provide will be impartial, authoritative and up to date, and that reasonable utterances of this kind will in the end be more listened to and believed than pronouncements which are obviously partial, and will be better understood than an ambiguous silence.[62]

The BBC, which was informed only on 11 August that its services would not be required for the Arabic broadcasts but that it might

The BBC foreign-language broadcasts

still be called upon to undertake Spanish and Portuguese transmissions, considered that the Foreign Office had merely suggested the Latin American service 'as a "smoke-screen", i.e. to disguise the anti-Italian intention which would have stood out so obviously if broadcasts in Arabic had been introduced alone'.[63] As later events were to prove, this judgement was not far wide of the truth. After all, if the professed aim of the Foreign Office was to broadcast impartial news, then why was the BBC not considered to be a suitable instrument for this purpose?

The Cabinet Committee on Arabic Broadcasting held its first meeting on 15 September 1937 under the chairmanship of Sir Kingsley Wood, minister of health but soon to become secretary of state for air. Present were senior officials from the Treasury and the Dominions, Colonial and India Offices, as well as the lord privy seal, Earl de la Warr; F. W. Phillips, director of telecommunications at the GPO; Sir Alexander Cadogan, shortly to replace Vansittart as permanent under secretary at the Foreign Office; A. S. Calvert, the Arabic expert who had recently joined the News Department; and Christopher Warner, also from the News Department. The BBC, however, was not invited to take part, a decision 'in regard to the wisdom and efficacy of which' Reith had 'considerable misgivings'.[64] This was partly because the BBC had launched an internal enquiry into the entire issue under the direction of C. A. L. Cliffe, the director of overseas programmes, whose report had attempted to determine whether or not propaganda in foreign languages had any appreciable influence on the listeners to whom it was directed. That report recognised that there was no categorical answer to this question:

> On the one hand, it may be urged that repeated propaganda of a blatant type, such as the Italian, can have no lasting influence on the intelligent [Footnote: 'It is the "intelligent listener" that the Foreign Office, on their own admission, are particularly anxious to reach...'] listener, who will realise that the constant stories of the infallibility and might of Italy cannot *all* be true, and will so come to discredit other news from the same source. Or is this attributing too much intelligence to the average listener? On the other hand, there is evidence at any rate of a general belief in the efficacy of foreign language broadcasts, furnished by the fact that new countries are constantly entering this field, a recent and notable addition being the Americans.[65]

Psychological rearmament, 1935–1939

With such experience at its disposal, as an irritated Reith commented, the Kingsley Wood committee would have to approach the BBC sooner or later: 'Meanwhile, the politicians and civil servants could sit and ask each other questions which only the BBC could answer.'[66]

The initial exclusion of the BBC was, in fact, deliberate. The Foreign Office had moved away from the original intention to conduct the Arabic broadcasts through the Empire Service and was now considering them the responsibility of the News Department. Indeed, on 17 September 1937, Calvert had begun to compile and despatch Arabic news bulletins to the Jerusalem medium-wave station for translation and transmission.[67] This temporary arrangement was to operate until the Cyprus station was erected, when broadcasting would begin on lines similar to those which already existed at Hong Kong and Ceylon.[68] It was maintained that the Arabic broadcasts should remain a responsibility of the government, because 'it would be a new departure to pay the BBC to send out political broadcasts' and that the BBC's cherished reputation for impartiality and its 'independent status' would suffer 'by saying what the Government told them to say'.[69] As Leeper explained when he attended the second meeting of the Kingsley Wood committee on 30 September,

> this country was being attacked and lies were being broadcast about our activities. It was essential that these should be dealt with. Although the Foreign Office had not the least intention of indulging in blatant propaganda of a virulent or offensive type and were fully seized with the advantages of restrained and sober corrective statements and the more suitable forms of counter-propaganda, it was inevitable that the messages for the Arabic broadcasts might, from time to time, be a subject of controversy. It was for this reason that the Foreign Office did not wish to ask the BBC to undertake responsibility for them.[70]

This was a significant admission, and although the committee did not challenge the assumption that the British government ought to embark upon broadcast propaganda, discussion invariably lapsed into debate concerning the nature and tone of that propaganda.

At the first two meetings of the Kingsley Wood committee, much time was devoted to consideration of possible sites for the proposed new station. There were three choices: Cyprus, India and Palestine. The latter was the first to be eliminated on political grounds.

The BBC foreign-language broadcasts

Warner presented the Foreign Office's objections: 'At Cyprus ... the British Government would be in a position, if they wished to do so, to say something which might be unpalatable to another country and face the consequences, but at Jerusalem they would have to be continually bearing in mind the restrictions arising out of the mandatory position.'[71] Although, following closer scrutiny of the mandatory position, it was discovered that there was nothing in the terms to prevent the broadcasting of an accurate news service,[72] the uncertain future position and the potentially explosive situation of Palestine made it a less desirable location. Moreover, the Foreign Office introduced a new consideration into the debate, namely that it had become important to begin broadcasting in short-wave in order to cover a much wider area than was at present possible from the medium-wave station at Jerusalem. This factor proved decisive in converting the Treasury from its preference for the cheaper alternative of Palestine. Having accepted the need for short-wave transmissions, the India Office was requested to examine the possibility of a site at a distance more suited to this purpose. Meanwhile, preliminary enquiries were to be made regarding the BBC's willingness to undertake news broadcasts in Spanish and Portuguese.[73]

When the committee convened for a second time, India was rejected as a possible site on financial as well as on political grounds. In order to reach Palestine and Syria from India, a short-wave station of some 500 kilowatts would be required, and this would cost approximately £200,000 to build, as compared with a 50-kilowatt station broadcasting on the medium-wave from Cyprus, which could be erected at a cost of only £50,000. The former would require at least two years for completion, whereas a station at Cyprus could be ready before the end of 1938.[74] The Indian government was also unwilling to help finance a project that would have little direct relevance to Indian subjects, while the future position of such a station would remain uncertain if federation was introduced. The existing Anglo-Indian tension provided another objection. Moreover, the project would cut right across the Indian government's existing plans for the development of a broadcasting service in that country. Finally, some doubts were expressed as to the possible effects of broadcast propaganda concerning questions of policy in Palestine which might offend Indian Muslims.[75.]

The third choice, and that most favoured by the Foreign Office from the outset, was Cyprus. But, here again, there were serious objections, chiefly of a technical nature. Although a station in the Mediterranean would be cheaper to build than in India and would also be more accessible to Foreign Office control (Cyprus being undisputed British territory), it would still prove an expensive project, particularly in regard to maintenance costs (as the Treasury constantly reminded the committee), and problems of control would remain.[76] More significantly, whereas India lay at an ideal distance for short-wave broadcasts to the Middle East, Cyprus was too near, because it was in the nature of short-wave transmission that it could not be received *within* a distance of a few hundred miles. This meant that short-wave broadcasts from Cyprus would not be received in northern Egypt, Palestine, Syria and Lebanon, although these areas were currently being served by the medium-wave station at Jerusalem. Conversely, if a medium-wave station was erected in Cyprus, its range would not be sufficient to reach areas beyond a distance of some 300 miles. Hence the signals would not be received in Iraq, the Persian Gulf, most of Arabia, southern Egypt and the Sudan. In short, Cyprus was unsuitable for broadcasts in Arabic because it was too near for short-wave transmission and yet too distant for medium-wave.

On further investigation it was discovered that there were more short-wave receiving sets in the Middle East than was at first believed, but the logical Foreign Office appeal for the construction of both a short-wave and a medium-wave transmitter in Cyprus[77] was dismissed by the Kingsley Wood committee on the grounds of expense, despite the possibility of also utilising Cyprus for the Latin American broadcasts. Because the Spanish and Portuguese broadcasts would largely consist of news, whereas the Arabic service would be more obviously propaganda, it was felt that it was essential to keep the two services quite separate so that the one did not impair the credibility of the other. The BBC remained the most natural authority to conduct news bulletins, but an alternative site for the Arabic propaganda station still had to be found. Possible stations in Uganda and Aden were dismissed as unsuitable,[78] and the committee was thus forced to come around to considering the possibility of broadcasting in Arabic from the United Kingdom.

Kingsley Wood was among the first to point out that there would be severe opposition to the operation of a government propaganda

The BBC foreign-language broadcasts

radio station in Britain, and that the BBC would not tolerate such a role should it be asked to conduct the work.[79] Even so, a short-wave station in Britain would be capable of reaching both the Middle East and South America, and it would provide a prestigious base for the broadcasts. Given the broadcasting monopoly, however, it was inconceivable that any authority other than the BBC would undertake the work, particularly as it already possessed short-wave transmitters at Daventry as well as five years of experience with the Empire Service. Nevertheless, the Dominions Office remained opposed to the Empire Service facilities being used for foreign-language broadcasts on the grounds that the credibility and development of the service would be jeopardised. The Dominions Secretary, Malcolm MacDonald, wrote:

> At present the Service enjoys great prestige, because it appears devoid of any suggestion of 'propaganda'. The Dominions would be quick to resent propaganda as such; and there is just a danger that if the BBC should embark upon foreign broadcasts suspicions would be aroused that this was the prime object of the whole service.[80]

The BBC, on the other hand, had already responded positively to preliminary enquiries concerning its willingness to undertake broadcasts in Spanish and Portuguese provided that they were to be restricted to news.[81] If the same co-operation was to be extended for the Arabic broadcasts, it was likely that the BBC would specify similar conditions concerning news rather than propaganda, in which case the Foreign Office's conception of the Arabic service would be fundamentally altered.

It was largely for this reason that the Foreign Office regarded the broadcasts in Arabic and in Spanish and Portuguese as two entirely separate propositions. The News Department remained only too aware that its British Official News Service was not sufficient to combat the intensive anti-British propaganda being conducted in South America. Nor had Reuters been able to make much of an impression. The Foreign Office believed that the BBC could play an important role because news bulletins in Spanish and Portuguese from such a respected source 'would certainly attract a number of listeners, and would certainly attract all those seriously interested in international affairs and whose opinion, even if they were not many in number, we should particularly wish to influence'.[82] Leeper subsequently elucidated the vital distinction between the tone and content of the proposed services:

> The Spanish and Portuguese speaking communities of South America were highly sophisticated and 'westernised' peoples and of an entirely different mentality and outlook from the Arabs. News broadcasts to Arabs, therefore, would need special treatment by a method of selection and omission – selections of such items of news as it was in the interest of this country to broadcast to the widest possible Arabic speaking audience, and the omission of news which, in the view of the Foreign Office, it would be inadvisable should it receive the emphasis that broadcasting by wireless would give. This was an innocent form of propaganda, but it was propaganda and as such was hardly suitable for the BBC.[83]

Although the Foreign Office would attempt to adhere to objectivity and impartiality, Leeper considered the difference in treatment a matter of 'cardinal importance'. It was essential to make an immediate start, and because the Foreign Office did not feel that there was 'anything degrading in using the most effective and most modern means of making ourselves understood', it was quite prepared to leave the South American broadcasts to the BBC. Much, however, would depend upon the attitude of the BBC itself, and it was for this reason that representatives of the BBC were invited to attend the third meeting of the Kingsley Wood committee on 4 October.

The corporation was represented by Reith, R. C. Norman (the chairman), Sir Noel Ashbridge (controller of engineering) and C. G. Graves (controller of programmes). Only the latter doubted the wisdom of foreign-language broadcasts on the grounds that they would seriously damage the reputation and prestige of the BBC. Reith summarised the arguments for and against as follows:

> Arguments in favour of foreign languages were chiefly of the 'why not' order: English lethargy; the English language not understood; foreign inaccuracies not contradicted; other countries were increasingly broadcasting languages other than their own, and even inhabitants of Empire territory were affected; a good deal that was unfriendly and untrue was broadcast, but no doubt some of the propaganda was so crude that it defeated its own object; constant dripping, however, wears away a stone.
> Arguments against: prestige; that our hands would be soiled and present high reputation would be tarnished by adopting the practice of other countries; it was a credit to England that there were not broadcasts other than in English today; the discredit of other countries would be transferred

The BBC foreign-language broadcasts

to England, to the BBC, and even to the existing Empire Service (there had even been suspicions in the Dominions when the Empire Service started); finally, it could not be undertaken as an experiment and then dropped.[84]

The arguments in favour were, in his opinion, more convincing, and he declared the BBC's willingness to undertake the Spanish, Portuguese and Arabic broadcasts, 'but in its own way'.[85] Norman then laid down six conditions: (1) the foreign-language broadcasts must not be allowed to impair the Empire Service, either in its present form or its future expansion; (2) if short-wave transmissions were to begin from the United Kingdom, they must be the responsibility of the BBC; (3) the new service must be done on a considerable scale and properly conducted, as a poor service would result in a loss of prestige; (4) something more than news bulletins would be required if listeners were to be attracted; (5) the Treasury would have to meet the cost, because domestic listeners could not be expected to pay for a foreign service out of their licence fees; (6) the BBC must enjoy the same freedom vis-à-vis its relationship with the government as with the Home Service.[86]

Leeper, who was pleasantly surprised by the BBC's attitude, stated that Reith and Norman had dispelled many of the Foreign Office's apprehensions. There were no immediate technical difficulties, although Reith did warn that two additional transmitters would eventually be required at a cost of £100,000. Nevertheless, there remained the delicate issue of the BBC's relationship with the Foreign Office. The BBC insisted that it must retain control over the broadcasts and 'not become merely the organ of the Government for broadcasting to the world'.[87] On the other hand, although party political criticism was not expected at home, the Foreign Office argued that because the broadcasts might raise serious questions concerning Britain's relations with other countries it should command an element of control in their compilation. The BBC conceded this point and stated that it would be possible to conduct the work according to its own standards while at the same time meeting the desiderata of the Foreign Office without a threat to its independence. With this assurance, the Foreign Office finally abandoned its preference for a government station in Cyprus.[88]

Kingsley Wood produced his report on 22 October. It was based almost entirely upon the discussions which had taken place in his committee during its first three meetings. He proposed the abandon-

Psychological rearmament, 1935–1939

ment of the Cyprus station and the transmission of foreign-language programmes from Britain by the BBC. Relations with the Foreign Office were to be embodied in the form of a 'gentleman's agreement', while the greater part of the cost of the new service would be borne by the Exchequer.[89] The report was considered by the Cabinet a week later and accepted in its entirety.[90] It was also decided that if a dispute occurred because the BBC refused to transmit material prepared by the Foreign Office, 'power remained for the Government to insist, though in that case the BBC were entitled to state that their announcement was made at the request of the Government'. By the same token, the government retained the right to prohibit any material desired by the BBC.[91] The so-called gentleman's agreement was later agreed on an oral basis, rather than in the exchange of letters first contemplated,[92] a decision which certainly pleased Warren Fisher, who congratulated Reith on resisting the Foreign Office's desire for something more tangible.[93] Meanwhile, the momentous decision was announced in the House of Commons.[94] Reith was triumphant; in his memoirs he described the new departure under the sub-title 'Projection at last'.[95]

Nothing but the truth?

Such was the obvious need for British overseas propaganda, particularly in the eastern Mediterranean, that by the winter of 1937–8 there were few objections to the proposed new measures. Indeed, it provided an issue on which the major political parties were united in their support. Clement Attlee, the leader of the Opposition, stated in the Commons that Italian propaganda was 'a form of warfare that attacks this country, attacks democracy, attacks all the ideals for which this country stands' and fully endorsed the government's plans to counteract it.[96] Prime Minister Chamberlain maintained:

> His Majesty's Government fully realise that ... the old stand-upon-your-dignity methods are no longer applicable to modern conditions and that, in the rough-and-tumble of international relations which we see today, it is absolutely necessary that we should take measures to protect ourselves from constant misrepresentation.[97]

The changing official attitude towards British participation in

The BBC foreign-language broadcasts

propaganda abroad, as reflected in these statements, was a significant development not only for the general concept of national projection but also in the process of psychological rearmament.

In the immediate short term, the repercussions were dramatic. During the negotiations for an Anglo-Italian rapprochement in the winter of 1937–8, the British government insisted that the cessation of Bari's hostile propaganda was an essential prerequisite to a political agreement.[98] This episode illustrated the important degree to which the British government now regarded propaganda as a factor in international affairs. The decision to make the termination of anti-British propaganda a condition of the negotiations was made after two months of monitoring the Bari broadcasts by the Foreign Office,[99] when the fundamental difference between the British and the Italian conception of propaganda had become apparent. The Foreign Office maintained that its work was based upon two basic assumptions:

(a) A full and forcible presentation of British news and views, especially of matters redounding to the credit of Great Britain and the Empire, recorded objectively and factually, though favourably by a process of selection and omission, and (b) a strict disregard of the propagandist activities of other countries, except in so far as actual misstatements, damaging to the interests of this country, necessitate immediate challenge and confutation.[100]

Italian propaganda, on the other hand, was designed

not so much to project, for the enlightenment of listeners in the Near and Middle East, the achievements of Italy at home in her social, economic and industrial life [which presumably would have been more acceptable] as to throw upon events abroad a light calculated to distort their true significance, and to emphasise selected features to the point of exaggeration at the expense of this and other countries.[101]

In reality, however, the difference between the Italian and the Foreign Office interpretation was slight. It involved merely a difference of emphasis. That the Foreign Office placed so much emphasis upon the 'process of selection and omission' was a clear indication that what it had in mind was propaganda by any definition.

The BBC's Arabic Service was inaugurated at Broadcasting House on 3 January 1938 in full ceremony and amidst a blaze of publicity.

Psychological rearmament, 1935–1939

The British press generally welcomed the new broadcasts. For example, in a leading article entitled 'News on the Air', *The Times* went to great lengths to emphasise the factual content of the service, disclaiming that it could be described as 'propaganda, properly so called'.[102] The Italian media were predictably hostile, referring to 'the British Wireless War against Italy'[103] conducted by 'Radio Eden'.[104] However, the Arabic Service was very nearly a disaster from the first broadcast. A news bulletin announced the execution of a Palestinian Arab for carrying a revolver and provoked considerable alarm both at home and in the Middle East. Leeper was furious. Not only was the BBC helping the Italians in their anti-British campaign but it also appeared to have completely disregarded the Foreign Office's insistence upon the careful selection and omission of news items that would excite Arab audiences. He minuted:

> 'Straight news' (a BBC expression) must not be interpreted as including news which can do us harm with the people we are addressing. That seems to me to be sheer nonsense... It was because the BBC had made such a song and dance about their moral purity (implying that the FO were immoral and impure) that we laid down these conditions at the Kingsley Wood Committee before agreeing that the BBC should be entrusted with the Arabic broadcasts.[105]

In fact, the whole affair was a storm in a teacup, because the announcement of the execution had already been included in an earlier news bulletin, broadcast in English by the Empire Service – a fact which appears to have gone unnoticed. Even so, the incident revealed the urgent need to clarify the somewhat vague terms of the 'gentleman's agreement'.

Confusion had mainly centred on the position of A. S. Calvert, who had been seconded from the Foreign Office to the BBC in December 1937.[106] The BBC wanted to establish that 'Calvert visits the FO as a servant of the BBC, and receives advice and information on our behalf; and that such advice and information can be accepted as a general rule only if it accords with BBC policy'.[107] The Foreign Office saw Calvert's role as similar to that of Kenneth Johnstone at the British Council. Although the BBC was quite happy to accommodate the views of the Foreign Office in regard to the Arabic broadcasts and did not 'like to contemplate our doing anything that the FO opposed', the corporation did wish to see Calvert 'endeavour to see things from our point of view as much as from theirs – and to ensure

The BBC foreign-language broadcasts

that the FO appreciated our point of view also'.[108] The BBC felt that its case was reinforced when, on 11 January, the German station at Zeesen transmitted a bulletin in English stating that two Arabs had been executed for the murder of a British archaeologist. In the opinion of one official, the German broadcast appeared 'to strengthen the absolute necessity of our reporting incidents of this kind in our bulletins. It so happens that news of these executions was not made available in London, and they may not, of course, have taken place; but this only strengthens our argument in favour of giving the *whole* truth as well as nothing but the truth.'[109] Whether or not the story was in fact true did not seem to matter; his point was that Britain could not afford to suppress unfavourable news when other countries were busy publicising it. Clark informed Calvert that 'the *omission* of unwelcome *facts* of news and the consequent suppression of truth runs counter to the Corporation's policy'.[110] The Foreign Office, on the other hand, favoured the truth, nothing but the truth and, *as near as possible*, the whole truth on the assumption that unwelcome news from less trustworthy foreign sources would be received with greater scepticism.

Closer co-ordination between the Foreign Office and the BBC was clearly essential if a compromise was to be reached. On 12 January 1938, Leeper and Warner met with Graves and Clark to work out the details. It was decided that copies of the English versions of the Arabic news bulletins would be sent to the Foreign Office daily, but on the day after transmission. This effectively gave the BBC total control over the service. However, to ensure a continued measure of Foreign Office influence, a meeting would take place every fortnight to review and supervise the work. Liaison by telephone was arranged so that the Foreign Office could relate any urgent information which it wished to see included in the broadcasts. Christopher Warner was to be made responsible for transferring such information to either Calvert or to Arthur Barker, the former diplomatic correspondent of *The Times* who had recently been appointed by the BBC as chief editor of the Foreign Language Service.[111]

The outcome of these arrangements was a much smoother working relationship between the Foreign Office and the BBC. The independence of the corporation had been preserved, and the Empire Service remained untarnished. The terms of the redefined 'gentleman's agreement' allowed for the omission of news items

Psychological rearmament, 1935–1939

which 'might have a harmful effect' if the Foreign Office so desired.[112] As Calvert wrote,

> The aim should be to cater for our Arabic-speaking audiences by presenting to them news of special Arab interest, in a setting of world news, and to put before the Arab world a presentation of this country, its political, social and economic life, which will create a favourable impression of Britain and the Empire in all their activities. This can only be done by a careful policy of selection of news items.[113]

Having secured the acceptance of this cardinal point, the Foreign Office thereafter experienced fewer differences of opinion with the BBC.

The BBC's inaugural broadcast in Spanish and Portuguese took place on 14 March 1938. The event attracted far less attention than the earlier experiment – partly because eyes were then focused upon Hitler's annexation of Austria. But the question of news broadcasts to South America constituted merely one piece in a complex jigsaw puzzle. The propaganda activities of France, Italy, Germany and the United States in that continent had been causing a severe headache in the News Department since the early 1920s. The counter-measures initiated by the Travel Association, the British Council, the Ibero-American Institute, the British Official News Service and Reuters were clearly proving inadequate to combat the effects of hostile propaganda, particularly in the sphere of trade.[114] The urgent need to increase the supply of British news abroad in general, and specifically to South America, was the subject of a memorandum submitted to the Cabinet by Anthony Eden in December 1937.

Eden drew special attention to the problems being encountered by Reuters in attempting to compete with the state-subsidised news agencies of other countries. Much of the trouble stemmed, he claimed, from the high costs charged by the GPO for the wireless transmission of Reuters messages from Rugby.[115] He therefore argued that it was in the national interest to find a means of aiding Reuters in their attempt to increase the supply of news originating from British sources. It was pointed out that London had been losing ground as a major distributing centre for world news and that if better facilities were made available editorial offices would be attracted back to Britain. This was essential because, he continued, 'It is, I think, indisputable that, in character and form, news items to some extent take their colour from the surroundings in which they are compiled, quite apart from deliberate garbling dictated by policy.'[116] News about Britain originating from foreign sources which were not always sympathetic to Britain was creating an adverse picture at a time when the government was trying to create the opposite effect.

The Cabinet considered Eden's memorandum on 15 December 1937, and it was decided that the Kingsley Wood Committee on Arabic Broadcasting should be given new terms of reference in order to consider means of improving and extending the dissemination of British news abroad, both by cables and by wireless.[117] Because the BBC was about to embark upon a Foreign Language Service, the urgent need was to examine the dissemination of news by cables. The committee was thus rechristened with the rather misleading title of the Cabinet Committee on Overseas Broadcasting, and held its first meeting on 4 January 1938. In fact, this proved to be the only meeting of the reconstituted committee before Kingsley Wood was replaced by the minister for the co-ordination of defence, Sir Thomas Inskip, and new terms of reference decided, terms which had no direct bearing on overseas propaganda during the remaining years of peace.[118] Nor did the committee submit a report or propose any positive recommendations.

Nevertheless, the Overseas Broadcasting Committee did discuss several issues pertinent to the question of British news abroad. Discussion at the only meeting centred on the position of Reuters and the views of its chairman, Sir Roderick Jones. Like many other interested observers, Jones was distressed at the shortage of British news available overseas. He wrote: 'It is not difficult to imagine the undesirable consequences, especially during any period of international tension, of having British political news, British Public Opinion and British newspaper comment presented to foreigners, not by a British organisation, but as seen through German, French, Italian and Japanese eyes.'[119] He argued that there was a genuine demand for 'quality news' of the kind for which Reuters was famous as an alternative to the poor but quantitative news supplied by less-respected sources. Jones therefore appealed to the government to, if not directly subsidise Reuters, then at least reduce the transmission costs to more favourable rates.[120] Like Reith at the BBC, Jones had been advocating increased government involvement in this subject for many years, and, also like Reith, he believed that it was conditional on the preservation of the independence of Reuters. Jones had certainly sensed the change in official attitudes towards such initiatives since 1937.[121] But his proposals were clearly of such a radical nature that the government was unwilling to rush into any further departures, at least at this stage, in its conduct of propaganda abroad.

While complicated negotiations between the government and Reuters continued, the Foreign Office ascertained that, contrary to previous assumptions, the degree to which the subsidised German and Italian news services to South America were drawn upon by the local press was negligible.[122] The newly instigated BBC broadcasts in Spanish and Portuguese appeared to be covering the field more than adequately. As a result, little progress was made with Reuters before September 1938, perhaps because before then few politicians were prepared to face the probable repercussions of a government subsidy in peacetime to a private organisation such as Reuters. Jones himself assumed that the delay was caused by ministerial preoccupation with the international crisis and with detailed departmental discussion.[123]

As in so many other areas of government, the Munich crisis provided the badly needed stimulus for the more urgent development of psychological rearmament. During the final week of September 1938, not only was Jones granted official permission to enlarge the Reuters wireless messages[124] but the BBC also introduced the first of its European-language broadcasts. As the crisis threatened to develop into war following Chamberlain's return from Godesberg, the BBC had, on 24 September, begun to initiate arrangements for a broadcast of news to Germany at short notice. Three days later, the Foreign Office warned the BBC that a translation of the Prime Minister's speech on the crisis would be required for European listeners, and, at short notice, the speech was broadcast on the medium-wave in German, French and Italian – at the expense of many regional programmes in the Home Service.[125] On the following day, the Foreign Office asked the BBC to continue the broadcasts. At a time when events were moving at such a rapid pace, radio provided the most efficient means for the immediate explanation of the British point of view. Indeed, such was believed to have been the success of the experiment that, on 3 October, Vansittart conveyed orally the

The BBC foreign-language broadcasts

request of Chamberlain and Lord Halifax that the BBC should continue the European-language news bulletins 'as a permanent commitment'.[126] In addition, the government began to provide Reuters with free transmission facilities for messages sent over and above the normal wireless service on the condition that Reuters would increase its output of British news.

The die was cast. During the months that followed, radio propaganda became an increasingly regular characteristic of international relations. After negotiations with the Foreign Office in December 1938, the BBC extended its European broadcasts from ten minutes to fifteen. At the end of January 1939, the German bulletin was extended to a half-hour programme, including talks. Hitler's response was to threaten retaliation if the BBC did not desist, and further reports from Germany seemed to indicate that the broadcasts were having 'a profound effect' and were 'more effective than anything we have attempted for a long time'.[127] In June 1939, Dr Hesse, the director of the DNB (the Nazi equivalent of Reuters), called at the Foreign Office and informed Charles Peake that the BBC broadcasts were 'annoying in ever-increasing measure Germans, not necessarily Nazi in their sympathies, who had previously been well disposed towards us'. Peake recorded:

> I ... asked Dr. Hesse whether the BBC German news was much listened to by Germans. He replied that it was, and the number of listeners was continually increasing. Indeed, that was why the Ministry of Propaganda had asked him to raise the question with me. I observed that it seemed odd if the news given were resented in Germany that it should be increasingly listened to. Dr. Hesse, who is not mentally very agile, could not think of any reply to this and said, after a pause, that this did not in any way affect his case.[128]

Neither the Foreign Office nor the BBC could have wished for a more satisfying result.

Despite such encouraging reports, it is only possible to speculate as to the precise effects of the BBC's foreign-language broadcasts during the two years of peace prior to the outbreak of the Second World War. They certainly provided an indication to people at home and abroad that Britain was beginning to take seriously the business of making herself understood, and they were, in this respect, vital to the process of psychological rearmament. As a War Office memorandum warned in April 1937, Italian propaganda was

Psychological rearmament, 1935–1939

causing British prestige to 'wane by default' and 'if we continue to leave the field free to our enemies in peace, our difficulties in the Near and Middle East will only be intensified in war'.[129] Britain was, by 1937, the only Great Power which did not employ foreign-language broadcasts. Just to be seen to be doing something in this direction was considered to be far more important than appearing to remain aloof and indifferent to the requirements of foreigners, particularly those under British rule. This factor was also considered to be more important than the appearance of conducting propaganda, although the very fact that the BBC and not the government was performing the task ensured at least a measure of credibility for the content of the broadcasts. To many foreigners the BBC may have been the mouthpiece of the British government, but listening to programmes prepared by Broadcasting House was more palatable to them than swallowing official propaganda emanating directly from Whitehall. It was partly for this reason that the BBC was prepared to take on (and defeat) the Foreign Office over the question of news selection and omission. The BBC accepted that such processes were a normal and indeed a necessary function of journalism, but it was not prepared to tolerate being told by a government department which items to select or omit. After all, it was Reith who maintained that 'news is the shocktroops of propaganda', a dictum that would have gained the full sympathy of the Foreign Office. But, initially, the Foreign Office was not prepared to trust the BBC's ability to select and omit news 'in the national interest', and the experience of the first Arabic broadcast merely seemed to confirm its view. However, once the struggle over editorial control had been settled by a clarification of the so-called gentleman's agreement, and as the BBC's experience increased with each broadcast, there developed a greater degree of trust and mutual co-operation in the cause of national projection. Indeed, by early 1939, the BBC had begun to draw much closer to the original Foreign Office conception of the broadcasts as articulated by Leeper, so much so that *The Times* was forced to print a leading article in defence of the Foreign Language Service.[130] By then, somewhat ironically, it was the turn of the Foreign Office to dampen down overenthusiasm, with Cadogan minuting that 'I think it may be expected that the BBC will mend their ways.'[131]

That the British government had been forced in the first place to request the BBC to initiate broadcasts in foreign languages was pri-

The BBC foreign-language broadcasts

marily the result of external stimuli, chiefly in the form of the Bari broadcasts. It has been suggested that 'Bari was popular because it was anti-British rather than because it was pro-Italian'.[132] Yet, as one observer wrote in April 1938 concerning the reception of anti-British propaganda in Palestine, 'While the indigenous population is only too happy to make use of the Italians as a stick with which to beat the mandatory power, they are not misled to any appreciable extent as to the aims and object of Italian propaganda.'[133] Another observer, who remained sceptical about the alleged success of Bari, claimed that it was only since the publicity afforded to the inauguration of the BBC's Arabic Service that people in Palestine had begun to listen to the Italian broadcasts. In Egypt, he argued, the Bari broadcasts were not considered a serious threat to British prestige, especially among the 'better classes', who nonetheless generally welcomed the BBC's response.[134] However, there were several complaints that the programmes were 'lifeless and dry' and that the Middle Eastern audience would remain small until transmission was begun on the more popular medium-wave.[135]

This may well have been true, but it had missed a vital point. Although radio was an ideal instrument for directly influencing large numbers of people in an area of such high illiteracy, the BBC's Arabic Service was not simply designed to appeal to a mass audience. As S. H. Perowne, the BBC's Arabic programme organiser, wrote in September 1938,

> ... we are not appealing to the man under the palm tree. He may, and probably does, listen to the news if he is lucky enough to be near a receiver, but it is ... certain that he listens to nothing else. Our listening body is drawn almost entirely from the Effendi class. That is to say, Government officials, school teachers, students and men and women of leisure and means. This is only natural, and in my opinion is far from regrettable. It is in the hands of this class that the destinies of their countries must lie for some time to come.

Moreover, he continued,

> ... although the strata of society to which we appeal are comparatively few, their importance is far greater than it would be in a western democracy, and I consider it justifiable to suggest that the Corporation should deliberately make the entertainment and conciliation of this group of listeners their primary object. It has certainly, I believe, been the experience of many of those who have been concerned in the administration of Oriental peoples that it is among the educated or semi-educated wealthier classes that the seeds of estrangement and suspicion are most easily sown, and we

Psychological rearmament, 1935–1939

are surely justified in exerting every legitimate effort to try to replace distrust by confidence, and that can only be done by converting ignorance into knowledge.'[136]

Such words could quite easily have been written by an employee of the British Council. But the BBC could only afford to contemplate gearing its broadcasts to such an audience during the brief respite provided by the signature of the Anglo-Italian Agreement of March 1938. In return for Britain's *de jure* recognition of the Italian conquest of Abyssinia, Italy promised to reduce the number of her 'volunteers' in Spain and to tone down the anti-British propaganda contained in the Bari broadcasts. But it was not long before Bari again began to champion the cause of Arab nationalism in the Near and Middle East, and when that happened the BBC could ill afford to ignore 'the man under the palm tree'.

The same condition applied to the European Service. In December 1938, Leeper informed Graves that 'the Government consider it of the greatest importance that every step should be taken to make your German news bulletins available to the maximum number of listeners'.[137] The BBC's view that 'truth and plain facts may be calculated to cause disaffection of a sort in Germany'[138] seemed to be borne out by Hitler's threat of January 1939 to retaliate in kind, a threat which was carried out in late March when the stations at Hamburg and Cologne began to transmit in English on medium-wavelengths.[139] Two months later, the Foreign Office reported that 'large sections of the German public' continued to listen to the BBC broadcasts, despite the possibility of imprisonment for between two and five years.[140]

Although the BBC's Foreign Language Service undoubtedly helped to correct some of the more outrageous Italian and German statements broadcast from Bari and Zeesen, it did not – nor could it be expected to – constitute a panacea for Britain's problems. As Sir Miles Lampson pointed out shortly after the Arabic broadcasts were begun, 'As long ... as our policy in Palestine remains unacceptable to the Arab world, the Italians must continue to have a very great advantage over us in propaganda. Palestine will remain a thorn in the flesh until our line is changed: it is in fact a veritable mill stone around our neck.'[141] In other words, no amount of propaganda could rectify the impression created by unpopular government or by unpopular policies. The European and South American services

The BBC foreign-language broadcasts

were handicapped by the same problem. But it was clear that something had to be done to explain the British point of view other than relying upon foreign governments to discredit themselves through wild exaggerations. Yet because the BBC entered the field of international broadcasting relatively late in the day, it was forced to play a defensive role, concentrating upon making the British case known and understood abroad through the dissemination of news, albeit after purposeful selection.

The BBC's foreign-language broadcasts were yet another price to pay for a country whose world-wide interests and commitments exceeded her capacity to defend them. Radio offered an ideal opportunity for binding those interests closer together and rallying foreign sympathy to the British cause. But for Britain its use was symptomatic of a declining power searching for new and alternative means of defending her prestige from constant attack. It was an attempt to preserve credibility not only for Britain but for democracy as a viable alternative to totalitarianism. The battle for foreign sympathy was, however, merely the prelude to a war in which that sympathy would be put to the test.

6

The Vansittart Committee for the Co-ordination of British Publicity Abroad

Early in 1938 British overseas propaganda was about to enter a critical phase of its development. The advancements made in the direction of national projection during the previous three years had undeniably been impressive, but despite the progress now being made by the British Council with the energetic Lord Lloyd at its helm, despite governmental approval for the inauguration of a foreign-language service by the BBC and despite the investigations of the reconstituted Kingsley Wood committee into the deficiencies which still existed in the distribution of British news abroad, there nonetheless remained much work to be done in the cause of psychological rearmament. Hitherto the tendency had been to tackle each individual part of the propaganda problem separately. The Travel Association had been set up to conduct tourist and trade propaganda and the British Council for cultural propaganda, and the BBC had agreed to broadcast news in foreign languages on behalf of the government. In this somewhat spasmodic manner, the official British machinery for conducting propaganda overseas had been gradually built up. It was, perhaps, the only way that progress in this direction could have been made in the face of at times overwhelming opposition from the more traditionally minded elements in Whitehall who could not – or would not – accept the need for such work. Yet there still remained an urgent need to approach the subject in its entirety. The machinery was by no means efficient or complete. In this respect, the establishment of the Committee for the Co-ordination of British Publicity Abroad in January 1938 was the first serious attempt to combine the activities of the various official and semi-official organisations engaged in the projection of Britain abroad with an effective utilisation of the available media. Previous attempts had proved either impracticable, largely because of the diverse evolution of Britain's involvement in propaganda abroad since the end of the First World War, or half-hearted, because the

The Vansittart committee

necessary motivation had been absent. In late 1937 the first of these factors remained a difficult problem to resolve; the second, however, no longer applied.

Co-ordination by committee

As the individual primarily responsible for the foundation of the British Council and for the acceptance of the idea of broadcasts in languages other than English, Rex Leeper was among the first to appreciate that increased centralisation was a prerequisite to further progress. He had probably first pondered at length over this question in July 1937 when he had expressed himself as 'strongly opposed to the establishment of a Ministry of Information in peacetime', largely because such an organisation, as then envisaged by the Committee of Imperial Defence, would exercise special powers on the home front.[1] Apart from the News Department's press work, Leeper believed that the Foreign Office should not involve itself in domestic propaganda. Instead he considered that the necessary machinery for an efficient peacetime programme of overseas propaganda was, in basic form, already available; it merely required a higher degree of co-ordination. Even so, Leeper recognised that this could not be achieved without first confronting certain fundamental issues relating to the kind of political system which existed, or which was desired, in Britain. He wrote:

> The main problem is how a democracy such as our own which desires to maintain the freedom of the press and to give as much room as possible to individual initiative can compete successfully with other countries which control not only their press but all other means of propaganda and publicity. It cannot be stated quite so simply as competition between a democracy and a totalitarian State, for other democracies such as France admit far more government control and initiative than here... One cannot therefore overlook the difficulties which may beset His Majesty's Government in attempting to organise the publicity of this country on lines which can hope to compete effectively with publicity in totalitarian States.[2]

Leeper's use of the word 'compete' may have been merely a slip of the pen; he had until now protested his belief that British propaganda should not enter into competition with the more heavily state-subsidised propaganda activities of other countries. But one might not unreasonably assume that such an expert in the use of publicity would have tended to choose his words more carefully. If so, this choice of word would appear to reflect his growing conviction that, in view of the fierce and unremitting anti-British propaganda of the Italian and German governments, Britain's counter-activities should now enter a new phase of 'propaganda for democracy' if psychological rearmament was to succeed. Britain must take the initiative in persuading the rest of the world that democracy was a more acceptable and more peaceful political ideology than Nazism or fascism. For the moment, however, his major preoccupation was how those organisations which already existed could be made more efficient for this task.

His search for a solution to the problems of overlapping and a lack of co-ordination which hampered the efficiency of British overseas propaganda resulted in a lengthy memorandum written on 2 January 1938. He began with the curious observation that

British rearmament has undoubtedly been the principal steadying factor in Europe in 1937 and has in large measure helped to balance the decline in French influence during that period. Unfortunately, our increased prestige in Europe has not been properly appreciated either at home or abroad. At home there has been a tendency to defeatism which has been vocal rather than representative, but which has been exploited by our rivals to do us damage, while we have done far too little to counteract the effects of this hostile propaganda.[3]

Leeper did not explain what indices or evidence he had used for such a statement. It was probably no more than mere impression. But it is nevertheless an interesting one, not only because of its assumption that national prestige in the context of the late 1930s rested to a large degree upon the condition of a nation's armaments or, in other words, upon 'power'. For there is also the assumption that 'prestige' was in some way divorced from 'power' in that the former did not necessarily follow naturally from the latter. If British rearmament really was believed to have been 'the principal steadying factor in Europe in 1937' – which is debatable – then why had British prestige not enjoyed the increase Leeper clearly believed it deserved? The answer, he suggested, was the readiness of the German and Italian governments to harness propaganda to their national policies in such a way as to deride or deprecate any British achievements. Leeper continued:

The German and Italian dictatorships regarded it as essential to accompany

The Vansittart committee

their material rearmament with an intensive propaganda not only to key their own populations up to the effort and sacrifices required, but to impress other countries with the effect being produced. We may dislike and criticise much of this propaganda and may rightly eschew many of the methods employed which are alien and repugnant to our own ways of thinking, but we should be rash to belittle its effects which have been widespread and highly injurious to ourselves and all that we stand for. This fact is slowly penetrating the House of Commons and the press, and still more slowly the sceptical minds of Whitehall.[4]

This latter remark was a reference to the long history of debate between the Foreign Office and the Treasury concerning the necessity for British propaganda abroad. On this issue Leeper was less than generous and, by implication, suggested that the present inadequacies were largely due to the continued reluctance of the Treasury to provide sufficient expenditure when it had been repeatedly requested, a view that was not entirely without justification. As Leeper wrote,

The Foreign Office have received all kinds of warnings from China to Peru, but the Treasury, in that calm collegiate atmosphere which prevails on the other side of Downing Street, has given slow and grudging support to the many applications we have made since we first approached them in 1930. Though to some extent we have succeeded in loosening their purse strings, we are still a very long way from receiving the funds which are required.[5]

It was, admittedly, the normal business of the Treasury to mind the public purse, and Leeper recognised that the problem had not simply been one of finance. Many of the old suspicions concerning the use of propaganda remained:

In England prejudices die more slowly than elsewhere and new methods are viewed with greater suspicion with the result that they meet with stubborn resistance until they can be proved to be necessary. Not only must the proofs be convincing, but time is required before people are willing to be convinced. The time lag which we are suffering from in our material rearmament is also appearing in what may be described as our psychological rearmament.[6]

Leeper was, however, optimistic that there now existed a solid foundation of support for this type of work, a feeling which, as will be discussed below, was entirely justified.

Leeper suggested that the main problem, caused by hostile propaganda 'busy representing us as a weak and tired nation, unwilling to

Psychological rearmament, 1935–1939

make sacrifices, uncertain and vacillating in all our policies', was essentially 'how we are to get other countries to see us as we should like to be seen; how to make them understand the British outlook, British institutions and British activities in different fields'.[7] More convinced than ever of the detrimental effects of foreign propaganda upon British interests and prestige, he warned that 'it is idle to imagine that we can safely let our case go by default'. While recognising that Britain's efforts would necessarily have to be conducted on a smaller scale than those of her rivals, he had no reason to doubt her capacity to undertake propaganda on a larger and more efficient scale than hitherto. But, he continued, 'where we are behind them is in realising that national publicity is as important in foreign policy as commercial publicity is in business'.[8]

Leeper sub-divided the subject of national propaganda into four basic categories. News and broadcasting were two which were the current object of investigation by the Kingsley Wood committee, and he was prepared to await the outcome before considering further action. Of the third category, cultural and educational propaganda, he wrote:

It is here that the chief progress has been made... It can be said without exaggeration that in the British Council we have the makings of a first-class organisation which works in the closest association with the Government. In this field alone has the Government (mainly the Foreign Office) succeeded in providing the kind of organisation which will adapt its programme entirely to national requirements.[9]

It will be recalled that Eustace Percy had resigned the chairmanship of the council only six months earlier partly because those national requirements were different from those for which the council had been established in 1934. The projection of Britain was becoming less important than the needs of psychological rearmament.

If Leeper expressed relative satisfaction with the progress thus far achieved in the three aforementioned categories, he was far from content with the attention which had been given by government to the important medium of film in national propaganda overseas, adding: 'nothing has been more unsatisfactory than the lack of machinery for getting useful British films shown abroad'.[10] He described the work of the Joint Films Committee of the British Council and Travel Association as a 'mere flea-bite' and proposed its replacement by some form of centralised organisation which

The Vansittart committee

would involve itself in the production and distribution of propaganda films on a comprehensive basis.

Leeper concluded his memorandum with a proposal for the establishment of a central co-ordinating committee, a government initiative which would serve to bring together all the various Whitehall departments and semi-official agencies engaged in propaganda abroad. He was particularly emphatic that the main authority to which this committee would be responsible should be the Foreign Office 'as the only department competent to judge what form our propaganda and publicity should take in foreign countries and where the chief effort should be made'.[11] Memories of the Foreign Office's unfortunate record of disputes first with the Ministry of Information in 1918 and then with the industrial elements represented in the British Council were undoubtedly still vivid in Leeper's mind.

The chairman he had in mind for the proposed committee was Sir Robert Vansittart, who, only a few weeks earlier, had been 'promoted', as Valentine Lawford put it, 'to a sort of newly discovered Siberia known as the post of Chief Diplomatic Adviser to the Government'.[12] It is possible that Leeper suggested Vansittart for the post as a means of bringing his former master and friend back from the diplomatic wasteland that many believed his new job would be. But Vansittart was a logical choice. Leeper had always found him sympathetic to his views concerning national projection and, more recently, psychological rearmament. Vansittart's successor as permanent under secretary at the Foreign Office, Sir Alexander Cadogan, was, on his own admission, largely ignorant of the News Department's work. When, in July 1937, Leeper had approached him with various proposals to develop its work, Cadogan had admitted that 'this is rather outside my beat, and I am not sufficiently familiar with the conditions to be able to offer a useful opinion'.[13] He then referred the matter to someone who could – Vansittart. Given Leeper's loyalty and friendship towards Vansittart, combined with the desire of both men to ensure Foreign Office control over the proposed co-ordinating committee, the choice of the chief diplomatic adviser as its chairman seemed ideal. It was, however, to prove something of a mixed blessing.

Leeper handed a copy of his memorandum to Eden, who read it while on holiday in the south of France early in January. The Foreign Secretary declared himself to be 'in full agreement with this excellent paper',[14] which is hardly surprising in view of the fact that Leeper had initially been moved to write it after a conversation he had had with Eden some weeks earlier when Parliament had expressed some concern for the issues involved.[15] Vansittart was also in complete agreement, and he reiterated his desire to undertake the chairmanship.[16] Accordingly, on 18 January, Eden submitted the proposal for the establishment of a co-ordinating committee to the Prime Minister along with a suggestion that an announcement be made in Parliament to show that the government was 'giving proper attention to the subject'. Eden added that the proposed committee 'seems to me ... to be the natural outcome of the preliminary work done so far'.[17] Chamberlain almost immediately replied that he agreed to the proposals 'in principle'.[18] This provided the signal for Leeper and Vansittart to begin their preliminary arrangements for the appointment and first meeting of the committee, the interests of the Foreign Office News Department being virtually guaranteed with the appointment of one of its senior officials, Christopher Warner, as secretary.[19]

The existence of the Vansittart Committee for the Co-ordination of British Publicity Abroad was announced by the Prime Minister in the House of Commons on 7 February 1938. Chamberlain stated that its main purpose would be 'to prevent overlapping and, by exchange of information among the bodies engaged in various forms of publicity abroad, to co-ordinate their programmes and activities'.[20] The announcement was favourably received by the House and by the press. *The Times*, for example, published a lengthy explanatory article justifying the need for the committee and expressing general support for its aims.[21] Vansittart personally received numerous letters of congratulations and offers of support from a wide range of different people and organisations.[22] The German press, however, greeted the news with less enthusiasm. The *Volkischer Beobachter* led the chorus of hypocritical indignation, invoking memories of British propaganda during the Great War, but with the substitution of Vansittart for Northcliffe.[23] Such comparisons were, of course, misleading. The Vansittart committee was not a propaganda department and had no executive powers. Nor did it conduct propaganda itself. Its function was purely advisory and aimed at the increased co-ordination of existing work.

The first meeting was scheduled to take place on 16 February. On

The Vansittart committee

that very same day there took place, coincidentally, a major debate in the House of Commons on the subject of British overseas propaganda. It was a non-party debate on a motion by a private member,[24] and was significant not least because it was the first major parliamentary discussion of British propaganda since August 1918. Indeed, the very occurrence of the debate, and the response it provoked, was testimony to the growing recognition of the need to accept propaganda as a permanent feature of peacetime British diplomacy. It was appreciated that Britain could no longer afford to neglect the use of publicity and that the government would need to take positive steps 'to present ourselves and our views, actions and motives to the world in their true colours, and to combat the insidious attacks which are being made upon us'.[25]

The debate was remarkable in many ways, not least because it took the subject of propaganda out of the realm of inter-departmental discussion and placed it firmly in the public forum. Many of the views and arguments expressed bore a striking similarity to those which had been put forward by the Foreign Office during the previous decade. Members of Parliament were prepared to talk about propaganda, and the importance of British involvement in it, in a manner that would have seemed inconceivable only a few years before. Harold Nicolson, for example, felt that 'We must, in contrast to the strident superlatives of Bari, put across something very sedative, very quiet, very calm – always seeing the other person's point of view and prepared to give way to it when he is right; never being angry; and always sympathetic. That is British culture, the capacity of being sympathetic.'[26] Earl Winterton, speaking on behalf of the government in his capacity as chancellor of the Duchy of Lancaster, stated that

> We shall never, let it be hoped, believe in propaganda in the bad sense... We believe in objectivity, in untainted news and sincere views, honestly expressed. But while that is so, neither the Government, the House, nor the country can afford to ignore the use of publicity or propaganda in which foreign governments engage – or the majority of them – sometimes quite legitimately, but sometimes decidedly otherwise, where the results are detrimental to British interests.[27]

The House welcomed the appointment of both the Kingsley Wood and Vansittart committees as positive and serious attempts to help rectify the deficiencies, while also advocating greater official support for the work of Reuters, the BBC, the British Council and the Travel Association. Even the Foreign Office News Department was applauded for its efforts.

Herbert Morrison described the debate as 'one of the most peaceful that we have ever had in the House of Commons',[28] and indeed the House enjoyed that rare event in the 1930s of unanimous support for the resolution, which, in its final form, stated

> That, having regard to the increasing activity of certain foreign Governments in the field of propaganda, political and cultural, by means of the press, broadcasting and films, this House being of opinion that the evil effects of state propaganda of a tendentious or misleading character can best be countered, not by retaliation, but by the widespread dissemination of straightforward information and news based upon an enlightened and honest public policy, urges the Government to give the full weight of its moral and financial support to schemes to further the wider and more effective presentation of British news, views and culture abroad.[29]

This may have been long-winded, but its point was clear enough. Moreover, if the House of Commons can be regarded, even remotely, as a barometer of informed public opinion, then in a period of just twenty years the attitude towards Britain's employment of national propaganda in peacetime had changed from open hostility to widespread support. The subject continued to leave an unpleasant taste in the mouths of many advocates, but the facts of modern diplomatic life could no longer be ignored. There undoubtedly remained a few critical opponents, but their numbers were as slight as had been the supporters of the Ministry of Information in 1918.

The outcome of the debate must have provided great encouragement to the members of the Vansittart committee, who had concluded their first meeting earlier the same day. Besides Leeper, Warner and Vansittart representing the Foreign Office, there were present senior officials from the Colonial Office, Post Office, Department of Overseas Trade and the Treasury, as well as representatives of the BBC, the British Council and the Travel Association. This was, in fact, the first occasion when members of these bodies, the principal official and semi-official interests engaged in the projection of Britain abroad, had met together around the same table. The chairman therefore took the opportunity to explain the aims of the committee and to familiarise himself with the views of those present. It was important, he said, to establish clear lines of demarcation, plan

The Vansittart committee

new forms of activity and encourage generally a wider sense of responsibility in the conduct of the work. Vansittart discovered that there was a unanimous desire for increased mutual co-operation. The BBC, for example, was prepared to collaborate with the British Council in helping to disseminate British culture through the Empire and Foreign Language services.[30] It was this unity of purpose which was to characterise the early work of the committee.

At the first meeting, it was decided that two areas in particular required immediate attention: trade publicity and the work of government press departments. An increase in the number of official press departments was a marked feature of British governmental administration during the inter-war period. In 1919 only the News Department of the Foreign Office had existed for the purpose of conducting press publicity. By 1923, seven government departments employed officials who specialised in the release of information to the British and foreign press or in conducting publicity in general – a development which had not initially been welcomed by the Treasury.[31] The number had increased steadily with the gradual acceptance of public relations as a legitimate function of the official bureaucracy,[32] and by 1938 more than a dozen government departments were equipped with press and publicity divisions, the total annual expenditure of which exceeded a quarter of a million pounds. Indeed, by comparison to the sums allocated to the War Office and to the Air Ministry, the Foreign Office News Department had become one of the least expensive to run.[33]

Official information, whether it concerned domestic or foreign affairs, was considered to be of interest to the world's press as a major source of news about Britain. It therefore contributed to the image or general impression abroad of the British way of life, or of its government, and the Vansittart committee was fully aware of its importance in the projection of Britain. But there had been very little collaboration among the various press offices from this point of view. If the output of the various press departments could be more closely co-ordinated than it had been to suit the needs of national projection, greater advantage would be made in future of the presence of foreign journalists in Britain by supplying them with non-political news which was likely to produce a favourable impression abroad of Britain's domestic condition.[34] As a result of this suggestion, a meeting of all official press officers was held at the Foreign

Psychological rearmament, 1935–1939

Office on 23 February to discuss improved inter-departmental cooperation in this matter. Vansittart explained to them that they afforded 'a channel through which other countries could be kept informed of what we were doing in respect, for example, of social legislation'.[35] Vansittart later recorded that the meeting 'had been extremely useful and that, as one of its results, improved contacts between Government Press and Publicity Officers and the foreign correspondents in London would be secured'.[36]

The second area which demanded the Vansittart committee's immediate attention, trade propaganda, turned out to be a much more difficult problem to resolve. Mullins, the DOT representative, pointed to the 'insufficient co-ordination in this country in the projection of our commercial achievements'.[37] Existing official trade and industrial propaganda was secured through co-operation among the DOT, the Foreign Office, the Board of Trade, the Treasury and the Exports Credit Guarantee Department, and indirectly through the Travel Association and the British Council. But this was a cumbersome process which achieved only minimal results. Nor was the situation helped by the fundamental differences of opinion within these organisations concerning the emphasis which should be placed upon specific advertising for individual products or on national publicity for British industrial achievements in general. These were the reasons behind a new DOT proposal to establish a central organisation which would supervise more efficiently the projection of British trade and industry. As one official pointed out, the existing arrangements were clearly inadequate: 'Publicity, if it is to be of any real value, cannot be effectively carried out by officials as part of their day to day duties. It is a highly technical job requiring a continuous survey over a field of enormous extent which could only be handled by some central authority.'[38] However, this was a double-edged problem. It was recognised that, whatever initiative the government might decide to take in this direction, the ultimate success of trade and commercial propaganda depended upon the efficiency of British industry in producing something to shout about. Indeed, the bulk of British trade propaganda currently being conducted was undertaken by individual firms or industrial associations with the object of promoting their own sales and profits. In a highly competitive business world, trade publicity in the national interest was of secondary, almost incidental, import-

The Vansittart committee

ance to them. It was because of this, and because there was little direct consultation between government and private enterprise on this issue, that Vansittart agreed with the DOT that a more concerted, mutually beneficial, effort was essential.

Accordingly, on 14 April 1938, Vansittart submitted to the Treasury a provisional proposal for the creation of a central organisation to conduct trade propaganda under the auspices of the DOT. This was intended to be a joint enterprise between public and private concerns, with a large proportion of the necessary funds being expected to derive from industrial subscriptions. In other words, this was to be a sort of trade propaganda version of the British Council. Vansittart, however, having learned the lessons of the council's early experience, resigned himself to the possibility that such an arrangement might involve the proposed organisation in publicity on behalf of individual products. This was the price the government would have to pay for its dependence upon private investment. But, he wrote, 'some considerable part of the publicity may ... well be of a kind which has not this particular appeal and is designed to enhance the general prestige of this country, and for this the cost may properly be regarded as a responsibility of the Government'.[39] Could it be denied that advertisements for Rolls Royce automobiles reflected upon the quality of British craftsmanship and engineering? Moreover, Vansittart argued, the degree to which the venture would attract private support would be determined by the level of official assistance, which would serve to encourage or deter industrial confidence.

In order to discuss this proposal in greater detail, an interdepartmental conference was convened at the Foreign Office on 25 April. There was a unanimous desire to see an increase in the quality and in the quantity of Britain's trade propaganda overseas, but Hale, speaking on behalf of the Treasury, pointed out that, 'according to general Treasury principles, propaganda benefiting a particular industry should normally be paid for by that industry'.[40] This factor was to provide the major obstacle to further progress.

At the inter-departmental conference, the DOT undertook responsibility for ascertaining the views held in leading industrial and commercial circles concerning their willingness to invest in a joint venture with the government to improve trade propaganda abroad. The results were disappointing. A report was produced for the benefit of the Vansittart Committee in which it was stated:

> On the question whether it is desirable that His Majesty's Government should participate in commercial and industrial publicity overseas, it will cause little surprise that commerce as distinct from industry (i.e. those which sell services as distinct from those who sell goods) has no interest in the establishment, or co-ordination by His Majesty's Government of commercial propaganda overseas.[41]

Industry, on the other hand, 'overwhelmingly favours the idea', but was less enthusiastic at the prospect of having to meet even part of the cost, claiming that trade propaganda was an integral component of 'prestige propaganda' and was therefore primarily a government responsibility. An impasse had been reached: the Treasury maintained that trade propaganda was a responsibility of industry, while industry insisted upon the reverse.

The Travel Association, whose aims include the stimulation abroad of demand for British goods and services but which saw itself as being in the business of 'prestige propaganda', seized upon the stalemate. The association had been desperately searching for an identity since its creation in 1929. With all the talk in the early 1930s of the projection of England, it had transformed itself into a body able and willing to undertake the task, only to be foiled by the creation of the British Council in 1934. When the Empire Marketing Board had been dissolved in the previous year, it had seen its newly created film unit as the logical successor in patronising the work of Grierson's documentary film movement, even appointing Grierson himself as film adviser and his sister Marion as controller of the unit. Now, in 1938, the Travel Association presented itself as the one body capable of providing the central authority being suggested for trade propaganda. Its qualifications were admirable, though not outstanding. It was the only semi-official body in existence even remotely concerning itself directly with trade propaganda, and, in the opinion of one supporter, it was 'the only group not under obligation to specialised commercial or political interests in a position to make detached films reflecting the national life of the country'.[42] But its work had been constantly hampered by a shortage of funds and possibly also by lack of an official champion in the DOT, which had not been prepared to fight for its cause in the same manner that the Foreign Office had done with the British Council. In sharp contrast to the dramatic increases afforded to the British Council's of-

The Vansittart committee

ficial grant, the Travel Association still received an annual sum of £5,000 – the same figure that had been awarded by the Treasury on its foundation. In the words of one member, 'whatever we may say in public, in private we must know that we are being swamped' by the council.[43] Meredith, the Travel Association's secretary, pointed out that it had been his organisation which had suffered from the lack of clear demarcational lines with the British Council, and he insisted that, 'apart from the waste and inevitable ill-will, I feel that the method of open publicity, advertising and information, of the Association is a necessary and important part of the projection of England'.[44] He was determined to see greater use being made of the association, particularly in the United States, where the British Council did not operate, but although he did manage to secure the support of the Vansittart committee in his appeal for a larger government grant, he was nevertheless disappointed by the committee's insistence that the Travel Association should in future confine itself to tourist publicity and not involve itself in cultural or trade propaganda.[45] Once again, the Foreign Office's somewhat limited conception of the association's work had prevailed.

'A very astonishing document'

Of the various questions examined by the Vansittart committee, that of film propaganda proved to be the one which required the most serious and detailed attention. Film was the only important medium which had not received the degree of official attention which its potential value in national propaganda overseas demanded. The value of film as a medium of peacetime propaganda had been recognised in British political circles since at least the mid 1920s, but its employment in the projection of Britain abroad left a great deal to be desired. The Empire Marketing Board, followed by the Travel Association and the Joint Films Committee, had devoted considerable attention to the subject, but had always in the last resort been hampered by the severe shortage of funds at their disposal.

The interest of government departments in film publicity was not a problem. Many of them, including the Ministries of Health, Labour and Transport, the Boards of Trade and Education, the Air Raids Precautions Department, the National Savings Committee

Psychological rearmament, 1935–1939

and the National Fitness Council, had all involved themselves in the production of documentary or information films relating to subjects with which they were concerned. However, only the General Post Office was directly concerned with the regular production of films for public exhibition and maintained its own film unit out of public funds for the purpose. The GPO had inherited the Empire Marketing Board's film unit on the latter's closure in 1933 and had made several films publicising its own work as well as that of other departments. For example, the GPO co-operated with the Ceylon Tea Propaganda Board in the making of Basil Wright's *Song of Ceylon* in 1934, while the unit's most famous, and certainly most celebrated, film for the Post Office was *Night Mail*, released in 1936. It was not usual for other government departments to produce or distribute films themselves, and, where collaboration with the GPO proved impossible, they had tended to rely upon the initiative and imagination of commercial producers or other private concerns such as the Gas, Light and Coke Company, Imperial Airways, the Pearl Assurance Company, Shell and the British Gas Authority. Edgar Anstey's celebrated film *Housing Problems* (1935) had been sponsored by the Gas, Light and Coke Company, whereas in 1936 and 1937 Imperial Airways had sponsored the making of *Heart of an Empire*, *The Future is in the Air* and *Air Outpost* by the Strand Film Company.

The Ministry of Agriculture was the only government department with a special annual Treasury grant enabling it to place orders with private concerns for the production of publicity films.[46] The service departments also took an active interest in the making of technical and training films, but these were hardly suitable for public exhibition overseas. Moreover, what may be said to have been Britain's major contribution to the international film industry between the wars, the documentary, was hardly likely to evoke the type of foreign interest which the entertainment films produced by Hollywood undoubtedly did. Documentary films dealing with housing problems, malnutrition or pollution in various parts of Britain were understandably considered unsuitable for overseas audiences. The Joint Films Committee regularly examined films sponsored by government departments but almost invariably concluded that none were suitable for distribution abroad.[47] Even the most outstanding documentary films of the late 1930s were vetoed: John Taylor's *The*

The Vansittart committee

Smoke Menace (1937) 'revealed too much that is unfortunate in our social system', whereas Basil Wright's *Children at School* (1937) was considered 'too informative to hold the interest of any but a relatively instructed audience'.[48] In short, the situation in so far as the projection of England through the medium of film was concerned was desperate.

The Foreign Office, the DOT and the Colonial, Dominions and India offices had all given the matter varying degrees of attention, but none had really come up with an adequate solution. Nor had the principal semi-official bodies concerned with the production and distribution of educational or publicity films (the Joint Films Committee, the Imperial Institute and the British Film Institute). The problem lay not so much with the channels of distribution – by 1938 the Travel Association had secured outlets in fifty-four countries[49] – but with the acute shortage of films suitable for foreign audiences which could also serve a definite propagandist purpose.[50] A similar situation existed with regard to newsreels, always 'far more convincing than any fabricated propaganda product'.[51] This problem was underlined in a letter to Vansittart from Richard de Rochement, the managing director of Time Incorporated's British company, The March of Time, in which he complained of the lack of governmental assistance and guidance in the production of newsreels.[52]

The response of the Vansittart committee was to appoint Roland Kenney, the Foreign Office's film expert, as its liaison officer with the various official and semi-official organisations interested in film. Kenney was also asked to investigate the entire question of British film publicity abroad with a view to improving the production and distribution of propaganda film material.[53] After two months of careful investigation, Kenney produced his report. There were three categories of film worthy of the committee's consideration: newsreels, feature films and documentaries. Kenney strongly urged greater official involvement in the making of newsreels, 'the most topical and therefore always of immediate importance', but pointed out that the main complaint of the five leading newsreel companies (Gaumont–British, Movietone, Pathé, Paramount and Universal) had been the payment of customs duties on all imported footage, most of which was not normally included in the final product. A wider selection of material in the finished newsreel would be possible, he maintained, if duties had to be paid only on the amount of

Psychological rearmament, 1935–1939

imported footage actually used rather than on the quantity received.[54]

Feature films were also considered to be of vital importance to the projection of Britain and certainly demanded a greater level of official consideration than they had received hitherto. Kenney continued:

> Where the newsreel may rouse passions and enthusiasms about contemporaneous events, and thus act immediately – if we may indulge in the jargon of psychology – on the instinctive parts of the mind, the Feature Film will strike subconscious chords and reinforce or modify prejudices or opinions already held, and thus in the long run make a more lasting impression.[55]

Finally, the documentary film was considered important because it appealed 'to the more conscious levels of the mind' and was therefore significant in view of its appeal 'to the more intelligent classes of the community'.[56]

Kenney did not consider it necessary to stimulate government departments into greater interest or involvement, because, he wrote, 'in most cases they are well aware of the value of film publicity and are prepared to help the film companies in any way possible'.[57] Nevertheless, in order to co-ordinate more efficiently the efforts of the various official, semi-official and private interests involved, he proposed the creation of a National Film Council which would effectively replace the Joint Films Committee of the British Council and the Travel Association as the body principally responsible for the overseas distribution of propaganda films. A National Film Unit would also be necessary to sponsor the production of films by well-known directors and production companies, but would not itself make films. It was only through such a council, Kenney believed, that national film propaganda abroad could be made more efficient, more economical and more suited to the requirements of national projection.[58]

Kenney's proposals formed the subject of almost the entire discussion at the Vansittart committee's second meeting on 27 April 1938. Hale, representing the Treasury, reminded those present of the existing policy laid down by the 1934 Select Committee on Estimates, namely that individual government departments were responsible for their own policy with regard to film publicity, subject always to Treasury sanction. He also warned that, because the proposed National Film Council 'would have control of a most power-

The Vansittart committee

ful instrument of national propaganda', its terms of reference must be clearly restricted to overseas propaganda in order to prevent it from being used as a political instrument at home. Having said that, however, Hale preferred instead to develop the existing work of the Joint Films Committee rather than create a new organisation for the purpose. The committee generally agreed that the danger of the council being used as a domestic propaganda instrument must be avoided, but nonetheless considered that the situation abroad merited such a body, and it therefore decided to push ahead with the proposal.

The Vansittart committee convened for a third time on 26 May, when the chairman announced that he was ready to submit a report within the next few days. The report, he said, would be based mainly on Kenney's proposals combined with the decisions already reached at the inter-departmental discussions on trade propaganda.[59] The manner of this announcement provided an ominous indication of Vansittart's future unorthodox behaviour. Although he had given advance warning of his next move, and even went to the trouble of obtaining the support of those present for several specific proposals, the Vansittart committee as a whole was not to be given the opportunity to discuss or amend the chairman's report before its submission. This was to prove the first of several unusual – almost dictatorial – steps taken by Vansittart acting independently of his committee, which was not called to meet again until the following December, and then only to be presented with the report and its outcome as a *fait accompli*.

Vansittart wrote his report on 28 May. There is some evidence to suggest that he did not exert himself unduly to accommodate the views of his committee, which he seems to have regarded as necessary merely to provide him with authoritative backing. The report contained several recommendations which had not been examined previously by the committee, and others to which it had already objected. Moreover, the highly personalised style employed is revealing; after beginning by using the word 'we', Vansittart before long reverted, perhaps subconsciously, to a more frequent use of the first person singular.

Vansittart had, in fact, preferred to work more in conjunction with the experts in the Foreign Office News Department than with the members of his committee. Together with Leeper, Warner and

Psychological rearmament, 1935–1939

Kenney, Vansittart had controlled the direction of the committee's investigations and had imposed the Foreign Office's conception of the necessary solutions upon its recommendations. The attention of the committee, which was originally based upon an idea by Leeper, was steered by Vansittart on to proposals made by Kenney. Warner, as secretary, was in a key position to influence the agenda, and all meetings, whether of the full committee or of specialist groups, had been held at the Foreign Office. It is hardly a coincidence, therefore, that the proceedings of the Vansittart committee, and the report itself, concentrated upon the areas which had been the subject of concern within the News Department for some time. Moreover, Vansittart clearly went beyond his original terms of reference, taking the opportunity in his report to recommend the promotion of Leeper to the position of assistant under secretary of state for Foreign Affairs.[60]

Vansittart's report, however, concentrated essentially upon the two most glaring deficiencies which existed in the peacetime propaganda machinery. Just as trade propaganda was the only aspect of national projection which had been almost entirely ignored, so film remained the only important medium which had not received concerted official attention. As a solution to both problems, Vansittart proposed the creation of centralised machinery. If this solution was accepted, he wrote, 'adequate interlocking machinery will be available, which will secure co-ordination between Government and private enterprise and between the different branches and media of publicity without any taint of Government control'.[61] The proposals were intended to provide Britain with a comprehensive system of national propaganda abroad with the capacity to undertake all forms of publicity by an efficient utilisation of the available media. But this would involve considerable sums of money. The organisation for trade propaganda, for example, which Vansittart believed should be entirely subsidised by the government, would require £15,000 for a six-month investigatory period, whereupon a sum of £100,000 per annum should be allocated to the DOT to maintain it. Vansittart pointed out that this sum was the equivalent of that already spent on publicity by industry, and also by the government on cultural propaganda. Only with such a figure could the danger be avoided of industry 'feeling that they were being treated as the "poor relation"'.[62]

The Vansittart committee

The proposed National Film Council would consist of representatives from the various film interests – official, semi-official and private. Its work would be carried out by a small permanent staff which would be responsible for planning and supervising the production of films made for the council by outside concerns, and for arranging distribution overseas. Vansittart estimated that a sum of £50,000 would be initially required to set up the council, which would then require an annual grant of £150,000 to keep it running. 'With such a sum', he wrote, 'excellent work could be done, but it would not be worth setting up the Council unless His Majesty's Government were prepared to devote an annual sum of that nature to its work.'[63] But in order to avoid any discrepancies in the existing machinery, Vansittart further proposed that a supplementary grant of £60,550 be allocated to the British Council to cover increased costs in the renting of accommodation, the recruitment of additional staff and the extension of cultural propaganda in the Near and Middle East. He also proposed an expansion of the Travel Association's tourist propaganda, and for this a grant of £50,000 a year would be required.

Vansittart next turned his attention to a matter 'of primary importance for the carrying out of our publicity abroad in its many aspects', but in doing so departed from his original terms of reference. He proposed the appointment of at least fifteen additional press attachés in those countries 'where it is important for political or commercial reasons that British publicity should be actively promoted'.[64] The expansion of the publicity machinery advocated in his report would make the presence of such officials essential if the work of those organisations which relied upon diplomatic cooperation – such as the British Council, the Travel Association and the projected National Film Council – was to be effectively supervised 'on the spot'. For, as Vansittart maintained,

> Publicity has now become as much a function of diplomacy as commerce, and I am convinced that Press Attachés are as necessary today as Commercial Secretaries ... I would urge that appointments should be made within the near future ... and that this recommendation should be regarded as an integral part of the scheme for publicity abroad.[65]

Vansittart had been advancing this thesis for some time; the problem had been convincing many of his fellow diplomats of its validity. In addition, however, he proposed that the unpaid chairman of the British Council, Lord Lloyd, should also be appointed president of the Travel Association when Lord Derby retired later in the year. This would provide a higher degree of integration of their work into the requirements of modern British diplomacy. For this dual role, Lloyd should receive a salary of £5,000 per annum for his services 'and the energies which he brings to them', which Vansittart considered 'quite indispensable to success'.[66]

In short, the total cost of Vansittart's proposals would amount to somewhere in the region of £550,000, but the chief diplomatic adviser believed that 'nothing really effective in this modern and competitive world can be achieved on less'. Exactly how he arrived at such a figure is not clear from the report. Instead, he merely cited in support of his proposals the House of Commons resolution of 16 February with the addition that, as a result of correspondence and conversations with numerous individuals, he considered that any decision to substantially increase expenditure on national publicity 'would not cause surprise – rather the contrary'.[67] Perhaps he was right, but Vansittart's next move was certainly the cause of considerable surprise.

He decided to send his report direct to the Prime Minister with a covering note which virtually demanded its immediate acceptance.[68] This was a tactical miscalculation. In pursuing such a direct approach, Vansittart was abandoning the normal diplomatic procedure whereby the report would first have been sent through the pyramidal administration of the Foreign Office, and then on to the Treasury before it even reached Chamberlain – a move which did not pass without disapproving criticism in the Prime Minister's office. One of the private secretaries informed Chamberlain: 'It is quite wrong to short-circuit the usual procedure like this ... It obviously requires further elucidation before you ought to be asked to bless it.'[69] This was indeed so. Vansittart's decision to send his report direct to the Prime Minister without the knowledge and prior approval of the Foreign Secretary was clearly a hopeless negation of ministerial responsibility. Despite the fact that Vansittart had simultaneously sent copies of his report to Warren Fisher and Sir John Simon at the Treasury, and to Cadogan and Halifax (Eden's replacement as Foreign Secretary since February) in the Foreign Office, he appeared to be dismissing the traditions of official bureaucracy. But

The Vansittart committee

the post of chief diplomatic adviser had no constitutional precedent, 'and the appointment was an anomalous one from the outset'.[70] Vansittart was possibly taking advantage of the anomaly to prove that he had direct access to the Prime Minister in his capacity as chief diplomatic adviser, a supposition to which the announced terms of his appointment lent some weight. Moreover, Chamberlain had personally approved the appointment of the Vansittart committee in January, and, following the departure of Eden, the Prime Minister might have appeared more responsive than Lord Halifax. The most likely explanation, however, would seem to have been Vansittart's desire to secure Chamberlain's immediate approval for his proposals in time for submission in the supplementary estimates in July. He was undoubtedly conscious of the Treasury's long record of obstruction over publicity matters, and he probably anticipated further opposition to the new proposals, which, by the standards of the 1930s, involved considerable expenditure. It therefore seems likely that Vansittart was attempting to avoid protracted negotiations and unnecessary delay in the implementation of questions which he felt required urgent attention. Yet there is also the possibility that he feared obstruction much nearer home; he was well aware that both Cadogan and Halifax were less committed to the cause of national publicity abroad than he would have liked them to be.

Whatever his real reasons, Vansittart's approach proved unsuccessful. In effect, he did the report more harm than good. Because the Prime Minister was not responsible for the sanctioning of large sums of money for this or that purpose, the report was sooner or later bound to go to the Treasury. On reading the report, Chamberlain minuted: 'This is really a very astonishing document to receive from a Civil Servant', and also stated that he was not prepared to consider the proposals before they had been processed through the normal channels or until he had heard the opinion of the Foreign Secretary.[71] Sir Horace Wilson, the government's chief industrial adviser, concurred, pointing out that it was for the Foreign Secretary, and not the chief diplomatic adviser, to decide whether or not the matter should be brought before the premier.[72] Chamberlain's reply to Vansittart incorporated these sentiments.[73] When, however, the report was referred back to the Foreign Secretary, Lord Halifax admitted that he was 'not competent to express an opinion upon the details of the proposals'.[74] Nevertheless, following a meeting with Vansittart and Lord Lloyd, he was sufficiently impressed with their insistence upon the urgency of the problem that he urged the Chancellor of the Exchequer, Sir John Simon, to give the report speedy consideration.[75] This was precisely the situation which Vansittart had wished to avoid. With the ball now firmly in the Treasury's court, the report was subjected to lengthy scrutiny, and detailed investigations dragged on for the rest of the year.

The Foreign Office played a relatively minor role in these investigations. The News Department, which regarded the report as definitive of its views, stubbornly maintained that it accepted the proposals *in toto* and could therefore see no reason for further discussion[76] – an attitude which did not enhance its popularity with a much more critical Treasury. Perhaps resentful of Vansittart's attempt to by-pass their opinions, Treasury officials subjected each and every proposal to a microscopic examination. And although many of Vansittart's recommendations were eventually accepted, as one historian has pointed out, 'the inference is that if he had put his ideas forward in the ordinary way and not like a bull in a china shop he might have got all that he wanted without delay'.[77]

Edward Hale, the Treasury's representative on the Vansittart committee, began the autopsy on the proposals and, with the assistance of Sir Alan Barlow,[78] produced a formidable case against their acceptance. Hale declared his opposition on a variety of different grounds. While accepting that there was a genuine need for increased trade propaganda and even that it was futile to expect any financial support from industry, he nonetheless remained sceptical that the proposed central body was the correct solution. He wrote:

I am far from convinced that an organisation on a nation-wide scale, whether purely Governmental or grant-aided, or financed wholly by private enterprise, is the proper way to tackle trade publicity. It is possible to 'project' England as a country of culture or as a place in which to take a holiday. But trade publicity must, to be effective, be carried out in terms of particular goods – motor cars, worsteds, steel, etc.[79]

He accordingly believed that each individual export trade should more properly conduct trade propaganda at its own expense, considering that industry rather than the nation would more directly profit from such work. 'If trade publicity is inadequate', he argued, 'that is not the responsibility of Government.' This view, diametri-

The Vansittart committee

cally opposed to that of Vansittart and the DOT, merely served to reinforce the deadlock already encountered by the Co-ordinating Committee on this question.

Hale was equally, if not more, opposed to the proposal to establish a National Film Council. This was because of the anomaly which such a body would produce in the existing publicity apparatus. British overseas propaganda was organised by reference to its variable forms, not by reference to media. Hence the British Council was responsible for cultural propaganda and the Travel Association for tourist propaganda, and it was proposed that a new body be created for trade propaganda. Hale believed that

If to this type of organisation you add a body concerned with publicity for all purposes but through one medium, viz. the film, you introduce an awkward cross-classification which seems to me to be wrong in principle and unlikely to work in practice. Such a body would tend, I would fear, to exalt the means above the end.[80]

This objection may simply have been the product of a tidy mind, and a conservative one at that, for Hale preferred instead to adhere to the existing policy as laid down in 1934 whereby it was the responsibility of each individual government department to decide what proportion of its funds should be devoted to the various media of publicity. But it is an example of the kind of scrutiny to which the Vansittart proposals were subjected. Moreover, Hale also opposed the suggested higher grants to the British Council and to the Travel Association. He argued that the council's work in the Middle East had become less important in view of the recent détente with Italy with the signing of the Anglo-Italian Gentleman's Agreement. As for the discrepancy between the rates of increased governmental support to the council and to the Travel Association, he pointed out that the latter had never 'intended to be a continuing one, and several efforts have been made to bring it to an end', efforts which had proved unsuccessful only because of 'very strong pressure' exerted by the interests involved. Besides, he wrote, the analogy between the two bodies was not a valid one:

The British Council is engaged on propaganda of an essentially political character, which does not benefit particular interests except in so far as it may encourage the tourist traffic. The propaganda of the Travel Association on the other hand is directly aimed at profit for the commercial

Psychological rearmament, 1935–1939

interests who house and transport visitors from overseas and ought to be paid for by those interests.[81]

In other words, Hale had entirely missed the point concerning the importance of foreign visitors to the projection of Britain.

He next turned his attention to Vansittart's other proposals. He stated that he was not opposed to the payment of a salary to Lord Lloyd but suggested that, in view of the Travel Association's jealousy of the council's income, he might not be welcomed as its president. Also on the question of personnel, Hale did not consider that Rex Leeper's present work justified his promotion. If the publicity machinery was to be expanded along lines envisaged by Vansittart, then his position would need to be re-examined. In the margin alongside this point, Warren Fisher minuted caustically: 'Mr. Leeper is already overpaid, though I would be prepared to pay him more as a pension', an indication of the extent to which the head of the News Department had upset people in high places by 1938.

The only proposal to which Hale found no objection was the increase in the number of press attachés, although he was not happy with Vansittart's failure to raise this matter at the Co-ordinating Committee. Yet he did concede that 'there is no doubt that in modern conditions press work has tended to grow in importance, and the diplomat who has no journalistic experience and whose stay at any post is not long enough to enable him to develop all the necessary contacts, is not an ideal instrument for the purpose'.[82]

After he had expressed point by point his specific objections to the Vansittart proposals, Hale concluded with several general observations which raised important political issues. For example, he warned that

> A sort of armament race in propaganda is developing, to which it is no easier to see finality than to the armament race itself... I am not suggesting that the propaganda race will ever involve figures at all comparable with those involved by the armaments race. But they will be large, and the camel's back is in no condition to take even straws lightly.[83]

Hale clearly believed that the economy, and not propaganda, was the fourth arm of defence. His concern over the propaganda race derived from the belief that the expenditure 'is dictated by your rivals and your effort can be only limited by exhaustion'. The Germans were estimated as currently spending the equivalent of £5

The Vansittart committee

million and the Italians £2 million on propaganda, 'and there is no reason to believe that growth has ceased'. The Vansittart proposals, he continued, had 'potentialities of growth sufficient to raise the issue whether it is better to conserve your strength or dissipate your energies by creating an impression'. Although the Foreign Office had repeatedly disclaimed any intention of imitating the scale or the manner of totalitarian propaganda, 'that is what we shall be sliding into'. It was an illusion to suppose that the Treasury could check the growth of British propaganda once it had been placed upon a larger scale, because 'if we accept the underlying philosophy of the Vansittart recommendations, the future level of expenditure will be settled by Germany'.[84]

Quite apart from financial objections, Hale stated his case against the report on political grounds. He pointed to the past efforts of government to avoid the appearance of direct involvement in propaganda; the BBC, the British Council and the Travel Association were autonomous or semi-autonomous bodies, and it was intended to deal with the problem of news distribution abroad through Reuters. If the organisations for trade and film propaganda were set up, they would be purely official bodies dependent entirely upon governmental support. There was also the additional danger that a National Film Council might be converted to include domestic propaganda and become influenced by party politics. Hale concluded with the following remarks, written in light of the recent weekend crisis of 20–2 May provoked by reports of German troop movements on the Czechoslovakian border:

There is no doubt that the general effect of Government propaganda in recent years has been to poison the international atmosphere. It may be replied that, from that point of view, the measures proposed are at least harmless. I do not believe that any propaganda is really harmless. Even if you are careful, in praising yourself, not to decry others, the unflattering implication is always there. 10 days ago, the British press acclaimed our diplomatic efforts in the cause of peace. That could be read as implying that Germany was on the point of aggression. It was so read in Germany, and bitterly resented. The example is worth quoting as showing how easily the most harmless publicity may give offence. Even apart from this danger, I fear that by entering the propaganda race, we shall intensify it.[85]

It was for this reason that Hale feared that any announcement by the British government of an increase in its overseas propaganda would be interpreted in Germany as a direct challenge, and because of this, he did not believe that

> in the long run it will be possible to combine the policy of appeasement with a forward policy in propaganda. Armaments may be infinitely more expensive than propaganda but they, at least, have the virtue of being dumb, and do not cause the same ill-will. From the point of view of appeasement, the propaganda race seems to me the more serious danger.[86]

Hale's views were favourably received in the Treasury. Unlike Vansittart's, however, they were motivated by a strong belief in the value of the policy of appeasement, and not by a fear of an impending war with Germany.

It is possible that the Vansittart report was deliberately subjected to lengthy examination by the Treasury in order to help provide a 'cooling off' period in Anglo-German relations at a time when the international atmosphere was severely strained in the wake of the Anschluss and the May crisis. When Lord Halifax wrote to Simon on 20 June reiterating his appeal for speedy consideration,[87] it failed to rouse the Treasury. Barlow criticised the News Department of the Foreign Office for its inflexible stand over the report and its unwillingness to discuss the proposals further. He also claimed, not without justification, that the figures quoted by Vansittart appeared to 'have no considered basis, but are merely guesses'.[88] Sir Richard Hopkins, another senior Treasury official, generally agreed with Barlow and Hale, although he was more prepared to accept 'the intrinsic merits of some (though not all) of the objects on which Sir R. Vansittart wishes to spend more money'.[89] Warren Fisher, however, considered 'the whole thing *very* amateurish' and was more inclined towards the critical views of Barlow and Hale.[90] Nevertheless, the Chancellor supported the more restrained view of Hopkins and asked his permanent under secretary to discuss a smaller sum with Vansittart.[91] Accordingly, Fisher charged Hale and Barlow with the task of opening negotiations with Vansittart for the purpose of providing some increase in expenditure on propaganda abroad.[92]

Barlow and Hale met Vansittart, Leeper and Warner on 30 June to inform them that the Treasury was not prepared to authorise the sums envisaged in the report, but that it was prepared to sanction an additional £50,000 for the remainder of 1938, with a further

The Vansittart committee

maximum figure of £100,000 for 1939.⁹³ Vansittart surprisingly, but realistically, conceded that under the present financial circumstances he would be prepared to accept the more moderate outlay. However, it can scarcely be contended that those circumstances had changed very much in the month which had elapsed since the report was written. By accepting the need for financial restraint, Vansittart was in fact playing into the hands of the Treasury. Similarly, his admission added credence to the suspicion that his figures had been compiled in a somewhat random manner. It was hardly surprising, therefore, that the permanent head of the Treasury and of the Civil Service, who had collaborated with Vansittart to great effect in the preparation of successive reports for the Defence Requirements Committee, should describe the whole thing as very amateurish. But, as Ian Colvin has written, the Treasury's influence in policy, 'invisible but persistent, is well illustrated in its criticism of the Vansittart proposals'.⁹⁴

Returning to the charge

The Vansittart report was a major event in the evolution of Britain's involvement in the conduct of propaganda abroad. It was, in many ways, the logical outcome of two decades of gradual, staggered and diverse growth in a controversial new area of governmental responsibility. It was a powerful attempt not only to extend the existing peacetime machinery but also to remove the deficiencies in the programme of national projection so that this task would be more efficiently co-ordinated and adapted to meet the conditions required for psychological rearmament. By 1938 propaganda had become a subject considered worthy of serious consideration at the highest levels of British government. The volatile combination of such a controversial figure as Vansittart with such a contentious activity as propaganda at a time of worsening international tension demanded no less. But what exactly did Vansittart achieve? It cannot simply be said that his report was a complete failure, because most of the proposals were, in fact, implemented – albeit on a smaller scale and at a later date than originally anticipated. In actual terms, a supplementary figure of £50,000 was secured for increasing British overseas propaganda in 1938, with the promise of a further £100,000 for work in 1939. This might well have been regarded as a significant increase, but, as Vansittart pointed out to his committee when it met for a fourth time in December 1938, this was a far cry from the half million pounds requested in his report.[95]

The British Council was the first to benefit, at least to outward appearances, from the report. In reality, however, the Treasury's award of a further £20,000, thereby bringing the council's governmental revenue to a total of £130,000 for 1938–9, was not due solely to Vansittart's efforts. Support for the council and sympathy for its aims were fairly widespread by 1938, and it had enjoyed dramatic annual increases in its income since its foundation four years earlier. Lord Lloyd had proved to be a formidable and influential chairman, quite capable of championing the cause of cultural propaganda by himself. However, with an absence of tact reminiscent of Vansittart, Lloyd had already attempted to short-circuit the Treasury's examination of the publicity proposals by a direct personal appeal to the Chancellor.[96] Lloyd was persistent in his appeals for a higher government grant as a method of asserting the growing independence of the British Council from the control of the Foreign Office. Nevertheless, he undoubtedly welcomed the efforts of Vansittart, with whom he shared many apprehensions concerning the menace posed by Hitler, in the council's cause. But it does appear that those efforts merely helped to reinforce the council's case rather than providing the sole reason for the increased financial support.

A much more obvious beneficiary of the Vansittart report was the Travel Association. A figure of £15,000 was awarded for tourist propaganda in 1939 – an increase of 200 per cent over the previous grant. The Treasury did, however, warn that in subsequent years the governmental grant would be related to outside subscriptions on a proportional basis – a qualification which was not welcomed by the Foreign Office.[97] The increase was nonetheless a welcome stimulus for the association, as indeed was the appointment of Lord Lloyd as president on 12 December 1938, succeeding the retiring Lord Derby. Lloyd held the new post simultaneously with his chairmanship of the British Council. This latter development did much to ease the tension and rivalry which had previously characterised relations between the two organisations.

From the point of view of the Foreign Office News Department, the most satisfying immediate outcome was the Treasury's willingness to authorise the appointment of additional press attachés to

The Vansittart committee

diplomatic missions abroad. In June 1938, Leeper had written that 'the Treasury have always opposed this in the past for reasons of economy and we have done our best to urge missions to carry on this work with their existing staffs. It has not been a success.'[98] With the increased output of material from the News Department, the British Council and the Travel Association, in addition to the demands of foreign journalists for official news, it had now become necessary to appoint more publicity experts at the receiving end of the process in order to ensure proper supervision of the different types of work being done and also to keep an ever watchful eye upon foreign opinion. The Treasury on this occasion was in agreement; it did not involve any question of principle – there already existed press attachés at the embassies in Paris, Rome and Berlin and at the consulate in New York. Accordingly, on 1 November 1938, the News Department canvassed the opinion of the various diplomatic missions abroad concerning the desirability of appointing press attachés on their staffs.[99] The replies proved generally enthusiastic about such a development.[100] The result was that, during the course of 1939, fifteen additional press attachés were appointed to such embassies as Athens, Belgrade, Lisbon, Santiago and Warsaw and in Scandinavia.

Much less satisfying was the failure to secure promotion for Leeper to the position of assistant under secretary. Leeper was in a unique position at the Foreign Office. He was the senior counsellor, and his knowledge and experience of British peacetime propaganda was unrivalled. He was due either for promotion or for an overseas appointment. Vansittart wished to avoid the latter because he considered Leeper irreplaceable. But Leeper's behaviour, particularly during the Munich crisis, had served only to antagonise many senior officials at both the Treasury and 10 Downing Street. Leeper himself described, many years later, an extraordinary conversation he had had with Horace Wilson shortly after Munich, during the course of which Wilson is alleged to have said to him: 'Some members of the Foreign Office say you are not loyal to the Government... If that is the impression you create you are not suitable for work in the Foreign Office in London... You have no future in the Foreign Office. You must seek that future abroad.'[101] Other than Leeper's memory, there is no evidence available to substantiate this episode, although Cadogan did complain that the Treasury were proving

Psychological rearmament, 1935–1939

rather unhelpful in his attempt to find for Leeper 'a niche on the landing' rather than 'kicking him downstairs'.[102] Sir John Simon replied that 'in our view the Department with an indispensable expert is in a dangerous position'.[103] He possibly regarded Vansittart's proposal as a ploy to keep one of his most loyal admirers in the Foreign Office. Cadogan, who had meanwhile taken Leeper off press work in order to take charge of the purely propaganda side of the News Department's work, was in a difficult position. He did not have a vacant position abroad appropriate to Leeper's rank, but if Leeper was permitted to stay in London, the Treasury was not prepared to authorise the creation of an additional under secretaryship. It would be too easy to suggest malevolence on the part of the Treasury. But the simple fact of the matter was that Leeper *was* indispensable, especially at a time when propaganda was being rapidly developed. Leeper therefore remained a counsellor, although he effectively functioned as an assistant under secretary in charge of propaganda throughout 1939. Yet this, in turn, created an anomaly, because Charles Peake, who had assumed Leeper's responsibilities for meeting with the press in October 1938, remained a first secretary in a post which normally merited the status of counsellor.[104] It is a tribute to the devotion of both men that they were prepared to be overworked and underpaid for their services until the outbreak of war.[105]

A much more successful outcome of the Vansittart report was achieved almost a year after it had been submitted. Neither the Foreign Office nor the DOT had been deterred by the initial reluctance of the Treasury to support the proposal for a centralised trade propaganda organisation. Indeed, in anticipation of the Vansittart report's acceptance, the DOT had already planned to establish 'a powerful committee' to prepare the ground for a programme of trade publicity overseas.[106] The Treasury opposed this development,[107] but in sharp contrast to the antipathy of the Foreign Office, the DOT proved more willing to negotiate a possible solution. On 28 June 1938, two of its officials, Edgecumbe and Mullins, went to see Barlow and Hale at the Treasury to present their case. They discovered that the Treasury feared the possibility of a hostile response to any announcement that British propaganda was being increased:

if propaganda was to be successful it would have to be conducted as discreetly as possible without giving rise to the suspicion that propaganda

The Vansittart committee

existed. Once the inauguration of the campaign were made known abroad, press correspondents through whom we hoped ... to distribute publicity articles would be on the look out for such articles, and there was every likelihood that articles which, were it not for the suspicion created in their minds by the flourish of trumpets, they would have accepted, they would no longer accept, regarding them as being propaganda ... It was no doubt quite easy to spend a very large sum of money on propaganda without achieving any considerable effect. In fact propaganda afforded one of the easiest methods of squandering money without return.[108]

Nevertheless, no matter how much the Treasury would have preferred it, the need for such work could not simply vanish. There remained a glaring deficiency in this aspect of national projection which became more acute as time went on. The DOT had found the Treasury 'far more sympathetic than one might have anticipated towards the proposal for the inauguration of a campaign of trade propaganda abroad'[109] but failed to submit an immediate proposal because of 'the leave season, during which, naturally the most senior officials here were playing Box and Cox: then the threatened international crisis began to assume serious proportions'.[110] When the DOT did finally submit its formal application on 14 October 1938,[111] the evidence and arguments in favour of initiating trade propaganda were such that the Treasury could no longer resist the appeal. Within a fortnight, a sum of £10,000 was set aside for the DOT to undertake the work, chiefly through the medium of the press. In reaching this decision, which was to be kept secret, the Treasury laid down that, 'as a matter of general principle, publicity on behalf of particular trades and industries, and aimed at benefiting those particular trades and industries alone, should not be conducted and financed through public funds'.[112] Vansittart informed his committee of this decision at its December meeting.[113]

Following a brief investigatory period, the DOT invited Robert Williamson, an industrial journalist with an expert knowledge of trade propaganda, to set up an Industrial Publicity Unit with the following terms of reference: 'To secure the insertion in newspapers published outside the United Kingdom of news items, special articles and illustrations calculated to project the achievement, enterprise and efficiency of the trade and industry of the United Kingdom as a whole and not particular trades or industries or individual concerns'.[114] The Industrial Publicity Unit officially came into being on

Psychological rearmament, 1935–1939

25 April 1939 and began its work unobtrusively, operating under the auspices of the DOT but clearly outside of it in order to avoid any ostensible connection with the government. Secrecy was essential to protect the credibility of the unit's propaganda.[115] Detailed information concerning the work of the unit is rare; the DOT appears to have given Williamson a virtual free hand in determining the direction of his activities. It is known that he established close contacts with the British Council, the Travel Association, Reuters, the BBC and the Federation of British Industries. Williamson also maintained a close link with the five major newsreel companies, 'suggesting to them subjects of industrial interest calculated to improve this country's industrial prestige'.[116] However, the unit's main concern was with press publicity, and by August 1939 Williamson had surpassed all initial expectations by securing the insertion of more than 10,000 industrial articles and news items in the foreign press.[117] The subject of these articles varied considerably, ranging from 'Going Gay in Cottons: Ginghams now elevated to evening wear' (issued to the empire press, 30 June 1939) to 'Britain builds still more ships' (issued to the foreign and empire press, 11 and 12 July 1939) and 'Three Continents buy British Pigs' (issued to the empire press, Egypt and Palestine, and to foreign farming papers, 16 August 1939).[118] The work continued into the war, but the unit, which had been set up on a one-year renewable contract, was absorbed into the Ministry of Information in 1940. Nevertheless, during the unit's four months of peacetime existence, a constructive attempt had been made to fill one of the most glaring deficiencies within the peacetime propaganda apparatus, albeit almost too late in the day to be of any real value.

The other major deficiency upon which the Vansittart report had concentrated, film propaganda, was not to receive even a remote measure of success, although this was not due to any lack of effort on the part of the various interests concerned. Following the Treasury's dismissal of the proposal to create a National Film Council, the Foreign Office News Department had continued to search for an alternative solution to the problem of the severe shortage of suitable propaganda films. Direct government control was clearly out of the question, not least because the 1938 Cinematograph Films Act was partly designed to create a strong and independent film industry free from the type of state control that existed in

The Vansittart committee

Soviet Russia or in Nazi Germany. But a peculiarly British variation of official influence over the film industry, or rather over certain sections of the industry which proved amenable to suggestions, did emerge. During 1937 and 1938, with the growing estrangement of Whitehall from the Griersonian section of the documentary film movement,[119] both the Foreign Office and the Joint Films Committee began to look towards the newsreels to shoulder the burden of British film publicity overseas. Clearly basing its assumption on the belief that news really did constitute the shocktroops of propaganda, the Joint Films Committee advocated 'the judicious exploitation of the newsreel, which is far more convincing than any fabricated propaganda product'.[120] Negotiations with the newsreel companies in both London and Paris were entered into during 1938 – in Paris, because it acted as the central exchange for news film among the various European countries.[121] The Joint Films Committee's aim was to secure an increased proportion of British news items in the newsreels which were distributed abroad. It was considered essential 'that news of this country should receive its proper share of attention in foreign film programmes and should not be edged off the screen by American items admitted for commercial reasons or subsidised items from other European states'.[122] It was perhaps partly for this reason that an initiative from the controversial American March of Time series to encourage a more effective use of its newsreels in the projection of Britain abroad was allowed to lapse.[123] March of Time films were considered too blatant in approach, and had frequently clashed with the British censors.[124] Besides, the British government would have little control over the editorial policies of an American company operating outside Britain.

This is not to suggest that the British government exercised direct control over the British newsreel companies. In many respects there was no need. The newsreels

featured and played up the ordinary, the orderly, the well-arranged aspects and events of the society around them, rather than the truly sensational. The newsreels laid stress on the points of similarity, identity of outlook and interests between the world of the government and that of their working-class regulars. Above all, they stressed the points of consensus rather than the points of conflict. The majority of newsreel editors, it should be added, did so by inclination as well as necessity.[125]

This statement applies, of course, mainly to the five leading newsreel companies – the complete opposite may be said to have applied to, say, the films of the radical wing of the Labour movement.[126]

In the early summer of 1938, the Joint Films Committee reached an agreement with Gaumont–British News. The committee agreed to pay a subsidy to the company in return for an undertaking by which Gaumont–British agreed to increase the number of British news items distributed abroad. Meanwhile, the committee agreed to support the efforts of the Newsreel Association to abolish the duties on newsreel footage.[127] In other words,

> For a moderate subvention, British news items will be made available over a far larger area than hitherto, and in some cases special news items will be worked up into a more extended form; for example, the recent record-breaking flight of the RAF could be worked up into a general essay on the achievements of British aviation, civil as well as military.[128]

It was largely due to the success of such an arrangement that the Joint Films Committee decided that its arrangements for the New York World Fair would be conducted 'mainly on a newsreel basis'[129] – a decision which was to create an outcry from the documentary film movement, which remained sceptical concerning the value of newsreels.

From the point of view of the Foreign Office, the problem of inadequate film publicity abroad remained. It might extend its co-operation to individual newsreel companies,[130] but this was still merely one aspect of a multi-sided question. The Foreign Office had renewed its pressure upon the Treasury in July and August of 1938 with the result that a compromise solution had been reached whereby the work of the Joint Films Committee was to be strengthened.[131] But this did not solve the problems deriving from a lack of co-ordination between government producers and private directors. There was still a shortage of films suitable for overseas propaganda. Accordingly, on 10 December 1938, Leeper appealed to the Treasury to reopen discussion on Roland Kenney's scheme for a National Film Council, because, he wrote, 'the problem of film propaganda is assuming considerable – almost alarming – proportions, and we cannot help but feel that it should be tackled on the lines of the Co-ordinating Committee's memorandum'.[132] Of the Joint Films Committee, he wrote:

> It is obvious that with their meagre resources, all they can do is but a drop in the ocean compared with what other countries are doing, or with the

The Vansittart committee

obvious needs of countries all over the world. The sum at the disposal of the Joint Committee for the current year for practically the whole world is £4,000!'[133]

Leeper therefore appealed for at least three times that amount, although he considered that a sum of £25,000 per annum would be more appropriate. To this, the Treasury merely retorted that it was the responsibility of the British Council and of the Travel Association to determine what proportion of their combined income should be channelled into the work of their Joint Films Committee.[134]

By February 1939, Vansittart had become more determined than ever to find a more effective solution. With almost crusading zeal, he wrote: 'I am convinced that we must return to the charge. It is in the national interest to do so; and I owe it to my Committee and to myself ... I am going to attack the Treasury again, even if I have to do it alone.'[135] Three months later, Vansittart wrote to the Treasury renewing the proposal for the establishment of a National Film Council, because, he wrote,

I feel that we cannot wait until economic and other circumstances would appear to indicate that the time is propitious from the point of view of the country's finances being in a satisfactory condition as, in my opinion, the need for national film publicity increases month by month, and the longer the problem of dealing with the matter on a comprehensive basis is delayed, the more difficult will it be to make up leeway should an emergency arise.[136]

As it turned out, Vansittart was not alone in his appeal. On 16 February, the Treasury received a letter from three MPs strongly urging the creation of a National Film Council because, they wrote, 'the time is ripe to raise and press this matter, in order that steps may be taken to inform the world of the strength and position of Great Britain and the British Empire and to counter the active anti-British propaganda that is so rife, especially in native territory in different parts of the world'.[137]

Hale suspected that Vansittart was behind this attempt to force the Treasury's hand. He remained opposed to the proposal largely for political reasons. He argued that, in the wrong hands, it would be too easy to convert the council into an instrument of political propaganda at home. Besides, he felt that the provisions of the 1932 Sunday Entertainments Act contained a more satisfactory solution.

Psychological rearmament, 1935–1939

Under this Act, it was a condition of Sunday opening that cinemas should surrender in whole or in part their profits for that day, 5 per cent of which would go to the Cinematograph Fund and the balance to charity. The receipts of the Cinematograph Fund were paid to the British Film Institute, the purpose of which was to encourage the use and development of film as a means of entertainment and instruction. But, Hale continued, a National Film Council which would inevitably become involved in domestic film production raised serious issues of a different nature:

> As long as the public is given nothing but what the film trade thinks that the public wants, the film trade, taking a pretty low view of the public taste, will continue to debase that taste and so justify their low taste. If it be objected that the film must be primarily entertainment and cannot be turned into 'uplift', the answer is that this is equally true of broadcasting where a monopolistic Corporation attempts with considerable success to provide education for the million mixed with wholesome entertainment. But if an attempt to influence the content of films is to be seriously made on a wide scale, it becomes important to ensure that whatever agency is used for this purpose is free from political influences, and with a voted grant depending from year to year on the goodwill of the Government of the day such freedom would be impossible.[138]

These objections were passed on to Sir Ralph Glyn, one of the MPs who had written to the Treasury, in April 1939,[139] although Glyn proved unsympathetic to the fears that a National Film Council 'might be prostituted for nefarious purposes should a Socialist Government be in Office. The argument that a disaster might occur if irresponsible people capture an excellent piece of new machinery has never impressed me very much!'[140]

Nevertheless, Hale stood firm in his opposition to the proposed council when the Vansittart committee met for the fifth time on 17 May. The Treasury, he stated, still preferred the alternative of developing the work of the Joint Films Committee, which would be in a much healthier position to tackle the problem of film propaganda abroad once the British Council's grant for 1939–40 had been increased to £400,000.[141] Hale summarised the Treasury's three fundamental objections to the proposed organisation:

> The first was that while you swop horses the coach necessarily stops. The second was that we preferred to give money for cultural propaganda for all media and leave the British Council to consider how much should be

The Vansittart committee

devoted to films and how much to other media. If we were asked for, say, £150,000 for a National Film Council, we should not feel certain that the money would not be better spent on some other form of propaganda. The third reason I gave was that the National Film Council, if constituted on the lines proposed, would inevitably tend to spread its activities into the home front, even if originally constituted for purposes of propaganda abroad; it would thus become a kind of BBC of the films.[142]

Hale's objections finally made their mark. The Vansittart committee was itself now divided on this issue. It was eventually decided to invite the British Council to explore the possibility of expanding the work of the Joint Films Committee before a final decision was reached, although it did not bode well for the proposal when the Treasury again refused to take up a call for a 'central Government committee' to regulate the commercial production and distribution of official propaganda films, this time voiced by powerful film trade interests in June.[143]

The outcome of the British Council's investigations was considered by the Co-ordinating Committee at its sixth and final meeting in July 1939.[144] It was pointed out that the Joint Films Committee had enjoyed an increase in its budget from a mere £400 in 1936 to £1,200 in 1937 and to £4,000 in 1938. Of this latest figure, however, £1,500 had been spent on adapting and re-editing existing films, whereas only £1,630 had been available for the purchase of new films.[145] The balance was all that remained for the production of additional films. Although the British Council intended to devote £25,000 to the Joint Films Committee for the remainder of 1939, most of this sum would be required to meet the cost of the British entries in the New York World Fair. Little would be available for the production of new films for the non-English-speaking world. Nevertheless, under strong Treasury pressure, it was decided to concentrate upon developing the work of the Joint Films Committee rather than to press ahead for a National Film Council, which, in view of the fact that this was to be the last meeting of the Co-ordinating Committee, would instead be considered by the Treasury's newly formed Overseas and Emergency Publicity Expenditure Committee.[146]

This body, known as the OEPEC, had been created in late June 1939 under the chairmanship of Sir Alan Barlow and with Mr J. Cairncross as its secretary.[147] It was designed for a dual purpose. In the first place, the OEPEC was authorised, 'subject always to the over-riding requirements of Parliamentary authority', to sanction expenditure for any requests to initiate peacetime propaganda abroad which required immediate attention. For example, a Foreign Office request for authority to implement an arrangement by which British official broadcasts would be recorded and distributed free in translation to Portuguese newspapers was sanctioned in June.[148] Further requests to finance the distribution of pamphlets 'which will enable the foreign reader to obtain a clearer view of British policy'[149] and to assist a South American radio station to relay the BBC's news bulletins in Spanish and Portuguese[150] were authorised in August.[151] The Foreign Office also requested sanction for a proposal to authorise the missions at Bucharest, Belgrade, Sofia, Athens and Budapest 'to spend up to £100 each, if necessary, to induce newspaper editors to print the articles ... calculated to put across the British point of view'. The censorship in those countries, 'which was due mainly to fear of German pressure, had recently relaxed somewhat as a result of our firm stand, and it was thought that, by offering the more favourably disposed editors a modest financial premium, they could be persuaded to take the risk, and publish the offending articles'.[152] Cairncross, who received this request, minuted: 'as we have already agreed to the "Operational Expenses" (i.e. palm-greasing) ... I do not think we need boggle at this further analogous charge'.[153]

The second function of the OEPEC was to provide speedy decisions to requests from the planners of the wartime Ministry of Information and other propaganda bodies. As the drift towards war became more and more irreversible, the OEPEC naturally concerned itself more with propaganda in the next war, although this preoccupation did not prevent it from finding time in August 1939 finally to discard the proposal for a National Film Council. The Joint Films Committee was to be the chosen official instrument of British overseas film propaganda – at least in what little was left of peacetime.[154]

Vansittart's proposal concerning film propaganda was the only major recommendation contained in his report of May 1938 which did not achieve implementation before the outbreak of the Second World War. Whereas British overseas film publicity undoubtedly improved during the final year of peace, as was clearly illustrated

The Vansittart committee

by the success enjoyed by the British Cinema Pavilion at the New York World Fair, it was not to receive the degree of official attention that its potential value as an instrument of propaganda demanded until the creation of the Crown Film Unit during the 1939–45 war.

However, the real significance of the Vansittart report lies largely in the reaction it provoked. The successful outcome of its proposals, albeit on a less ambitious scale than had been originally anticipated, was achieved far too late in the day to prove of any real value in so far as the projection of Britain in peacetime was concerned. Yet the proposals did play an important role in the process of psychological rearmament at home in that they helped to re-educate the Treasury and various other sections of the Whitehall bureaucracy as to the importance and, indeed, necessity of conducting national propaganda abroad in a serious and systematic manner.

Nevertheless, what was clearly a milestone in the evolution of Britain's information services and propaganda activities very nearly became a millstone around the neck of the Foreign Office. It is not difficult to appreciate why Vansittart had become impatient with the bureaucratic procedure. His report was the culmination of two decades of Foreign Office pressure for increased British publicity and propaganda, and the manner of its submission was symptomatic of mounting frustration on the part of those News Department officials directly involved at the apparent reluctance of the Treasury to accept the facts as they had been presented. Yet it was precisely for this reason that the Treasury was not initially well disposed towards accepting the report, or at least not at its face value. For a small but influential group of officials who did not share Vansittart's fear of impending disaster, the proposals of the Co-ordinating Committee raised serious financial and political issues which could not be hurriedly dismissed. They also aroused a deep-rooted historical antipathy towards the concept of propaganda as a function of British government, as well as doubts concerning the wisdom and necessity of interfering with such an unpredictable force as public opinion, at least in peacetime. Its opponents chose, in other words, to see the dangers rather than the benefits of national propaganda. Had Vansittart not acted like 'a bull in a china shop', one can only speculate whether his proposals might have been more sympathetically received at the initial stages, and possibly even have earned more rapid approval. But it is unlikely that this would have been the case. The necessary conviction required to authorise large sums of taxpayers' money on such a controversial and intangible activity was not present until the period immediately following the Munich crisis.

It was Munich which, above all, provided the much-needed stimulant to the gradual process of erosion which had been taking place upon official prejudice against British peacetime involvement in propaganda abroad since the end of the First World War. Twenty years on, the brink of war had served to concentrate the official mind upon the inadequacies of policies pursued in the past. Thereafter, Treasury opposition to further expansion of the peacetime propaganda machinery evaporated as if by magic. With the inherent deficiencies of the existing system so blatantly exposed by the crisis, the process of psychological rearmament was dramatically accelerated. The appointment of the additional press attachés, the increased grants to the British Council and the Travel Association, and the creation of the Industrial Publicity Unit were all indicative of the trend away from the long-term concept of national projection towards a more urgent short-term approach to the problem of winning friends and influencing people. This was essentially the reason why, with the notable exception of the National Film Council, all of the major Vansittart proposals had been put into effect by the outbreak of war in September 1939.

Without entering into an argument similar to that which still rages concerning the time factor gained for the rearmament programme by the Munich Agreement, it does appear almost certain that Britain would not have been prepared to embark successfully upon a war of words against the enemy in September 1938. But then again, it could hardly be said that the Ministry of Information was ready for the tasks which lay before it when war actually did break out.[155] Nevertheless, just as the peacetime propaganda organisations benefited greatly from the experience of Munich, and from the extra time gained, so also did the planners of the shadow wartime machinery, who were able to recognise and go some way towards rectifying the deficiencies exposed in their preparations.

Munich did illustrate one significant factor: that no amount of propaganda, however well conducted, could, by itself, disguise the realities of British foreign policy. Actions and deeds counted for

The Vansittart committee

much more. Britain may have saved Europe from the horror of another war, at least temporarily, but the means to achieve that end soon began to raise serious doubts. Once the euphoria had subsided, it became apparent to British propagandists that they would now have to compensate in some way for a loss of national prestige abroad, particularly in the smaller countries whose sympathies lay with the Czechs. The British case required explanation now more than ever before. Leeper believed, however, that this could be achieved simply by using the existing apparatus 'to the full and to regard publicity in its different forms as an integral part of policy, to be given full weight and consideration in any new examination of our position in the world and the measures which should be taken to secure and strengthen it'.[156] The implication was that, hitherto, the work of the peacetime propaganda agencies had only approximately paralleled the broad trends of British foreign policy. Leeper reiterated this view on 10 October 1938 when he appealed to Cadogan and Halifax to regard publicity 'as an integral part of our programme for national defence and national recovery'.[157] Leeper did have a point. While successful propaganda should always follow policy, the tendency in Britain had been to regard propaganda as something clearly apart from the central issues of foreign policy. Propagandists in the diplomatic service or those working for the British Council had been forced to justify or explain the reasons why this or that decision had been reached without being consulted beforehand by the policy-makers. This was, of course, much less of a problem in a dictatorship which exercised a rigorous state control over the media and other organs of publicity than in a democracy which cherished such traditions as freedom of speech and freedom to criticise. But it was a problem which demanded a long-overdue examination.

On 22 October 1938, Leeper developed his views concerning a possible solution. He wrote:

If we decide to bring publicity into the centre of the picture, we can make it the hand-maiden of policy and use it to strengthen our position in those areas of the world where we feel we must be specially active... Our foreign policy, stated in general terms, is to be a combination of reconciliation and security. Our publicity abroad should likewise reflect this combination. We should make it known abroad, through all the channels at our disposal, and we should emphasise those aspects of our policy in the countries where it is most important that they should be emphasised. We should also decide in what areas it is most important for us to conduct active publicity, thereby concentrating rather than dispersing our efforts.[158]

Apart from Germany, Leeper considered that the primary targets for attention should be those countries 'where our trade is most important' as well as Scandinavia, Holland, Belgium, the Dominions and South America. 'Elsewhere we should maintain enough publicity to preserve our position without exaggerating what can be done there.'[159] Strangely, there was no mention of the Far East, an area which had never really received the consistent attention of the peacetime propaganda machinery commensurate with the scale of British interests there. This was possibly because Leeper believed that

> The issues have been simplified by the fact that we and the French have withdrawn from a number of uncertain commitments in Central and South Eastern Europe. We have both come back to Western Europe and the Mediterranean, and so far as Europe is concerned, we are unlikely to be involved in anything which does not affect our immediate interests. We know that our European problem is to protect our country from direct attack and to maintain our position in the Mediterranean and the Near East.[160]

Although the German invasion of Prague in March 1939 created a different set of criteria, Leeper's point was clear enough. Munich had made it essential for Britain to strengthen her influence and position in those areas which were likely to prove invaluable in the event of war. It had now become even more important for Britain to conduct immediate political propaganda alongside the cultural and commercial work of the British Council and the Travel Association in a determined attempt to reassure potential allies of British goodwill while reinforcing the will of present friends to resist the advance of extremist totalitarian ideologies.

It was for this reason that, during the final year of peace, British overseas propaganda tended to concentrate upon such areas as South America, Portugal, Turkey, Egypt, Iraq, Palestine, Italy, Spain and the countries of south-east Europe. This propaganda attempted not only to portray Britain as a viable exponent of advanced democracy and a much more formidable power than foreign propaganda would have people in those countries believe, but also to convince foreign opinion that British words were not merely the hollow protests of a declining power. This became a much easier task after the British government's decision to guaran-

The Vansittart committee

tee Poland, Greece and Romania. Here at last appeared to be the diplomatic proof that Britain meant what she said. The problem then was how to convince foreign opinion of this fact.

7
Propaganda for war

In 1914 Britain had entered the First World War almost completely unprepared for the conduct of propaganda in foreign countries. That this was not the case on the outbreak of the Second World War was largely because of developments which occurred between 1935 and 1939.

The rapid growth of the peacetime machinery during this quinquennium, from the foundation of the British Council to the creation of the Industrial Publicity Unit, has already been discussed. These organisations were, however, designed to promote Britain's prestige in a peaceful, albeit troubled, world. It did not automatically follow that they would be called upon to undertake British overseas propaganda in time of war, when an entirely different set of conditions would require different solutions. Moreover, from an organisational point of view, one of the chief lessons to be drawn from the experience of the Great War was that if inter-departmental rivalry, overlapping and inefficiency were to be avoided in any future conflict, it would be advisable to centralise the conduct of all official propaganda under one roof. As the very appointment of the Vansittart Co-ordinating Committee in 1938 revealed, the record of the peacetime agencies was not a good one in this respect.

Parallel to, but quite distinct from, the expansion of the peacetime apparatus, a sub-committee of the Committee of Imperial Defence was secretly working out the details for the establishment of a Ministry of Information to take charge of all propaganda – both at home and abroad – in the event of war. Although this development was not directly concerned with the peacetime projection of Britain, it nonetheless remains necessary to examine the planning process because of its implications for those organisations already in existence. Attention in this chapter will therefore be focused essentially upon the preparations for propaganda abroad in wartime.

Propaganda for war

Preparations for war

If the necessity for conducting propaganda abroad in peacetime was fully recognised only in the 1930s, the value of propaganda as an effective weapon of warfare had been widely appreciated in Britain as early as 1918. The conviction that British propaganda conducted by Lord Beaverbrook's Ministry of Information and notably by Lord Northcliffe's enemy propaganda department at Crewe House had played a decisive part in the achievement of victory over the Central Powers virtually served to guarantee its revival in any future war. However, at the close of the 'war to end all wars' such a possibility seemed inconceivable. Just as the British armed forces were gradually reduced, so also was the wartime propaganda machinery dismantled in optimistic anticipation of a lasting peace when, it was hoped, neither would be necessary. Although the News Department of the Foreign Office had survived partly to provide a basic skeleton upon which to build in future should the need arise, the likelihood of it being so used seemed remote. It was only as the lofty idealism of the immediate post-war era came to be progressively undermined by the aggressive policies of Japan, Italy and Germany that the prospect of another major war had to be recognised as a distinct possibility. And there was every reason to suspect that propaganda would play an even greater role in the next war than it was believed to have done in the last.

There was nothing unreasonable about this assumption. The fears (albeit exaggerated, as it turned out) of the impact of aerial bombardment upon the morale of the civilian populace, combined with the anticipated nature of the exigencies of total war, plus the advent of the first truly 'mass' media in the form of radio and film, all suggested that propaganda was likely to prove of critical importance in the waging of any future war. Its peacetime exploitation by the totalitarian regimes merely served to reinforce this conviction. When, therefore, British defence planners were forced to consider the question of contingency plans for a war which it was hoped would not come in the wake of the painfully slow death of the Geneva Disarmament Conference, the abandonment of the Ten Year Rule and the production of the Defence Requirements Committee's first major report, it was felt that Britain would need to be sufficiently well equipped from the outset to engage in a war of words.

Psychological rearmament, 1935–1939

The precise events leading up to this decision remain somewhat vague. During the summer of 1935, as the CID was preparing for the impending crisis with Italy over Abyssinia, one of its sub-committees was deliberating over the delicate question of censorship in time of war. It was recognised that propaganda and censorship were twin sisters; some system for issuing news would be required to work alongside the system for controlling it.[1] Accordingly, C. P. Robertson, press attaché at the Air Ministry, appears to have taken the initiative in proposing that plans for the creation of a Ministry of Information should be put under way so that 'we should not merely start off in the case of a future conflict where we ended in the last'.[2] In September 1935, Robertson produced a lengthy memorandum which began:

> The History of the Great War ... emphasises the high importance which publicity eventually attained as a means of maintaining, and, indeed, strengthening the solidarity of the Home, Dominion and Colonial Fronts, of influencing favourably Allied and Neutral opinion, and of breaking down the resistance of the enemy peoples, both soldiers in the field and civilians at home.[3]

But, he argued, the wartime system had been deficient from an organisational point of view largely because of the diversity of the bodies involved in propaganda, such as Crewe House, the Ministry of Information, the National War Aims Committee and the Press Bureau. In other words, his point was that in any future war official propaganda must be conducted from under one roof. Centralisation was, in Robertson's opinion, an essential precondition of success. If he derived this view from the example of Goebbels's ministry in Germany, there is no indication that this was the case. Indeed, as Ian McLaine has pointed out, references to the German propaganda organisation are extremely rare in the records of the shadow Ministry of Information, 'and [there is] no reference whatsoever to Goebbels by name'.[4] But, at the same time, the British planners were undoubtedly influenced to a greater or lesser extent by the alleged efficiency of the German machine, even though they were planning for a pluralistic society.

Robertson's memorandum was considered by the CID on 14 October 1935, when it was decided to establish a sub-committee to prepare plans for the establishment of a Ministry of Information on

Propaganda for war

the outbreak of war.⁵ The chairman was to be Sir John Colville, then parliamentary secretary to the Department of Overseas Trade, who became parliamentary under secretary of state for Scotland in the following month. His sub-committee boasted an impressive membership: Warren Fisher of the Treasury and Vansittart of the Foreign Office; Sir Russell Scott, the permanent under secretary at the Home Office and his counterpart at the Dominions Office, Sir Edward Harding; J. A. G. Troup and Major-General J. G. Dill, respectively the directors of Naval and Military Intelligence; Sir Donald Banks and Sir John Reith, the directors-general of the GPO and of the BBC; C. L. Courteney, deputy chief of the Air Staff; and Sir Maurice Hankey, secretary to the Cabinet and to the CID. Rex Leeper and Stephen Gaselee from the Foreign Office were also present in view of their experience in propaganda. Warren Fisher informed the only member who was not a government official – Sir John Reith – that it was 'as strong a CID committee as had ever been called'.⁶ This may well have been so, but it was also true that few of its members had any detailed knowledge or experience of propaganda. This was perhaps the reason why meetings of the sub-committee turned out to be infrequent; only five full meetings were convened between 1935 and 1939, three of which were held within nine months of its creation. Rather, the detailed planning was undertaken largely by subordinate officials.

Those officials were faced with a formidable task for an alarming eventuality. Yet although the character of the next war would almost certainly be radically different from that of the last, the planners had only the precedent of the Great War upon which to base their new structure – unless, of course, they chose to model their organisation upon that of Goebbels. If that was in fact what happened, as Michael Balfour has argued, a ridiculous situation ensued: 'in the war of words the British imagined that they were copying from the Germans something which the Germans imagined they had copied from the British!'⁷ But it is difficult to see what other alternatives were available to them, even if it did mean that the planners began their work from a misleading premise. The assumption that Britain's war propaganda had been highly successful either in bringing the United States into the war in 1917 or in bringing Germany to her knees the following year tended to be exaggerated by contemporaries, whether friend or foe. If the lessons of the past were to prove of any real value for the future, they had first to be discovered. This proved easier said than done, because the records of the various wartime organisations had largely been destroyed in 1920 or 'lost' in the years that followed. Detailed information on the wartime experiment was simply not available. Instead, the planners were forced to consult the memoirs of such former participants as E. T. Cook (*The Press in Wartime*, 1920), Douglas Brownrigg (*Indiscretions of the Naval Censor*, 1920) and Sir Campbell Stuart (*Secrets of Crewe House*, also 1920). The rather absurd situation which resulted was reflected in the plea of one official, who wrote, after being reduced to consulting an article on propaganda in the *Encyclopaedia Britannica*, 'there must be experts somewhere'. He described the search for information as 'rather like completing a Chinese puzzle, with the key pieces missing'.[8] Consequently, the planning proceeded from the basis of information gleaned from subjective secondary sources which testified to the unqualified success of the wartime experiment and encouraged the belief that little more than increased centralisation would be required in future. Robertson's warning went unheeded. Because those sources helped to perpetuate the wartime reputation for success without really challenging the assumptions upon which that reputation was based, the second Ministry of Information would, it seemed, merely turn out to be a more streamlined version of the first after all.

The outcome might well have been different, however, if the Foreign Office had originally been allowed to have its way. At the first meeting of the CID sub-committee on 25 October 1935, Leeper (speaking on behalf of the absent Vansittart) challenged the basic assumption of Robertson's memorandum that the proposed Ministry of Information should be an entirely separate entity. As an alternative, he argued, the Foreign Office News Department should constitute the nucleus of any future wartime organisation. He considered that in the News Department, with its reservoir of resident experts and expertise as well as its links with the British Council and the Travel Association, there already existed an ideal basic structure capable of expansion and conversion to wartime requirements.[9] Under Leeper's scheme, it would merely be necessary to appoint a large advisory committee which would maintain close contacts with the BBC, the Foreign Office and other government departments. In effect, Leeper's proposal amounted to the reintroduction of a system

Propaganda for war

which had existed in 1917 under the Department of Information, a system which had enabled the Foreign Office to control the direction and policy of British overseas propaganda.[10]

The scheme divided the sub-committee. Hankey, Gaselee and, if to a lesser degree, the chairman considered the peacetime apparatus as capable and worthy of expansion and conversion in the event of war. But theirs was a minority view. Warren Fisher considered the proposal 'too parochial and narrow' and dismissed it as beyond the sub-committee's terms of reference, which clearly were designed to create a separate ministry. He also pointed out that the experience of the News Department was limited to propaganda abroad in peacetime. There was no guarantee that its staff could undertake home propaganda and censorship in time of war. Fisher's views gained the support of the majority, and it was decided that smoother running and greater efficiency would ensue if the ministry was created as a unit apart from the existing machinery and free from the interference of any Whitehall department. The implication was that a return to the 1918 system was infinitely preferable to a return to the arrangements which had existed before the Ministry of Information had taken charge of propaganda from the Foreign Office.

That the planners were subsequently prepared to accept the 1918 model as a blueprint for their work was entirely understandable, particularly in view of the fact that the planning was essentially conducted on a part-time basis by civil servants who were already overworked in their normal duties. Small wonder, therefore, that progress was slow. Leeper, for example, who was appointed assistant director-general designate responsible for the planning of a News Division in March 1937, was forced to withdraw his services a year later because, he wrote, it was 'impossible to give any real attention to these matters'.[11] His counterpart in the proposed Administrative Division, W. P. Hildred, decided to carry on, but warned that the planning 'can only be kept moving in present circumstances by a few of us putting in ghastly hours, risking their health, sacrificing leisure, and possibly prejudicing their positions in their own departments'.[12] It is thus hardly surprising that the planners chose the more convenient alternative of basing their efforts upon what they considered to be the most efficient of wartime precedents, especially when their sources of information gave them little reason for starting afresh.

Psychological rearmament, 1935–1939

At its first meeting, the CID sub-committee had appointed a planning sub-committee under Leeper's chairmanship to examine the preliminary arrangements for the proposed ministry. Leeper's influence upon the planning was to prove considerable, because it was on the basis of his proposals put forward in December 1935 that the foundation was to be laid.[13] The second and third meetings of the full sub-committee, held in February and July 1936, were devoted to discussing Leeper's proposals,[14] and the outcome was a report, dated 27 July 1936, which was to remain the basis of the planning until the outbreak of war. The main function of the Ministry of Information would be

> to present the national case to the public at home and abroad in time of war. To achieve this end it is not only necessary to provide for the preparation and issue of National Propaganda, but also for the issue of 'news' and for such control of information issued to the public as may be demanded by the needs of security.[15]

The final decision to bring the preparations into effect would rest with the government of the day, but it was to be made independently of the precautionary phase provided for in the War Book. The ultimate responsibility for bringing the question before the Cabinet would rest with the Home Secretary.

The report went on to describe in some detail the proposed organisation of the ministry, which was to be the centre for 'the distribution of all information concerning the war' and would endeavour

> firstly, to make use, as far as is practicable, of the publicity facilities which exist in normal times, secondly, to secure the co-operation of publicity services outside the Government Departments, e.g. the Press, the British Broadcasting Corporation and the Film Companies; and thirdly, to produce a system of censorship which is not unnecessarily irksome to those whose activities are subject to it.[16]

In accordance with these aims, it was decided to proceed with the planning in two distinct phases. The first would provide for the creation of a News Division, a Control (or Censorship) Division and an Administrative Division. The second stage, to begin as soon as the first was completed, would see the addition of a Publicity and of an Intelligence Division. Each of these five divisions would be supervised by an assistant director-general who would be responsible to

Propaganda for war

the director-general designate, a post second only in rank to the designated Minister of Information. An advisory committee would also be appointed to ensure the closest possible co-operation between government and private publicity concerns.[17]

The man chosen for the post of director-general designate, to be responsible for the overall supervision of the planning, was Sir Stephen Tallents, author of *The Projection of England* and currently director of public relations at the BBC, a post to which he had been appointed after three years in charge of public relations at the GPO. Reith claimed the credit for nominating Tallents,[18] who continued his duties at the BBC. Reith had himself been offered the job, but had refused because it did not conform to his own conception of his possible future role.[19] In Tallents, he saw a man who was not only well qualified to deal with the planning but who would also champion the cause of the BBC in the tricky question of its wartime relationship with the ministry. Tallents took up his new duties in October 1936 following the complete acceptance of the report by the CID.[20]

A year after the appointment of the sub-committee, therefore, a fundamental organisational structure had been conceived. However, progress was thereafter achieved at a much slower pace, although this was was not the result of any lack of effort on the part of Tallents or the handful of men whom he gathered around him to conduct the work. Indeed, their hands were largely tied by the 1936 report's somewhat rigid conception of the proposed ministry, and also by decisions reached before they had been appointed. For example, in September 1935, another CID sub-committee had recommended that, in the event of war, the Ministry of Information would assume effective control over broadcasting and over the BBC.[21] This proposal was embodied in a report[22] and approved by the CID on 14 October 1935 — nearly a fortnight before the first meeting of the sub-committee to prepare plans for a Ministry of Information. This decision meant that a disproportionate amount of time was devoted by the planners to working out the wartime structure of the BBC and of its position in regard to the Ministry. And whereas broadcasting would undoubtedly prove to be a vital weapon in wartime propaganda, there were other important aspects which demanded detailed examination, but which were denied due consideration at first because of the determination of Reith and Tallents to ensure that the BBC was effectively exploited while its autonomy was preserved.

A dress rehearsal

By the summer of 1937 the first stage of the planning was complete. This heroic effort was due largely to the efforts of the codifying sub-committee, which had continued the preparations where Leeper's original planning sub-committee had left off in 1936.[23] Even so, following a year and a half of deliberations, a conclusion was reached which should have been apparent from the outset, namely that 'given the changes in the speed, scope and method of communications which have taken place since 1918, few of the activities developed between 1914 and 1918 could be adopted without modification in any war of the future'.[24] Moreover, although the preparations for the News, Administrative and Control divisions were well under way in accordance with stage one of the planning process, the plans existed more in the minds of the men responsible for their implementation than in any tangible procedure. Leeper, for example, contemplated that in the event of war the Foreign Office News Department would form the nucleus of the ministry's News Division, which was to be responsible for the dissemination of 'hot news' through the press, radio and newsreels. This, at least, was the idea in theory. But with the single exception of the BBC, the various organs of publicity were completely unaware of the role that the government was contemplating for them in wartime. Moreover, Leeper was anxious to bring the British Council into the picture and asked Tallents to consult Bridge,[25] but despite a preliminary meeting in December 1937, little progress was achieved pending further examination by the planners.[26]

In short, a crucial stage in the planning had been reached. In February 1938 Tallents felt that although 'considerable progress' had been made with regard to the ministry's wartime relationship with government, 'it is important that the preparatory process should be extended beyond the limits of Government Departments and the BBC, so as to enlist representatives of such interests as the press and the film industry in the discussion of the machinery appropriate to the changed conditions of 1938'.[27] He warned that the planning was not sufficiently well advanced to enable the ministry to spring into existence if a sudden emergency arose, underlining the point by con-

Propaganda for war

trasting the relative unpreparedness of the shadow ministry with the more advanced preparations of the service departments. He wrote:

> Even in a war in which the actual operations were geographically restricted, public opinion might come to be engaged on a world-wide front, and might materially affect its issue. Our preparations for the conduct of war on land, by sea and in the air, are the concern of powerful existing departments, and their planning [is] the subject of continuous study by specialised staffs. Our preparations for the conduct of wartime operations of great possible variety and extent in the field of public opinion have no comparable peacetime basis, and their planning is dependent on a handful of men, all, with one exception, very fully employed on other work.[28]

Tallents therefore appealed for a greater sense of urgency and official support for his work.

His views were considered by the full CID sub-committee at its fourth meeting in March 1938, when Tallents requested authority to open negotiations with outside publicity concerns. Despite the risk of premature leakage concerning the existence of this highly secret work, it was decided to grant him permission to consult representatives of the press, news agencies and film companies provided he exercised the maximum discretion.[29] It was further decided that the ministry would be reconfirmed as the proper centre for all governmental wartime propaganda, at home and abroad, and that consequently there would be no transfer of work from the peacetime agencies, whether official or semi-official, 'unless experience proved this to be desirable'.[30] These important decisions were ratified by the CID on 12 May 1938.[31]

It was at this point that the planning began to move away from the original conception based upon the 1918 precedent, where propaganda had been conducted at home and in allied, neutral and enemy countries. During the late spring and early summer of 1938, a vital distinction between overt and covert propaganda began to emerge. Preparations for the Ministry of Information continued essentially along the Reithian concept of propaganda based upon accurate news in readiness to conduct overt, or 'white', propaganda, i.e. that which was disseminated by an attributable official agency. However, in the wake of the Anschluss, 'when Hitler's annexation of his Austrian homeland made imminent danger plain, the British began afresh to turn some official attention toward irregular and clandestine warfare'.[32] An entirely different set of priorities and

Psychological rearmament, 1935–1939

techniques would be required for propaganda designed to foster disaffection against the enemy. As M. R. D. Foot has written;

> Clandestine operations are probably quite as old as war, if not quite as respectable; the Trojan horse provides the classic example... But by 1938 the days of irregular warfare as a normal tactic of imperial expansion and defence were past, and half forgotten; no organisations conducting it survived and there was no readily available corpus of lessons learned or of tried operators in the field.[33]

This deficiency began to be rectified when preparations for covert, or 'black', propaganda (i.e. that conducted by an unattributable official source) were initiated about eighteen months before the actual outbreak of war.

Information relating to this development in the twilight area of government between military intelligence and political propaganda is not freely available, but it does appear that two organisations designed to conduct 'black' propaganda came into being during the summer of 1938. The first of these, established by MI6 and known as Section D, was set up 'to investigate every possibility of attacking potential enemies by means other than the preparation of military forces'.[34] It seems that Section D was concerned with espionage and subversive propaganda and what was described as 'moral sabotage'; it 'handled the unavowable' and, together with another outfit known as GS(R), seems eventually to have evolved into the Special Operations Executive (SOE) during the war.[35]

Slightly more is known about the second department launched by the Foreign Office at about the same time. This came to be known as Department EH after the initials of its headquarters at the Imperial Communications Committee in Electra House on the Victoria Embankment. The initial credit for laying the groundwork for this body, which was eventually to evolve into the Political Warfare Executive (PWE), appears to belong to Rex Leeper, who had withdrawn earlier in the year from the planning of the Ministry of Information to concentrate upon this matter and upon his normal peacetime duties. Despite his role in inaugurating the preparations for political warfare, however, it seems that Leeper had made too many enemies to earn him the wartime job of controller. On 1 April 1938, he informed his close friend Bruce Lockhart that he was bitterly disappointed 'not to be the man' in charge of the work, and that he had no desire 'to be Number Two'.[36] The man who was chosen to supervise the planning was Sir Campbell Stuart, currently chairman of the Imperial Communications Committee at Electra House and formerly Northcliffe's right-hand man at the department of enemy propaganda at Crewe House in 1918. Stuart was called in to direct the plans in the penultimate week of September 1938 (probably the 24th; the date remains vague).[37] He later recalled that he had received a personal invitation to take charge of Electra House from the Prime Minister through the intermediary channel of Warren Fisher. 'It was not a post I desired', he wrote, 'but it seemed the organisation of 1918 had impressed the powers that be in this possible second war, and I was told that it was considered to be my duty to accept.'[38] Department EH, sometimes known as Department CS after the initials of its chief (thereby giving it a secret-service flavour), began its work in complete secrecy, but too late to prove effective when the possible need of it arose at the height of the Czechoslovakian crisis.

Munich did, in fact, provide a valuable dress rehearsal for the shadow propaganda organisations, but their preparations were, quite frankly, found to be hopelessly inadequate. Important decisions concerning appointments, accommodation and demarcation of duties had yet to be resolved, while the ministry's relationship with the existing peacetime agencies had still not been clarified. The ministry was partially mobilised on 26 September amidst confusion and uncertainty. Its planners had still not consulted the media, and they also seemed unaware of the plans in progress for black propaganda. The British Council had been approached only on 16 September,[39] and it thus comes as no surprise to find Tallents admitting to Leeper a week later that the important foreign section of the Publicity Division 'was not yet organised'.[40] Arrangements were hurriedly made to transfer certain staff, facilities and duties from the Foreign Office News Department to the ministry to perform this role in the event of war, but in view of the general confusion Chamberlain's third flight to Germany provided a most welcome respite for the planners. Despite the optimistic reassurances of Lord Stanhope, Colville's successor as Minister of Information Designate, that 'we would have given a good account of ourselves',[41] the fact remains that the shadow organisation was hopelessly ill prepared for war in September 1938.

Even so, an encouraging measure of success had been achieved through rapid improvisation. In the months after the Anschluss, the planners had turned their attention to an analysis of German public opinion in order to ascertain the most effective methods which might be employed in the event of a sudden emergency. Early in September 1938 one observer, Stephen King-Hall, had informed Tallents that he had recently received 'a good deal of reliable information from Germany and there is no doubt that the home front is shaky'. Moreover, he continued,

> Although it is not within the terms of reference of our committee, I am convinced that a moment might arrive when the whole situation might be saved by an immediate and nation-wide appeal to the German people. If we are involved in war, a shower of pamphlets over Germany should precede a shower of bombs over the Ruhr (I hope we've got the bombers).[42]

Subsequent reports confirmed that German public opinion, starved of uncensored news by the Nazi regime, would prove susceptible to what was tantamount to 'propaganda with facts'.[43] This was partly the motivating factor behind the BBC's decision to broadcast the Prime Minister's speech on 27 September,[44] and indeed of the inauguration by the BBC of news bulletins in several European languages.[45] But in so far as pamphlets and leaflets were concerned, even if the bombers had been available, the Air Ministry had not been consulted as to its willingness to release the necessary men and machines for what would obviously be a highly dangerous mission. There was thus a real danger, as King-Hall had warned, that 'if the crisis gets worse ... we may be caught with our trousers down'.[46]

Essentially, the problem lay in the confusion which existed over the role of the existing peacetime agencies being prepared for propaganda in war in relation to that of the Ministry of Information. At what precise moment was the latter to assume responsibility from the former? Before the outbreak of war, or immediately after? If the ministry sprang into existence prior to a formal declaration of war, it might provoke a political outcry at home, particularly if the emergency was averted at the last minute. It would also provide the enemy with advance warning of what to expect in so far as propaganda was concerned, thus presenting him with an opportunity to prepare for, say, a leaflet raid, which in turn would merely increase the dangers involved in such a mission. If, on the other hand, the peacetime machinery was left in charge right up until the outbreak

Propaganda for war

of hostilities, serious confusion might result from the wartime organisation suddenly taking over without any prior co-operation or advance preparation.

A compromise solution had been reached during the Czech crisis. The CID invited the Foreign Office to undertake the preparation of a suitable leaflet which might be used as soon as war was formally declared. The conclusions drawn from the most recent investigations into the state of opinion in Germany suggested that the war should be presented as a fundamental clash of ideals between democracy and totalitarianism, between freedom and oppression. The theme to be adopted was similar to that employed by Crewe House in 1918, namely the destruction of the governing regime rather than of the German people themselves. The latter were to be presented with a clear and accurate exposition of the true facts in order to show that the war was not in the interest of the ordinary German, who must accordingly rise up against the Nazi regime which had brought the war upon him.[47] Such an appeal, it was argued, would have to be made to all levels of German society by the provision of facts otherwise denied them. Having thus been incited to revolution, the German people could then sue for peace and return to the community of civilised nations. Moreover, it was felt that, at the initial stage of the conflict, the bombing of selective targets should only take place 'after it has been made obvious to all the world that alternative methods of using the aeroplane had been tried'.[48] It was in this way that a propaganda raid could also serve to bring the force of neutral opinion to bear against the Nazi regime.

The pamphlets that were hurriedly drafted in the final week of September fully reflect the belief that the German people were deeply divided and on the verge of rejecting Hitler's regime. On 27 September, the Foreign Office made arrangements with the Air Ministry and with the Stationery Office to print, in German, ten million leaflets which would be dropped by the RAF immediately war was declared, but not before.[49] The Foreign Office leaflet read as follows:

Message to the German People

Mr. Chamberlain, the British Prime Minister, went to Berchtesgaden to help settle the return of 3½ million Sudetens to the Fatherland. The British, French and Czech Governments were ready to negotiate the transfer by peaceable means, so that those who wished to join the Reich could do so.

Psychological rearmament, 1935–1939

The settlement could have been carried out without bloodshed and Britain and France have guaranteed that the territory shall be handed over in the course of a few weeks which are necessary to enable this to be done in an orderly manner.

But the Führer wanted more, and thus the German nation is involved by Herr Hitler in a war which will have spread far and wide, although he could have had what he wanted without shedding a drop of German blood.[50]

In contrast to this measured, almost innocuous, statement, other leaflets were drafted, such as this one prepared by an unattributable source:

Hitler and his lot mean everlasting war. What is the result of his five years' rule? This five years' mockery has come to a grisly end. Now you are paying the bill for this demented Government. We attack you with a heavy heart...

German people! We are not fighting you but your leader. We know you have been deceived and defrauded by him. If you can release yourselves from his leadership, which sets the world in flames so as to conquer it, we promise you a decent peace and the way to an honourable future...

German Mothers! Hitler butchers you and your children simply in order to gratify his megalomaniac desire for power. It is all the same to him – he has no children.[51]

Although it was the former which gained official sanction, the latter does appear to indicate that plans for psychological warfare were also well under way. However, despite some experimental leaflet raids carried out by the RAF in the North of England,[52] none were printed on a large scale, nor, of course, were any actually dropped over Germany. Chamberlain's visit to Munich pre-empted such a course of action. Nevertheless, it was subsequently learned that, on 26 September, Major Grand, the head of Section D, had been instructed (by whom is not known) to secure the dissemination of leaflets in German 'through all channels outside this country' – presumably this meant the Secret Intelligence Service – 'and had apparently got a few of them into Germany'.[53] Further evidence or confirmation of this event is not available. Nor is it known what Electra House was doing during these critical days, although it does appear that Campbell Stuart had hardly begun to gather his staff together when the Prime Minister 'felt that in the Munich meeting he had achieved world peace, and I was instructed to suspend my operations.'[54]

Propaganda for war
Putting out more flags

Of the many deficiencies exposed in the planning process by the Munich crisis, Tallents recognised that the most urgent need was to establish much closer co-operation with existing government departments involved in propaganda. Writing to the Air Ministry on 4 October, he stated: 'Last week's dress rehearsal for the Ministry of Information taught us various lessons, but the sharpest and most urgent of them was the need of properly co-ordinated arrangements for the conveyance of information into enemy countries.'[55] He therefore decided to accelerate his preparations so that the ministry would be capable of efficiently springing into action at a moment's notice. On 5 October contact was established, seemingly for the first time, with Section D in order to establish clear lines of demarcation in the conduct of enemy propaganda, black or white, and thus avoid the danger of overlapping. Major Grand informed A. P. Ryan, the secretary of the CID sub-committee planning the Ministry of Information, that he was contemplating four types of propaganda activity:

a) *Broadcasting*: by broadcasting outside this country, e.g. from Luxembourg, etc....
b) *The Press*: by indexing papers with the names of correspondents in all allied and friendly countries adjacent to enemy territory, and taking steps to introduce desirable material into them.
c) By *leaflets distributed by any and every means* – balloons, carrier pigeons, commercial travellers, communists ... seamen ... social democrats...
d) By *whispering campaigns* which were most effective in the last war.[56]

Little more is known about the activities of Section D during the final year of peace, except that in November 1938 Grand invited Hilda Matheson, director of talks and news at the BBC from 1926 to 1932, to set up a Joint Broadcasting Committee in order to examine the possibilities of broadcasting propaganda 'from stations outside Great Britain, primarily to Germany but also to any other countries which proved available'.[57] Matheson began her work for a six-month experimental period in February 1939. She toured Europe and, on her return, discontinued an unprofitable arrangement recently made with Radio Luxembourg and instead 'advised the formation of a "good-will" committee to sponsor broadcasts arranged

Psychological rearmament, 1935–1939

through the broadcasting authorities of friendly countries, while the possibilities of other means of getting programmes into Germany were explored'.[58] The Joint Broadcasting Committee was the result. Matheson established contact with Leeper at the Foreign Office but worked under the auspices of Section D. Her liaison officer with the planners of the Ministry of Information was Guy Burgess,[59] but the peacetime work of this black propaganda unit remains a tantalising mystery.

Meanwhile, Tallents continued to establish contact with other interested concerns. On 6 October 1938, he conferred with Major E. K. Page and Major W. T. Stephenson (who later became 'Intrepid') to initiate a liaison with Military Intelligence.[60] Shortly afterwards, Tallents also entered into negotiations with the Secret Intelligence Service (SIS), and it was eventually decided that

> Dissemination by overt means, i.e. the BBC, RAF dropping leaflets, etc., will be arranged between the Ministry of Information and the Departments concerned. All subterranean dissemination and dissemination from neutral countries, excepting, of course, the usual diplomatic channels of communication, should be the responsibility of the SIS.[61]

It was also agreed that the Secret Service would advise on the content of any propaganda material prepared by the ministry.[62]

Of the various branches of government approached by Tallents, the Foreign Office proved the most reluctant to accept the demarcations laid down by him and, in the months following Munich, there developed a great deal of mutual antipathy. Although it had long been recognised that the Ministry of Information would assume responsibility for overt propaganda in foreign countries from the Foreign Office on the outbreak of war, the events of September 1938 had served to cloud the issue somewhat. Now there was to be a separate body for black propaganda (Section D) and one for enemy propaganda (Electra House). Moreover, on 27 September, the Treasury had approved a Foreign Office proposal to recreate the Political Intelligence Department for the collection of information of value to the propagandists and to the government as a whole.[63] Leeper, who had been a member of the original PID during the Great War, was placed in charge of the new arrangements, and, with Christopher Warner acting as his assistant, he had begun to

Propaganda for war

recruit a small nucleus staff of specialists in the field of international affairs. Leeper also revised the methods of procedure for those sections of the News Department which were not to be handed over to the Ministry of Information in the event of war.[64] Nevertheless, as long as peace prevailed, it was the Foreign Office and not the ministry which was formally responsible for British overseas propaganda.

Once the Munich Agreement had been signed, the immediate concern was for the maintenance of peace, although it was recognised that the preparations for war would have to continue in case the worst came to the worst. Moreover, for the purposes of peacetime propaganda, Germany resumed the status of a 'foreign' rather than an 'enemy' country (at least for the moment) and was thus a Foreign Office responsibility. Leeper, who was taken off press work in October partly so that he might devote his considerable experience solely to propaganda matters, continued the wartime preparations already begun by the Foreign Office, such as the PID,[65] but was now concerned for the safety of the peacetime machinery, which he had largely developed. He believed that now, more than ever before, propaganda could be utilised in a manner beneficial to British interests and the preservation of peace. In appealing for increased effort along these lines, he wrote that such work 'should, I plead, remain under the control of the Foreign Office in peacetime through the machinery which has been gradually built up in light of experience'.[66] This was written in anticipation of a possible decision to establish a Ministry of Information in peacetime, a suggestion which was now being put forward in some quarters[67] and one to which Leeper was vehemently opposed, not least because he considered that the existing organisations were more than capable of handling any increased burden of work. Eighteen months earlier, when a similar call was heard in some circles, Leeper had written: 'Do not let us think in terms of a Ministry of Information in peacetime. It simply wouldn't work. It is one of the necessary evils of war.'[68] He remained convinced of this despite the lessons of Munich.

Tallents was not entirely in agreement. In November 1938, he proposed that the terms of reference for the planning of the Ministry of Information should now be revised to accommodate its operation prior to, rather than immediately after, the outbreak of hostilities. He proposed a six-stage mobilisation process, the first three stages

Psychological rearmament, 1935–1939

to take place in peacetime. Of the first stage, which Tallents termed 'Undisturbed Peacetime Conditions', he wrote:

> Nothing has struck me more forcibly in my recent exploration of this field than the emphasis spontaneously and separately laid by representatives of all three Service Departments on the need in present continental conditions, in which the boundaries between peace and war are so largely obliterated, of an efficient peacetime centre for the close study of 'enemy' public opinion, and the conveyance through channels appropriate in peace of truth about events and British policy to both 'enemy' and other foreign countries. They have recognised that the country needs specialised armament in the world of opinion not less than in that of munitions of war, and have bluntly remarked that such an equipment might well make the difference between future war and peace.[69]

The process of psychological rearmament, it seemed, was well under way in the months after Munich.

The second stage, which Tallents described as 'Peacetime Conditions Disturbed by Factors which might lead to War', provided for the establishment of machinery to conduct propaganda immediately prior to a possible outbreak of war in a last-ditch attempt to save the peace while all other avenues were being exhausted. This, in other words, would require partial mobilisation of the ministry. Stage three would provide for complete mobilisation 'immediately preceding a decision for peace or war'.[70] Tallents further sought authority for the advance preparation of material, such as propaganda leaflets, so that they might be ready for use at short notice.[71] These, briefly, were the recommendations which Tallents intended to submit to the fifth meeting of the full sub-committee scheduled to take place on 14 December.

Leeper found them completely unacceptable. He reminded Ryan that not only was the Foreign Office responsible for the conduct of all propaganda abroad in peacetime but was also in charge of the study of foreign opinion. The News Department, he wrote, had already examined methods of disseminating the British point of view into Germany in consultation with the Berlin embassy, the British Council and the SIS, and was about to submit its own proposals to the Cabinet. Leeper added:

> It seems to me quite useless to prepare material which, on account of the shifting nature of the political situation, will be out of date almost immediately; the actual preparation of material could be done at very short notice

on the basis of information available to the Foreign Office and the particular line of policy laid down *ad hoc* by the Cabinet.[72]

He accordingly requested that his objections to Tallents's scheme be recorded at the CID sub-committee meeting the following week. In the meantime, however, he devoted his energies to securing the acceptance of his own alternative proposals for increased propaganda by the existing peacetime machinery.

The Foreign Office proposals were embodied in a memorandum, signed by Lord Halifax (but almost certainly written by Leeper) and dated 8 December 1938. Many of the recommendations were based upon the findings of Charles Bridge, secretary-general to the British Council, who had recently returned from a trip to Germany undertaken with a view to improving Anglo-German cultural relations.[73] The Nazi government, it was believed, feared counter-propaganda to such an extent that any British activity in this direction 'should be unobtrusive and unprovocative, as the German Government will do their best to counteract it or even stop it, but it also means that our propaganda, if wisely done, may produce a big effect'.[74] The effective approach to adopt could therefore be the dissemination of accurate news mixed with explanatory comment rather than criticism of German policies or behaviour. Central to this argument was the assertion that 'if Europe may have to choose between a Pax Germanica or a Pax Britannica, the issue may to some extent – and perhaps to a considerable extent – be determined by the success of British propaganda not only in the countries surrounding Germany, but in Germany itself'.[75] In the immediate short term, several proposals were put forward: increasing the BBC news bulletins in German from ten to fifteen minutes; the provision of reciprocal broadcasting facilities; the encouragement of personal contacts between British and German businessmen; the opening of a Travel Association office or of a British Information Bureau in Berlin; the publication by the British Council of a monthly periodical in German with some such title as 'Digest of British Achievement'; and the purchase of broadcasting time on foreign radio stations such as Radio Luxembourg (which was also being examined by Section D). In the long term, the Foreign Office advocated further development of the British Council's cultural and educational activities in Germany through student exchanges, lecture tours and so on. 'Money so spent', it was argued, 'may rightly be regarded as an important item in our general defence programme.'[76]

The Cabinet considered these proposals on 14 December. Halifax reassured his colleagues that by propaganda he meant methods 'of making known the British point of view as impartially, simply and impressively as could be'.[77] He expressed his opposition to the creation of a Ministry of Information in peacetime on the grounds that any propaganda emanating from an official source would automatically be considered suspect by the recipient – always a major problem with overt propaganda, no matter how truthful or factual it may be. Chamberlain admitted that he had not really given much thought to these matters, but was personally favourably disposed towards the idea of broadcasts from foreign radio stations. Other ministers expressed some doubts concerning the suitability of the Foreign Office News Department serving as the nerve-centre for such work in peacetime, because its press guidance in the past 'had not always been in complete harmony with Government policy' – possibly a reference to Leeper's recent behaviour during the Munich crisis which had resulted in him losing his job as press spokesman. It was also pointed out that Lord Lloyd, chairman of the British Council, had, 'on occasion, been a severe critic of Government policy'.[78] Halifax rushed to the defence of the existing arrangements, stating that

> As regards the instrument of carrying out Government propaganda he was satisfied that the Government's policy in this matter must be under the general direction of the Foreign Office, and he accepted full responsibility for whatever emanated from the News Department of the Foreign Office. He thought that it would be very unjust that, merely because Lord Lloyd was a critic of the Government's policy in certain respects, the value of the publicity work which he had undertaken for this country should in any way be under-rated.[79]

After some further discussion, however, Sir John Simon, the Chancellor of the Exchequer, stated that he was unwilling to accept the Foreign Office proposals until they had been subjected to closer scrutiny by the Treasury, whereupon the Cabinet decided to defer any decision until the following week.[80]

That same day, 14 December, the CID sub-committee on the Ministry of Information met to consider Tallents's proposals. Grave concern was expressed at the lack of preparedness during the

Propaganda for war

Munich crisis, and Tallents himself was heavily criticised. Sir Warren Fisher, in the chair pending the appointment of a successor to the retired Stanhope, poured cold water over the six-stage mobilisation plan, adding that he would 'deprecate the formation of a nucleus on any large scale'. He warned that the shadow Ministry of Information must not be allowed to 'usurp in peacetime the functions of existing agencies or Departments, which should remain responsible for working out their own plans'.[81]

This came as a bitter disappointment to Tallents. Leeper's objections had prevailed, and he reassured the sub-committee that the recently expanded News Department would be sufficiently able to cope in any future emergency. Indeed, once it had been decided that all departmental preparations for the next war were to be carried out by the individual government departments concerned, many of Tallents's proposals were rendered superfluous, especially those advocating the partial mobilisation of the ministry in peacetime. Apart from a decision to increase the number of full-time officials engaged in the planning process from one to three, the only outcome of the meeting with which Tallents could have been remotely satisfied was the decision to appoint a new sub-committee under the chairmanship of Sir Campbell Stuart to re-examine the entire question of enemy propaganda in time of war. Yet this was poor consolation for a man who had devoted a considerable part of the past two years of his life to the planning of the Ministry of Information. As it turned out, the meeting proved to be his parting shot. Shortly afterwards, Tallents was dismissed as director-general designate only to be replaced in an astonishing decision by a man with no previous experience of propaganda, Sir Ernest Fass, the public trustee. Although the exact reasons for his dismissal remain obscure, it appears that Tallents was chosen as the natural scapegoat for the Munich débâcle. He had been associated with the preparations in a detailed manner longer than any other individual, during which time he had antagonised enough high-ranking officials to warrant his replacement, at least in their eyes, by a man who was less willing to rock the Whitehall boat. But in the absence of any clear evidence, the episode must remain, as Reith put it, 'all very odd'.[82] Conversely, Leeper's satisfaction with the outcome of the sub-committee meeting could only have been enhanced when, a week later, the Cabinet approved the Foreign Office proposals to

Psychological rearmament, 1935–1939

expand the peacetime machinery, with the single reservation of reciprocal broadcasting.[83]

Sir Ernest Fass did not prove a success, although he was certainly more willing than Tallents had been to accommodate the views of the various interested government departments. Sir Samuel Hoare, the Home Secretary, reluctantly assumed overall responsibility for the planning, although his commitment to the cause was, as he later admitted in his memoirs, half-hearted to say the least.[84] In other words, both men were entirely unsuited to the enormous task of rectifying the serious deficiencies which the Munich crisis had exposed.

On 26 January 1939, the first and only formal meeting of Campbell Stuart's sub-committee was convened at Electra House in order to decide the next phase of the planning in so far as enemy propaganda was concerned. Discussion largely centred on a lengthy memorandum written by Leeper in which he described the work currently being undertaken by the peacetime apparatus under the auspices of the Foreign Office News Department.[85] Following oral amplification by Leeper, the Foreign Office was confirmed as the authority properly responsible in peacetime for the conduct of overseas propaganda and for the study of foreign opinion.[86] On the outbreak of war, different arrangements for the conduct of enemy propaganda would come into force, which were to be the responsibility of Campbell Stuart. Meanwhile, Leeper was to discover the views of the British Council concerning the possible role of cultural propaganda in wartime, while the negotiations between the BBC and the Air Ministry over the role of broadcasting and leaflets in enemy propaganda were to be accelerated.[87]

Campbell Stuart continued his preparations in strict secrecy. Arrangements were made to move his organisation from Electra House to Woburn Abbey on the outbreak of war.[88] A small nucleus staff was recruited and organised into sub-sections for each potential enemy country, while close contacts were established with the service departments, the Foreign Office, the BBC and the shadow Ministry of Information, from which Campbell Stuart was completely separate.[89] In February 1939, negotiations with the BBC were initiated to discuss the technical problems involved in broadcasting to enemy countries without interfering with the Home Service.[90] Alternative methods of distributing propaganda were also investigated but not disclosed 'in the public interest'.[91]

Propaganda for war

The Foreign Office also began to re-examine its own position, and that of the peacetime propaganda machinery, in light of these recent developments. The wartime role of the British Council was considered a question of urgent priority, and, on 30 January 1939, Charles Bridge submitted his views concerning the value of certain cultural activities in wartime.[92] Yet Bridge was labouring under a misconception, because, as Fass pointed out in his reply, the question whether the British Council was to be kept in being in time of war had not yet been decided.[93] Fass therefore requested Leeper to summon an inter-departmental meeting to discuss this question; although he recognised that many of the council's activities would be valuable in wartime, the Ministry of Information would have to be responsible for them.[94] At a preliminary meeting held on 15 February, the ministry planners declared that they would take over the council's lecture work, its press office and its responsibility for prestige articles. If it was decided to allow the council to continue, it would remain in charge of students, books and periodicals, and the preparation of *Britain Today*. But it was decided that the council's work would cease in enemy countries, 'and indeed in any sphere save, perhaps, such activities which, not being direct propaganda, might serve as background for such'.[95]

The wartime role of the council was further considered at a conference held on 17 February by the three full-time planners of the ministry – Fass, A. P. Waterfield and J. B. Beresford – along with Leeper and Hale. It was eventually decided that the ministry would take over the council, although its name and idea would be preserved 'for use within certain limits in order to make it easy to resuscitate the Council after the war assuming that to be the future policy of His Majesty's Government'.[96] The ministry would assume responsibility for any cultural work which could readily be converted for political propaganda purposes. As for the purely cultural and educational activities, it was decided that 'while these should be carried out under the control of the Ministry (in so far as it might be thought necessary to continue them at all) they should be carried out on behalf of the non-existent Council'.[97] Lord Lloyd, who had not been consulted, rather surprisingly accepted these decisions without question when informed of them by Leeper.[98] He may not have taken them too seriously in the absence of written confirmation. Lloyd was initially requested not to inform his executive committee

Psychological rearmament, 1935–1939

of the arrangements, ostensibly because of the secrecy which surrounded the planning but really because, as in the case of the BBC's board of governors, the executive committee would disappear in wartime. However, when Lloyd was asked for written confirmation he rather curiously replied that, 'in the circumstances, I must clearly agree with any proposals and wishes put forward by His Majesty's Government'.[99] Why Lloyd accepted this critically important decision for the future of the council so meekly is not clear from the available records.

In the event, the war did not witness the end of the British Council. During the summer of 1939, while the British Council was enjoying the mixed blessings of a still higher government grant and the start of Lord Beaverbrook's critical press campaign, Lloyd and Bridge managed to persuade the planners of the Ministry of Information to change their mind. It was recognised that the council did have a genuine contribution to make in wartime, particularly in fostering sympathy and friendship among allied and neutral peoples. In August, Waterfield recorded that at a recent conference on propaganda 'we went a great deal further by way of agreeing that the Council's cultural activities should continue during the war than had ever been contemplated in previous discussions on the subject'.[100] In effect, this meant that the British Council entered the war with the same relationship to the Ministry of Information as had existed with the Foreign Office in peacetime.[101] But Lloyd, after what appears to have been a momentary loss of concentration earlier in the year, soon regained his composure to champion the cause of a separate wartime identity for the council. The Ministry of Information was unlikely to survive the war. Lloyd was determined that a similar fate would not befall the British Council. He therefore fought to avoid being tarred with the same brush of the ministry's propaganda in order to protect the council's credibility in anticipation of the return of peace. The 1940 Royal Charter was a significant victory in this battle.

During the spring and summer of 1939, the Foreign Office was busy expanding its peacetime propaganda activities along the lines laid down by the Vansittart report and those approved by the Cabinet in December 1938. The burden of this work fell heavily upon Leeper. He was personally in charge, on the one hand, of reconstituting the Political Intelligent Department and of organising

Propaganda for war

the transfer of Foreign Office propaganda to the Ministry of Information in time of war, and, on the other hand, for all News Department dealings with the British Council, the Industrial Publicity Unit, the Travel Association, the BBC, Reuters and Campbell Stuart's Electra House. In January 1939, he had appealed for increased staff to assist him in this work, claiming that 'I cannot extend my hours of work any further because there simply are not any further hours to find.'[102] Moreover, he argued, because propaganda 'is now coming to be regarded as an essential and important adjunct' to British foreign policy,

> If we do not perform our part adequately and show that we attach importance to it, it will be taken out of our hands with unfortunate results. There are many sharks outside the Foreign Office waiting to take it from us and I think that I can truthfully say that I have had a good deal more knowledge and experience than they have, having worked on it now for ten years in succession, having founded the British Council over four years ago and having initiated the fight for the foreign language broadcasts at a time when the BBC were opposed to them and having won from a reluctant Treasury authority to appoint 14 new Press Attachés abroad.[103]

Leeper might well be forgiven this self-congratulatory outburst. It was largely accurate anyway. His achievements were undeniably impressive, particularly as in almost every case he had been confronted with constant obstruction from quarters which had not recognised the importance of propaganda as early as he had. However, now that many of his ideas were beginning to gain much wider acceptance, Leeper was slowly being squeezed out of the picture. Despite the support of Cadogan,[104] he was forced to continue his labours with inadequate staff and facilities until June 1939, when he was made to swallow perhaps the most bitter pill of all.

Given these difficult conditions, it was not surprising that Leeper's progress with the organisation of the Political Intelligence Department was slow. And yet by February 1939 he had earmarked twelve experts for wartime service, including Bruce Lockhart, E. L. Woodward, Harold Nicolson and G. M. Gathorne-Hardy. His team was recruited from various walks of life in order to avoid the criticism often levelled against the Great War PID, namely that it had been a 'collection of lecturers in vacuo'.[105] Each member was to be responsible for a geographical sub-section dealing with an area or country about which he possessed detailed knowledge and experience. The PID as a whole was to be responsible for the collection, classification and analysis of all information relating to political matters abroad in order to provide an up-to-date appraisal on any question referred to it.[106] A weekly summary of the political situation in each country would be prepared on the basis of information gathered through normal diplomatic channels and by an arrangement made with the Royal Institute of International Affairs at Chatham House. For this purpose, Chatham House would receive a small Treasury grant-in-aid.[107] On 23 February, Leeper assured the planners of the wartime organisation that the PID would not duplicate any of the functions of the Collecting Division of the Ministry of Information because its reports were designed primarily for Cabinet use, whereas the Collecting Division's information was ultimately designed for public consumption. Leeper also took this opportunity to explain the proposed liaison arrangements between the Foreign Office and the ministry: Charles Peake for the ministry's News Division; Kenneth Johnstone for the Publicity Division; Christopher Warner for the Collecting Division; and Michael Huxley for Campbell Stuart's Research Division.[108] Thus, four officials would be responsible for ensuring smooth working relations between the two departments, as compared with just one, Stephen Gaselee, in 1918. Otherwise, the PID was virtually an exact revival of its predecessor.

Despite the considerable improvements which had taken place in the planning of propaganda in the next war, it must be said that much work remained to be done if the work was to be conducted on an efficient scale. The preparations were still being conducted at a relatively leisurely pace. The German invasion of Prague in March 1939 was to provide the necessary injection of urgency and realism which had not always been evident before, even after Munich.

Leeper's efforts at the Foreign Office were to be considerably aided in May 1939 when the Prime Minister authorised the appointment of a ministerial committee comprising the Foreign and Home secretaries, along with the minister for the co-ordination of defence, to consider 'what steps should be taken during peace to counteract anti-British propaganda and to institute a more active policy of British publicity overseas'.[109] Although, once again, there appears to be no available record of any formal proceedings for this committee, Sir Samuel Hoare did submit a report to the Cabinet with the full approval of Halifax. Hoare made two recommendations:

(i) to strengthen and expand the News Department of the Foreign Office by the addition of staff whose duty it will be to watch foreign press and broadcasts, to supply material for telegrams and articles, and to prepare (or cause to be written by outside experts) press articles presenting the antidote to anti-British propaganda, and
(ii) to explore and give effect to other means of giving publicity abroad to the British case and attitude through all the channels available.[110]

Hoare also suggested removing two of the major obstacles which had hitherto bound the hands of the wartime planners, namely the obligation of secrecy and the lack of funds made available to the shadow organisations (which had so far been carried on the Secret Service vote). Moreover, because the Ministry of Information was being designed partly to take over all responsibility for propaganda abroad from the Foreign Office in the event of war, it had now become important to ensure 'continuity between the peace-time activities of the Foreign Office in relation to publicity abroad and the work that will in war fall upon the Ministry of Information'.[111] This recognition was certainly long overdue and was the main reason for the Treasury's establishment of the OEPEC.[112] It might have proved even more significant had Leeper been placed in charge. Instead, Hoare suggested that the ill-cast Fass should be replaced as director-general designate by Lord Perth, the recently retired ambassador to Rome. Hoare claimed to appreciate that any public announcement of these measures would almost certainly be 'badly received in Germany as a fresh proof of British hostility and determination to press forward with an "encirclement" policy', but he nonetheless felt that the importance of being seen to be doing something positive in this direction now far outweighed the possibility of a hostile German reaction.[113]

The news of Perth's appointment created, in Oliver Harvey's words, 'a real scandal'. Perth was certainly an unusual choice. Although he had enjoyed a long and distinguished diplomatic career, he could hardly have claimed to be well grounded in propaganda techniques. He had, of course, served in Geneva as secretary-general to the League of Nations before taking up the Rome embassy, during which time he undoubtedly experienced League publicity and Italian propaganda, but there is no indication that he took an active interest in either. Harvey believed that Perth had 'wangled' this new job, which was all the more scandalous in his opinion because

> meanwhile he is to sit in the Foreign Office as a special Under-Secretary for publicity with £2,900 a year (i.e. his pension plus £1,000) and do or try to do the work which Rex Leeper has built up and been doing to universal satisfaction and which by rights he should continue to do as an Under-Secretary. It is a ramp of Sam Hoare and Horace Wilson, with the tacit and really unforgivable acquiescence of H[alifax].[114]

Like Tallents before him, Leeper had made too many enemies. The two leading exponents of British overseas propaganda during the 1930s had paid the price for championing an unpopular cause before the requirements of national defence dictated that such work was essential.

The Cabinet first considered Hoare's proposals on 7 June. The Minister of Information Designate stated that the 'transition from peace to war arrangements would be greatly eased by the appointment of Lord Perth in the dual capacity'.[115] This was a matter of opinion, and a decision was deferred until the following week, although not before several ministers had expressed the view that Hoare's package did not go far enough because the proposals were mainly confined to the increased dissemination of news when what was really needed was a large-scale propaganda campaign to save the peace.[116] The contrast with views expressed only months before by the same men could hardly be more marked.

When the Cabinet again met to discuss this issue a week later, it emerged from the meeting unanimous in its support for Hoare's proposals.[117] The reasons for this change of heart are unknown. Much of the discussion centred on the precise terminology of a parliamentary announcement. It was important to emphasise that the Ministry of Information would only come into being once war had been declared while at the same time to show that the government was giving its full support to the conduct of British propaganda in peacetime. Chamberlain added that many of the defects in the existing arrangements stemmed from the fact that no one individual had been responsible for the supervision of propaganda as a whole. This, he believed, would now be rectified by the appointment of Lord Perth.[118]

The Prime Minister was mistaken. Perth did not prove to be a

Propaganda for war

success. Indeed, when Chamberlain announced the new measures in the House of Commons on 15 June, thereby revealing the existence of the plans for a Ministry of Information for the first time publicly, he was subjected to a series of difficult questions concerning Perth's appointment. In reply to one concerning Perth's qualifications for his new post, the Prime Minister tamely replied that Perth had acquired 'a great deal of experience in connection with publicity' during his tenure in Geneva. But Perth's Geneva experience predated the advent of Nazi propaganda on an international scale. Chamberlain may only have made matters worse by refusing to reply to further questions concerning Perth's alleged sympathies towards 'Fascist countries'.[119] *The Times* did manage to rally to the support of the government, but, in a leading article praising the new measures, rather cynically defended Perth by claiming that it was to be counted among his qualifications that he is 'not a professional publicist. The press would have more reason to distrust the new Department of the Foreign Office if he were.'[120]

This latter remark was a misinformed reference to the recent reorganisation of the Foreign Office News Department. Perth was to have little contact with the press; his main task was supervising the other methods of propaganda. The press work of the Foreign Office, which had been the responsibility of Charles Peake since the previous October, was now separated from the main News Department, although it remained directly under Cadogan. Peake was to continue his normal press work until the outbreak of war, when he would remain an integral part of the Foreign Office. As for the remaining duties of the News Department, such as the British Official News Service and supervision of the British Library of Information at New York, these now became the responsibility of Lord Perth, assisted by Leeper and thirteen additional propaganda specialists.[121] Collectively, they were henceforth to be known as the Foreign Publicity Department of the Foreign Office, which would be transferred to the Ministry of Information on the outbreak of war.

As it turned out, the fast-moving events of the summer of 1939 rendered the new peacetime arrangements superfluous. Hardly had the Foreign Publicity Department begun to develop its propaganda activities, greatly aided in the process by the quick financial decisions of the OEPEC, when it was confronted with an entirely different set of criteria with the Nazi–Soviet Pact, the German invasion

Psychological rearmament, 1935–1939

of Poland and the declaration of war. Like many of the other measures, it had been created far too late in the day to serve any positive peacetime purpose. All it could really do was to ensure that those propaganda activities which had been built up over the previous ten years could be converted to a war footing smoothly and efficiently if the Ministry of Information decided to utilise them in its war of words.

The Ministry of Information entered the Second World War hopelessly ill prepared for the enormous tasks which lay before it. Despite the considerable progress which had been made during the final year of peace, so much more work remained to be done. Small wonder that it was considered something of a public joke, at least until Brendan Bracken took over as minister in 1941. The same could not be said, however, of the enemy propaganda department. At least the preparations in that quarter were sufficiently well advanced to enable the RAF to drop six million leaflets over Germany on the night of 3–4 September 1939.

Why was it that, despite five years of pre-war planning, Britain entered the war of words in September 1939 not speechless, as she had effectively been in August 1914, but certainly inarticulate? It was not simply because new machinery tends to need running in before it can begin to operate smoothly and effectively, for, as recent research has shown, Goebbels's Ministry of Propaganda, which had after all had six years of practice, also entered the war in chaos and confusion.[122] Nor would it be entirely accurate to attribute the planning deficiencies of the Ministry of Information solely to inter-departmental rivalry and squabbling, although that undoubtedly played its part. Perhaps the answer lies in the fact that psychological rearmament was not sufficiently well advanced at home until the spring and summer of 1939. Before then, few were prepared to accept the idea that a Ministry of Information would actually be needed. A Ministry of Information did, after all, mean war.

The dress rehearsal of Munich should have been the critical factor in accelerating the process of psychological rearmament in so far as the wartime planning was concerned, and in many respects it was. But by comparison with the rapid expansion of the peacetime propaganda machinery in the months that followed, progress was far less dramatic. Increased propaganda in an attempt to preserve

Propaganda for war

the peace so dearly bought at Munich was one thing, but to accept that a Ministry of Information, and therefore war, was inevitable was quite another. Prague shattered that illusion. By then, however, Tallents had been chosen as the sacrificial lamb on the altar of the Munich post-mortem, and Leeper was shortly to follow the same route. The two principal architects of British overseas propaganda, both in peacetime and in laying the groundwork for propaganda in the next war, had paid the price for having their worst fears confirmed. After ten years of campaigning repeatedly for increased official commitment to a programme of national propaganda overseas, both men had made too many enemies in the process to merit a significant role in the machinery which they had largely created. The fall from grace of their patrons, Reith and Vansittart, did not help matters. In 1938, Reith left the BBC to become chairman of Imperial Airways, a move which served to undermine Tallents's position in the shadow Ministry of Information. Without Reith to champion his cause at the higher levels, Tallents's rows with existing government departments and with people such as Campbell Stuart merely served to highlight the grave deficiencies which existed in the planning process. Somebody had to attract the lightning generated by the storm clouds of Munich. The conductor of *The Projection of England* made an admirable choice. Similarly, the official who had been chiefly responsible for converting Tallents's ideas into practice suffered the consequences of his own personal convictions. Having associated himself so closely with Vansittart for most of the 1930s, Leeper's light began to fade with that of his patron during the period of the former permanent under secretary's cries from the diplomatic wilderness. It was not just that Leeper had overstepped the mark of a permanent official during the Munich crisis. After February 1938, the Foreign Office was no longer the garden of Eden in which the seeds planted by Leeper could flourish and blossom, despite the efforts of the Vansittart report to propagate them.

The officials chosen to replace Tallents and Leeper, Fass and Perth, were not the right men to rectify the deficiencies. Not only did they lack detailed knowledge and experience of propaganda, but they also lacked genuine commitment. Regardless of the steadily increasing support in Parliament and in the press for Britain's growing involvement in overseas propaganda, Fass and Perth, like Halifax and Cadogan, represented a generation of British public ser-

Psychological rearmament, 1935–1939

vants which could not reconcile itself to accepting such work as a legitimate peacetime activity of British government. 'Propaganda' remained a dirty word which left an unpleasant taste in the mouths of English gentlemen. Reassurances that it was the only antidote to the virus being spread by hostile totalitarian propaganda, or that it was really based upon 'information' and was thus 'educational', or even that it was based upon the truth, nothing but the truth and, as near as possible, the whole truth, failed to sweeten the bitter pill which people such as Tallents and Leeper were attempting to administer. The only problem was that, by the late 1930s, its use could no longer be avoided in peace as in war. No matter how much its opponents would personally have preferred otherwise, the unavoidable conclusion they were forced to reach was that propaganda had become a fact of modern political and diplomatic life.

Conclusion

One of the characteristic features of Britain's overseas propaganda between the wars was that it began, almost without exception, as a direct response to the activities of other countries. It was thus, strictly speaking, counter-propagandist in the widest sense. In view of the widespread dislike and suspicion of propaganda, it would not be too unreasonable to suggest that, had the British government been left entirely to its own devices, it would not have embarked upon such work out of preference. This might have been because, as Leeper suspected, new ideas were anathema to the official mind[1] or, as Percy Loraine believed, because of 'a fundamental English inability to understand the force of ideas and the danger of leaving their shaping in the hands of others'.[2] It may simply have been because of misguided prejudice. It was certainly true that British officials invariably misunderstood what Leeper and his fellow advocates of increased official involvement in propaganda meant by the word in the British context. It was not that the protagonists in the debate failed to explain clearly their interpretation. They did, after all, go to considerable lengths to emphasise the essential differences between British overseas propaganda and that conducted by other governments. It was more a case of the antagonists not being able to accept the idea of propaganda by Britain, even for Britain, as a matter of principle. This was because the acceptance of the need to conduct national propaganda abroad meant, fundamentally, the acceptance of Britain's declining position in international affairs.

Until the final decades of the nineteenth century, Britain's supremacy in the world was considered to be so self-evident that there was felt to be little call for a programme of propaganda overseas. Although countries such as France and Germany had already begun to utilise propaganda as an instrument of national policy, it was not until the First World War that the British government was forced seriously to consider means for the control and influence of foreign

Conclusion

opinion. Having embarked upon such a course with the establishment of the News Department and Wellington House, the British soon discovered a peculiar talent for such work, and by 1918 they had graduated with honours with the establishment of the Ministry of Information and Crewe House. On the return of peace, however, the unfortunate failure to distinguish between propaganda in war and the Foreign Office's conception of propaganda in peace led to the withdrawal of public funds from services which had they been modified and continued to meet the requirements of the post-war world, might have rendered invaluable support to the representation of Britain abroad.

Although Britain emerged from the First World War both relatively and absolutely weaker than when she had entered it, it was only following a decade of virtual inactivity in a field to which others were devoting increasing attention that the implications of the post-war reduction for British interests and prestige became sufficiently apparent to prompt a reversal of policy. By then, however, the British government had lost the initiative in propaganda that it had gained in 1918. It meant that when Britain did decide to re-enter the field, British prestige had to be rescued not only from current abuse but also from the consequences of past neglect. Organisations such as the Travel Association and the British Council, however, had to defend national interests and prestige with only very limited financial resources. There was much to be said for the argument that qualitative rather than quantitative propaganda was more effective, but it was nonetheless a financially expedient argument. Despite the rapid expansion of the work during the late 1930s, as reflected by the dramatic increase in the British council's official grant from £5,000 in 1935 to £330,000 in a period of just four years, Britain's peacetime propaganda was conducted on a much smaller scale than that of her rivals. Admittedly, British propaganda was designed to perform an entirely different function from that of, say, totalitarian propaganda, but Leeper still had a valid point when he wrote in October 1938 that 'hitherto we have merely nibbled at the problem and have treated it as a necessary evil rather than as something positively valuable'.[3]

Twenty years earlier, the Foreign Office had tried in vain to convince those who disliked propaganda that it could be utilised to serve a positive role in the promotion of British interests and in the

Conclusion

cause of international peace and understanding. Although the Foreign Office repeatedly disclaimed any intention of emulating the scale or the character of foreign propaganda, greater support for the work of the News Department and the various semi-official agencies working under official auspices was not more readily forthcoming during the 1920s and early 1930s, because of fear that this would be precisely what would happen. Then, suddenly, in the wake of the failure of the Disarmament Conference and the resurgence of a powerful Germany under Hitler, a breakthrough was reached. Early in 1934, Leeper met with Warren Fisher, who told him that he 'attached the greatest importance to my particular department in the F.O. and that for his part he wanted to do everything to strengthen it'. 'We covered the whole ground of my work in the conversation', Leeper wrote, 'and at the end of it I found that he was prepared to give me everything I had been struggling for for some years.'[4] The Treasury, which had played the role of keeper of the official conscience since the end of the First World War in so far as propaganda was concerned, had now come to accept that 'the projection of England' was an essential part of diplomacy, although many of its less senior officials remained convinced that propaganda was an expensive substitute for good government. However, after the creation of the British Council, more money was made available, and the Foreign Office was, perhaps, too quick to see the Treasury as the *bête noire* and too slow to remember that it was the Treasury's role to keep close tabs on the official purse.

By the late 1930s, there was a strong suspicion that the Foreign Office was attempting to establish what would amount, in effect, to a peacetime Ministry of Information. Such fears were not to be allayed by statements to the contrary made by Leeper. For example, he wrote in November 1938:

Our scheme looks on paper complicated and piecemeal. I claim that it is on the right lines and very cheap. It builds on existing foundations, associates non-official effort with official activities, where appropriate, in the traditional way, and eliminate the internal dangers which would attend the creation of a vast publicity machine under unified Government control.[5]

Even so, the proposals contained in the report of the Vansittart Committee for the Co-ordination of British Publicity Abroad merely served to enhance this suspicion, because, had they been

Conclusion

accepted without question, the Foreign Office would have commanded a large propaganda apparatus that could quite easily had been adapted to encompass domestic as well as foreign propaganda while also being capable of conversion for the purpose of conducting propaganda in wartime.

This was politically unacceptable not only to those who disliked propaganda on principle but also to the opponents of the Foreign Office in general and of Leeper and Vansittart in particular. It also proved unacceptable to the planners of the Ministry of Information, who were only too aware of the problems posed by the Foreign Office to their predecessors during 1918 when, just as the Foreign Office had resented the incursions of Beaverbrook and Northcliffe into the field of diplomacy, so also had the ministry and Crewe House resented the Foreign Office's involvement in propaganda. A similar situation was to recur during the early years of the Second World War. But although the Foreign Office had clearly demonstrated during the inter-war period that propaganda and diplomacy were not necessarily incompatible, as Northcliffe had once suspected, many continued to believe that they were. This, essentially, was what Edward Hale at the Treasury meant when he argued that it was impossible to combine a forward policy in propaganda with the policy of appeasement. This may also have been the reason why the Treasury dragged its feet over the Vansittart report. Moreover, despite Leeper's repeated reassurances that the Foreign Office was concerned only with overseas propaganda, and his constant opposition to the establishment of a Ministry of Information in peacetime, the Treasury remained unconvinced – perhaps, at least in part, because such utterances came from an official who was widely suspected of conducting propaganda against the government's appeasement policy through his dealings with the press.

The line separating domestic and overseas propaganda, at least in a liberal democracy is not always clearly defined. The British media provided a mirror of events in Britain for foreign observers. If Fleet Street or Broadcasting House – free of government control but often amenable to official influence – decided to inform the British people of certain events in another country, events which the governing regime of that country did not wish to see publicised, it could seriously affect the course of diplomacy. Leeper, like Willert before him, recognised this and attempted to keep the press and the BBC

Conclusion

fully informed with a regular supply of accurate news in an attempt to ensure that the media appreciated the possible repercussions of irresponsible behaviour (that is, from the point of view of diplomacy). If the media, recognising this, still decided to press on with their investigations, there was little that the Foreign Office could do – other than threaten to withdraw its facilities to the 'guilty' party and apologise to the foreign government. But in order to avoid such embarrassments, the News Department of the Foreign Office attempted to cultivate an atmosphere of mutual understanding and co-operation so that the one understood the problems and requirements of the other. This situation could also serve the process of national publicity in so far as the British media were speaking to the foreigner.

In 1938, Leeper described the functions of his department as being 'not only the supply of day to day news, but to educate the different organs of publicity along the lines of the foreign policy pursued by the Government'.[6] But because of the nature of his dealings with the press, it is difficult to assess in any exact terms whether or not he did in fact abuse his position as Foreign Office press officer to secure publicity for his personal views. During Chamberlain's premiership, he was certainly suspected of such abuse. Leeper himself admitted that 'the connections of the News Department both with the press and with the B.B.C. are now so close that it can conduct this work quietly and smoothly without giving the impression of propaganda'.[7] Regardless of the controversy which surrounded Leeper's role, from the point of view of the government's involvement in psychological rearmament, this was a highly satisfactory state of affairs. Few could take exception to the seemingly innocuous dissemination of accurate news and information in response to a genuine demand on the part of foreign, particularly influential, observers. But because the Foreign Office's propaganda was directed to opinion-makers rather than direct to mass opinion itself, camouflage was essential. Nor, in an age when propaganda was being universally exploited by all the leading powers, could exception really be taken to the dissemination of 'straight news' which was of benefit to British interests. Yet there were those opponents who, with the experience of the Great War behind them, and with their experience of totalitarian propaganda before them, tended to look for something more sinister. Leeper's behaviour,

Conclusion

especially in his dealings with the press, seemed to confirm their worst fears.

Asa Briggs has correctly stated that words do not win wars.[8] The Foreign Office learned in the 1930s that they could not save the peace. Actions will always count for much more. But those actions have first to be discovered, and for this purpose the facilities for publicity have to be made available. Having accepted this fundamental desideratum, it became important for the British government to ensure that the information passing through the channels of communication was of a nature beneficial to the interests of the source. Because that source was official, its credibility would automatically be considered suspect. Goebbels himself recognised that official propaganda known to be such is almost worthless unless, of course, you are already preaching to the converted. The Foreign Office worked on the assumption that it had a critical audience to convert partly because of the impression being created by hostile propaganda but partly because of the consequences of British actions. In other words, it was feared that foreign propaganda might drive home the realities of decline. British overseas propaganda, therefore, attempted to persuade foreigners that Britain was not the declining power that totalitarian propaganda maintained, when in reality she was.

In 1918, one British official argued that 'really effective propaganda, by which ... I ... mean the exercising of influence on the intellectuals and politicians of a country, is something subtle and essentially secret'.[9] It was perhaps largely for this reason that many people in Britain insisted that the government did not conduct propaganda but rather that its work was publicity. To have accepted its existence would merely have served to draw foreign attention to it, thereby jeopardising its credibility. Yet the subtlety of British overseas propaganda between the wars derived from its secrecy. Sources of official information, like the channels of communication through which that information passed, were carefully disguised. The accuracy of the information was a further method of disguise, because, during the First World War, 'propaganda' had come to be associated in the popular mind with 'lies'. But through a careful process of selection and omission, British propaganda never assumed the proportion of the whole truth.

Propaganda, like secret intelligence, has become an essential part

Conclusion

of the equipment of the modern state. So long as other countries are prepared to employ such activities in their conduct of foreign policy, the state which does not is simply inviting disaster. Although, during the 1930s, the British comforted themselves in the belief that their propaganda was publicity, and that anyway they had only been forced to resort to such an 'un-English' activity in order to defend themselves and democracy against the worst excesses of totalitarianism, the fact remains that it has been the British government itself which had, between 1914 and 1918, demonstrated the enormous power of propaganda, a lesson which was not lost on Adolf Hitler or his fellow dictators.

Notes

Unless otherwise stated, all primary source references relate to material in the Public Record Office, Kew, London.

Select bibliography

Index

Notes to pp. 2–16

Introduction

1. W. Irwin, *Propaganda and the News: or, What Makes You Think So?* (New York, 1936) p. 3.
2. B. Russell, *Free Thought and Official Propaganda* (Conway memorial lecture, London, 1922).
3. J. A. C. Brown, *Techniques of Persuasion: From Propaganda to Brainwashing* (Harmondsworth, 1963) p. 21.
4. R. Taylor, *Film Propaganda: Soviet Russia and Nazi Germany* (London, 1979) p. 25.
5. Russell, pp. 33–4.
6. Minute by R. Kenney, 19 February 1931. FO 395/448, P 334/3/150.
7. W. Osterling to the editor, *The Times*, 20 November 1936.
8. *The Times*, 20 March 1935.
9. Hansard, 5th series, vol. 350, 28 July 1939, col. 1871. The speaker was J. P. L. Thomas, Eden's former parliamentary private secretary, who had resigned with the Foreign Secretary in February 1938.
10. Memorandum by R. A. Leeper, 22 October 1938. Enclosed in Leeper to Cadogan, 22 October 1938. FO 800/396.
11. Hansard, 5th series, vol. 343, 15 February 1939, cols. 1866–7. The speaker was Mr Emmott.

1. The Foreign Office and the press

1. B. Akzin, *Propaganda by Diplomats* (Washington, 1936); O. J. Hale, *Publicity and Diplomacy – With Special Reference to England and Germany, 1890–1914* (Gloucester, Mass., 1964).
2. Z. Steiner, *The Foreign Office and Foreign Policy, 1898–1914* (Cambridge, 1969) pp. 172–91.
3. Enquiry regarding press and postal censorship in time of war. CAB 38/28/3. See also P. Towle, 'The Debate on Wartime Censorship in Britain, 1902–14' in B. Bond and I. Roy (eds.), *War and Society: A Yearbook of Military History* (London, 1975).
4. P. M. Taylor, 'Publicity and Diplomacy: The Impact of the First World War upon Foreign Office Attitudes towards the Press' in D. Dilks (ed.), *The Retreat from Power* (2 vols., London, 1981) I.
5. Memorandum by Lord Curzon, 26 March 1919. FO 366/787, 32759.
6. J. Margach, *The Abuse of Power: The War between Downing Street and the Media from Lloyd George to Callaghan* (London, 1978).
7. Memorandum by G. B. Beak, 'Policy and Propaganda', 2 December 1918. FO 395/301, 00409.
8. Memorandum by S. A. Guest, 24 January 1919. FO 395/301, 00409.
9. C. H. Montgomery to Treasury, 16 November 1920. FO 366/790, 2800. Undated Treasury note on the News Department. T 162/42, E 2826.
10. Lord Vansittart, *The Mist Procession* (London, 1958) p. 249.

Notes to pp. 16–22

11 Ibid. p. 273.
12 K. Jones, *Fleet Street and Downing Street* (London, 1920) p. 341.
13 Lord Hardinge, *Old Diplomacy* (London, 1947) p. 263.
14 Jones, p. 341.
15 Margach, pp. 15–22.
16 *History of 'The Times'*, IV: *The 150th Anniversary and Beyond, 1912–48* (London, 1952) pt II, p. 604.
17 Lord Riddell, *An Intimate Diary of the Peace Conference and After, 1918–23* (London, 1933), entry for 15 February 1921.
18 Hansard, 5th series, vol. 144, 18 July 1921, cols. 1747–9.
19 E. Crowe to R. Graham, 22 July 1921. FO 395/362, P 1612/1612/150.
20 *History of 'The Times'*, op. cit., pp. 606–7.
21 Minute by A. W. A. Leeper, 12 November 1921. FO 395/362, P 2548/1612/150.
22 Memorandum by Tyrrell, 'The Foreign Office and the Press', 10 December 1921. FO 800/329, Pp/21/1.
23 Ibid.
24 Ibid.
25 Ibid. For further details of Kerr's position see J. R. M. Butler, *Lord Lothian* (London, 1960) pp. 81–3.
26 Memorandum by Tyrrell, op. cit.
27 Memorandum by Crowe, 14 December 1921. FO 800/329, Pp/21/1.
28 Ibid.
29 Ibid.
30 J. D. Gregory, *On the Edge of Diplomacy: Rambles and Reflections, 1902–28* (London, 1928) pp. 267–9.
31 Memorandum by P. A. Koppel, 10 February 1922. FO 366/783.
32 R. Graham to Treasury, 2 April 1919. FO 366/787, 32759.
33 Ibid.
34 Memorandum by Koppel, 20 August 1920. FO 366/790, 2800.
35 Memorandum by Koppel, 10 February 1922. FO 366/783.
36 H. Knatchbull-Hugessen, *Diplomat in Peace and War* (London, 1949) p. 54.
37 V. Lawford, *Bound for Diplomacy* (London, 1963) pp. 309–15.
38 For an excellent example of these reports see the correspondence between Mendl and Tyrrell (1924) in FO 800/220; between Mendl and Lord Crewe (1926) in FO 800/330. Mendl's reports for 1929 are in FO 395/434, as indeed are those of the Rome press attaché, Mr McClure.
39 Lord Strang, *The Foreign Office* (London, 1955) p. 111.
40 Lord Burnham to V. Wellesley, 28 May 1919. FO 395/303, 81477.
41 Lord Hankey, *Diplomacy by Conference: Studies in Public Affairs, 1920–46* (London, 1946) p. 173.
42 A. Willert, *Washington and Other Memories* (Boston, 1972) pp. 150–61.

43 Riddell, *An Intimate Diary*, entries for 24 and 29 March and 3 May 1919.
44 Ibid., entry for 12 December 1921.
45 Willert to his wife, 10 December 1921. Arthur Willert Papers, Yale University Library (hereafter cited as Willert MS, Yale UL) box 6, F 324.
46 Willert to his wife, 24 November 1921. Florence Willert Correspondence, Willert MS, Yale UL, box 6, F 233.
47 Willert to his wife, 2 January 1922. Florence Willert Correspondence, Willert MS, Yale UL, box 6, F 236.
48 Willert to Tyrrell, 19 January 1922. Willert MS, Yale UL, box 5, F 194.
49 Hankey, p. 173.
50 Willert to his wife, 2 January 1922. Willert MS, Yale UL, box 5, F 194.
51 Willert, *Washington and Other Memories*, p. 162.
52 Memorandum by Willert, 17 December 1924. Willert MS, Yale UL, box 13, F 38.
53 Willert to F. Villiers, 17 December 1924. Willert MS, Yale UL, box 13, F 38.
54 The Dominions Information Office was wound up in 1933 following the Statute of Westminster. *The Records of the Foreign Office, 1782–1939* (PRO Handbooks, No. 13, HMSO, 1969) p. 23.
55 Willert, *Washington and Other Memories*, p. 164.
56 Gregory, *On the Edge of Diplomacy*, p. 260.
57 Willert, *Washington and Other Memories*, pp. 168–9.
58 R. K. Middlemas and A. J. Barnes, *Baldwin* (London, 1969) pp. 344–5.
59 Willert, *Washington and Other Memories*, p. 169.
60 Willert to J. D. Gregory, 3 June 1925. Willert MS, Yale UL, box 3, F 88.
61 Ibid.
62 Willert, *Washington and Other Memories*, p. 168.
63 The largest, the Central Department, then employed eleven officials. FO 366/850, 2272.
64 FO 366/850, 1654.
65 Ibid.
66 C. Malone to A. Henderson, 9 July 1929; minute by Willert, undated. FO 395/438, P 1014/1014/150.
67 Minute by Willert, 2 December 1926. FO 800/259.
68 Minute by C. J. Norton, 15 May 1928. FO 395/432, P 817/817/150.
69 Minute by Willert, 11 June 1929. FO 395/436, P 703/703/150.
70 Willert to Mendl, 15 January 1929. FO 395/435, P 57/57/150.
71 Ibid.
72 Ibid.
73 Ibid.

74 A. Willert, 'British News Controls', *Foreign Affairs*, 17, 4 (1939) 722.
75 Willert, *Washington and Other Memories*, pp. 172–3. For an example of Henderson's skill and frankness in his dealings with the press see the record of his press conference of 31 August 1929. FO 395/434, P 1334/53/150.
76 The arrangements are to be found in FO 395/440–2.
77 Memorandum by Willert, 17 December 1924. FO 366/821. Willert to Mendl, 15 January 1929. FO 395/435, P 57/57/150.
78 Willert, *Washington and Other Memories*, p. 181.
79 Ibid. p. 185.
80 Memorandum by Willert, 27 November 1934. Willert MS, Yale UL, box 4, F 169.
81 Willert, *Washington and Other Memories*, p. 184.
82 R. H. Ullman, *Anglo-Soviet Relations, 1917–21, I: Intervention and the War* (Princeton, 1961) p. 60.
83 For further details see A. Headlam-Morley et al. (eds.), *Sir James Headlam-Morley: A Memoir of the Paris Peace Conference, 1919* (London, 1972).
84 For a little-known but highly informative biographical tribute see H. Nicolson, 'Allen Leeper', *Nineteenth Century and After*, 118 (1935) 473–83.
85 Willert to Vansittart, 26 February 1934. Willert MS, Yale UL, box 14, F 57.
86 K. Young (ed.), *The Diaries of Sir Robert Bruce Lockhart, 1915–38* (London, 1973), entry for 30 August 1933.
87 Memorandum by R. A. Leeper, 12 October 1932. FO 395/458, P 2143/2/150.
88 Ibid.
89 Ibid.
90 Ibid.
91 An example of the links forged by Leeper with Harold Whates and T. W. Hutton of the *Birmingham Post* during this period is described by A. J. Anthony Morris, 'The *Birmingham Post* and Anglo-German Relations, 1933–35', *University of Birmingham Historical Journal*, 11, 2 (1968) 193.
92 One example of a meeting between Leeper and an editor (of the *Manchester Guardian*) survives in A. J. P. Taylor (ed.), *Off the Record: W. P. Crozier's Political Interviews, 1933–43* (London, 1972) pp. 3–7. The interview is dated 4 November 1933.
93 J. Harvey (ed.), *The Diplomatic Diaries of Oliver Harvey, 1937–40* (London, 1970), entry for 7 November 1937.
94 Ibid., entry for 8 November 1937.
95 Young (ed.), *Bruce Lockhart Diaries*, entry for 20 December 1937.
96 Record of a conversation between Herr Hitler and Lord Halifax, 19 November 1937. Enclosed in Neurath to N. Henderson, 20 Novem-

ber 1937. *Documents on German Foreign Policy, 1918–45*, Series D, vol. 1.
97 Lord Avon, *Memoirs: Facing the Dictators* (London, 1962) p. 182; J. Harvey (ed.), *Oliver Harvey Diaries*, p. 60.
98 Eden to Lord Perth, 2 December 1937; Eden to Perth, 23 December 1937. CAB 21/558. See also ch. 5.
99 Memorandum by Leeper, 2 January 1938. FO 395/596, P 359/359/150.
100 Margach, *The Abuse of Power*, ch. 4.
101 Memorandum by Leeper, 2 January 1938. FO 395/596, P 359/359/150.
102 Hankey to Vansittart, 3 November 1937. CAB 21/558.
103 See Eden's account of this episode in Lord Avon, *Memoirs: Facing the Dictators*, pp. 511–14.
104 H. J. Wilson to Hankey, 7 January 1938. CAB 21/558.
105 Cadogan to Eden, 26 January 1938. FO 954/13, It/38/3.
106 J. Harvey (ed.), *Oliver Harvey Diaries*, entry for 12 February 1938.
107 Young (ed.), *Bruce Lockhart Diaries*, entry for 1 April 1938.
108 D. N. Dilks (ed.), *The Diaries of Sir Alexander Cadogan, 1938–45* (London, 1971) entry for 7 May 1938.
109 R. Barrington-Ward to G. Dawson, 13 October 1938. Barrington-Ward MS, Archives of *The Times*.
110 Lord Gladwyn, *Memoirs* (London, 1972) p. 97.
111 M. Gilbert and R. Gott, *The Appeasers* (London, 1963) p. 164; W. S. Churchill, *The Gathering Storm* (London, 1948) p. 278; R. K. Middlemas, *The Diplomacy of Illusion: The British Government and Germany, 1937–39* (London, 1972) p. 388; I. Colvin, *Vansittart in Office* (London, 1965) pp. 266–7.
112 Viscount Templewood, *Nine Troubled Years* (London, 1954) p. 318.
113 Minute by Leeper for Cadogan, 30 September 1938. FO 800/396.
114 Ibid.
115 Ibid.
116 Memorandum by Peake, 5 August 1939. FO 366/1072, 8902/1976/504.
117 Ibid.
118 C. Howard Smith to E. Hale, 1 September 1939. FO 366/1072, 8902/1976/504.
119 Minute by Leeper, 26 April 1939. FO 800/315, H/XV/155.
120 For an examination of the attitude of the British press towards the question of Germany in the late 1930s see F. R. Gannon, *The British Press and Germany, 1936–39* (Oxford 1971).
121 D. McLachlan, *In the Chair: Barrington-Ward of 'The Times', 1927–48* (London, 1971) p. 128.
122 Ibid. p. 129.
123 Iverach McDonald to author, 12 January 1980.
124 Ibid.

125 Other than his correspondence with Charles Bridge, currently in the possession of the British Council, and with his family, which is in the possession of Miss V. A. Leeper in Australia.
126 Young (ed.), *Bruce Lockhart Diaries*, entry for 24 November 1935.
127 Colvin, *Vansittart in Office*, pp. 45–6.
128 A. L. Kennedy to N. Ebbutt, 20 May 1935. Kennedy MS, Archives of *The Times*.
129 Young, *Bruce Lockhart Diaries*, entry for 31 March 1937.
130 Ibid., entry for 14 October 1937.
131 Ibid., entry for 2 November 1937.
132 Minute by Cadogan, 28 November 1938. FO 800/396.
133 London, 1950.
134 Willert, 'National Advertisement', *Fortnightly*, January 1939, pp. 3–4.
135 CAB 23/10, 561 (1) 1 May 1919.
136 P. E. P., 'Government Public Relations', *Planning*, 1, 14 (1933); P. E. P., 'Government Information Services', *Planning*, 10, 213 (1943).
137 R. Pound and G. Harmsworth, *Northcliffe* (London, 1959) p. 769.

2. The Foreign Office and propaganda abroad

1 See Professor Michael Balfour's recent contribution to this debate in the opening chapter of his *Propaganda in War, 1939–45* (London, 1979).
2 Cited in ibid. p. 8.
3 Cited in R. Pound and G. Harmsworth, *Northcliffe* (London, 1959) p. 670.
4 J. D. Squires, *British Propaganda at Home and in the United States from 1914 to 1917* (Cambridge, Mass., 1935) p. 77.
5 P. M. Taylor, 'The Foreign Office and British Propaganda during the First World War', *Historical Journal*, 23 (1980) 875–98.
6 P. M. Taylor, 'Publicity and Diplomacy' in D. Dilks (ed.), *The Retreat from Power* (2 vols., London, 1981) I.
7 Hansard, 5th series, vol. 109, 5 August 1918, cols. 947–1035.
8 Memorandum by Beaverbrook, 'The Functions of the Ministry of Information on the Cessation of Hostilities', 16 October 1918. CAB 24/67, GT 6007.
9 Ibid.
10 Ibid.
11 CAB 23/8, 501 (11) 13 November 1918.
12 C. Stuart, *Secrets of Crewe House: The Story of a Famous Campaign* (London, 1920) p. 202.
13 H. Wickham Steed, *The Fifth Arm* (London, 1940) p. 41.
14 Steed, *Through Thirty Years* (2 vols., London, 1924) II, p. 248.

Notes to pp. 47–55

15 *The History of 'The Times'*, IV: *The 150th Anniversary and Beyond, 1912–48*: pt 1 (London, 1952) pp. 385–6.
16 Ibid. pp. 384–98. Lloyd George recalled: 'I thought the suggestion dangerous in the extreme. Indirectly it would have given him [i.e. Northcliffe] great power in the direction and control of our policy ... I curtly told him to go to Hades.' *Memoirs of the Peace Conference* (2 vols., New Haven, 1939) I, p. 176.
17 Pound and Harmsworth, p. 653.
18 A. J. P. Taylor, *Beaverbrook* (London, 1972) p. 137.
19 P. M. Taylor, 'The Foreign Office and British Propaganda'.
20 Minute by Sir H. Newbolt, 17 January 1919. FO 395/301, 00346.
21 Steed, *Through Thirty Years*, II, p. 250
22 Memorandum by Wellesley, 'The Reconstruction of the Foreign Office', 30 November 1918. FO 395/297, 001377.
23 'Notes on the Liquidation of the Ministry of Information'. INF 4/1B.
24 W. Tyrrell to Sir H. Batterbee, 30 December 1918. FO 395/297, 0012.
25 Minute by Gaselee, 28 January 1919. FO 395/301, 00409.
26 Cited in minute by Tilley, 31 January 1919. FO 395/301, 00409.
27 Memorandum by G. B. Beak, 'Policy and Propaganda', 2 December 1918. FO 395/301, 00409.
28 Memorandum by S. A. Guest, 24 January 1919. FO 395/301, 00409.
29 Ibid.
30 Minute by C. Harmsworth, 6 February 1919. FO 395/304, 00848.
31 Note of proceedings at a meeting held on 20 March 1919 to consider the future of British propaganda abroad. FO 395/297, 001377.
32 Ibid.
33 Memorandum by Lord Curzon, 'Proposed News Department of the Foreign Office', 26 March 1919. FO 366/787, 53464.
34 Ibid.
35 See the proposed outline plan of organisation in FO 366/787, 32759.
36 Ibid.
37 Sir R. Graham to Treasury, 2 April 1919. FO 366/787, 32759.
38 Minute by Gaselee, 8 February 1919. FO 366/787, 32759.
39 Note of proceedings of a conference held at the Treasury, 14 May 1919. FO 395/297, 002006.
40 Ibid.
41 Foreign Office circular despatch, 19 May 1919. FO 395/304, 00848.
42 T. C. Heath to Tyrrell, 31 May 1919. FO 366/787, 82638.
43 Ibid.
44 Memorandum by J. W. Headlam-Morley, 28 October 1919. Enclosed in Headlam-Morley to Tyrrell, 28 October 1919. FO 371/4382, 619.
45 Minutes by Hardinge and Curzon, 31 October 1919. FO 371/4382, 619.
46 The immediate post-war decisions relating to the News Department

must be considered in the wider context of Foreign Office reconstruction. For further details see Z. Steiner and M. L. Dockrill, 'The Foreign Office Reforms, 1919–21', *Historical Journal*, 17, 1 (1974) 131–56.
47 Koppel to Tyrrell, 20 August 1920. FO 366/790, 2800.
48 Hardinge to Curzon, 27 August 1920. FO 366/790, 2800.
49 Minute by Curzon, 7 September 1920. FO 366/790, 2800.
50 S. King-Hall, *Chatham House* (London, 1937) pp. 10–16; see also Arnold Toynbee's account in his *Experiences* (Oxford, 1969) pp. 60–5.
51 Memorandum by Koppel, 13 October 1925. FO 366/821, 8039.
52 Memorandum by Gregory, 'Reconstruction of Press and News Department', 21 February 1925. FO 366/783.
53 Ibid.
54 Ibid.
55 Willert to Gregory, 3 June 1925. Arthur Willert MS, Yale UL, box 3, F 88.
56 Unsigned memorandum on the News Department, 29 January 1915. FO 371/2555, 12567.
57 Jones to Montgomery, 19 February 1919. FO 395/305, 36447.
58 Minute by Gaselee, 20 February 1919. FO 395/305, 36447.
59 Ibid.
60 Note by Montgomery, 20 February 1919. FO 395/305, 36447.
61 R. Graham to T. C. Heath, 26 March 1919. FO 395/305, 36447.
62 Wellesley to Lord Burnham, 22 May 1919. FO 395/303, 74559.
63 Minute by Norton, 18 January 1928. FO 395/426, P 121/16/150.
64 Foreign Office circular despatch, 7 April 1919. FO 395/305, 001361.
65 Memorandum by Koppel, 20 August 1919. FO 366/790, 2800.
66 Unsigned memorandum, 'British Wireless Services', undated. FO 395/306, 003877.
67 Ibid.
68 FO 395/305, 001605.
69 Minute by W. Guinness, 1 June 1920. FO 395/312, P 359/101/150.
70 Memorandum by Koppel, 20 August 1920. FO 366/790, 2800.
71 Minute by Guinness, 10 April 1920. FO 395/312, P 101/101/150.
72 Numerous such complaints are to be found in FO 395/312, although one News Department official believed that 'the more "criticism" we receive from South American Legations on the subject of our bi-weekly news messages, the more ridiculous the Legations make themselves'. Minute by C. Duff, 18 June 1920. FO 395/312, P 359/101/150.
73 Koppel to R. Macleay (Buenos Aires), 18 November 1920. FO 395/313, P 1350/101/150.
74 Minute by W. Ridsdale, 13 July 1921. FO 395/360, P 1409/56/150.
75 FO 395/360, P 2266/56/150.
76 Minute by Ridsdale, 7 January 1922. FO 395/369, P 42/25/150.

Notes to pp. 63–72

77 R. Jones, *A Life in Reuters* (London, 1951).
78 Minute by Ridsdale, 21 February 1922. FO 395/369, P 338/25/150.
79 Memorandum by Koppel, 10 February 1922. FO 366/783.
80 Ibid.
81 Minute by Koppel, 22 February 1922. FO 395/369, P 346/25/150.
82 Memorandum by Koppel, 10 February 1922. FO 366/783.
83 Ibid.
84 Minute by Gaselee, 18 September 1922. FO 395/370, P 1744/26/150.
85 Minute by Tyrrell, 18 September 1922. FO 395/370, P 1744/26/150.
86 R. Jones, p. 456.
87 Minute by Norton, 9 November 1928. FO 395/426, P 1602/14/150.
88 Memorandum by Norton, 5 December 1928. FO 395/426, P 1679/14/150.
89 Cited in Memorandum by Duff, 21 September 1928. FO 395/425, P 1381/8/150.
90 Willert to E. F. Crowe (DOT), 18 December 1928. FO 395/426, P 1679/14/150.
91 Minute by Duff, 12 December 1928. FO 395/426, P 1679/14/150.
92 Minute by Ridsdale, 14 November 1929. FO 395/433, P 1641/3/150.
93 R. A. Leeper to Treasury, 9 April 1935. FO 395/522, P 529/9/150.
94 Ibid.
95 R. V. Nind Hopkins to Foreign Office, 8 May 1935. FO 395/522, P 529/9/150.
96 Memorandum by Eden, 'British News Abroad', 8 December 1937. CAB 24/273, CP 301(37).
97 Ibid.
98 CAB 23/90, 47 (37) 6, 15 December 1937.
99 A. Willert, *The Road to Safety: A Study in Anglo-American Relations* (London, 1952) pp. 69ff.
100 Ibid. p. 83.
101 Pound and Harmsworth, *Northcliffe*, p. 550.
102 *'The Times' History of the War* (London, 1920) XXI, pp. 103–8.
103 Drummond to P. Kerr, 1 January 1919. FO 800/329, US/19/1.
104 W. Wiseman to Tyrrell, 4 March 1919. FO 395/297, 001377.
105 Ibid.
106 Ibid.
107 Tilley to Lord Reading, 10 April 1919. FO 395/297, 001377.
108 Reading to Foreign Office, 16 April 1919. FO 395/297, 00206.
109 Foreign Office memorandum, 9 February 1934. FO 395/515, P 582/267/150.
110 Ibid.
111 A. Chamberlain to Esme Howard, 25 January 1927. FO 800/260.
112 New York; Knopf, 1927.
113 New York; Liveright, 1930.
114 Cambridge, Mass; Harvard University Press, 1935.

115 Fletcher to Willert, 10 May 1928. FO 395/437, P 732/ 732/150.
116 Ibid.
117 Minute by Willert, 9 January 1930. FO 395/440, P 30/1/150.
118 Minute by Leeper, 13 January 1933. FO 395/476, P 99/26/150.
119 Minute by Duff, 23 January 1935. FO 395/523, P 12/12/150.
120 Minute by Duff, 7 February 1935. FO 395/523, P 393/12/150.
121 Minute by Duff, 8 February 1935. FO 395/523, 466/12/150.
122 Vansittart to Reith, 26 February 1935. FO 395/523, P 393/12/150.
123 Reith to Vansittart, 8 March 1935. FO 395/523, P 393/12/150.
124 J. Nock, 'A New Dose of British Propaganda', *American Mercury*, 42 (December 1937) 482.
125 R. Lindsay to Leeper, 10 July 1938. FO 395/616, P 2345/1157/150.
126 Annual report of the British Library of Information for 1938. Enclosed in Fletcher to Leeper, 20 January 1939. FO 395/640, P 491/35/150.
127 Ibid.
128 Minute by Corley Smith, 8 February 1939. FO 395/640, P 491/35/150.
129 Lindsay to Leeper, 21 March 1939. FO 395/640, P 1164/36/150.
130 Minute by? (illegible) 18 April 1939. FO 395/640, P 1164/36/150.
131 Lindsay to Leeper, 20 April 1939. FO 395/647B, P 1404/105/150.
132 T. C. Heath to Tyrrell, 31 May 1919. FO 366/787, 82638.
133 H. O. Lee, 'British Propaganda during the Great War 1914–1918', undated (probably 1919). INF 4/4A.
134 *The Times*, 22 February 1918.
135 Hansard, 5th series, vol. 109, 5 August 1918, cols. 947–1035.
136 R. K. Middlemas and A. J. Barnes, *Baldwin* (London, 1969) p. 68.
137 H. Nicolson, *Curzon: The Last Phase 1919–25* (London, 1934) p. 2.
138 R. Marrett, *Through the Back Door: An Inside View of Britain's Overseas Information Services* (London, 1968) p. 21.
139 R. A. Leeper, 'British Culture Abroad', *Contemporary Review*, 148 (1935) 201.
140 Minute by Tilley, 24 October 1919. FO 395/304, 00848.

3. Commercial propaganda and the concept of national projection

1 CAB 23/12, 627 (5), 3 October 1919.
2 CAB 23/25, 18 (21) 12, 12 April 1921. See also CAB 23/25, 22 (21) appendix IX (3) 15 April 1921.
3 I am grateful to Timothy Hollins for permitting me to see his article 'The Conservative Party and Film Propaganda between the Wars', to be published in *English Historical Review*.
4 'Political Propaganda Experiments', *The Times*, 13 April 1926.
5 R. D. Casey, 'The National Publicity Bureau and British Party Propaganda', *Public Opinion Quarterly*, 3 (1939) 624.
6 B. Thomson, *The Scene Changes* (London, 1939) p. 387.

Notes to pp. 84–93

7 Tyrrell to Koppel, 23 August 1920. FO 366/790.
8 J. A. S. Grenville, *The Major International Treaties* (London, 1974) p. 140.
9 See CAB 23/64, 28 (30) 1, 21 May 1930; CAB 23/65, 64 (30) 1, 28 October 1930; CAB 23/71, 27 (32) 2, 11 May 1932; CAB 23/71, 32 (32) 5, 8 June 1932; Hansard, 5th series, vol. 300, 17 April 1935, cols. 1838–40.
10 Lord Vansittart, *The Mist Procession* (London, 1958) p. 40.
11 Conference held at the Treasury, 14 May 1919. FO 395/297, 002006.
12 Minute by W. Guinness, 1 June 1920. FO 395/312, P 359/101/150.
13 Ibid.
14 Minute by Koppel, 28 June 1920, on memorandum by C. L. Duff, 'Propaganda by the film in Spain, Portugal, Central and South America', 24 June 1920. FO 395/313, P 578/482/150.
15 Memorandum by Koppel, 20 August 1920. FO 366/790.
16 Ibid.
17 BT 60/21/2, DOT 33429/5 (1928).
18 BT 60/21/2, DOT 33429/4 (1928).
19 Memorandum by Duff, 9 April 1920. FO 395/312, P 477/7/150.
20 Ibid.
21 Capt. Hopper to Duff, 2 June 1920. FO 395/312, P 477/7/150.
22 The pen-names 'Andrew Blackmore' and 'Joseph Martin' were used by A. M. Byrne, a journalist and copywriter for a firm of publicity agents, in writing the weekly *London Letter* and the special weekly article. Notes on the work of the News Department, 8 April 1931, BT 61/46/1, DOT E 13168, OPC/1.
23 Minute by Wellesley, 16 March 1921. FO 800/329, FE/21/1.
24 Minute by Tyrrell, 17 March 1921. FO 800/329, FE/21/1.
25 Minute by E. L. Mercier, 19 December 1928. BT 61/33/6, DOT E 11068.
26 Ibid.
27 Ibid.
28 Minute by Willert, 30 January 1928. FO 395/425, P 149/14/150.
29 A. Longden, 'British Art Exhibitions at Home and Abroad', 31 October 1935. BT 60/44/3, DOT 5215.
30 Ibid.
31 Ibid.
32 Willert to E. F. Crowe, 14 December 1928. FO 395/435, P 468/57/150.
33 Memorandum by Duff, 21 February 1928. FO 395/425, P 272/14/150.
34 Minute by Meredith, 9 January 1929. BT 61/33/6, DOT E 11068.
35 Minute by Pickthall, 16 January 1929. BT 61/33/6, DOT E 11068.
36 Minute by Eddison, 21 January 1929. BT 61/33/6, DOT E 11068.
37 Minute by G. H. Lloyd, 21 January 1929. BT 61/33/6, DOT E 11068.
38 Crowe to Willert, 28 March 1929. FO 395/435, P 468/57/150.

39 Meredith to Willert, 11 February 1929. FO 395/435, P 215/178/150.
40 Ibid.
41 P. C. Rice to Treasury, 9 January 1929. BT 61/54/2, DOT E 14888.
42 R. V. Nind Hopkins to DOT, 25 January 1929. BT 61/54/2, DOT E 14888.
43 Meredith to Willert, 11 February 1929. FO 395/435, P 215/178/150.
44 Speech by the Earl of Derby at the Mansion House, 20 December 1928. Enclosed in Meredith to Willert, 11 February 1929. FO 395/435, P 215/178/150.
45 Ibid.
46 Application form for membership of the Travel Association, April 1929. BT 61/54/2, DOT E 14888.
47 Meredith to Willert, 11 February 1929. FO 395/435, P 215/178/150.
48 BT 61/35/9, DOT E 11528.
49 DOT circular despatch signed by E. F. Crowe, 11 May 1929. FO 395/435, P 629/178/150.
50 Memorandum enclosed in Meredith to Kenney, 1 August 1929. FO 395/435, P 1140/178/150.
51 Ibid.
52 Ibid.
53 Speech by Lord Derby at the Mansion House, 20 December 1928.
54 Memorandum enclosed in Meredith to Kenney, 1 August 1929. FO 395/435, P 1140/178/150.
55 Ibid.
56 *The Times*, 22 August 1929.
57 Ibid. 13 December 1929.
58 Willert to Treasury, 3 December 1929 and reply of 6 December 1929. T 161/966, S 9178.
59 Meredith to Fletcher, 4 March 1929. FO 395/435, P 298/178/150.
60 Norton to Fletcher, 5 April 1929. FO 395/435, P 298/178/150.
61 Crowe to Willert, 28 March 1929. BT 61/33/6, DOT E 11068.
62 *The Times*, 24 December 1929.
63 Memorandum enclosed in Meredith to Kenney, 1 August 1929. FO 395/435, P 1140/178/150.
64 H. Goad, 'The Commercial and Spiritual value of British Institutes abroad', 1928. BW 2/4, F 11,855, GB/2/1.
65 Memorandum by Charles Duff, 14 November 1929. FO 395/434, P 1665/5/150.
66 *Proceedings of the Imperial Conference*, 1926, Cmd. 2768, p. 53.
67 Memorandum by Hatton, 'Industrial Propaganda and Interest Films', 14 May 1928. BT 60/21/2, DOT 33429/28 (A), BWD 7084/28.
68 Ibid.
69 Notes by Ingram regarding films and comments by Hatton, 9 June 1928. BT 60/21/2, DOT 33429/2/28.
70 Memorandum by Hatton, 9 December 1929. BT 60/21/2, DOT 33429/28 (B).

71 P. Swann, 'The British Documentary Film Movement, 1926–46', University of Leeds Ph.D. thesis, 1979, p. 196.
72 BT 60/26/2, DOT 26538.
73 Report of the British Economic Mission to South America, 18 January 1930. FO 371/14178, A 1908/77/51.
74 Ibid.
75 BT 31/38/3, DOT E 12003/1929.
76 Hansard, 5th series, vol. 249, 12 March 1930, cols. 1363–426.
77 Trade Propaganda Committee, interim report, 6 August 1930. BT 61/40/1, DOT E 12251.
78 Ibid.
79 Ibid.
80 Ibid.
81 Ibid.
82 BT 60/25/5, DOT E 25003.
83 Memorandum by Pickthall, 6 April 1933. BT 59/16, DC 398.
84 Ibid.
85 *Third Annual Report of the Empire Marketing Board, 1928–29* (HMSO, 1929) EMB 19, p. 5.
86 L. S. Amery, *My Political Life* (3 vols., London, 1953–5) II, p. 352.
87 For further details see Swann, op. cit.; G. Huxley, *Both Hands: An Autobiography* (London, 1970) pp. 125–53; P. Rotha, *Documentary Diary: An Informal History of the Documentary Film, 1928–39* (London, 1973) ch. 3; F. Hardy (ed.), *Grierson on Documentary* (London, 1966); Arts Enquiry, *The Factual Film* (Oxford, 1947); P.E.P., 'British Documentary Films', *Planning*, 11, 228 (1944).
88 *Fifth Annual Report of the Empire Marketing Board, 1930–31* (HMSO, 1931) EMB 41, p. 8.
89 Note by Rice, 'Propaganda re. UK Trade Overseas', 4 March 1931. BT 61/46/1, DOT E 13125.
90 Oversea Propaganda Committee, minutes, 1st meeting, 24 March 1931. BT 61/46/1, DOT E 13168.
91 Oversea Propaganda Committee, minutes, 2nd meeting, 27 March 1931. BT 61/46/1, DOT E 13168.
92 Memorandum by Lloyd, 'Inter-Departmental Publicity Committee', 28 March 1931. BT 61/46/1, DOT E 13168.
93 Ibid.
94 Ibid.
95 Memorandum by ? (illegible signature) 30 March 1931. BT 61/46/1, DOT E 13168.
96 Ibid.
97 Report of the Oversea Propaganda Committee. BT 61/46/1, DOT E 13168.
98 Ibid.
99 Ibid.
100 P. M. Taylor, 'British Official Attitudes towards Propaganda

Abroad, 1918–39' to be published in a collection edited by D. W. Spring and Nicholas Pronay entitled *Film, Politics and Propaganda*.
101 Report of the Oversea Propaganda Committee. BT 61/46/1, DOT E 13168.
102 Minute by Lloyd, 3 June 1931, BT 61/46/1, DOT E 13168.
103 Minute by Lloyd, 19 July 1931. BT 61/46/1, DOT E 13168.
104 J. H. Thomas to G. M. Gillett, 9 July 1931, BT 61/46/1, DOT E 13168.
105 Minute by A. Edgecumbe, 13 July 1931. BT 61/46/1, DOT E 13168.
106 Gillett to Thomas, 27 July 1931, BT 61/46/1, DOT E 13168.
107 Ibid.
108 Thomas to Gillet, 12 August 1931. BT 61/46/1, DOT E 13168.
109 *Sixth Annual Report of the Empire Marketing Board, 1931–32* (HMSO, 1932) EMB 53, p. 100.
110 *Seventh Annual Report of the Empire Marketing Board, 1932–33* (HMSO, 1933) EMB 63, p. 102.
111 P. M. Taylor, 'The Projection of Britain: British Overseas Publicity and Propaganda, 1914–39, with Particular Reference to the Work of the News Department of the Foreign Office', University of Leeds Ph.D. thesis, 1978, p. 201.
112 A. C. D. Rivett, 'The Empire Marketing Board: A Tribute, a Lament and a Hope', *Australian Rhodes Review*, March 1934, pp. 8–19.
113 *The Times*, 9 August 1933.
114 See, for example, the minute by Crowe of 9 February 1933. BT 61/51/2, DOT E 14169.
115 DOT memorandum enclosed in Edgecumbe to G. S. Baily, 5 September 1932. BT 61/51/2, DOT E 14169.
116 J. M. Lee, 'The Dissolution of the Empire Marketing Board, 1933: Reflections on a Diary', *Journal of Imperial and Commonwealth History*, 1 (1972–3) 49–57.
117 London: Faber and Faber, 1932.
118 *The Projection of England*, p. 11.
119 Ibid. pp. 16–17.
120 Ibid. p. 37.
121 Ibid. p. 39.
122 Ibid. pp. 39–40.
123 Ibid. pp. 41–4.
124 'A New Art for New Ideas: Public Relations', *The Times*, 9 October 1933.
125 *The Projection of England*, pp. 41–2.
126 'H.M.G. and the Travel Association', enclosed in Meredith to Derby, 18 September 1934. BT 61/58/4, DOT E 15716.
127 Ibid.
128 The figure of £3,000 was originally sanctioned for 1934–5, but, following strong protests, it was restored to £4,000. From 1935 to December 1938, the sum remained constant at £5,000. BT 61/58/4, DOT E 15716.

Notes to pp. 114–24

129 Memorandum on the work of the Travel and Industrial Development Association of Great Britain and Northern Ireland, 1934. FO 395/520, P 3841/1749/150.
130 Ibid.
131 Ibid.
132 Ibid.
133 Cited in ibid.
134 Ibid.
135 Ibid.
136 FO 395/520, P 3841/1749/150.
137 Minute by Kenney, 6 December 1934. FO 395/520, P 3841/1749/150.
138 Minute by Leeper, 7 December 1934. FO 395/520, P 3841/1749/150.
139 Minute by Kenney, 21 December 1934. FO 395/520, P 3841/1749/150.
140 C. Bridge to Leeper, 11 August 1937. BW 2/213, GB/30/1.
141 BT 60/51/2, DOT 23198/6/1937.
142 Minute by H. O. Chalkey, 16 September 1937. BT 60/51/2, DOT 23198/6/1937.
143 Enquiry into non-theatrical distribution of industrial documentary films abroad, July 1937. BW 2/35, GB/3/86.
144 H. P. Croom-Johnson to Leeper, 25 March 1938. BW 2/213, GB/30/1.
145 Croom-Johnson to Bridge, 15 November 1937. BW 2/35, GB/3/86.
146 See Swann, 'The British Documentary Film Movement', pp. 210ff for a discussion of this campaign.
147 Ibid. p. 219.
148 Butler to Duff Cooper, 23 May 1940. BW 4/62, TGB/6/12.
149 Louis Beale, report on the British Pavilion for the period 30 April–12 June 1939. BT 60/52/4, DOT 23198/253/37.
150 Ibid.
151 *The Projection of England*, pp. 14–15.
152 Quoted by Swann, op. cit., p. 194.
153 Cited in memorandum on the work of the Travel Association, 1934. FO 395/520, P 3481/1749/150.
154 K. Martin, *Editor: A Volume of Autobiography, 1931–1945* (London, 1968) p. 210.
155 R. A. Leeper. 'British Culture Abroad', *Contemporary Review*, 148 (1935) 202.
156 Ibid., p. 203.
157 *The Mercury*, April 1937, pp. 610–17.
158 Hoare to H. Kennard, 8 November 1935. FO 395/529, P 3900/267/150.
159 J. Grierson, 'Propaganda for Democracy', *The Spectator*, 11 November 1938. Cited in Swann, op. cit. p. 220.

Notes to pp. 124–34

160 J. Grierson, 'Propaganda in its Working Clothes', *World Film News*, 3 (1938) 254. Also cited in Swann, p. 221.

4. Cultural propaganda and the British Council

1. G. Moorhouse, *The Diplomats: The Foreign Office Today* (London, 1977) p. 342.
2. R. E. McMurray and M. Lee, *The Cultural Approach: Another Way in International Relations* (Chapel Hill, 1947) pp. 9–21.
3. P. G. Lauren, *Diplomats and Bureaucrats: The First Institutional Responses to Twentieth-Century Diplomacy in France and Germany* (Stanford, 1976) p. 185.
4. Ibid. pp. 190–7; McMurray and Lee, pp. 12–21.
5. Cited in McMurray and Lee, pp. 44–5.
6. Cited in ibid, pp. 46–7.
7. Lauren, pp. 197–203.
8. R. A. Leeper, 'British Culture Abroad', *Contemporary Review*, 148 (1935) 201.
9. Report of a departmental committee of the Department of Information, 9 April, 1918. INF 4/5.
10. Ibid. col. 25.
11. Ibid. col. 48.
12. Ibid. col. 57.
13. Memorandum by V. Wellesley, 30 November 1918. FO 395/297, 001377.
14. Ibid.
15. Minute by Newbolt, 17 January 1919. FO 395/301, 00346.
16. Minute by G. H. Mair, 26 January 1919. FO 395/301, 00346.
17. Note by C. Harmsworth, 31 January 1919. FO 395/301, 18222.
18. Minute by S. Gaselee, 5 February 1919. FO 395/301, 18222.
19. Ibid.
20. Newbolt to Harmsworth, 1 June 1919. FO 395/301, 002272.
21. Report of a Treasury conference to discuss propaganda, 14 May 1919. FO 395/297, 002006.
22. T. C. Heath to Foreign Office, 31 May 1919. FO 366/787, 82638.
23. *Accounts and Papers (Miscellaneous)* No. 8, 1920, Cmd. 672.
24. Ibid.
25. Ibid.
26. Minute by? (illegible signature) 14 June 1920. T 161/132, S 11065.
27. Minute by? (illegible signature) 21 June 1920. T 161/132, S 11065.
28. Minute by F. J. Salter, 16 July 1920. T 161/132, S 11065.
29. Ibid.
30. Minute by F. Phillips, 16 July 1920. T 161/132, S 11065.
31. G. L. Barstow to Lord Curzon, 26 July 1920. T 161/132, S 11065.
32. Memorandum by the Western Department of the Foreign Office,

Notes to pp. 134–41

'French policy with regard to propaganda in foreign countries', 1 December 1920. FO 371/5465, W 814/814/17.
33   Ibid.
34   Memorandum by Curzon, 9 February 1921. CAB 24/119, CP 2569.
35   Minute by J. Headlam, 19 March 1921. T 161/132, S 11065.
36   Unsigned memorandum for the Chancellor of the Exchequer, 21 March 1921. T 161/132, S 11065.
37   CAB 23/26, 49 (21) 14 June 1921.
38   Minute by P. A. Koppel, 3 December 1921. FO 395/369, N 13180/260/59.
39   Cited in McMurray and Lee, *The Cultural Approach*, p. 49. See also J. Hiden, 'The Weimar Republic and the Problem of the Auslandsdeutsche', *Journal of Contemporary History*, 12, 2 (1977) 273–89.
40   FO 371/5465, W 814/814/17.
41   Cited in McMurray and Lee, p. 49.
42   Cited in ibid, p. 57.
43   F. C. Barghoorn, *The Soviet Cultural Offensive: The Role of Cultural Diplomacy in Soviet Foreign Policy* (Princeton, 1960) p. 17.
44   E. Percy, 'Britain Abroad', *The Times*, 16 November 1936.
45   Memorandum by C. Duff, 5 October 1928. FO 395/432, P 1433/1433/150.
46   Memorandum by Calder, 3 July 1928. FO 395/432, P 1433/1433/150.
47   Minute by E. M. B. Ingram, 11 July 1928. FO 395/432, P 1433/1433/150.
48   Ibid.
49   Minute by A. Willert, 11 July 1928. FO 395/432, P 1433/1433/150.
50   Minute by Calder, 3 August 1928. FO 395/432, P 1433/1433/150.
51   Minute by Norton, 11 August 1928. FO 395/432, P 1433/1433/150.
52   Minute by Willert, 13 August 1928. FO 395/432, P 1433/1433/150.
53   Cultural propaganda, 1919–35. FO 431/1, introductory memorandum.
54   Ibid.
55   Ibid.
56   Memorandum by R. A. Leeper, 2 April 1931. FO 395/449, P 772/4/150.
57   Gaselee and Fletcher to A. Henderson, 15 July 1931. FO 395/449, P 1757/3/150.
58   FO 431/1, introductory memorandum.
59   Vansittart to MacDonald, 28 April 1931. Ramsey MacDonald Papers, PRO 30/69/1/287.
60   Ibid.
61   MacDonald to Vansittart, 29 April 1931. PRO 30/69/1/ 287.
62   Ibid.
63   Circular despatch signed by Sir A. Henderson, 30 April 1931. FO 395/449, P 772/4/150.

Notes to pp. 142–50

64 Memorandum by Leeper, 2 April 1931. FO 395/449, P 772/4/150.
65 Circular despatch signed by Lord Reading, 26 September 1931. FO 395/449, P 2217/4/150.
66 Ibid.
67 Ibid.
68 FO 431/1, introductory memorandum.
69 Ibid.
70 All figures quoted are taken from an unsigned memorandum entitled 'Propaganda by the Great Powers' enclosed in British Council to G. Locock, 15 May 1935. BW 2/84, 22504, GB/8/1.
71 Minute by Duff, 29 July 1935. FO 395/522, P 2512/5/150.
72 Memorandum by Leeper, 23 April 1934. FO 395/504, P 1255/9/150.
73 Ibid.
74 Ibid.
75 Memorandum by Leeper, 18 June 1934. FO 395/505, P 1887/9/150.
76 Ibid.
77 Ibid.
78 Minute by Vansittart, 19 June 1934. FO 395/505, P 1887/9/150.
79 Memorandum by Pickthall, 'The Technical and Commercial Training in the United Kingdom of foreign students', 6 April 1933. BT 59/16, DC 398; FO 395/494, P 920/834/150.
80 BT 59/16, DC 398/8.
81 BT 60/40/5, DOT 32423.
82 Ibid.
83 Memorandum by Pickthall, 6 April 1934. BT 59/16, DC 398.
84 Minute by Mullins, 26 June 1934. BT 59/29, DC/CR/1.
85 Enclosure in Kenney to Pickthall, 3 August 1934. FO 395/505, P 2330/9/150.
86 Overseas Trade Development Council, minutes, 11 July 1934. BT 59/29, DC/CR/1.
87 Ibid.
88 Ibid.
89 Enclosure in Kenney to Pickthall, 3 August 1934. FO 395/505, P 2330/9/150.
90 Meredith to Derby, 27 August 1935. BC. Hereafter, all references marked 'BC' refer to papers in the possession of the British Council at Spring Gardens, London. I am indebted to the former secretary, Mr Irvine Watson, for first drawing my attention to this correspondence in 1976.
91 Leeper to Wrench, 5 November 1934. FO 395/505 P 3151/150.
92 Wrench to Leeper, 6 November 1934. FO 395/505, P 3151/9/150.
93 Meredith to Derby, 27 August 1935. BC.
94 Leeper to Bridge, 14 November 1934. BC.
95 Leeper to Bridge, 23 November 1934. BC.
96 Minute by Sir J. Simon, undated. FO 395/505, P 3253/9/150.

Notes to pp. 150–6

97 Executive, Finance and Agenda committees (hereafter EFA) minutes, vol. I, BC 1, 5 December 1934. BC.
98 The deteriorating position of British culture in Scandinavia had been brought to the attention of the DOT following a tour by Ramsden in 1933, and of the News Department following a tour by Roland Kenney in 1934. The report of Kenney's mission can be found in FO 395/505, P 1795/9/150 and that of Ramsden in BT 59/16, DC 398/13.
99 Memorandum by Leeper, 14 March 1935. BC.
100 Leeper to Bridge, 11 March 1935; Leeper to Bridge, 24 June 1935. BC.
101 Vansittart to Sir E. Crowe, 8 July 1935. BC.
102 For further details of the early financial problems, and of the dispute between the diplomatic and industrial factions, see P. M. Taylor, 'Cultural Diplomacy and the British Council, 1934–39', *British Journal of International Studies*, 4, 3 (1978) 244–65.
103 Leeper to Bridge, 18 July 1935, BC.
104 Foreign Office memorandum, 'The British Committee for Relations with Other Countries', December 1934. FO 395/505, P 3531/9/150.
105 EFA, minutes, vol. I, FA, 4, 18 December 1935. BC
106 A. J. S. White, *The British Council: The First Twenty Five Years* (London, 1965) p. 10. This booklet was produced for the internal use of the council.
107 Draft memorandum and articles of association, 1934–5. BW 2/121, F 5708, GB/14/1.
108 Speech delivered at the council's inaugural meeting at St James's Palace, 2 July 1935. BW 2/61, F 243, GB/4/43: The Prince of Wales was not entirely correct. The United States government did not embark upon a programme of overseas cultural relations until 1938. FO 395/575, P 2438/80/150. However, private endowments from such organisations as the Rockefeller Foundation and the Carnegie Corporation were meanwhile potent forces for the spread of American culture abroad.
109 News Department memorandum on cultural propaganda, 8 February 1935. FO 395/527, P 411/267/150.
110 Undated memorandum by Leeper (probably 1935). BC.
111 'The Students Committee of the British Council'. FO 431/1, no. 14.
112 EFA, minutes, vol. I, BC 8, 10 October 1935. BC.
113 For the complete list see FO 395/517, P 938/881/150.
114 Report for the Ibero-American Institute for 1934 by P. Guedalla, 5 March 1935. FO 395/517, P 938/881/150.
115 Leeper to Sir F. Holt, 8 December 1934. BW 2/12, F 114, GB/3/30.
116 Speech at St James's Palace, 2 July 1935. BW 2/61, F 243, GB/4/43.
117 EFA, minutes, vol. I, EC 7, 11 July 1935. BC.
118 Memorandum by the Ibero-American Institute, 29 July 1935. BW 2/142, F 906, GB/16/68.
119 Minute by Bridge, 8 August 1938, BW 2/14, F 116, GB/3/30.

Notes to pp. 156–61

120 2 vols., Oxford, 1938. The book was written with the aid of a council grant of £400 on the condition that the introduction would be translated into Spanish and Portuguese for distribution to Latin America. British Council report for the second quarter of 1938. BC.
121 Minute by Bridge, 12 January 1939. BW 2/15, F 117, GB/3/30.
122 Meredith to Derby 27 August 1935. BC.
123 Ibid.
124 First meeting of the Joint Broadcasting Committee, 25 June 1936. BW 2/30, F 162, GB/3/80.
125 Ibid. In the event of requests from foreign radio stations for reciprocal broadcasting arrangements, the British Council would have to emphasise that it had no influence over the BBC 'and absolutely no control over the composition of their programmes'. Memorandum on the broadcasting of British gramophone records, 4 July 1936. BW 2/106, F 427, GB/9/6.
126 Lord Riverdale to Derby, 19 February 1936. Enclosed in EFA, minutes, vol. I, E 13. BC. See also the record of an informal meeting with representatives of the Travel Association held on 8 April 1936. BW 2/142, F 906, GB/16/68.
127 For further details see the introduction to F. Thorpe and N. Pronay, *British Official Films in the Second World War: A Descriptive Catalogue* (London, 1980).
128 For further details on the GPO film unit see P. Swann, 'The British Documentary Film Movement, 1926–46', unpublished Ph.D. thesis, University of Leeds, 1979.
129 Arts Enquiry, *The Factual Film* (Oxford, 1947) p. 12.
130 F. Hardy (ed.), *Grierson on Documentary* (London, 1966), p. 23.
131 Second meeting of the Joint Films Committee, 8 July 1936, BW 2/35, F 171, GB/3/86.
132 Fourth meeting of the Joint Films Committee, 23 March 1937. BW 2/35, F 171/1, GB/3/86.
133 EFA, minutes, vol. III, FA 26, 6 April 1937. BC.
134 Fifth meeting of the Joint Films Committee, 1 October 1937. BW 2/35, F 171/1, GB/3/86. The BFI, founded in 1933, served as a general clearing house for information on all film matters at home and abroad, particularly with regard to educational and cultural aspects.
135 BW 2/35, F 171/1, GB/3/86.
136 The DOT was partly answerable to the Board of Trade, which was responsible for any legislation affecting the production, distribution and exhibition of all films.
137 H. P. Croom-Johnson to Bridge, 15 November 1937. BW 2/35, F 171/1, GB/3/86.
138 Ibid.
139 A report on film distribution obtained by the Travel Association for films provided by the committee, and for its own films in Britain, May 1938. BW 2/35, F 171/1, GB/3/86.

140 Leeper, 'British Culture Abroad', p. 202.
141 Tyrrell to Sir E. Peacock, 30 January 1935. BS 2/55, F 7866, GB/4/1.
142 Tyrrell to the editor of *The Times*, 26 March 1935.
143 Draft speech by Tyrrell to the Rotary clubs, undated. BW 2/113, F 12506, GB/12/7.
144 Tyrrell's statement to the Chancellor, 27 January 1936. BW 2/109, F 8412, GB/9/9.
145 E. Percy, *Some Memories* (London, 1958) p. 160.
146 Leeper to Bridge, 30 April 1936. BC. Leeper added: 'He is a great worker. You will find him with ideas of his own ... very precise and very much on the spot. He used to be rather impatient with people who do not come quickly to the point, but he may have become more tolerant. But he is absolutely straight and above board.'
147 E. Percy, 'Britain Abroad: A New Council of Culture', *The Times*, 16 November 1936.
148 British Council pamphlet, 'The work of the Council', BW 2/112, F 516, GB/12/6.
149 E. Percy, 'The Projection of Britain: Intellectual Co-operation', *Mercury*, April 1937, p. 612.
150 Percy to Eden, 8 June 1937. FO 395/554, P 2485/138/150.
151 Ibid.
152 Memorandum by K. Johnstone, 'Foreign Cultural Propaganda and the threat to British interests abroad', 19 February 1937. FO 395/534, P 823/160/150.
153 Ibid.
154 Johnstone to Leeper, 7 April 1937. BW 2/58, F 235, GB/4/40a.
155 Minute by Leeper, 18 February 1937. FO 395/554, P 823/160/150.
156 Minute by Vansittart, 24 February 1937. FO 395/554, P 823/160/150.
157 Eden to Chamberlain, 13 November 1936. FO 395/536, P 407/15/150.
158 Chamberlain to Eden, 15 March 1937. FO 395/554, P 823/160/150.
159 Eden to Chamberlain, 16 March 1937. FO 395/554, P 823/160/150.
160 Vansittart to Fisher, 17 June 1937. BC.
161 Eden to Simon, 16 June 1937. BC.
162 Simon to Eden, 12 July 1937. FO 395/554, P 3015/138/150.
163 Eden to Simon, 26 July 1937. FO 395/554, P 3015/138/150.
164 Leeper to Bridge, 23 June 1937. BC.
165 Eden to Chamberlain, 1 July 1937. BC.
166 Chamberlain to Lloyd, 17 November 1937. BC.
167 Hansard, 5th series, vol. 330, 21 December 1937, cols. 1893–803.
168 Lloyd to Eden, 22 December 1937. T 161/807, S 35581/03/38/1.
169 Eden to Simon, 23 December 1937. T 161/907, S 35581/03/38/1.
170 Ibid.
171 Note by Hale, 11 January 1938. T 161/907, S 35581/03/38/1.
172 Note by Simon, 12 January 1938. T 161/907, S 35581/03/38/1.

Notes to pp. 169–78

173 Sir P. Loraine to Sir J. Simon, 9 November 1933. FO 371/17034, J 2790/2790/16.
174 Memorandum by Mr Galt, 'The conflict of English and French educational philosophies in Egypt', enclosed in Loraine to Simon, 9 November 1933. FO 371/17304, J 2790/2790/16.
175 L. Pratt, *East of Malta, West of Suez: Britain's Mediterranean Crisis, 1936–39* (Cambridge, 1975).
176 Memorandum by Johnstone, 'British cultural propaganda in the Mediterranean area', 10 October 1936. BW 2/85, F 399, GB/8/2.
177 Lampson to Foreign Office, 30 April 1937. FO 395/554, P 2130/160/150.
178 Memorandum by Johnstone, 10 October 1936. BW 2/85, F 399, GB/8/2.
179 Ibid.
180 Memorandum by Johnstone, 11 May 1937. BW 2/222, F 9578, GB/37/1.
181 Speech by Bridge to the conference of the Association of Special Libraries and Information Bureaux, October 1937. BW 2/113, F 12506, GB/12/7.
182 Report of a tour of the Mediterranean and Near East by the chairman and secretary-general of the British Council, March–April 1938. BW 2/223, F 9579, GB/37/1.
183 Unsigned memorandum, 'The British Council and the maintenance of British influence abroad', September 1938. CAB 16/130.
184 Memorandum by Leeper for Vansittart, 14 March 1935. BC.
185 E. H. Carr, *Propaganda in International Politics*, Oxford Pamphlets on World Affairs, no. 16 (Oxford 1939) p. 21.
186 Leeper to Phipps, 23 January 1936. FO 395/539, P 106/106/150.
187 Ibid.
188 Phipps to Eden. 7 February 1936. British Council Confidential Papers, F 3454, G/8/1. BC.
189 Memorandum by D. Russell, 'Reasons for increasing British propaganda in Germany', 6 October 1938. Confidential Papers, F 3455, G/8/1.
190 Ibid.
191 D. Ellwood, '"Showing the World What It Owed to Britain": The British Council and Cultural Propaganda, 1935–45', paper delivered to the Imperial War Museum Conference on Film, Politics and Propaganda, 1918–45, March 1979.
192 For an attempted appraisal see F. Clements, 'The British Council in Europe', *Quarterly Review*, 273 (1939) 133–45.
193 C. Forbes Adam, *The Life of Lord Lloyd* (London, 1948) p. 285.
194 White, *The British Council*, p. 25.
195 Cited in Adam, *Lloyd*, p. 283.

Notes to pp. 181–90

5. The BBC foreign-language broadcasts

1. The bibliography contains a list of contemporary works.
2. Lord Avon, *Memoirs: Facing the Dictators* (London, 1962) p. 182.
3. Leeper to Bridge, 9 May 1935. BC.
4. I. Colvin, *Vansittart in Office* (London, 1965) pp. 74–5.
5. For a detailed study see D. Waley, *British Public Opinion and the Abyssinian War, 1935–36* (London, 1975).
6. Memorandum by Leeper, 1 January 1936. FO 395/538, P 224/46/46/150.
7. Ibid.
8. Ibid.
9. Ibid.
10. Minute by Vansittart, 4 January 1936. FO 395/538, P 224/46/150.
11. Ibid.
12. Barrington-Ward to Dawson, 14 January 1936. Barrington-Ward MS. Archives of *The Times*.
13. Ibid.
14. Memorandum by Leeper. 27 January 1936. FO 395/541, P 332/332/150.
15. Ibid.
16. Ibid.
17. Minute by Vansittart, 1 February 1936. FO 395/541, P 332/332/150.
18. M. Gilbert, *Winston S. Churchill, 1922–39* (London, 1976) pp. 724–6.
19. W. N. Medlicott, *Britain and Germany: The Search for Agreement, 1930–37* (London, 1969).
20. A. L. Kennedy to Deakin, 16 February 1936. Kennedy MS. Archives of *The Times*.
21. Cited in J. Hale, *Radio Power: Propaganda and International Broadcasting* (London, 1975) p. xiii.
22. J. B. Whitton and J. H. Hertz, 'Radio in International Politics' in H. L. Childs and J. B. Whitton (eds.), *Propaganda by Short-wave* (Princeton, 1942) p. 7.
23. Z. A. B. Zeman, *Nazi Propaganda* (2nd edn. Oxford, 1973) pp. 85–140.
24. Ibid. pp. 51–4; Whitton and Hertz, pp. 11–12.
25. Zeman, ch. 5; Whitton and Hertz, pp. 12–15.
26. O. W. Riegel, 'Press, Radio and the Spanish Civil War', *Public Opinion Quarterly*, 1 (1937) 131–41.
27. *Propaganda in International Politics*, Oxford Pamphlets on World Affairs, no. 16 (Oxford, 1939) p. 20.
28. League of Nations Assembly, Council, Circular Letters & Documents, 1936–39. Category xii A, 1936, C 37 (1936).
29. Explanatory note on the draft convention in ibid. C 399, M 252 (1936) xii C.

30 League convention concerning the use of broadcasting in the cause of peace, 23 September 1936 in ibid. C 399, M 252 (1936) xii C article 1.
31 Ibid., article 5.
32 Viscount Cranborne, under secretary of state for foreign affairs, signed for Britain. The Italian delegate withdrew from the discussions on 22 September.
33 A. Briggs, *The History of Broadcasting in the United Kingdom*, II: *The Golden Age of Wireless* (Oxford, 1965) pp. 370–83.
34 J. C. W. Reith, *Into the Wind* (London, 1949) p. 191.
35 Briggs, pp. 146–7.
36 Reith to Vansittart, 28 January 1930. FO 395/540, P 327/1/150.
37 C. Stuart (ed.), *The Reith Diaries* (London, 1975), entry for 14 February 1934.
38 W. Irwin, *Propaganda and the News: or, What Makes You Think So?* (New York, 1936) p. 258.
39 Reith, *Into the Wind*, p. 278.
40 Hale, *Radio Power*, p. 49.
41 Briggs, pp. 393–4.
42 *Report of the Broadcasting Committee, 1935*. Cmd. 5091 (1936) paras. 115–24.
43 Briggs, p. 395.
44 C. A. MacDonald, 'Radio Bari: Italian Wireless Propaganda in the Middle East and British Countermeasures, 1934–38', *Middle Eastern Studies* 13, 2 (1977) 195–207.
45 Whitton and Hertz, 'Radio in International Politics', pp. 27–8; S. Bent, 'International Broadcasting', *Public Opinion Quarterly*, 1, 4 (1937) 117–21; J. Coatman, 'Broadcasting News', *Quarterly Review*, 268, 531 (1937) 118–28.
46 A. J. Mackenzie, *Propaganda Boom* (London, 1938) p. 139.
47 BBC Archives, R 34/399; E 2/245.
48 BBC Archives, R 34/399, paper 4; Foreign Office memorandum, 'Proposed broadcasts in foreign languages by the BBC', 10 February 1937. FO 395/546, P 121/20/150.
49 Batterbee to Vansittart, 8 January 1937. FO 395/546, P 672/20/150.
50 BBC Archives, R 34/399, paper 2.
51 Notes of a meeting to discuss the use of foreign languages in the empire Service, 13 April 1937. BBC Archives, R 34/399.
52 Minute by Leeper, 14 June 1937. FO 395/547, P 2682/10/150.
53 Minute by Vansittart, 14 June 1937. FO 395/547, P 2682/10/150.
54 BBC Archives, R 34/399.
55 Minutes of the sub-committee, June 1937, and report, July 1937. BBC Archives, R 34/399.
56 Hansard, 5th series, vol. 321, 2 March 1937, cols. 196–7; vol. 321, 3 March 1937, cols. 337–8; vol. 321, 25 March 1937, cols. 3110–78; vol. 324, 7 June 1937, cols. 4087–9; vol. 325, 23 June 1937, cols.

1177–8; vol. 325, 28 June 1937, cols. 1618–19.
57 Memorandum by Eden, 13 July 1937. CAB 24/270, CP 185 (37).
58 CAB 23/89, 31 (37) 6.
59 CAB 23/89, 32 (37) 7, 28 July 1937.
60 Foreign Office memorandum, 'Proposed broadcasting station in Cyprus', 29 July 1937. CAB 27/641, ABC (37) 2.
61 Foreign Office memorandum, 13 September 1937. CAB 27/641, ABC (37) 4.
62 Ibid.
63 The Cliffe report, 'The Use of Foreign Languages in the Empire Service', September 1937. BBC Archives, E 2/245.
64 Reith to Phillips, 17 September 1937. CAB 27/641, ABC (37) 6.
65 The Cliffe report. BBC Archives, E 2/245.
66 Reith, *Into the Wind*, p. 290.
67 Foreign Office notes, 28 September 1937. CAB 27/641, ABC (37) 10.
68 These stations were under the immediate control of the local government. Both the administrative and the technical staffs were government employees, responsible to the station director. The programmes were drawn up locally under the supervision of broadcasting committees.
69 Arabic Broadcasting Committee, 1st meeting 15 September 1937. CAB 27/641, ABC (37).
70 Arabic Broadcasting Committee, 2nd meeting, 30 September 1937. CAB 27/641 ABC (37).
71 Arabic Broadcasting Committee, 1st meeting, 15 September 1937. CAB 27/641, ABC (37).
72 Foreign Office memorandum, 13 September 1937. CAB 27/641, ABC (37) 5.
73 Arabic Broadcasting Committee, 1st meeting, 15 September 1937. CAB 27/641, ABC (37).
74 Memorandum by the India Office, 6 September 1937. CAB 27/641, ABC (37) 3.
75 Ibid.
76 Foreign Office control could only be exercised through the Colonial Office and the governor of Cyprus.
77 Foreign Office memorandum, 'Proposed broadcasting station in Cyprus', 13 September 1937. CAB 27/641, ABC (37) 5.
78 Arabic Broadcasting Committee, 2nd meeting, 30 September 1937. CAB 27/641, ABC (37).
79 Ibid.
80 Memorandum by MacDonald, 28 September 1937. CAB 27/641, ABC (37) 8.
81 Reith to Phillips, 17 September 1937. CAB 27/641, ABC (37) 6.
82 Foreign Office memorandum, 'Broadcasts in Spanish and Portuguese', 13 September 1937. CAB 27/641, ABC (37) 4.

Notes to pp. 202–9

83 Arabic Broadcasting Committee, 3rd meeting, 4 October 1937. CAB 27/641, ABC (37).
84 Ibid.; see also BBC Archives, E 2/245, G 110/37.
85 Ibid.; see also Reith, *Into the Wind*, p. 292.
86 Ibid.
87 Ibid.
88 Ibid.
89 Report of the Cabinet Committee on Arabic Broadcasting, 22 October 1937. CAB 24/271, CP 274 (37).
90 CAB 23/90, 39 (37) 9, 27 October 1937.
91 Ibid.
92 CAB 23/90, 40 (37) 1, 3 November 1937.
93 Stuart (ed.), *Reith Diaries*, entry for 5 November 1937.
94 Hansard, 5th series, vol. 328, 29 October 1937, col. 501.
95 *Into the Wind*, pp. 290–3.
96 Hansard, 5th series, vol. 330, 21 December 1937, col. 1796.
97 Ibid. col. 1803.
98 Eden to Perth, 2 December 1937 and 23 December 1937. CAB 21/558; see also Lord Avon, *Memoirs: Facing the Dictators*, p. 431.
99 Summaries of the Bari broadcasts, illustrating their persistence and virulence, transmitted in the winter of 1937–8 can be found in FO 371/21836.
100 Memorandum by Calvert, 20 October 1937. CAB 21/558.
101 Ibid.
102 *The Times*, 3 January 1938.
103 *The Times*, 5 January 1938.
104 Perth to Foreign Office, 11 January 1938. FO 395/557, P 292/2/150.
105 Minute by Leeper, 8 January 1938. FO 395/557, P 69/2/150.
106 Note by J. B. Clark, 21 December 1937. BBC Archives, E 2/254.
107 Note by Clark, 31 December 1937. BBC Archives, E 2/254.
108 Record of a conversation with Calvert, 7 January 1938. BBC Archives, E 2/254.
109 Note by Clark, 'News Policy', 12 January 1938. BBC Archives, E 2/254.
110 Clark to Calvert, 18 January 1938. BBC Archives, E 2/39/1.
111 Minute by Leeper, 12 January 1938. FO 395/557, P 69/2/150; BBC Archives, E 2/254: record of a meeting at the Foreign Office on 12 January 1938.
112 Leeper to Graves, 18 January 1938. FO 395/558, P 332/2/150.
113 Calvert to Clark, 18 January 1938. BBC Archives, E 2/39/1.
114 Minute by J. Balfour, 'German activities in South America', 26 July 1938. FO 371/21457, A 6012/3182/51.
115 Memorandum by Eden, 8 December 1937. CAB 24/273, CP 301 (37).
116 Ibid.
117 CAB 23/90, 47 (37) 6.
118 The new terms of reference empowered the committee to look into

the questions of advertising broadcasts and relay services and wire broadcasting. CAB 27/641.
119 Aide-mémoire by Jones, 23 November 1937. CAB 27/641, ABC (37) 13.
120 Overseas Broadcasting Committee, 4th [sic; should be 1st] meeting, 4 January 1938. CAB 27/641, ABC (37).
121 R. Jones *A Life in Reuters* (London, 1951) pp. 457–60.
122 Foreign Office memorandum, 'Sources of foreign news appearing in the principal South American newspapers', 4 April 1938. CAB 27/641, ABC (37) 16.
123 R. Jones, pp. 460–2.
124 G. Storey, *Reuters' Century, 1851–1951* (London, 1951) p. 211.
125 Briggs, *Golden Age*, p. 645.
126 Undated, unsigned memorandum, 'Broadcasting of news bulletins in European languages'. BBC Archives, E 9/12/1.
127 Enclosure in a letter from 'an anti-Nazi' to Lord Halifax, 2 May 1939. FO 800/315, H/XV/159.
128 Unsigned minute, 1 July 1939. BBC Archives, E 9/12/5.
129 Cited in MacDonald, 'Radio Bari', p. 201.
130 *The Times*, 25 February 1939.
131 Cadogan to N. Henderson, 28 February 1939. FO 800/270.
132 MacDonald, 'Radio Bari', p. 198.
133 Memorandum by one of the oil companies (unnamed), 9 April 1938. FO 371/21915, E 2118/21189/89.
134 J. Heyworth-Dunne, 'A report on Arabic broadcasting in Egypt and Palestine with special reference to the Arabic broadcasts from London', 20 January 1938. INF 1/716; BBC Archives, E 2/39/1.
135 J. Heyworth-Dunne, supplementary report, May 1938. INF 1/716; BBC Archives, E 2/39/1.
136 Memorandum by S. H. Perowne, 'Proposals for the Development of the Arabic Broadcast Service', 2 September 1938. BBC Archives, E 2/39/1.
137 Leeper to Graves, 23 December 1938. BBC Archives, E 9/12/1.
138 Note by Clark, 6 October 1938. BBC Archives, E 9/12/1.
139 *The Times*, 23 March 1939.
140 Warner to Frost, 3 May 1939. FO 395/647B, P 1583/105/150.
141 Lampson to L. Oliphant, 26 January 1938. FO 371/21834, E 749/50/65.

6. *The Vansittart committee*

1 Memorandum by R. A. Leeper, 13 July 1937. FO 395/546, P 3261/1/150.
2 Ibid.
3 Memorandum by R. A. Leeper, 'Co-ordination of British Publicity Abroad', 2 January 1938. FO 395/596, P 359/359/150.

Notes to pp. 219–28

4 Ibid.
5 Ibid.
6 Ibid.
7 Ibid.
8 Ibid.
9 Ibid.
10 Ibid.
11 Ibid.
12 V. Lawford, *Bound for Diplomacy* (London, 1963) p. 271.
13 Minute by Cadogan, 14 July 1937. FO 395 /546, P 3261/1/150.
14 Minute by Eden, 8 January 1938. FO 395/596, P 359/359/150.
15 Minute by Leeper, 4 January 1938. FO 395/596, P 359/359/150.
16 Minute by Vansittart, 19 January 1938. FO 395/596, P 359/359/150.
17 Eden to Chamberlain, 18 January 1938. FO 395/596, P 359/359/150.
18 Chamberlain to Eden, 19 January 1938. FO 395/596, P 359/359/150.
19 Minute by Leeper, 22 January 1938. FO 395/596, P 476/359/150.
20 Hansard, 5th series, vol. 331, 7 February 1938, cols. 670–1.
21 *The Times*, 8 February 1938.
22 This correspondence is in FO 395/597.
23 N. Henderson to Foreign Office, 9 February 1938. FO 395/597, P 786/359/150.
24 Mr Lees-Jones, MP for Blackley.
25 Hansard, 5th Series, vol. 331, 16 February 1938, cols. 1909–10.
26 Ibid. col. 1932.
27 Ibid. col. 1944.
28 Ibid. col. 1953.
29 Ibid. col. 1969.
30 Committee for the Co-ordination of British Publicity Abroad (hereafter CBPA), 1st meeting, 16 February 1938. FO 395/597, P 965/359/150.
31 Treasury memorandum on publicity, 28 July 1923. T 162/42, E 2862.
32 P.E.P., 'Government Public Relations', *Planning*, 1, 14 (1933).
33 'Publicity services in Government Departments', April 1938. FO 366/1029, X 3097/431/504.
34 CBPA, 1st meeting, 16 February 1938. FO 395/597, P 965/359/150.
35 Minute by? (illegible signature), 25 February 1938. BT 59/25, DC 592.
36 CBPA, 2nd meeting, 27 April 1938. FO 395/601, P 1964/359/150.
37 CBPA, 1st meeting, 16 February 1938. FO 395/597, P 965/359/150.
38 'Publicity in relation to trade', CBPA 1, enclosed in Mullins to Vansittart, 16 February 1938. FO 395/597, P 965/359/150.
39 Vansittart to Fisher, 14 April 1938. T 161/933, S 42850/1.
40 Inter-departmental meeting on publicity overseas for UK trade and industry, 25 April 1938. FO 395/600, P 1692/359/150.
41 DOT report on trade publicity, 18 May 1938. FO 395/602, P 2081/359/150; BT 59/25, DC 592.

Notes to pp. 228–38

42 A. Elton in *World Film News*, 2, 5 (1937) 32.
43 Meredith to Warner, 9 February 1938. FO 395/597, P 975/359/150.
44 Ibid.
45 CBPA, 1st meeting, 16 February 1938. FO 395/597, P 965/359/150.
46 'Documentary films for overseas propaganda purposes', enclosed in R. Reid Adam to Vansittart, 14 February 1938. FO 395/597, P 937/359/150.
47 'The Joint Films Committee and its work', November 1938. BW 2/214, GB/30/1.
48 Ibid.
49 'The projection of Britain overseas', enclosed in Meredith to Warner, 18 February 1938. FO 395/597, P 968/359/150.
50 Memorandum enclosed in Reid Adam to Vansittart, 14 February 1938. FO 395/597, P 937/359/150.
51 'The Joint Films Committee and its work', November 1938. BW 2/214, GB/30/1.
52 Rochemont to Vansittart, 9 February 1938. CBPA 3, FO 395/597, P 965/359/150.
53 Memorandum by Kenney, 'National Film Publicity', 14 April 1938. FO 395/601, P 1748/359/150.
54 Ibid.
55 Ibid.
56 Ibid.
57 Ibid.
58 Ibid.
59 CBPA, 3rd meeting, 26 May 1938. FO 395/602, P 2083/359/150.
60 'Report of the Co-ordinating Committee for British Publicity Abroad', 28 May 1938. FO 395/602, P 1948/359/150.
61 Ibid.
62 Ibid.
63 Ibid.
64 Ibid.
65 Ibid.
66 Ibid.
67 Ibid.
68 Vansittart to Chamberlain, 28 May, 1938. PREM 1/272.
69 Minute by O. S. Cleverly, 28 May 1938. PREM 1/272.
70 N. Rose, *Vansittart: Portrait of a Diplomat* (London, 1978) p. 212.
71 Minute by Chamberlain, 29 May 1938. PREM 1/272.
72 Minute by Wilson, 31 May 1938. PREM 1/272.
73 Chamberlain to Vansittart, 31 May 1938. PREM 1/272.
74 Halifax to Simon, 1 June 1938. T 161/933, S 42850/2.
75 Ibid.
76 Memorandum by J. A. Barlow, 23 June 1938. T 161/933, S 42850/2.
77 C. Cruickshank, *The Fourth Arm: Psychological Warfare, 1938–45* (London, 1977) p. 11.

Notes to pp. 238–48

78 Joint second secretary at the Treasury, 1938–48.
79 Note by Hale, 2 June 1938. T 161/933, S 42850/2.
80 Ibid.
81 Ibid.
82 Ibid.
83 Ibid.
84 Ibid.
85 Ibid.
86 Ibid.
87 Halifax to Simon, 20 June 1938. T 161/933, S 42850/2.
88 Memorandum by Barlow, 23 June 1938. T 161/933, S 42850/2.
89 Memorandum by Hopkins, 24 June 1938. T 161/933, S 42850/2.
90 Minute by Fisher, 24 June 1938. T 161/933, S 42850/2.
91 Minute by Simon, 26 June 1938. T 161/933, S 42850/2.
92 Minute by Fisher, 27 June 1938. T 161/933, S 42850/2.
93 Memorandum by Hale, 5 July 1938. T 161/933, S 42850/2.
94 I. Colvin, *The Chamberlain Cabinet* (London, 1971) p. 133.
95 CBPA, 4th meeting, 15 December 1938. T 161/933, S 42850/2.
96 Note by Simon, 17 June 1938. T 161/907, S 35581/03/38/1.
97 CBPA, 4th meeting, 15 December 1938. T 161/933, S 42850/2.
98 Minute by Leeper, 1 June 1938. FO 395/601, P 1880/359/150.
99 Foreign Office circular despatch, 1 November 1938. FO 395/604, P 2385/359/150.
100 FO 395/604, P 3068/359/150.
101 Lord Birkenhead, *Halifax* (London, 1965) pp. 424–5.
102 Cadogan to Halifax, 28 November 1938. FO 800/396.
103 Simon to Halifax, 11 November 1938. FO 800/396.
104 C. Howard Smith to Hale, 30 May 1939. FO 366/1071, X 5389/1876/504.
105 For a description of the difficult conditions under which Peake was forced to work, see his memorandum of 5 August 1939. FO 366/1072, X 8092/1976/504.
106 Minute by A. Edgecumbe, 1 June 1938. BT 59/25, DC 613.
107 Minute by Barlow, undated. BT 59/25, DC 613.
108 Memorandum of interview at the Treasury regarding trade propaganda abroad, by A. Edgecumbe, 26 June 1938. BT 59/25, DC 592.
109 Ibid.
110 Edgecumbe to Hale, 14 October 1938. BT 59/25, DC 592.
111 J. H. Jones to Treasury, 14 October 1938. BT 61/72/9, DOT E 188773.
112 R. V. Nind Hopkins to DOT, 27 October 1938. BT 61/71/3, DOT E 18436.
113 CBPA, 4th meeting, 15 December 1938. T 161/933, S 42850/2.
114 Mullins to Williamson, 15 April 1939. BT 61/71/9, DOT E 188773.
115 Note by T. St Quintin Hall, 1 May 1939. BT 61/72/9, DOT E 188773.
116 Memorandum by Lord Halifax, 'Foreign Publicity', 10 July 1939. CAB 24/288, CP 153 (39).

117 Williamson to Mullins, 9 December 1939. BT 61/71/3, DOT E 18436.
118 For the reports of the Industrial Publicity Unit see BT 59/25, DC 592.
119 P. Swann, 'The British Documentary Film Movement, 1926–46', unpublished Ph.D. thesis, University of Leeds, 1979.
120 'The Joint Films Committee and its work', November 1938. BW 2/214, GB/30/1.
121 Joint Films Committee minutes, 1 October 1937. BW 2/35, GB/3/8.
122 'The Joint Films Committee and its work', November 1938. BW 2/214, GB/30/1.
123 Minute by Kenney, 9 June 1938. FO 395/597, P 936/359/150.
124 N. Pronay, 'British Newsreels in the 1930s, II: Their Policies and Impact', *History*, 57 (1972) 66.
125 Ibid. p. 67.
126 I am grateful to Mr T. Ryan of the University of Leeds for providing me with information on this subject, which forms the basis of his forthcoming doctoral thesis.
127 Joint Films Committee minutes, 2 June 1938. BW 2/35, GB/3/86.
128 'The Joint Films Committee and its work', November 1938. BW 2/214, GB/30/1.
129 H. P. Croom-Johnson to K. Johnstone, 11 November 1938. BW 2/214, GB/30/1.
130 Minute by Kenney, 14 September 1938. FO 395/622, P 2645/2645/150.
131 Minute by Hale, 25 July 1938; Warner to Hale, 11 August 1938. T 161/933, S 42850/2.
132 Leeper to Barlow, 10 December 1938. T 161/933, S 42850/2.
133 Ibid.
134 Minute by Hale, 14 December 1938. T 161/933, S 42850/2.
135 Minute by Vansittart, 14 February 1939. FO 395/660, P 356/282/150.
136 Vansittart to Hale, 12 May 1939. T 161/933, S 42850/2.
137 Thelma Cazalet, John Wardlaw-Milne and Ralph Glyn to N. Chamberlain, 16 February 1939. T 161/948, S 46284.
138 Minute by Hale, 5 April 1939. T 161/948, S 46284.
139 Minute by O. S. Cleverly, 6 April 1939. T 161/948, S 46284.
140 R. Glyn to Lord Dunglass, 16 May 1939. T 161/948, S 46284.
141 CBPA, 5th meeting, 17 May 1939. FO 395/660, P 2947/281/150.
142 Memorandum by Hale, 18 May 1939. T 161/933, S 42850/2.
143 E. Rowe Dutton's record of a meeting with Sir Michael Bruce, 3 June 1939. T 161/562, E 19011/2.
144 CBPA, 6th meeting, 25 July 1939. T 161/933, S 42850/2. Vansittart was replaced by Lord Perth as chairman for this meeting. Perth had recently been placed in charge of the newly created Foreign Publicity Department of the Foreign Office. For further details see chapter 7.
145 British Council memorandum, 'The work of the Joint Films Com-

mittee and how these activities can be expanded', July 1939. FO 395/660, P 2974/281/150.
146 CBPA, 6th meeting, 25 July 1939. T 161/933, S 42850/2. In fact, Lord Perth had already referred the matter to the Treasury prior to the final meeting of the Co-ordinating Committee, which was not informed of this move. Perth to Hale, 24 July 1939. FO 395/661, P 3324/281/150.
147 T 162/858, E 39140/1.
148 OEPEC, 2nd meeting, 30 June 1939. T 162/858, E 39140/1.
149 Memorandum by Leeper, 18 July 1939, OEPEC Paper 15. T 162/858, E 39140/2.
150 Memorandum by Leeper, 19 July 1939, OEPEC Paper 16. T 162/858, E 39140/2.
151 OEPEC, 5th meeting, 4 August 1939. T 162/858, E 39140/2.
152 Minute by J. Cairncross, 31 August 1939. T 162/858, E 39140/2.
153 Ibid.
154 Memorandum by Hale, 5 August 1939, OEPEC Paper 23. T 161/933, S 42850/2.
155 I. McLaine, *Ministry of Morale: Home Front Morale and the Ministry of Information in World War II* (London, 1979).
156 Memorandum by Leeper, undated (probably early October 1938). FO 800/396.
157 Memorandum by Leeper, 10 October 1938. FO 800/396
158 Memorandum by Leeper, 22 October 1938. FO 800/396.
159 Ibid.
160 Ibid.

7. Propaganda for war

1 Balfour, *Propaganda in War, 1935–45* (London 1979) p. 53.
2 Memorandum by C. P. Robertson, 12 September 1935. CAB 16/127, MIC 2.
3 Ibid.
4 Ian McLaine, *Ministry of Morale: Home Front Morale and the Ministry of Information in World War II* (London, 1979) pp. 12–13.
5 CAB 16/127, MIC 1.
6 C. Stuart (ed.), *The Reith Diaries* (London 1975) p. 122.
7 Balfour, p. 54.
8 H. V. Rhodes to Tallents, 12 July 1938. INF 4/1 A.
9 CID sub-committee to prepare plans for the establishment of a Ministry of Information, 1st meeting, 25 October 1935. CAB 16/127.
10 P. M. Taylor, 'The Foreign Office and British Propaganda during the First World War', *Historical Journal*, 23 (1980) 875–98.
11 W. P. Hildred to Tallents, 8 February 1938. INF 1/1.
12 Ibid.
13 Note by Leeper's planning sub-committee, 21 December 1935. CAB 16/128, MIC (Sub) 1.

Notes to pp. 266–72

14 CID sub-committee to prepare plans for the establishment of a Ministry of Information, 2nd meeting, 28 February 1936; 3rd meeting, 16 July 1936. CAB 16/127.
15 Report of the CID sub-committee, Paper no. 1253 B, 27 July 1936. PREM 1/388.
16 Ibid.
17 Ibid.
18 J. C. W. Reith, *Into the Wind* p. 304.
19 Balfour, p. 55.
20 CAB 16/129, MIC (CC) 1.
21 CID sub-committee on the general policy of broadcasting in time of war, 3rd meeting, 25 September 1935. CAB 16/120.
22 1 October 1935. CAB 16/120, BW 14.
23 Codifying sub-committee, 1st meeting, 10 June 1937. CAB 16/129, MIC (CC).
24 Progress report by S. G. Tallents, 23 February 1938. CAB 16/127, MIC 10.
25 Leeper to Tallents, 23 November 1937. INF 1/442.
26 Tallents to G. C. North, 14 December 1937. INF 1/442.
27 Progress report by Tallents, 23 February 1938. CAB 16/127, MIC 10.
28 Ibid.
29 CID sub-committee to prepare plans for the establishment of a Ministry of Information, 4th meeting, 18 March 1938. CAB 16/127, MIC 12.
30 Ibid.
31 CAB 16/127, MIC 12.
32 M. R. D. Foot, *S.O.E. in France* (London, 1966) p. 1.
33 Ibid.
34 Ibid. p. 2.
35 Ibid. p. 3; B. Sweet-Escott, *Baker Street Irregular* (London, 1965).
36 K. Young (ed.), *The Diaries of Sir Robert Bruce Lockhart, 1915–38* (London, 1973) p. 389.
37 See Tallents's account in his memorandum of 7 November 1938. CAB 16/127, MIC 15.
38 Campbell Stuart, *Opportunity Knocks Once* (London, 1952) p. 185.
39 Tallents's confidential notes on the British Council, September 1938. INF 1/442. Bridge to Lloyd, 16 September 1938. BC.
40 Note of a discussion between Tallents and Leeper held on 27 September 1938. INF 1/442.
41 McLaine, *Ministry of Morale*, p. 16.
42 King-Hall to Tallents, 5 September 1938. FO 898/2.
43 Unsigned memorandum, 'Propaganda in Germany: a memorandum on the dissemination of ideas among the German people to weaken their fighting power in war', 19 September 1938. CAB 16/127, MIC 14.
44 CAB 16/127, MIC 15.

45 A. Briggs, *The History of Broadcasting in the United Kingdom*, II: *The Golden Age of Wireless* (Oxford, 1965) p. 645.
46 King-Hall to Tallents, 5 September 1938. FO 898/2.
47 Note by King-Hall, 28 September 1938. FO 898/1.
48 Memorandum by Vernon Bartlett on propaganda in Germany, 27 September 1938. FO 898/1.
49 Minute by H. Knatchbull-Hugessen, 27 September 1938. FO 898/1.
50 Enclosed in a record of a meeting in Mr Leeper's room, 27 September 1938. FO 898/1.
51 Draft leaflet, 27 September 1938. FO 898/1.
52 Memorandum by Tallents, 'Information in Enemy Countries', 7 November 1938. CAB 16/127, MIC 15.
53 Ryan to Tallents, 5 October 1938. FO 898/1.
54 Campbell Stuart, *Opportunity Knocks Once*, p. 185.
55 Tallents to Sir Donald Banks, 4 October 1938. FO 898/1.
56 Ryan to Tallents, 5 October 1938. FO 898/1.
57 Memorandum on the Joint Broadcasting Committee, 24 August 1939. Appendix to OEPEC paper 82. T 162/858, E 39140/4.
58 Ibid.
59 Ibid.
60 Record of a meeting at the BBC, 6 October 1938. FO 898/1.
61 Henniker-Heaton to Fass, 25 January 1939. FO 898/1.
62 Ibid.
63 Ibid.
64 Memorandum by Warner, 6 October 1938. FO 395/624. P 2853/2853/150.
64 Minute by Leeper, 30 September 1938. FO 800/396.
65 See FO 395/624, P 2960/2853/150.
66 Minute by Leeper, 10 October 1938. FO 800/396.
67 Sidney Rogerson, head of public relations at ICI, whose book *Propaganda in the Next War* was published in September 1938, appealed for the peacetime establishment of a central propaganda agency. He was speaking in an address to the National Book Fair at Earl's Court. *The Times*, 15 November 1938. Rogerson was a member of a group of advertising and industrial publicity experts who were campaigning for a role in any national propaganda organisation that might be created. O'Brien to Leeper, 30 November 1938. BC. These men were apparently unaware of the plans in progress for the Ministry of Information, knowledge of which had by then become an open secret in informed political circles.
68 Minute by Leeper, 31 May 1937. FO 395/556, P 2264/2264/150.
69 Memorandum by Tallents, 7 November 1938. CAB 16/127, MIC 15.
70 Ibid.
71 Ibid.
72 Leeper to Ryan, 7 December 1938. CAB 16/127, MIC 18.
73 Memorandum by Bridge, 'The development of cultural relations

Notes to pp. 279–86

with Germany', 25 November 1938. British Council Confidential papers, F 3455, G/8/1. BC.
74 Memorandum by Halifax, 'British propaganda in Germany', 8 December 1938. CAB 24/281, CP 284 (38).
75 Ibid.
76 Ibid.
77 CAB 23/96, 59 (38) 5, 14 December 1938.
78 Ibid.
79 Ibid.
80 Ibid.
81 CID sub-committee to prepare plans for the establishment of a Ministry of Information, 5th meeting, 14 December 1938. CAB 16/127.
82 Reith, *Into the Wind*, p. 341.
83 21 December 1938. CAB 23/96, 60 (39) 3.
84 Viscount Templewood, *Nine Troubled Years* (London, 1954) pp. 420–1.
85 Memorandum by Leeper, 'British publicity abroad', 20 January 1939. CAB 16/130, MIC (P) 2.
86 Undated draft report by Campbell Stuart. CAB 16/130, MIC (P) 5.
87 CID sub-committee on propaganda in foreign countries in time of war, 1st meeting, 26 January 1939. CAB 16/130, MIC (P).
88 Balfour, *Propaganda in War*, pp. 88–9.
89 Memorandum by Campbell Stuart, 8 February 1939. CAB 16/130, MIC (P) 3.
90 Ibid.
91 Undated draft report by Campbell Stuart. CAB 16/130, MIC (P) 5.
92 Bridge to Fass, 30 January 1939. INF 1/442.
93 Fass to Bridge, 9 February 1939. INF 1/442.
94 Fass to Leeper, 9 February 1939. FO 395/647A, P 542/105/150.
95 Note of a meeting held on 15 February 1939. INF 1/442.
96 Note of a conference held at the Treasury, 17 February 1939. T 161/907, S 35581/06.
97 Ibid.
98 Minute by Leeper, 24 February 1939. FO 395/647A, P 662/105/150.
99 Lloyd to Leeper, 25 March 1939. FO 395/647 A, P 1078/105/150.
100 Waterfield to Bridge, 30 August 1939. INF 1/442.
101 Unsigned memorandum on the British Council, 29 August 1939. OEPEC paper 30, T 162/858, E 39140/3.
102 Minute by Leeper, 15 January 1939. FO 366/1071, X 1976/1976/504.
103 Ibid.
104 Cadogan to Sir James Rae, 27 January 1939. FO 366/1071, X 1976/1976/504.
105 FO 366/1071, X 1976/1976/504.
106 Warner to Woodburn, 17 February 1939. INF 1/718.
107 Note of a conference at the Treasury, 17 February 1939. T 161/907, S 35581/06.

Notes to pp. 286–98

108 Note of a discussion with the Foreign Office on the functions of the PID and its relations with the ministry, 23 February 1939. INF 1/718. See also I. S. Macadam to Leeper, 4 August 1939. T 162/858, E 39140/3.
109 Memorandum by Hoare, 2 June 1939. CAB 24/287, CP 127 (39).
110 Ibid.
111 Ibid.
112 Draft Treasury minute, June 1939. T 162/858, E 39140/1.
113 Memorandum by Hoare, 2 June 1939. CAB 24/287, CP 127 (39).
114 J. Harvey (ed.), *The Diplomatic Diaries of Oliver Harvey, 1937–40* (London 1970) entry for 24 May 1939. See also the entries for 7 and 29 May.
115 7 June 1939. CAB 23/99, 31 (39) 12.
116 Ibid.
117 14 June 1939. CAB 23/99, 32 (39) 9.
118 Ibid.
119 Hansard, 5th series, vol. 348, 14 June 1939, cols. 1499–503.
120 *The Times*, 16 June 1939.
121 C. Howard Smith to Hale, 30 May 1939. FO 366/1071, X 5389/1976/504.
122 R. E. Herzstein, *The War That Hitler Won: Nazi Propaganda* (London, 1979).

Conclusion

1 Minute by Leeper, 18 February 1937. FO 395/554, P 823/160/150.
2 Loraine to Simon, 9 November 1933. FO 371/17034, J 2790/2790/16.
3 Memorandum by Leeper, 22 October 1938. FO 800/396.
4 Leeper to his father, 4 January 1934. I am grateful to Miss V. A. Leeper for drawing my attention to this letter.
5 Leeper to Barlow, 25 November 1938. FO 395/605, P 3307/359/150.
6 Memorandum by Leeper, undated.
7 Ibid.
8 See the opening sentence of *The History of Broadcasting in the United Kingdom*, III: *The War of Words* (London, 1970).
9 ? (illegible signature) to R. Jones, 25 March 1918. INF 4/6.

Select bibliography

UNPUBLISHED PRIMARY SOURCES
Administrative and departmental records
Public Record Office, Kew, London

British Council
- BW 2 (selected files).
- BW 4 (selected files).

Cabinet Office
- CAB 4 Miscellaneous memoranda (selected files).
- CAB 16 Ad-hoc sub-committees of enquiry (selected files).
- CAB 21 Cabinet registered files (selected volumes).
- CAB 23 Cabinet minutes (1916–39).
- CAB 24 Cabinet memoranda (1916–39).
- CAB 27 Committees: general series to 1939 (selected files).
- CAB 38/23 CID standing sub-committee enquiry regarding press and postal censorship in time of war.
- CAB 48 Committee of Imperial Defence (selected files).

Department of Overseas Trade
- BT 59 (selected files).
- BT 60 (selected files).
- BT 61 (selected files).

Foreign Office
- FO 336 Chief Clerk's Department (selected files).
- FO 371 General correspondence (selected files).
- FO 395 News Department (666 files).
- FO 431 Cultural propaganda (4 files).
- FO 898 Political Warfare Executive (selected files).

Information
- INF 1 Ministry of Information, 1939–45 (selected files).
- INF 4 War of 1914–18 (11 files).

Prime Minister's Office
- PREM 1 (selected files).
- PREM 3 (selected files).

Treasury
- T 160 Finance (selected files).
- T 161 Supply (selected files).
- T 162 OEPEC (selected files).

Select bibliography

British Council, Spring Gardens, London
Minutes of the Executive, Finance and Agenda committees, 1934–9.
Confidential papers, 1934–9.
Annual reports.

BBC Archives, Caversham Park, Reading
Foreign general files
    E2/245–99   Arabic broadcasts.
    E2/300–23   Spanish and Portuguese broadcasts.
    E9/12/1–5   European News Service.

Private collections

Public Record Office, Kew, London
    FO   800/149–58   Lord Curzon.
    FO   800/197   Lord Robert Cecil.
    FO   800/203–13   Lord Balfour.
    FO   800/220   Sir William Tyrrell.
    FO   800/223   Lord Reading.
    FO   800/243   Sir Eyre Crowe.
    FO   800/256–63   Sir Austen Chamberlain.
    FO   800/264–71   Sir Nevile Henderson.
    FO   800/280–4   Sir Arthur Henderson.
    FO   800/285–91   Sir John Simon.
    FO   800/293–4   Sir Alexander Cadogan.
    FO   800/295   Sir Samuel Hoare.
    FO   800/309–28   Lord Halifax.
    FO   800/329, 383–99   General and miscellaneous collections: ministers and officials: private office, 1915–24, 1931–41.
    FO   800/330   Marquess of Crewe.
    FO   954   Lord Avon.
    PRO   30/69   Ramsay MacDonald.

British Council, Spring Gardens, London
Correspondence between Charles Bridge and Rex Leeper (marked BC). These papers are held in the office of the Secretariat in the British Council's London headquarters. I am indebted to the former secretary, Mr Irvine Watson, for bringing these papers to my attention in 1976.

Archives of 'The Times', New Printing House Square, London
R. Barrington-Ward MS.
G. Dawson MS.
A. L. Kennedy MSS and diary.

Select bibliography

Lord Northcliffe MS.
H. Wickham Steed MS.
A. Willert MS.

Yale University Library, New Haven, Connecticut, U.S.A.

A. Willert papers.

Rex Leeper's letters to his family

I am grateful to Miss V. A. Leeper for sending me copies of these letters from Australia.

PUBLISHED PRIMARY SOURCES

Parliamentary Debates (Commons) 5th series, 1919–39.
Annual Reports of the Empire Marketing Board, 1927–33 (HMSO, 1927–33).
Command papers
    Cmd. 672 (1920) *Accounts and Papers (Miscellaneous) No. 8. Report of the Foreign Office Committee on British Communities Abroad.*
    Cmd. 1589 (1922) *Third Report of the Committee on National Expenditure.*
    Cmd. 2768 (1926) *Proceedings of the Imperial Conference.*
    Cmd. 3718 (1930) *Proceedings of the Imperial Conference.*
    Cmd. 4175 (1932) *Proceedings of the Imperial Economic Conference.*
    Cmd. 5091 (1936) *Report of the Broadcasting Committee.*
    Cmd. 9138 (1954) *Summary of the Report of the Independent Committee of Enquiry into the Overseas Information Services.*
    Cmd. 2276 (1964) *Report of the Committee on Representational Services Overseas.*
Documents on German Foreign Policy, 1918–45, Series C and D (HMSO, 1946–).
Documents on British Foreign Policy, 1919–39, 2nd and 3rd series (HMSO, 1946–).
The Times, 1919–39

PUBLISHED SECONDARY SOURCES

Although not all the works listed here have been cited in the text, they are included in this bibliography because of their invaluable contribution in providing background information. Place of publication is London unless stated otherwise.

Select bibliography

Memoirs, diaries and autobiographies

Amery, L. C. M. S., *My Political Life* (3 vols., Hutchinson, 1953–5).
Avon, Earl of, *Memoirs* (3 vols., Cassell, 1960–5).
Baker White, J., *The Big Lie* (Evans Bros., 1955).
Brittain, H., *Pilgrims and Pioneers* (Hutchinson, n.d.).
Brownrigg, D., *Indiscretions of the Naval Censor* (Cassell, 1920).
Bruce Lockhart, R., *Comes the Reckoning* (Putnam, n.d.).
Churchill, W. S., *The Gathering Storm* (Cassell, 1948).
Clarke, T., *My Northcliffe Diary* (Gollancz, 1931).
Coote, C., *Editorial* (Eyre and Spottiswood, 1965).
Delmer, S., *An Autobiography* (2 vols, Secker and Warburg, 1962).
Dilks, D. N. (ed.), *The Diaries of Sir Alexander Cadogan, 1938–45* (Cassell, 1971).
Duff Cooper, A., *Old Men Forget* (Hart-Davis, 1953).
Eckersley, R., *B.B.C. and All That* (Low, n.d.).
Fyfe, H., *Sixty Years of Fleet Street* (Allen, 1949).
Gladwyn, Lord, *Memoirs* (Weidenfeld and Nicolson, 1972).
Gregory, J. D., *On the Edge of Diplomacy: Rambles and Reflections, 1902–28* (Hutchinson, 1928).
Halifax, Lord, *Fulness of Days* (Collins, 1957).
Hankey, Lord, *The Supreme Control at the Paris Peace Conference, 1919* (Allen and Unwin, 1963).
Hardy, F. (ed.), *Grierson on Documentary* (Faber and Faber, 1966).
Harvey, J. (ed.), *The Diplomatic Diaries of Oliver Harvey, 1937–40* (Collins, 1970).
Headlam-Morley, A., R. Bryant and A. Cienciala (eds.), *Sir James Headlam-Morley: A Memoir of the Paris Peace Conference, 1919* (Methuen, 1972).
Huxley, G., *Both Hands: An Autobiography* (Chatto and Windus, 1970).
Jones, R., *A Life in Reuters* (Hodder and Stoughton, 1951).
Knatchbull-Hugessen, H., *Diplomat in Peace and War* (Murray, 1949).
Lawford, V., *Bound for Diplomacy* (Murray, 1963).
Leeper, R. A., *When Greek Meets Greek* (Chatto and Windus, 1950).
Lloyd George, D., *War Memoirs* (2 vols., Odham, 1933–4).
  Memoirs of the Peace Conference (2 vols., New Haven: Yale University Press, 1939).
McDonald, I., *A Man of the Times* (Hamish Hamilton, 1976).
Martin, K., *Editor: A Volume of Autobiography, 1931–1945* (Hutchinson, 1968).
Percy, E., *Some Memories* (Eyre and Spottiswood, 1958).
Reith, J. C. W., *Into the Wind* (Hodder and Stoughton, 1949).
Riddell, Lord, *An Intimate Diary of the Peace Conference and After, 1918–23* (Gollancz, 1933).
Stuart, Campbell, *Opportunity Knocks Once* (Hodder and Stoughton, 1952).
Stuart, Charles (ed.), *The Reith Diaries* (Collins, 1975).

Select bibliography

Sweet-Escott, B., *Baker Street Irregular* (Methuen, 1965).
Templewood, Viscount, *Nine Troubled Years* (Collins, 1954).
Toynbee, A., *Experiences* (Oxford University Press, 1969).
Vansittart, Lord, *The Mist Procession* (Hutchinson, 1958).
Wickham Steed, H., *Through Thirty Years* (2 vols., Heinemann, 1924).
Willert, A., *Washington and Other Memories* (Boston: Houghton Mifflin, 1972).
Young, K. (ed.), *The Diaries of Sir Robert Bruce Lockhart, 1915–38* (Macmillan, 1973).

Biographies

Adam, C. F., *The Life of Lord Lloyd* (Macmillan, 1948).
Beveridge, J., *John Grierson: Film Master* (Macmillan, 1979).
Birkenhead, Lord, *Halifax* (Hamilton, 1965).
Boyle, A., *Only the Wind Will Listen: Reith of the B.B.C.* (Hutchinson, 1972).
Butler, J. R. M., *Lord Lothian* (Macmillan, 1960).
Churchill, R. S., *Lord Derby, King of Lancashire* (Heinemann, 1959).
Colvin, I., *Vansittart in Office* (Gollancz, 1965).
Cross, J. A., *Sir Samuel Hoare: A Political Biography* (Cape, 1977).
Feiling, K. G., *The Life of Neville Chamberlain* (Macmillan, 1946).
Fowler, W. B., *British–American Relations, 1917–18: The Role of Sir William Wiseman* (Princeton (N.J.): University Press, 1969).
Gilbert, M., *Winston S. Churchill, 1922–39* (Heinemann, 1976).
McLachlan, D., *In the Chair: Barrington-Ward of 'The Times', 1927–48* (Weidenfeld and Nicolson, 1971).
Middlemas, R. K. and A. J. Barnes, *Baldwin* (Weidenfeld and Nicolson, 1969).
Nicolson, H., *Curzon: The Last Phase, 1919–25* (Constable, 1934).
Owen, F., *Tempestuous Journey: Lloyd George, His Life and Times* (Hutchinson, 1954).
Pound, R. and G. Harmsworth, *Northcliffe* (Cassell, 1959).
Rose, N., *Vansittart: Portrait of a Diplomat* (Heinemann, 1978).
Saxon Mills, G. H., *There Is a Tide . . . The Life and Work of Sir William Crawford* (Heinemann, 1954).
Taylor, A. J. P., *Beaverbrook* (Hamilton, 1972).
Wrench, J. E., *Geoffrey Dawson and Our Times* (Hutchinson, 1955).

Other books

Akzin, B., *Propaganda by Diplomats* (Washington, D.C.: Digest Press, 1936).
Albig, W., *Public Opinion* (McGraw-Hill, 1939).
Aldgate, A., *Cinema and History: British Newsreels and the Spanish Civil War* (Scolar, 1979).
Arts Enquiry, *The Factual Film* (Oxford: University Press, 1947).
Aster, S., *1939: The Making of the Second World War* (Deutsch, 1972).

Select bibliography

Aston, G., *Secret Service* (Faber and Faber, 1930).
Astor, M., *Tribal Feeling* (Murray, 1963).
Balfour, M., *Propaganda in War, 1939–45* (Routledge and Kegan Paul, 1979).
Barghoorn, F. C., *The Soviet Cultural Offensive: The Role of Cultural Diplomacy in Soviet Foreign Policy* (Princeton (N.J.): University Press, 1960).
Bartlett, F. C., *Political Propaganda* (Cambridge: University Press, 1940).
Bernays, E. L., *Crystallising Public Opinion* (Boni and Liveright, 1923).
  Propaganda (New York: Liveright, 1928).
  Public Relations (Norman: University of Oklahoma Press, 1952).
Black, J. B., *Organising the Propaganda Instrument: The British Experience* (The Hague: Martinus Nijhoff, 1975).
Blanco White, A., *The New Propaganda* (Gollancz, 1939).
Briggs, A., *The History of Broadcasting in the United Kingdom* (Oxford: University Press, 1961–); vol. I, *The Birth of Broadcasting* (1961); vol. II, *The Golden Age of Wireless* (1965); vol. III, *The War of Words* (1970).
Brown, J. A. C., *Techniques of Persuasion: From Propaganda to Brainwashing* (Harmondsworth: Penguin, 1963).
Bruntz, G. C., *Allied Propaganda and the Collapse of the German Empire in 1918* (Stanford (Calif.): University Press; London: Humphrey Milford and Oxford University Press, 1938).
Camrose, Viscount, *British Newspapers and their Controllers* (Cassell, 1947).
Carr, E. H., *Propaganda in International Politics* (Oxford Pamphlets on World Affairs, no. 16, Oxford: University Press, 1939).
Childs, H. L. and J. B. Whitton, (eds.), *Propaganda by Short-wave* (Princeton (N. J.): University Press, 1942).
Clark, F., *The Central Office of Information* (Allen and Unwin, 1970).
Cockburn, P., *The Years of 'The Week'* (Harmondsworth: Penguin, 1971).
Cohen, B. C., *The Press and Foreign Policy* (Princeton (N.J.): University Press, 1963).
Colvin, I., *The Chamberlain Cabinet* (Gollancz, 1971).
Cook, E. T., *The Press in Wartime* (Macmillan, 1920).
Craig, G. A. and F. Gilbert, *The Diplomats, 1919–39* (Princeton (N.J.): University Press, 1953).
Crawford, W. S., *How To Succeed in Advertising* (World's Press News, 1931).
Cruickshank, C., *The Fourth Arm: Psychological Warfare, 1938–45* (Davis-Poynter, 1977).
Doob, L. W., *Propaganda: Its Psychology and Technique* (New York: Holt, 1935).
Ellul, J., *Propaganda: The Formation of Men's Attitudes* (New York: Vintage Books, 1973).
Fielding, R., *The March of Time, 1935–51* (New York: Oxford University Press, 1978).

Select bibliography

Foot, M. R. D., *S.O.E. in France* (HMSO, 1966).
Fraser, L., *Propaganda* (Oxford: University Press, 1957).
Germany between Two Wars: A Study in Propaganda and War Guilt (Oxford: University Press, 1944).
Friedmann, O., *Broadcasting for Democracy* (Allen and Unwin, 1942).
Gannon, F. R., *The British Press and Germany, 1936–39* (Oxford: University Press, 1971).
Gilbert, M. and R. Gott, *The Appeasers* (Wiedenfeld, 1963).
Granzow, B., *A Mirror of Nazism: British Opinion and the Emergence of Hitler, 1929–33* (Gollancz, 1964).
Grenville, J. A. S., *The Major International Treaties* (Methuen, 1974).
Haigh, A., *Cultural Diplomacy in Europe* (Strasbourg: Council of Europe, 1974).
Hale, J., *Radio Power: Propaganda and International Broadcasting* (Elek, 1975).
Hale, O. J., *Publicity and Diplomacy – With Special Reference to England and Germany, 1890–1914* (repr. Gloucester, Mass.: Peter Smith, 1964). (Originally published New York: University of Virginia Institute for Research in the Social Sciences, 1940.)
Hankey, Lord, *Diplomacy by Conference: Studies in Public Affairs, 1920–46* (Benn, 1946).
Hardinge, Lord, *Old Diplomacy* (Murray, 1947).
Hargrave, J., *Words Win Wars* (Wells Gardner, Darton & Co., 1940).
Herzstein, R. E., *The War That Hitler Won: Nazi Propaganda* (Hamish Hamilton, 1979).
Hood, P., *Ourselves and the Press* (Lane, 1939).
Irwin, W., *Propaganda and the News: or, What Makes You Think So?* (New York: McGraw-Hill, 1936).
Isaksson, F. and L. Furhammar, *Politics and Film* (Vista, 1971).
Jenkins, R., *Government, Broadcasting and the Press* (The Granada Guildhall lecture, Hart-Davis, 1975).
Jones, K., *Fleet Street and Downing Street* (Hutchinson, 1920).
King-Hall, S., *Chatham House* (Oxford, New York and Toronto: Oxford University Press, 1937).
Lambert, R. S., *Propaganda* (Nelson and Sons, 1938).
Lauren, P. G., *Diplomats and Bureaucrats: The First Institutional Responses to Twentieth Century Diplomacy in France and Germany* (Stanford, Calif.: Hoover Institution Press, 1976).
Lippmann, W., *Public Opinion* (Allen and Unwin, 1922).
Lloyd, Lord, *The British Case* (Eyre and Spottiswood, 1939).
Low, R., *The History of the British Film, 1918–29* (Allen and Unwin, 1971).
Lumley, F. E., *The Propaganda Menace* (New York: Appleton-Century, 1933).
McCallum, R. B., *Public Opinion and the Last Peace* (Oxford: University Press, 1944).
Macdonald, N. P., *Hitler over Latin America* (Norwich: Jarrold, 1940).

Select bibliography

Mackenzie, A. J., *Propaganda Boom* (Gifford, 1938).
McLaine, I., *Ministry of Morale: Home Front Morale and the Ministry of Information in World War II* (Allen and Unwin, 1979).
McMurray, R. E. and M. Lee, *The Cultural Approach: Another Way in International Relations* (Chapel Hill: University of North Carolina Press, 1947).
Margach, J., *The Abuse of Power: The War between Downing Street and the Media from Lloyd George to Callaghan* (W. H. Allen, 1978).
Marrett, R., *Through the Back Door: An Inside View of Britain's Overseas Information Services* (Pergamon, 1968).
Medlicott, W. N., *Britain and Germany: The Search for Agreement, 1930–37* (Athlone Press, 1969).
Middlemas, R. K., *The Diplomacy of Illusion: The British Government and Germany, 1937–39* (Weidenfeld and Nicolson, 1972).
Moorhouse, G., *The Diplomats: The Foreign Office Today* (Cape, 1977).
Ogilvy-Webb, M., *The Government Explains* (Allen and Unwin, 1965).
Peterson, H. C., *Propaganda for War: The Campaign for American Neutrality, 1914–17* (New York: Kennikat, 1939).
Pratt, L., *East of Malta, West of Suez: Britain's Mediterranean Crisis, 1936–39* (Cambridge: University Press, 1975).
Riegel, O. W., *Mobilizing for Chaos: The Story of the New Propaganda* (New Haven: Yale University Press, 1934).
Roetter, C., *Psychological Warfare* (Batsford, 1974).
Rogerson, S., *Propaganda in the Next War* (Geoffrey Bles, 1938).
Rotha, P., *Documentary Diary: An Informal History of the Documentary Film, 1928–39* (Secker and Warburg, 1973).
Russell, B., *Free Thought and Official Propaganda* (Conway memorial lecture, Watts and Co., 1922).
Salmon, L. M., *The Newspaper and Authority* (New York: Oxford University Press, 1923).
Seymour-Ure, C., *The Press, Politics and the Public* (Methuen, 1968).
The Political Impact of the Mass Media (Constable, 1974).
Smith, A. (ed.), *British Broadcasting* (Newton Abbot: David and Charles, 1974).
Smith, P. (ed.), *The Historian and Film* (Cambridge: University Press, 1976).
Squires, J. D., *British Propaganda at Home and in the United States from 1914 to 1917* (Cambridge, Mass.: Harvard University Press, 1935).
Steiner, Z., *The Foreign Office and Foreign Policy, 1898–1914* (Cambridge: University Press, 1969).
Storey, G., *Reuters' Century, 1851–1951* (Max Parrish, 1951).
Strang, Lord, *Home and Abroad* (Deutsch, 1956).
The Foreign Office (Allen and Unwin, 1955).
Stuart, Campbell, *Secrets of Crewe House: The Story of a Famous Campaign* (Hodder and Stoughton, 1920).

Select bibliography

Sussex, E., *The Rise and Fall of British Documentary* (Berkeley: University of California Press, 1975).
Tallents, S. G., *The Projection of England* (Faber and Faber, 1932).
Post Office Publicity (GPO, 1935).
The Birth of British Documentary (Film Centre, 1968).
Taylor, A. J. P., *The Trouble Makers: Dissent over Foreign Policy, 1798–1939* (Panther, 1969).
Taylor, A. J. P. (ed.), *Off the Record: W. P. Crozier's Political Interviews, 1933–43* (Hutchinson, 1972).
Taylor, R., *Film Propaganda: Soviet Russia and Nazi Germany* (Croom Helm, 1979).
Thompson, G. P., *Blue Pencil Admiral: The Inside Story of the Press Censorship* (Sampson, 1947).
Thompson, N., *The Anti-Appeasers: Conservative Opposition to Appeasement in the 1930s* (Oxford: University Press, 1971).
Thompson, O., *Mass Persuasion in History: An Historical Analysis of the Development of Propaganda Techniques* (Edinburgh: Harris, 1977).
Thomson, B., *The Scene Changes* (Collins, 1939).
Thorpe, F. and N. Pronay, *British Official Films in the Second World War: A Descriptive Catalogue* (Oxford: Clio Press, 1980).
Tilley, J. and S. Gaselee, *The Foreign Office* (Putnam, 1932).
Times, The, *History of 'The Times'* (5 vols., Printing House Square, 1932–52): vol. III, *The Twentieth Century Test, 1884–1912* (1947); vol. IV, *The 150th Anniversary and Beyond, 1912–48* (1952).
Tomlinson, J. D., *The International Control of Radiocommunications* (Geneva: Université de Genève, 1938).
Ullman, R. H., *Anglo-Soviet Relations, 1917–21,* I: *Intervention and the War* (Princeton (N.J.): University Press, 1961).
Waley, D., *British Public Opinion and the Abyssinian War, 1935–36* (Temple Smith, 1975).
Watt, D. C., *Personalities and Policies* (Longman, 1965).
Wellesley, V., *Diplomacy in Fetters* (Hutchinson, 1944).
White, A. J. S., *The British Council: The First Twenty Five Years.* (British Council, 1965).
Whitton, J. B. and A. Larson, *Propaganda: Towards Disarmament in the War of Words* (New York: Oceana, 1974).
Wickham Steed, H., *The Press* (Harmondsworth: Penguin Special, 1938).
The Fifth Arm (Constable, 1940).
Willert, A., *Aspects of British Foreign Policy* (New Haven: Yale University Press, 1929).
The Frontiers of England (Heinemann, 1935).
The Road to Safety: A Study in Anglo-American Relations (Verschoyle, 1952).
Willert, A., B. K. Long and H. V. Hodson, *The Empire in the World* (Oxford: University Press, 1937).
Williams, D., *Not in the Public Interest* (Hutchinson, 1965).

Select bibliography

Williams, F., *Dangerous Estate: The Anatomy of Newspapers* (Longman, 1957).
Zeman, Z. A. B., *Nazi Propaganda* (Oxford: University Press, 1964; 2nd edn, 1973).

Articles

Ainsworth, G., 'The New York World Fair: Adventure in Promotion', *Public Opinion Quarterly*, 3 (1939) 694–704.
Albert, E., 'The Press in Nazi Germany', *Contemporary Review*, 154 (1938) 693–9.
Beales, C., 'Totalitarian Inroads into Latin America', *Foreign Affairs*, 17, 1 (1938) 78–89.
Beloff, M., 'The Projection of Britain Abroad', *International Affairs*, 47, 3 (1965) 478–89.
  'The Whitehall Factor: The Role of the Higher Civil Service, 1919–39' in G. Peele and C. Cook (eds.), *The Politics of Reappraisal, 1918–39* (Macmillan, 1975).
Bent, S., 'International Broadcasting', *Public Opinion Quarterly*, 1, 4 (1937) 117–21.
Berchtold, W. E., 'The World Propaganda War', *North American Review*, 238 (1934) 421–30.
'British News by Wireless', *Round Table*, 29, 116 (1939) 719–31.
Casey, R. D., 'The National Publicity Bureau and British Party Propaganda', *Public Opinion Quarterly*, 3 (1939) 623–34.
Chalmers Mitchell, P., 'Propaganda', *Encyclopaedia Britannica*, 11th edn.
Clements, F., 'The British Council in Europe', *Quarterly Review*, 273 (1939) 133–45.
Coatman, J., 'Broadcasting News', *Quarterly Review*, 268, 531 (1937) 118–28.
Coggeshall, R., 'Diplomatic Implications of International News', *Journalism Quarterly*, 2, 2 (1934) 141–59.
  'Peace Conference Publicity: Lessons of 1919', *Journalism Quarterly*, 19, 1 (1942) 1–11.
Crucy, F., 'The Diplomat and the Journalist', *Nation and the Athenaeum*, 6 June 1925, pp. 288–90.
Dafoe, J. W., 'Public Opinion as a Factor in Government' in Q. Wright (ed.), *Public Opinion and World Politics* (Chicago: University of Chicago Press, 1933).
Ellwood, D. W., '"Showing the World What it Owed to Britain": Foreign Policy and Cultural Propaganda, 1935–45' in D. W. Spring and N. Pronay (eds.). *Film, Politics and Propaganda, 1918–45* (Macmillan, 1981).
Frankel, C., '"Culture", "Information", "Foreign Policy"', *Public Administration Review*, Nov.–Dec. 1969, 593–600.

Select bibliography

Garnett, M., 'Propaganda', *Contemporary Review*, 147 (1935) 574–81.
Grierson, J., 'Film Propaganda Technique', *Kine Weekly*, 18 December 1930, p. 35.
  'One Foot of Film Equals One Dollar of Trade', *Kine Weekly*, 8 January 1931, p. 87.
  'Propaganda: A Problem for Educational Theory and for Cinema', *Sight and Sound*, 2 (1933) 119–21.
  'The EMB Film Unit', *Cinema Quarterly*, 1 (1933) 203–8.
  'Introduction to a New Art', *Sight and Sound*, 3 (1934) 101–4.
  'Propaganda in its Working Clothes', *World Film News*, 3 (1938) 254–5.
  'World's Fair and Royal Visit Are Our Greatest Opportunities in 1939', *Kine Weekly*, 12 January 1939, p. 44.
Hiden, J., 'The Weimar Republic and the Problem of the Auslandsdeutsche', *Journal of Contemporary History*, 12, 2 (1977) 273–89.
Hollins, T., 'The Conservative Party and Film Propaganda between the Wars', *English Historical Review* (forthcoming).
Huxley, A., 'Dictators' Propaganda', *Spectator*, 20 November 1936.
  'Notes on Propaganda', *Harper's Magazine*, 174 (1936) 32–41.
Lee, J. M., 'The Dissolution of the Empire Marketing Board, 1933: Reflections on a Diary', *Journal of Imperial and Commonwealth History*, 1 (1972–3) 49–57.
Leeper, R. A., 'British Culture Abroad', *Contemporary Review*, 148 (1935) 201–7.
MacDonald, C. A., 'Radio Bari: Italian Wireless Propaganda in the Middle East and British Countermeasures, 1934–38', *Middle Eastern Studies*, 13 (1977) 195–207.
McLachlan, D., 'The Press and Public Opinion', *British Journal of Sociology*, 6 (1955) 159–75.
Martin, K., 'Public Opinion: Censorship during the Crisis'; *Political Quarterly*, 10, 1 (1939) 128–34.
  'Public Opinion and the Wireless', *Political Quarterly*, 10, 2 (1939) 180–6.
  'The Ministry of Information', *Political Quarterly*, 10, 4 (1939) 502–16.
Morris, A. J. A., 'The *Birmingham Post* and Anglo-German Relations, 1933–35', *University of Birmingham Historical Journal*, 11, 2 (1968) 191–201.
Nicolson, H., 'Allen Leeper', *Nineteenth Century and After*, 118 (1935) 473–83.
  'Modern Diplomacy and British Public Opinion', *International Affairs*, 14 (1935) 599–614.
  'British Public Opinion and Foreign Policy', *Public Opinion Quarterly*, 1, 1 (1937) 53–63.
  'The British Council, 1934–55', *21st Annual Report of the British Council* (British Council, 1955).
Nock, J., 'A New Dose of British Propaganda', *American Mercury*, 42 (1937) 482–6.

Select bibliography

Percy, E., 'The Projection of Britain: Intellectual Co-operation', *Mercury*, April 1937, pp. 610–17.
P[olitical and] E[conomic] P[lanning], 'Government Public Relations', *Planning*, 1, 14 (1933).
   'The Future of Foreign Publicity', *Planning*, 10, 213 (1943).
   'Government Information Services', *Planning*, 10, 213 (1943).
   'British Documentary Films', *Planning*, 11, 228 (1944).
Potter, P. B., 'League Publicity: Cause or Effect of League Failure?' *Public Opinion Quarterly*, 2 (1938) 399–412.
Pronay, N., 'British Newsreels in the 1930s, I: Audiences and Producers', *History*, 56 (1971) 63–72.
   'British Newsreels in the 1930s, II: Their Policies and Impact', *History*, 57 (1972) 63–72.
Riegel, O. W., 'Press, Radio and the Spanish Civil War', *Public Opinion Quarterly*, 1 (1937) 131–41.
Rivett, A. C. D., 'The Empire Marketing Board: A Tribute, a Lament and a Hope', *Australian Rhodes Review*, March 1934, 10–19.
Robertson, J. C., 'The Origins of British Opposition to Mussolini over Abyssinia', *Journal of British Studies*, 1969, 122–42.
Rose, E. J. B., 'The Press and International Tensions', *International Affairs*, 38, 1 (1962) 52–62.
Saerchinger, C., 'Radio as a Political Instrument', *Foreign Affairs*, 16, 3 (1938) 244–58.
Sanders, M. L., 'Wellington House and British Propaganda during the First World War', *Historical Journal*, 18, 1 (1975) 119–46.
Scott, C. P., 'The Function of the Press', *Political Quarterly*, 2, 1 (1931) 59–117.
Seymour-Ure, C., 'The Press and the Party System between the Wars', in G. Peele and C. Cook (eds.), *The Politics of Reappraisal, 1918–39* (Macmillan, 1975).
Siegel, S. N., 'Radio and Propaganda', *Air Law Review*, 10, 2 (1939).
Steele, R. W., 'Preparing the Public for War: Efforts to Establish a National Propaganda Agency, 1940–41', *American Historical Review*, 75 (1970) 1640–53.
Steiner, Z. and M. L. Dockrill, 'The Foreign Office Reforms, 1919–21', *Historical Journal*, 17, 1 (1974) 131–56.
Stenton, M. 'British Propaganda and the Raison d'Etat, 1935–1940', *European Studies Review*, 10 (1980) 47–74.
Taylor, P. M., 'Cultural Diplomacy and the British Council, 1934–39', *British Journal of International Studies*, 4, 3 (1978) 244–65.
   'British Official Attitudes towards Propaganda Abroad, 1918–39' in D. W. Spring and N. Pronay (eds.), *Film, Politics and Propaganda* (Macmillan, 1981).
   '"If War Should Come": Preparing the Fifth Arm for Total War, 1935–39', *Journal of Contemporary History*, 16 (1981) 27–51.
   'Publicity and Diplomacy: The Impact of the First World War upon

Select bibliography

Foreign Office Attitudes towards the Press' in D. Dilks (ed.), *The Retreat from Power* (2 vols., Macmillan, 1981), vol. 1, pp. 42–63.

'Techniques of Persuasion: Basic Groundrules of British Propaganda in the Second World War', *Historical Journal of Film, Radio and Television*, 1, 1 (1980).

'The Foreign Office and British propaganda during the First World War', *Historical Journal*, 23 (1980) 875–98.

'The New Propaganda Boom', *International History Review*, 2, 3 (1980) 485–502.

Towle, P., 'The Debate on Wartime Censorship in Britain, 1902–14' in B. Bond and I. Ray (eds.), *War and Society: A Yearbook of Military History* (Croom Helm, 1975).

Willert, A., 'The Foreign Office from Within', *Strand Magazine*, February 1936, pp. 398–405.

'England's Duty', *Atlantic Monthly*, January 1937, pp. 96–104.

'Ambassadors to Britain', *Strand Magazine*, November 1937, pp. 42–52.

'British News Abroad', *Round Table*, 27, 107 (1937) 533–46.

'Publicity and Propaganda in International Affairs', *International Affairs*, 17, 6 (1938) 809–26.

'The Crisis', *Contemporary Review*, 154 (1938) 385–92.

'National Advertisement', *Fortnightly*, January 1939, pp. 1–7.

'European Background', *Journal of the Royal United Services Institution*, February 1939, pp. 153–63.

'British News Controls', *Foreign Affairs*, 17, 4 (1939) 712–22.

Younger, K., 'Public Opinion and British Foreign Policy', *International Affairs*, 40, 1 (1964) 22–35.

UNPUBLISHED THESES

Swann, P., 'The British Documentary Film Movement, 1926–46', University of Leeds Ph.D., 1979.

Taylor, P. M., 'The Projection of Britain: British Overseas Publicity and Propaganda, 1914–39, with Particular Reference to the Work of the News Department of the Foreign Office', University of Leeds Ph.D., 1978.

Index

Abyssinian crisis, 31–2, 164, 169–70, 183–4, 186, 191, 192, 262
Admiralty, 58
Advisory Committee for the Promotion of International Relations, 150
Agence Service Reuter, *see* Reuters
Air Ministry, 225, 262, 272–3, 275, 282
Air Raids Precautions Committee, 229
Alexander, A. V., 176
Allenby, Lord, 79
Alliance Française, 122, 126, 143
All Peoples Association, 113, 137, 143, 144, 146, 148, 149
All Union Society for Cultural Relations with Foreign Countries, 136
America Latina, 88
Amery, L. C. M. S., 104
Anderson, Sir Alan, 103, 146
Anglo-German Naval Agreement, 31
Anglo-Soviet Trade Agreement, 84
Anstey, Edgar, 230
Argentine Association of English Culture, 101
Ashbridge, Sir Noel, 202
Ashfield, Lord, 94
Associated Press News Agency, 99
Association of British Chambers of Commerce, 91, 95
Association Grande-Bretagne, 116
Attlee, C., 176, 204

Baldwin, Stanley, 24, 33, 53, 137, 167
Balfour, A. J., 49, 51, 69
Balfour, Sir Arthur, 101, 151
Banks, Sir Donald, 263
Bari radio station, 192, 193, 194–5, 205, 213, 214
Barker, Arthur, 39, 207
Barlow, Sir Alan James, 238, 242, 246, 253
Barrington-Ward, R. W. 36, 40, 185–6
Batterbee, Sir Harry, 193
Beak, George, 49
Beale, Louis, 95
Beaverbrook, Lord, 12, 13, 18, 45–7, 284, 296
Bell, Oliver, 159
Beresford, J. B., 283
Bliss, Arthur, 155
Board of Education, 137, 143, 146, 154, 229
Board of Trade, 86, 91, 94, 143, 146, 154, 226, 229
Bracken, Brendan, 290
Brazilian Centenary Exhibition, 91
Bridge, Charles: joins APA, 148; joins British Council, 150–1, appointed secretary-general, 154, 157; friendship with Leeper, 152; tension with Guedalla, 156–7; on council's work, 171; consultation with Tallents, 268; trip to Germany (1938), 279; on wartime role of council, 283–4
Britain, F., 94

Index

Britain Today, 177, 283
British Broadcasting Corporation, 110, 113, 153, 189, 192, 224, 241, 264, 267–8, 284, 291, 296; Empire Service, 66, 110, 191–4; work in USA, 74–5; co-operation with British Council, 158, 223; role in psychological rearmament, 187; foreign-language broadcasts, 42, 66, 171, 181ff; 216, 272, 279; Home Service, 202, 210; connection with Foreign Office, 191–2, 201, 204–8, 297; wartime role, 266, 277, 282, 283
British Commercial Gas Association, 159
British Council, 104, 122, 181, 182, 187, 206, 208, 216, 217, 236, 241, 257, 260, 264; foundation, 6, 41–2, 116, 123, 125, 139ff; organisation, 152ff; co-operation with Ibero-American Institute, 155–6; with Travel Association, 116–18, 157–9; aims, 153, 188, 258; audience, 121, 160–1; income, 150, 162, 164, 166, 169, 228–35, 244–5, 252, 256, 294–5; conceptions of work, 161–3, 239; film, 158–61, 253; work in Middle East, 167, 169–72, 193, in Germany, 174–5; Paris Exhibition (1937, 122; Chamberlain's support for, 168; relationship with shadow Ministry of Information, 268, 271, 278–9; wartime role, 282–5; *see also* Lloyd' Lord
British Empire Trade Exhibitions, 103, 155
British Film Institute, 159, 160, 231, 252
British Gas Authority, 230
British Industries Fair, 90–1
British Institutes at Paris and Florence, 144

British Library of Information at New York, 68–77, 289
British Official News Service, 20, 55, 57–68, 88, 99, 189, 201, 208, 214, 289
British Petroleum, 159
Brittain, Sir Harry, 95
Brownrigg, Douglas, 264
Bruce Lockhart, Robert, 33, 35, 270, 285
Brussels Exhibition, 91
Bryant and May, 88
Buchan, John, 13, 46, 47
Burgess, Guy, 276
Burnham, Lord, 21
'Buy British' movement, 104

Cadogan, Alexander, 197, 236, 257, 285, 289, 291; view of R. A. Leeper, 35, 41, 245–6; on BBC, 212; on News Department, 221, 237
Calvert, A. S., 197, 198, 206, 207, 208
Cecil, Lord Robert, 49
Ceylon Tea Propaganda Board, 230
Chamberlain, Sir Austen, 13, 24, 27, 42, 72
Chamberlain, Neville, 122, 166, 167, 168, 273; as Chancellor of the Exchequer, 142, 162, 165; tension with Eden, 34–5; on hostile propaganda, 204; on BBC, 210–11, 272; on appointment of Vansittart committee, 222; receipt of Vansittart's report, 236–8; Munich crisis, 271, 273–4; confesses ignorance of propaganda, 280; appoints ministerial committee on propaganda, 286; appointment of Lord Perth, 288–9
Chanak crisis, 23
Chatham House (Royal Institute of International Affairs), 55
Churchill, Winston, 167, 187

Index

Cinematograph Acts, 122, 248
Cinematograph Fund, 252
cinema vans, 83
Clark, J. B., 207
Clerk, Sir George, 115
Cliffe, C. A. L., 197
Colonial Empire Marketing Board, 110
Colonial Office, 23, 193, 197, 224, 231
Colville, Sir John, 263, 271
'Come to Britain' movement, 93
Committee of Imperial Defence, 12, 217, 260, 262–7, 269, 272–3, 275, 279, 280
Committee on Economic Co-operation, 104
Committee on Education and Training, 146
Committee on International Understanding and Co-operation, 146
Committee on Trade and Industry, 101
Conservative Party, 83
Cook, E. T., 264
Cooke, F. H., 94
Courteney, C. L., 263
Crewe House, 12, 45, 78, 131, 181, 262, 271, 272, 294; relationship with FO, 296; liquidation, 13; reputation, 44, 261; post-war role, 46–8
Cromer, Lord, 169
Croom-Johnson, H. P., 160
Crowe, E. F., 92–3
Crowe, Sir Eyre, 18, 19, 23, 24, 42, 57
Crown Film Unit, 255
Cultural Relations Committee, 144, 147
Cunliffe-Lister, Sir Philip, 94
Curzon, Lord, 16, 18, 29, 55, 59 63; on Britain's prestige, 78; recreation of News Department, 51, 53, 54; attacked by The Times, 17; support for Tilley report, 134–5
Cyprus, 199, 200, 203, 204
Czechoslovakian crisis, see Munich crisis

D'Abernon, Lord, 100, 103, 139, 140, 146, 155
Daily Chronicle, 18, 25, 78
Daily Telegraph, The, 18, 21, 177
Dalziel, Sir Davison, 18
Dante Alighieri Society, 136, 143
Dawnay, Sir Alan, 158
Dawson, Geoffrey, 34, 40
Defence Requirements Committee, 261
Deller, Sir Edwin, 147, 150
Department of Information, 128, 265
Department of Overseas Trade, 98, 107, 112, 137, 147, 224, 263; creation, 86; post-war role in propaganda, 54, 87, 89; press articles, 89–90; exhibitions, 90–1, 155; commercial propaganda, 92–3, 103, 161; and Travel Association, 94–5; Trade Propaganda Committee, 101–2, 105; Oversea Propaganda Committee, 105–9; desire to undertake trade propaganda, 110; attitude to British Council, 117, 148–9; film propaganda, 87, 99–100, 160–1, 231; New York World Fair, 117–19; trade propaganda, 226–8; 231; Industrial Publicity Unit, 234, 246, 247–8
Derby, Lord, 93–4, 96, 158, 236, 244
Dill, J. G., 263
Directorate of Germanism Abroad and Cultural Relations, 135
Disarmament Conference, 28, 190, 261, 295

Index

Dominions Information Department, 23, 57, 108
Dominions Office, 104, 108, 193, 197, 201, 231
Donald, Robert, 78
Drummond, Sir Eric, *see* Perth, Lord
Dundas, C. A. F., 152

Eden, Anthony, vii, 31, 32, 35, 43, 188, 206, 237, 291; relationship with Rex Leeper, 30, 41; on Leeper, 182; on Italy, 33; suspicion of No. 10, 34; rift with Chamberlain, 34–5; support for Reuters, 67, 208–9; support for British Council, 165–6; on psychological rearmament, 185–6; on BBC, 195
Edgcumbe, A., 246
Electra House, 270, 271, 274, 276, 282, 285
Eliot, Sir Charles, 132
Empire Marketing Board, 103–14, 121, 125, 143, 159, 228–30
English-Speaking Union, 137, 146
exhibitions, 90–1, 155
Export Credit Guarantee Department, 226

Fass, Sir Ernest, 281, 282, 283, 287, 291
Federation of British Industries, 91
film, 111, 116, 118–19, 120–1; in USA, 73–4; for trade propaganda purposes, 88, 99, 100, 102; Travel Association film unit, 114–15, 158–61; National Film Council, 229–33, 239, 248–55
Film Centre, 159–60
Fisher, Sir Warren, 142, 166, 204, 236, 263, 265, 271; on Leeper, 240; on Vansittart report, 242; on shadow Ministry of Information, 281; on News Department, 295
Fletcher, Angus, 71, 72–3, 74, 140

Foreign Agents Registration Act, 75
Foreign Office, 5, 6, 11; regains control over propaganda, 13; relations with press, 11ff; propaganda overseas, 44ff; tension with Lloyd George, 16–18; press attachés, 20–1, 51, 244–5; concept of propaganda, 66, 130, 131–2, 148, 161; propaganda in the USA, 68, 70–1; film unit, 88; representative British literature, 155; and Travel Association, 93ff; and British Council, 125, 152ff; *see also* News Department
Foreign Publicity Department (FO), 5, 6, 288–9
France, 21, 36, 101, 107, 126–7, 134, 139, 169–70, 184, 189, 191, 221

Gas, Light and Coke Co., 230
Gaselee, Stephen, 53, 59, 65, 131, 140, 263, 286
Gathorne-Hardy, G. M., 285
Gaumont–British Newsreel Co., 231, 250
General Post Office, 110, 224, 267; and British Official News Service, 63–4, 67; and film, 119, 145, 159, 208, 230
Geneva Economic Conference, 102
Germany, 15, 31–3; 38, 40, 44, 46–7, 49, 58, 63, 67, 83, 88, 100–1, 103, 116, 122, 124, 127, 129, 135–6, 139, 162, 172, 173, 174, 184–8, 189, 191, 192, 208, 210–11, 214, 218, 222, 241, 242, 249, 254, 259, 261, 267, 268
Gibson, Sir Herbert, 97
Gilbey, E. W., 63
Gillett, G. M., 101, 108, 109
Glyn, Sir Ralph, 252
Goebbels, Joseph, 262, 263, 298
Graham, Sir Ronald, 20

Index

Grand, Major Laurence, 274, 275
Grandi, Count, 33
Graves, Cecil, 158, 202, 207, 214
Gregory, J. D., 19, 23, 56–7
Grierson, John, 124, 160, 228, 249
Grierson, Marion, 228
Guedalla, Philip, 155–6, 159, 161
Guest, S. A., 49, 50

Hacking, Douglas, 94
Hale, Edward, 283, 296; on trade propaganda, 227; on film propaganda, 232–3; on Vansittart report, 238–42; on National Film Council, 251–3
Halifax, Lord, 211, 236, 257, 287, 288; visit to Germany, 33; on propaganda, 35, 237, 291; on Vansittart report, 242; supports increased propaganda, 279–80
Hall, H. Noble, *see* Noble Hall, H.
Hankey, Sir Maurice, 21, 34, 263, 264
Harding, Sir Edward, 55, 263
Hardinge, Lord, 16, 55
Harmsworth, Cecil, 51, 53, 130
Harvey, Oliver, 32, 34, 287–8
Hatton, G. E. C., 99–100
Havas News Agency, 63, 65, 88, 99
Headlam-Morley, J. W., 54–5
Henderson, Arthur, viii, 27, 43, 139
Hildred, W. P., 265
Hitler, Adolf, 3, 31, 40, 76, 83, 162, 164, 167, 182, 183, 186–8, 244, 269, 274, 295; meeting with Halifax, 33–4; on British wartime propaganda, 44, 299; Anschluss, 208; threats to BBC, 211, 214
Hoare, Sir Samuel, 29, 32, 36, 123–4, 183; assumes responsibility for shadow Ministry of Information, 282; report on propaganda, 286–8
Hopkins, Sir Richard, 242
Huxley, M. H., 286

Ibero-American Institute, 143, 144, 155–7, 208
Imperial Airways, 230, 291
Imperial Chemical Industries, 146
Imperial Communications Committee, 271
Imperial Conferences: (1923), 103; (1926), 99, 103; (1930), 104
Imperial Institute, 231
Imperial Press Conference, 95
Imperial Relations Trust, 159
Imperial War Museum, 88
India, 167, 199, 200
India Office, 199, 231
Industrial Publicity Unit, 6, 247–8, 256, 260, 285
Ingram, E. M. B., 25
Inskip, Sir Thomas, 209
Institute for Cultural Relations with Foreign Countries, 136
Italy, 31–3, 34, 67, 83, 101, 116, 136, 169–71, 173, 174, 183–6, 189, 191, 197, 208, 258, 261, 262

Japan, 67, 173, 186, 261
Jerusalem, 198, 199, 200
Johnstone, Kenneth, 152, 164–5, 170–1, 106, 286
Joint Broadcasting Committee (Section D), 275–6
Jones, Kennedy, 16
Jones, Sir Roderick, 59, 65, 209, 210
Jury, Sir William, 159

Kennedy, A. L., 41, 188
Kenney, Roland, 116, 117, 231–3, 234, 250
Kerr, Philip, 18
King-Hall, Stephen, 272
Koppel, Percy, 88, 135; as head of News Department, 20, 21, 55–6; reform of News Department, 55; on British Official News Service, 62–4; transfer to Dominions

Index

Information Department, 57
Korda, Alexander, 116

Lampson, Sir Miles, 170, 214
Lasswell, Harold, 72
Laughton, Charles, 116
Lawford, Valentine, 221
League of Nations, 15, 24, 25, 32, 50, 72, 78–9, 183–7, 188, 190–1, 287
Leeper, Allen, 17, 18, 20, 29, 63
Leeper, Reginald (Rex):
  background, 28–9; joins News Department, 139; view of Simon, 29; relationship with Vansittart, 30, 182–7, with Cadogan, 35, with Halifax, 35, with Eden, 30 41, with Bridge, 148, 152; views on Chamberlain, 35–6, on Percy, 163, on Tyrrell, 163; tension with Wrench, 148–9; on British press, 29–30, 33–4, 37, 38, 39–40; suspicion of press manipulation, 34, 35, 157; on Britain, 79, 128, 161; on Italy, 31–3, 35–6; on Germany, 31, 35–6, 172, 174, 182–8; on propaganda in Germany, 214; on progaganda in USA, 74; on cultural propaganda, 141–2, 172; on need for cultural propaganda, 122–3; on Travel Association, 116–17; foundation of British Council, 113, 114, 116, 143ff; on British Council, 154; on Ibero-American Institute, 156; on BBC, 193ff; psychological rearmament, 182–8; on Treasury, 165, 219, 295; on British rearmament, 218; and Vansittart committee, 217ff; expansion of British Official News Service, 66–7; behaviour during Munich crisis, 36–7; and shadow Ministry of Information, 262–8, 278–81; recreation of PID, 276–7, 285–6; scandal over Perth's appointment, 287–9; influence of, 41–2, 178; appraisal of career, 40–2; *see also* News Department; British Council; Foreign Office
Lindsay, Sir Ronald, 74, 76, 77
Lister, S. J., 94
Litvinov, Maxim, 29, 33
Lloyd, Lord, 216, 240; appointed chairman of British Council, 167; experience, 167–8; relationship with Chamberlain, 168; on cultural propaganda, 177–8; work in Middle East, 169, 171; as a critic of government, 280; gains respect for council, 176–7; increased grant, 238; becomes president of Travel Association, 244; on wartime role of council, 283–4
Lloyd George, David, 38, 48; and press lords, 13, 14, 17, 45; tension with Foreign Office, 16, 18; relations with Riddell, 22, with Northcliffe, 47; departure, 19, 23, 27
Local Authorities (Publicity) Act, 114
London Naval Conference (1930), 27, 73
London Publicity Club, 115
Loraine, Sir Percy, 169, 293
Lothian, Lord, *see* Kerr, Philip
Lunn, William, 105
Luxembourg, Radio, 158, 275, 279

McDonald, Iverach, 39–40
MacDonald, Malcolm, 201
MacDonald, Ramsay, 27, 83, 98, 140–1
Mackenzie, Compton, 156
Mair, G. H., 58
Manchester Guardian, 27
March of Time, 231, 249
Marconi Company, 58, 60, 64, 189

Index

Martin, Kingsley, 121–2
Masefield, John, 155
Matheson, Hilda, 275–6
Mendl, Sir Charles, 21
Mercier, E. L., 95
Meredith, L. A. de L., 92, 95, 97, 117, 148–9, 157, 229
Military Intelligence, 270, 276; *see also* Secret Intelligence
Ministry of Agriculture, 230
Ministry of Blockade, 86
Ministry of Health, 229
Ministry of Information: (1918), 12, 13, 45, 46–7, 59, 78, 130, 159, 181, 221, 224, 261; establishment of second, 42, 110, 217, 248, 256, 260ff
Ministry of Labour, 229
Ministry of Transport, 229
Montgomery, C. H., 57, 59
Morning Post, 18
Morrison, Herbert, 224
Mosley, Sir Oswald, 101
Movietone, 231
Mullins, C., 226, 246
Munich crisis, 36, 75, 172, 175, 210, 256, 268ff
Mussolini, Benito, 25, 31, 83, 164, 183–4, 186, 193

Nash, N. E., 63
National Film Council, 232, 235, 239, 241, 248, 250–2, 254, 256
National Fitness Council, 230
National Publicity Bureau, 5, 83
National Savings Committee, 229
National War Aims Committee, 45, 262
Navy League, 167
Neutral Press Committee, 58
Newbolt, Sir Henry, 128, 129–32, 140
News Europe, The, 29
News Department of the Foreign Office, 22, 23, 29, 43, 69, 107, 125, 154, 188; wartime creation and work, 12; amalgamation with PID, 13–14; post-war cuts, 15, 25, 54–5, 79, 87, 225; press attachés, 20–1; procedures with press, 26–7, 37–8; limits to work, 26, 39, 130; international conferences, 23; post-war position, 49–52; reorganisation of (1925), 56–7, 85; British Official News Service, 57–68; and Reuters, 59-60; and BLI, 71–7; and commercial propaganda, 92–3; and Travel Association, 97, 116; and cultural propaganda, 132ff; and British Council, 152ff; work in 1930s, 38; special arrangement with *The Times*, 39–40; 'gentleman's agreement' with BBC, 204, 205–8; tension with BBC, 74–5, 191, 206–7; recreation of PID, 276–7, 285–6; ForeignPublicity Department, 287–90; *see also* Leeper, Reginald
News of the World, 16
Newspaper Proprietors' Association, 16, 33, 95
Newsreel Association, 119, 250
Nicolson, Harold, 223, 284
Noble Hall, H., 115–16, 121
Norman, R. C., 202, 203
Northcliffe, Lord, 12, 13, 17, 18, 45, 46, 47, 271, 296; view of public relations officers, 43; view of own wartime achievement, 44; plans for post-war propaganda, 47; head of War Mission, 69; accused of debasing 'propaganda', 73; death, 19; compared with Vansittart, 222
Norton, Clifford, 25, 26, 60, 65, 138

O'Brien, E. D., 177
Overseas Broadcasting Committee,

Index

209
Overseas Emergency Publicity Expenditure Committee, 253–4, 287, 289
Overseas League, 146
Overseas Propaganda Committee, 105–6, 109, 110
Overseas Trade Development Council, 146, 147

Page, E. K., 276
Palestine, 167, 193, 194, 199, 200, 213–14, 248, 258
Paramount, 231
Paris Exhibition (1937), 121–2
Paris Peace Conference (1919), 13, 22, 51, 78, 136
Pathé, 231
Peake, Charles, 36–7, 38, 211, 246, 286, 289
Pearl Assurance Company, 230
Percy, Lord Eustace, 123, 137, 162–4, 166, 220
Perowne, S. H., 213
Perth, Lord, 69, 287–9, 291
Phillips, F. W., 197
Phipps, Sir Eric, 174–5
Pickthall, C. M., 92–3, 95, 151
Pilgrim Society, 95, 112
Pole, Sir Felix, 94
Political Intelligence Department, 13–16, 20, 29, 54–5, 276, 277, 284–6
Political Warfare Executive, 270
Power, Sir John, 176
press attachés, 20, 21, 25, 51, 61, 245; *see also* Mendl, Sir Charles
Press Bureau, 12, 262

Quai d'Orsay, 11, 126, 136

Ramsbottom, J. W., 147, 150
Ramsden, Sir Eugene, 146, 147, 150, 154, 176
Reading, Lord, 71, 142
Reith, Sir John, 9; concept of propaganda, 3; relationship with Foreign Office, 74–5, 191–2; overseas broadcasting, 191; on Empire Service, 192; Kingsley Wood committee, 197–8, 202–4, 209–10, 212, 263, 267; *see also* British Broadcasting Corporation
Reuters: Agence Service Reuter, 58–60; post-war contract with Foreign Office, 60; international news agency agreements, 63, 65; inability to compete with rivals, 64–5; Treasury reluctance to subsidise, 67; Eden's support for, 67–8; work in Latin America, 99, 201, 208; and Kingsley Wood committee, 209–10; subsidy awarded, 211
Riddell, Lord, 16, 17, 22, 95
Ridsdale, William, 63, 66
Robertson, C. P., 262, 264
Rochemont, Richard de, 231
Rodd, Sir Rennell, 131
Rome 2 RO 4 radio station, 193
Rootes, William, 147, 150
Rothermere, Viscount, 18
Royal Air Force, 273, 274, 276, 290
Royal Institute of International Affairs (Chatham House), 55
Royal Navy, 119, 193
Royal Society of Literature, 130–1
Rumbold, Sir Horace, 166–7
Russia, *see* Soviet Union
Ryan, A. P., 275

Scott, Sir Russell, 263
Secret Intelligence Service, 274, 276, 277, 278
Section D, 270, 274, 275, 276, 279
Selfridge, Gordon, 94
Shell-Mex, 159, 230
Simon, Sir John: row with Willert, 27–8; Leeper's view of, 29; on foundation of British Council, 150; and British Official News Service, 67; as Chancellor of the

Index

Exchequer, 166; on British Council, 169; Vansittart proposals, 236, 237, 242, 244; on Leeper, 246; on plans to increase propaganda, 280

Soviet Union, 15, 36, 84, 102, 107, 122, 136, 172, 174, 189, 191, 249

Special Operations Executive, 270

Spectator, The, 146

Stanhope, Lord, 270, 281

Steed, H. Wickham, *see* Wickham Steed, H.

Stephenson, W. T., 276

Steward, George, 25, 27, 38

Strand Film Co., 230

Stresemann, Gustav, 136

Stuart, Campbell, 46, 264, 271, 274, 281, 282, 285, 286

Sunday Entertainments Act, 252

Sunday Times, 34

Sutherland, Sir William, 18

Tallents, Stephen, x, 106, 288, 291–2; personality, 110; as secretary of EMB, 103–4; *The Projection of England*, 111–14, 119–22; as director-general, shadow Ministry of Information, 267, 269, 271, 272; post-Munich enquiry, 275–81; dismissed, 281; influence, 110, 115, 122, 125, 140, 178

Taylor, John, 230

Thomas, J. H., 104, 108, 109

Thompson, Sir Ernest, 103, 146

Tilley, John, 79, 132–5, 144

Times, The, 41, 46, 69, 78, 120, 188; attacks on Lloyd George and Curzon, 17; releases Willert to Foreign Office, 22; accused of pro-German sympathies, 31; leaks, 34; on Travel Association, 96–7; on British Council, 6; on demise of EMB, 109; on public relations, 112–13; views of assistant editor on News Department, 35, 185–6; on BBC Arabic service, 206; defends foreign-language service, 212; on Vansittart committee, 222

Trade and Industry Committee, 146

Trade Propaganda Committee, 101–2, 105, 108

Travel Association, 104, 106, 107, 112, 125, 216, 236–41, 244, 264; creation, 93–5; work, 96–7; in France, 115–16; in South America, 208; audience, 121; revenue, 114, 235; and DOT, 110; film unit, 114–15, 145, 159; Joint Films Committee, 158–61, 220; attitude to cultural propaganda, 148; resentment of British Council, 149; 158; co-operation with British Council, 157–9

Treasury, 92, 102, 110, 237; opposition to post-war propaganda, 15, 20, 64, 77, 79, 219; cuts in News Department, 25, 52–5, 87, 131; contract between Foreign Office and Reuters, 59–60; expansion of British Official News Service, 67; on cultural propaganda, 131–2, 139–40; opposition to Tilley report, 133–5; grants to British Council, 150, 162, 164, 166, 168–9; on Kingsley Wood committee, 197, 199, 200, 202; on Vansittart committee, 224; on Vansittart report, 238, 242ff; PID, 276; OEPEC, 253–4, 287, 289

Trentham, E. N. R., 102

Troup, J. A. G., 263

Tweedsmuir, Lord, *see* Buchan, John

Tyrrell, Sir (later Lord) William, 20, 21, 27, 43, 53, 55, 65, 90,

Index

130, 167; as head of News and Political Intelligence Department, 13–14, 51; on post-war relations between Foreign Office and press, 17–18; relationship with Willert, 23–4, with Baldwin, 24, with Rex and Allen Leeper, 29; becomes permanent under secretary, Foreign Office, 57; ambassador in France, 115; as chairman of British Council, 150, 161–2; compared with Percy, 163; on link between labour and foreign policy, 84

Ullswater committee, 192
Union of Democratic Control, 15
United Press News Agency, 63, 65, 99
United States of America, 22, 44, 58, 68–77, 88, 97, 104, 117, 174, 208, 263
Universal, 231
Unwin, Stanley, 155

Vansittart, Sir Robert, 25, 34, 35, 43, 142, 149, 150, 151, 157; press work as Curzon's private secretary, 16; relationship with Allen Leeper, 29, with Rex Leeper, 30–1, 40, 182–7; on Italy, 32; on Abyssinian crisis, 183; inspires press, 40–1; reprimands Reith, 74–5; on economic diplomacy, 87; on cultural diplomacy, 140–1, 145; support for British Council, 146, 165–6; on psychological rearmament, 185–7; on BBC, 194; Committee to Co-ordinate British Publicity Abroad, 216ff
Vaughan Williams, Ralph, 155
Verein für das Deutschtum im Ausland, 127
VOKS, 136
Volkischer Beobachter, 222

Vyle, Sir Gilbert, 95

Wall Street crash, 101
War Book, 266
Warner, Christopher, 76, 197, 199, 207, 222, 224, 233, 242 276, 286
War Office, 225
Warr, Earl de la, 166–7, 197
Washington Conference (1921–2), 17, 22
Waterfield, A. P., 283, 284
Webster, Professor C. K., 156
Wellesley, Victor, 48, 57, 90, 129–30, 131
Wellington House, 20, 44, 68, 294
White, A. J. S., 177
Wickham Steed, H., 46–8
Wigram, Ralph, 40
Wilberforce, Robert, 71
Willert, Arthur, 37, 72, 179, 296; joins News Department, 21–2, 51, 55; at Washington Conference, 22–3; relations with 10 Downing Street, 23, 27; relationship with Tyrrell, 25; publicity for Locarno, 24; becomes head of News Department, 23, 57; press relations, 25–6, 73; row with Simon, 27–8; retirement, 28; on Leeper, 29; wartime work, 69; on commercial propaganda, 92; on cultural propaganda, 138
Williamson, Robert, 247, 248
Wilson, Sir Horace, 179, 237, 245, 288
Wilson, Woodrow, 15
Winterton, Earl, 223
Wiseman, Sir William, 69–70
Wolff Bureau, 63, 99
Wood, Kingsley, 68, 195–204, 206, 209, 216, 220, 223
Woodward, E. L., 177, 284
World Fair, New York, 117–19, 250, 253, 255

Index

Wrench, Sir Evelyn, 146–51
Wright, Basil, 231

Zeesen radio station, 189, 207, 214
Zinoviev letter, 84